Part of the proceeds of the sale of this book will be donated to Provites, an association which devotes itself to the defense, and promotion of Italian grape varieties.

| | |
|---|---|
| Text | PATRICIA GUY |
| Editing of publishing project | MARIO BUSSO - CARLO VISCHI |
| Selection of winemakers and wines | MARIO BUSSO - CARLO VISCHI - PATRICIA GUY |
| Typical Italian recipes | CHIARA BUSSO |
| Public relations | ELISA ZANOTTI |
| Concerns coordination | PIERA MERLO |
| Technical collaboration | MAURIZIO GILY |
| Territorial collaboration | LORETTA BELLUSSI, PAOLA COPPO, CARLA DEIOSSO, MATTEO FERRARESI, MARGHERITA CORDERO, LUCIANO VISCHI, PIER MICHELE ARNOLFO, ROBERTA ROCCHI |
| Photographs | STEFANO SCATÀ, ARCHIVIO 2SNC, ARCHIVIO GRIBAUDO, FRANCESCO BUSSO |

Regional cartography on distribution of vineyards is based on that found in the book *Vitigni d'Italia* by Antonio Calò, Attilio Scienza and Angelo Costacurta, Calderini Edagricole Editions; 2001.
Special thanks to Professor Attilio Scienza for his collaboration.

Many thanks for the contribution and the iconographical materials to:
Consorzio Vino Nobile di Montepulciano, Consorzio Vini Valtellina, Consorzio Garda Classico, Consorzio Tutela Vini di Montefalco, Consorzio Chianti, Consorzio Chianti Classico, Consorzio Chianti Rufina, Consorzio Chianti Colli Fiorentini, Consorzio Tutela Oltrepò Pavese, Consorzio Tutela Reggiano, Consorzio della Denominazione San Gimignano, Consorzio del Vino Brunello di Montalcino, Consorzio Tutela del Soave e Recioto di Soave, Consorzio Marchio Storico dei Lambruschi Modenesi, Consorzio per la Tutela del Vino Lessini Durello, Ente Vini Bresciani, Ente Tutela Vini di Romagna, Consorzio Tutela Valcalepio, Consorzio Tutela Vini Valpolicella, Consorzio Tutela Vini Orvieto, Consorzio Franciacorta, Consorzio di Tutela Vini Prosecco di Conegliano e Valdobbiadene, Consorzio Tutela Vini di Barletta, Consorzio Tutela Vini Collio, Consorzio Tutela Colli Orientali del Friuli, Consorzio Tutela Vini Asti e Monferrato, Consorzio Tutela Brachetto d'Acqui, Consorzio Tutela Asti, Consorzio Tutela Vini Oltrepò Pavese, Consorzio Tutela Montescudaio, Associazione Vignaioli del Trentino, Associazione Vignaioli Piemontesi, Enoteca Regionale del Roero, Associazione Consorzi Vini Lombardia ASCOVILO.

Special thanks to: Gianluigi Biestro, President of Unione Nazionale tra Associazioni dei Produttori Vitivinicoli and general director of Associazione Vignaioli Piemontesi and to the concerns Pellegrino, Feudo Principi di Butera and to Consorzio di Tutela Vini Colli Orientali del Friuli for the permit to use their own photographs.

This book was realized with the contribution of Consorzio per la Tutela del Formaggio Grana Padano.

Copyright © 2003 by Edizioni Gribaudo
Published by Tide-mark Press, Ltd.
Windsor, Connecticut

All Rights Reserved under International and Pan American Copyright Conventions

First North American Edition

Library of Congress Cataloging-in-Publication Data
Guy, Patricia
Wines of Italy
p. 356   cm.
Includes Index

ISBN: 1-55949-881-1  Hardcover Edition

Library of Congress Control Number: 2003106323

Printed in Italy
Proprietà letteraria e artistica
© Edizioni Gribaudo, Savigliano (Cn)
Tel. 0172.712221 Fax 0172.375319
edizioni.gribaudo@libero.it
First edition 2002

| | |
|---|---|
| Project manager | VALERIO COSTANZIA |
| Editing | GIUSEPPE GABUTTI |
| Graphics | FEDERICO CARLO PEVERADA |
| Drawings | ROBERTO PIROLA |
| Photocomposition | GI.MAC - SAVIGLIANO (CN) |
| Printed by | GRAFICHE BUSTI, COLOGNOLA AI COLLI (VR) |

Patricia Guy

# WINES OF ITALY

## il gusto italiano del vino

CUCINA
Il GUSTO!
ITALIANA
TIDE-MARK

# Man, the Climate, the Grape Variety and the Territory

*by Gianluigi Biestro*

Chairman of UNAVINI (National Union of Associations of Wine Producers)

The elements which are fundamental to the production of a great wine are: man, the climate, the grape variety and the territory.

At first glance this book is about grape varieties but in actual fact attention has also been dedicated to describing the other elements that become their essential corollary. The combination of these factors has made some wines unique and unrepeatable: so much so that some grape varieties can only be grown in particular areas, while the exposure and composition of some soils unmistakably characterize some great wines which are typical only in some areas. In this way Nebbiolo is characteristic to Piedmont, and Nero d'Avola to Sicily, unlike international grape varieties which adapt to cultivation anywhere.

The link between the grape variety and the territory in Italy is sometimes so close that the two elements seem to live in symbiosis and their identity and image are inseparable: Ribolla, Picolit and Tocai are synonymous with Friuli; Verdicchio cannot be from anywhere other than the Marches; Primitivo and Negroamaro go hand in hand with Puglia; Gaglioppo is Calabria, to mention just a few examples which represent some of the pieces in a complex and highly original puzzle. Reading one or two chapters it is easy to see that the research has been carried out paying meticulous attention to detail, providing elegant descriptions and historical particularities on the grape varieties and offering tasteful serving suggestions along with characteristic recipes.

The linearity and clarity of the texts with the descriptive passage from grape variety to wine, followed by wine-gastronomy combinations make this book enjoyable and easy to read.

Unavini has decided to use this publication for its first important promotional campaign as it offers an idea of the expanse of Italian wine-growing and justifies the over three hundred denominations of origin existing today.

The technical skills involved in working the vineyards and producing wines make it possible to see considerable improvements in quality, year by year, with the evolution of the whole spectrum of oenological production. Therefore, it is important to carry out adequate promotional activities throughout the country to further enhance the great heritage of vines and vineyards and to encourage the consumption of wines of increasingly high quality.

A big thanks to the authors and editors for their hard work in the name of our associations.

# Rediscovering Lost Flavors

*by Patricia Guy*

A change is taking place in Italy's vineyards which will affect both the way you drink and the way you think about wine. In the last ten years, producers – both large and small – have been tramping the fields and hills of their zones seeking out native vines, and in this way rediscovering lost pieces of their viticultural heritage.

Using modern technology, winemakers are now able to fully express the potential of these grapes. The results of their dedicated research are arriving in wine shops around the world, and offer wine lovers a luscious range of flavors and fragrances unavailable from any other country.

Talking about wine and sharing our impressions is part of the pleasure of tasting and drinking. And, of course, wines are easy to talk about when they remind us of something specific – Cabernet Sauvignon is black currant, Sauvignon Blanc is gooseberry. Too often difficulties arise in distinguishing Italian varieties precisely because we have not yet selected words to define them.

When you taste a wine from an Italian variety, I want you to close your eyes, inhale deeply and really think about its fragrance before you take your first mouthful. What are the connections it brings to mind? Perhaps mature Garganega reminds you of ripe pears, or maybe the scent of Alpine flowers emerges from a glass of Carema. Then take a generous amount of wine in your mouth and swish it around, letting it reach every taste bud. Allow yourself the freedom to discover the flavors of these original wines: that tangy burst of blackberries in Marzemino, the touch of white chocolate which defines a well-made Picolit, and the enticing sweetly bitter taste of the pulp near the cherry stone of young Sangiovese.

Italian wines are usually intended to be enjoyed with food. These wines are not the husky, dusky, wood-laden numbers which strut off with the prizes. Rather they are the kinds of wines that you can invite home to dinner. To help get you started with choosing the right dishes to accompany these new fragrances and flavors, I have included recipes with suggested wine pairings. Italians also recognize a category of wines which is woefully overlooked in most English-speaking nations: *vini da meditazione*. This simply means that some intensely flavored wines are meant to be served outside of mealtimes, with good conversation and good friends.

More than one hundred Italian varieties are described in this book. They were selected on the basis of their use (either on their own or as part of the blend) in Italy's most famous wines, their commercial success on the international market, and their palate-pleasing potential. Following each description, there is a list of the DOC and DOCG wines, as well as the most interesting non-DOC blends which feature the variety. You will also find a brief selection of producers. They were chosen by virtue of the consistent quality of their wines, and for their ability to clearly express the characteristics of the grape variety. In some cases, production is so limited that there are no more than two or three individuals working with the variety. For others – notably Nebbiolo, Sangiovese and Barbera – a complete list of top-notch producers would simply be too long to include. In such cases, I have, for the most part, listed the names of those which will be most readily available on foreign markets. When you taste a wine you like, I urge you to make a note of the producer's name. In this way you can develop you own catalogue of trusted winemakers and favorite wine styles.

This book is intended to help wine drinkers take their first steps through the kaleidoscopic world of Italian grape varieties. Let each new wine be an opportunity to explore your senses and your intellect and let it, too, be an opportunity for conviviality – because that is what enjoying wine is all about.

# A Thousand and One Desires

*by Mario Busso and Carlo Vischi*

*Tasting a wine in the company of a friend
is like sharing in the enjoyment of his
happiness all the time he is in our home*
"Physiology of Taste" by Brillat-Savarin

Time doesn't stand still and wine is alive, just like life. It evolves, following the natural rhythms of change. Wine lives off the sensitivity of the producers and taste, and both these sensations evolve like fashion, art and any other creative action.

Nature doesn't make wine, man is the creator; nature makes the grape wither and turn to seed, man intervenes and makes wine, but he must always be present, from the selection of the clone to vinification, from the use of the grape variety which best suits his cultural concept, to the obvious impositions of the market. Until not so long ago, to second that which was described as international taste, Italian producers were tempted by a sort of general standardization to compete on the international scene, with the same arms as the French, Californians and Australians.

Then, at last they began to reflect!

It was possible to make great wines from native grape varieties, those which have become part of tradition thanks to their ampelographic traits, which would brilliantly tell the story of the "Enotria tellus", in other words a Wineland, in other words Italy, all over the world.

This was not exclusively concerned with the need to renew the image of Italian wine, but was mainly due to the desire to confirm the real identity of the nation's wine-producing sector.

On the subject of the identity of a wine, it was necessary to present the different aspects that characterize Italy for the market and modern consumers.

As Ampelio Bucci, an industrial consultant, said when asked for his opinion regarding the project stage of a wine, "…we have the richest artistic heritage in the world, …Italy is the country of real beauty and goodness; … in the international market there is a need for authenticity, naturalness and variety; Italy is the country of variety; paradoxically one shouldn't even talk about Italian wine…"

Italy can therefore rightfully satisfy very different types of curiosity, styles of drinking and needs in terms of taste. Italy is the country of diversity, the country of the arts, and these arts include that of expressing the multiform, kaleidoscopic variety of the world of grape varieties, a polyhedral multitude of versions that can satisfy, in vinification, the taste of "A Thousand and One Desires".

It is important for producers to know how to plan their diversity and, if possible, their uniqueness, trying to occupy particular and exclusive spaces in the area of attentive, modern consumerism.

The idea of all things simple, healthy and authentic accompanies that of refined wisdom and opposes the standardization of the multicolored and ambiguous scents, flavors and knowledge of hidden or declared persuaders. Oenological luxury, like gastronomic luxury, almost always eludes "photocopied information". The luxury and rarity of a choice are often reserved for the notebook of research which marks the desire for knowledge starting with the advice given in guides, but also, and most importantly, knows when to abandon them in favor of personal emotions and strongly subjective hedonism.

Supported by an army of wine enthusiasts, professional tasters and frank hedonists, we set off on a tour of Italy's cellars and wine store tables, tasting wines using the methods suggested by modern tasting techniques. While the methodologies used led us to make more or less objective assessments with consistent results, nothing was more interesting and more appropriate than understanding the wine from the point of view of pleasure, capturing its importance within the culture of its homeland and the sensations which emerged during the tasting sessions.

In this way we have satisfied a thousand and one desires.

The long list that follows contains no "excommunications", just the clear address of those producers who seem to have been struck by the incurable human ambition to take their commitment further, focusing on continued improvement.

In this list we have followed three assessment criteria and used them to indicate several producers.

The wines which made a positive impression in terms of voluptuousness, intensity and richness, have been given Cupid's arrows.

We thought it would be curious and interesting to mark some producers with the sign of the new moon, as they are emerging in the market with a symbiotic combination that binds the personality and strength of the wine with the producer who makes it, together with the grape variety and the territory in which they are located. The third criterion was that of indicating some wineries which combine quality and quantity with a price policy that encourages the general consumer and young people to approach wine without economic fears. They honor Italian oenology, offering an approach to wine which quenches the thirst for everyday drinking but also makes an ideal accompaniment to the recipes presented when entertaining at home.

# A Quality Choice

Creating awareness in the consumer and presenting the products that best represent the diversity of Italy to the market. Exploiting products with ancient origins, handed down from generation to generation thanks to the sensitivity of numerous producers who search for quality and enhance unique flavors, bearing witness to the identity of a territory.

These are the aims of the author and editors of Vigneto Italia, which the Consorzio Tutela Grana Padano (Consortium for the Defense of Grana Padano) shares in full, with the same enthusiasm with which it has been operating for almost half a century in order to guarantee and disseminate, in Italy and the world, the quality and uniqueness of a great Italian dairy product: GRANA PADANO.

Emblem of a millenary tradition, the history of this DOP cheese has always been totally linked with the identity of a precise, protected production area.

Common intentions this strong gave birth to the desire to participate in the creation of this new published work.

I hope that in the "country of diversity", that which the authors call "the festival of taste" will continue to privilege quality as the foundation of its choices.

The mission of the Consortium for the Defense of Grana Padano has always focused on this, combining the concept of quality with the commitment to the safety and defense of the consumer.

*Consorzio per la tutela del Formaggio Grana Padano*

# A Synopsis of Italian Viticultural History

Vines were growing in Italy long before the beginning of recorded time. The fossilized remains of prehistoric vine leaves and grape clusters have been found throughout the country.

Some vineyard sites date from the Bronze Age, leading scientists to believe that man was already making wine here on a regular basis at that time. Wine was more than a beverage in these early days: it was thought to possess a mystic power and it played an important role in the religious lives of the ancient tribes who inhabited the peninsula.

grape seeds and cultivation and winemaking techniques, they brought the cult of Dionysus, son of Zeus and god of Wine and Revelry. These original colonies prospered by trading (among other things) local wine with Greek colonies in Africa and with their mother country.

The Magna Greacia vineyards expanded rapidly and the vines that were introduced

*Various types of ancient craters*
*(Museum of Archeology*
*of Agrigento and Lipari)*

## THE ETRUSCANS

The Etruscans arrived in Italy from Asia Minor around 800 B.C. Their first colonies were in the Tuscan area of the Maremma. At the peak of their power, in the 6th and 7th centuries B.C., they controlled the whole of northern Italy from the Tiber to the Alps. They planted vineyards throughout their domain.

## THE GREEKS

The Greeks arrived on Italian shores around 750 B.C., establishing the first colonies of Magna Greacia along the coast of the Ionian sea and on the island of Sicily. Along with

(the antecedents of such varieties as Aglianico, Grecanico and Greco) thrived in their new home.

The early Greeks cultivated their vines at the base of trees and left them to grow close to or even along the ground. This method was later employed by the Romans who colonized Southern Italy and examples of the practice can still be seen on the Sicilian island of Pantelleria.

In Northern and Central Italy, it was more common to follow the Etruscan practice of training vines to grow between the trunks of tallish trees.

## THE ROMANS

By the 5th century, Herodotus and other Greek historians had begun to refer to the area of Southern Italy as *Oenotria*, the land of wine. This name soon spread to the whole of the peninsula as the Romans brought the culture of vine growing to the most far-flung parts of Italy and wine consumption began to increase.

*or when the East wind drives*
*Most vehemently on the ships, to know*
*How many rollers reach the Ionian strand."*

(Virgil, *Georgics, Book II Of Trees*,
lines 122-128 T. F. Royds, Translator)

Pliny lists around a hundred grapes by names and sums up the remainder with the words *"innumera atque infinita."*

The aristocracy began investing in vine growing, with Columella claiming that at least fifteen slaves were required for every 100 jugers, in other words, for every 25 hectares of vines. The Romans based their viticultural techniques on Greek models, sowing Greek grape seeds alongside the many indigenous vines. Virgil declared that there were so many of these local varieties as to render them uncountable:

*"He who would number them,*
*the same would wish*
*To tell the tale of sand that Zephyr stirs*
*On Libya's waste,*

The Romans often planted vineyards and fruit orchards on the same plots of land. Trees were an indispensable part of vine growing in those days, as Virgil's graphic description of vine husbandry reveals:

*"When all is safely planted,*
*it remains*
*To draw the earth about the roots,*
*and ply*
*Stern hoes; or deeply drive*
*the frequent plough,*
*And e'en through vineyards guide*
*the straining steer.*

3

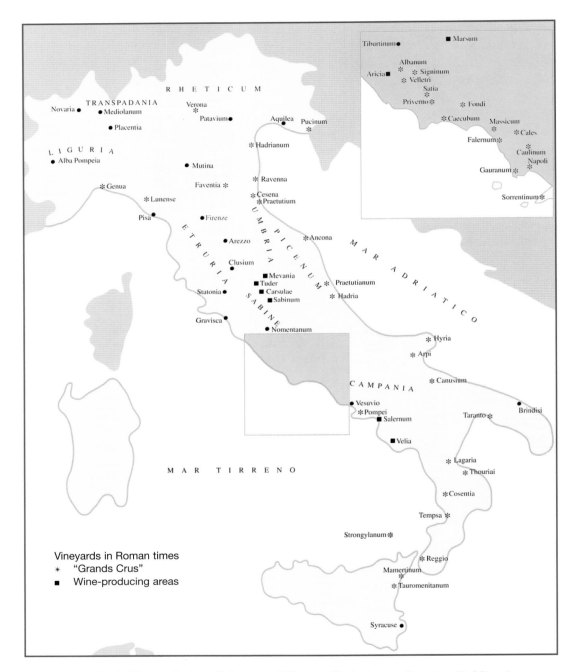

*From Nicola Trapani's* Art, Culture and Tasting Techniques, *Enovitus Publications*

*Then must you furnish shafts*
*of barkless wand,*
*Smooth reeds and ashen poles*
*and stalwart forks,*
*That the young plant, relying on their strength,*
*May rise to mock the winds, and,*
*climbing higher,*
*Attain the topmost storey of the elm.*

*And while sweet childhood's bloom*
*is on the leaves,*
*Spare yet their tenderness;*
*while the vine-spray*
*Leaps blithely into foamless seas of air*
*Unbridled, unrefrained, no pruner's blade*
*May violate the vine; only the leaves*
*Must with bent finger-tips be nicely thinned."*

(Virgil, *Georgics, Book II Of Trees*
424-438 T. F. Royds, Translator).

This Roman period saw the emergence of the first *terroirs*, produced in areas that became renowned for their exceptional quality. The most celebrated of these was undoubtedly *Falerno* produced on the Lazio-Campania border. Other famous wines of Roman times include *Cecubo* (from Salento), *Pucino* (produced between Aquileia and Trieste), *Retico* (from Verona), *Genova* (from Liguria), *Adriatico* (from the Marche) and *Luna* and *Florentinum* from Tuscany.

Early winemaking methods were simple but effective: the harvested grapes were piled into a stone or wooden trough. The free-run juice was collected and set aside to be made into the highest quality wine. Then the grapes were trod underfoot to make wine for everyday drinking. Torque presses squeezed out the last few drops of juice. The crusty residue which remained was pressed into blocks and sold to the poor and to slaves who added water to it to make "instant" wine.

Pressed wine was filtered by using wicker baskets, then left to ferment in large terracotta amphorae, called *doliums*. These generally contained from six hundred to one thousand litres. Each container was buried three-quarters underground to keep temperatures low and constant. The resulting wine was cloudy and thus fining with egg whites or fresh goats milk was carried out.

Once this work was finished, the wine was transferred into other containers and left there until the end of the Vinalia festival at the end of April. The *doliums* were opened and tasting began only after an offering was made to the gods. Even in those times, professional "sommeliers" – known as haustores – existed. They classified wines by color: *album* (white), *fulvum* (yellow), *purpureum et sanguieum* (red), *ater* or *niger* (black) and *halveolum* (rosé).

The wines were also classified according to structure: *fugiens* (low alcohol), *imbecille* (weak), *consistens, solidum et forte* (concentrated, dense and full-bodied), *asper et acutum* (acidic), *generosum et pingue* (generous and rich), *validum et firmum* (easily conserved), and *sordidum et vile* (which, I believe, needs no translation).

Where there are sommeliers, it follows that

*Medieval miniatures on a vine-growing theme*

there are also wine critics freely dispensing their opinions. During the heyday of the Roman Empire Falernian was by far the most popular wine: it earned a mention from Pliny, Martial and Horace, to name but three. Pliny even referred to three different categories of Falernian wine – one alcoholic and rough, one weak, with the third style steering a middle course between the other two. He also said that the wine was at its best at between 10 and 20 years from the vintage.

Virgil, in addition to setting out specific details of the types of soil, exposure, climatic conditions and viticultural methods that are best suited to specific varieties, also offered his warnings as to the effect certain wines were likely to have on an over-imbiber; as we can see from this translation by H. Warner Allen: "There are Thasian vines as well as the white Maraeotic, the one better suited to a heavy, the other to a light soil. The Psythian grapes are best pressed as raisins for dessert wine, and the Lageos, for all its seeming lightness, will make your legs fail beneath you and tie your tongue."
The Roman technique referred to above as "grapes pressed as raisins" is still in common

use throughout Italy today. This procedure is called *appassimento* and the resulting wines are known as *passiti*. These tend to be rich, full-bodied and highly alcoholic. In their Southern colonies, the Romans left the ripe grapes to dry on the vine. In cooler, more humid climates, they harvested the fully ripe bunches and left them to dry in well-ventilated lofts. These drying grapes were sometimes braided and hung from the ceiling.
Today, *appassimento* is used to produce superb dessert wines, such as Torcolato and the Reciotos, Passitos and Vin Santos. This process is also used in the production of rich, dry red wines, of which Amarone is the best-known example. Due to the increasing interest in wine made in this way, the National Centre for Passsito Wines was established in the Umbrian town of Montefalco in 2002. The goal of this new organization is to collect and monitor all research on the process and to establish a display of *passito* wines, with the intention of providing comparative tastings.

The terracotta amphorae used for the fermentation, storage and transport of wine typically held around 40 litres, although some vessels were much larger, measuring 3 meters high by

*More miniatures and capital letters from the same period*

1 meter across. The insides of these vessels were usually sealed with resin or pitch. These containers were closed with corks and sealed with the insignia of the vendor at the moment of sale in order to guarantee the quality of the product. This Roman practice of closing a container with cork fell into disuse, largely forgotten after the fall of the Empire, and did not come into popular use again until the middle of the 16th century. The technique of glassblowing originated in Syria and spread throughout the Roman Empire. Evidence indicates that the Romans also occasionally kept wines in small glass vessels. Once again, our "modern ideas" were already being practiced by the noble Romans.

## THE MIDDLE AGES

The chaos that emerged from the fragmentation and subsequent collapse of the Roman Empire virtually put an end to what had been a thriving international wine trade. However, wine drinking continued apace, at least within the walls of monasteries and in the courts of enlightened monarchs. Vine growing and wine making were carried out principally by religious orders. Techniques remained those inherited from the Romans, with grapes being pressed by foot. Only the large estates run by the aristocracy and the church were equipped with wine presses.

In the 5th century, inhabitants along the coast of what is now the Gulf of Venice fled to a small island in the lagoon to escape the Barbarian invasions. Their collections of huts eventually became the glorious city of Venice. The Venetians earned their reputation as master navigators and traders. By the end of the 6th century, Venice was providing spices, fabrics and other Oriental products to all of Italy. In 1202 the Venetian armada conquered Constantinople, thereby consolidating the city's control of all the important trade routes. Thus, the Venetians acquired a virtual international monopoly on wine trading. Famous wines of the time were Greco from Naples, Patti from Sicily and Turpia and Cutrone from Calabria.

## THE RENAISSANCE

The Republic of Venice continued to expand its territory. However, when Venice lost control of Crete, and the sweet wine that island produced, its merchants were forced to seek wine sources closer to home. They developed the areas around Verona and those in the hills south of Padua, encouraging the production

*A miniature from the 14th century
(Cesanatense Library, Rome)*

of *passito* wines, which withstood the rigors of transport better than wines made from fresh grapes.

Toward the end of the 1400s, Florence began to realize the economic importance of grape growing and wine making. At this time, the noble families of Frescobaldi, Antinori and Mazzei (of Castello di Fonterutoli) expanded their interests to include wine production.

The 16th century saw the reintroduction of glass bottles. Stoppered with cork and wrapped in straw, these vessels radically changed wine commerce.

In this era Italy was forced to adapt both to changes in the economic climate that arose from the founding of the United States of America and the new competition from the wines of Portugal, Spain and France. The transfer of trade routes from the Mediterranean to the Atlantic – the latter controlled by the Dutch and the English – led to the development of the wines of Madeira, Jerez, Malaga, Alicante and the Canary islands. In the meantime, new winemaking techniques evolved, particularly in Bordeaux, where the improvement in quality came about through vine selection and an increase in number of plants planted per hectare.

In the 17th and 18th centuries Italy was not yet a united country, and therefore every major power wanted to stake its claim on the peninsula. The Austro-Hungarian Empire, the House of Savoy and Napoleon all marched troops through the vineyards. With no secure political system in place, trading in wine was difficult.

## 19TH CENTURY

Cyrus Redding writes in his magnificent book, *A History and Description of Modern Wines* (published in 1833), "The wines of Italy have not obtained that character which might be expected, if the excellence of the grape, and the congeniality of the climate to the culture of the vine, be duly considered. The wines of modern Italy are all made for home consumption. The interests of commerce, which lead to competition, have not yet interfered to improve them."

By the 1880s Cabernet and Merlot were already well established in Friuli and the northeastern regions in general, and from here they spread throughout the country. The 19th century also saw an increased interest in the classification of vine varieties. Acerbi laid the foundations of modern ampelography with his treatise "Delle viti italiane", in which he devised a methodical and scientific system for vine classification. A few years later Di Rovascenda wrote a decisive essay entitled "Universal Ampelography."

Despite the proliferation of research, the 19th century proved to be difficult for vinegrowers. Producers throughout Europe faced continual crises as vine diseases followed by ruinous infestation wreaked havoc in the vineyards.

One of the prime causes of massive devastation was *phylloxera vastatrix*, a vine louse whose fiendish lifestyle makes it virtually impossible to arrest. This brazen bug, it has been conjectured, found its way from America to a greenhouse in Hammersmith on the leaves of

*Professions: making the vats (second half of 15th century)*

an ornamental shrub. By 1868 it had infected the vineyards of Bordeaux; by 1884 it had destroyed most of viticultural France and had caused great damage to Austro-Hungary, Germany, Spain, Italy, Portugal and Madeira. Initially, Italy sought to profit from France's woes, and between 1870 and 1890, the nation's wine production doubled and some 80% of its population made a living from vine growing, wine-making and trading.

But the voracious parasite finally took its toll: the phylloxera scourge continued unabated until the late 1880s when scientists realized that the only way to impede this louse was to graft local vines onto American rootstock. This worked because the American plants had existed for centuries along with phylloxera and had, over time, developed an immunity to it. Grafting and replanting required tremendous investments of time and money, and the first few phylloxera-free vintages did not appear until the late

1890s. Italian vineyards (as well as those of other European countries) were drastically altered as heartier and higher yielding vines were replanted to replace diseased vines. Other vineyards were abandoned altogether.

## 20th CENTURY
The World Wars created devastation of another sort, virtually bringing viticulture to a standstill in some areas of Italy as vineyards were destroyed and family estates fragmented. A war never ends neatly with the signing of a peace agreement; the ravages and deprivations can linger for decades. After World War II, there was simply no money to be made in wine, and most fit young people were forced to move to the cities in order to find work to support their families. During this period, land in some areas became virtually worthless, and many of the abandoned vineyards and farms were snapped up by businessmen and foreigners who built summer homes on the land.

*Professions: transporting the grapes (second half of 15th century)*

Other areas were given over to the production of more profitable crops.

G.I.s took back certain scraps of European culture and lore, among them, the idea that "Soave" was a term for light, dry whites, while "Chianti" was synonymous with cheap, dry reds. During the 1950s, one suspects, wines bearing these well-known names may have come from all over the country and from any manner of grapes in order to satisfy the emerging markets. It has taken the Chianti zone – through consistent and concerted effort – decades to revitalize its wines and its image. And Soave, with the exception of a few truly outstanding producers, is still struggling to achieve the recognition it deserves.

During the 1960s, in an effort to shore up the rapidly declining reputation of Italian wines and bring production regulations into line with European community standards, the Italian government set up a system of wine laws, which basically codified the existing realities of historic production zones with regard to yields, grape varieties and boundaries. As the DOC (Denominazione di Origine Controllata) laws were based on "tradition" – which sometimes stretched no further back than the 1930s, and thus accommodated 20th century mass production practices – the government decided to create DOCG regulations for certain zones. The "G" stands for *Garantita* and is supposed to serve as a guarantee of high quality. To receive the "G" rating, wines from a zone must be submitted to tasting panels and show consistently high standards. It also requires that producers work together and agree on just what those standards should be. This is not an easy task. There are, therefore, some truly outstanding wines, which could easily meet the most rigorous criteria but which do not, as yet, enjoy official DOCG approval.

The IGT (Indicazione Geografica Tipica) designation was added to the laws governing Italian wine in 1992 in an attempt to bring order to the much misunderstood "Vino da Tavola" category. IGT wines are firmly linked to their zone of production. Their labels must include the name of the region (or more limited locality) in which they are made. Producers may also include the grape variety/varieties and vintage if they wish.

In the 1980s and 1990s, wishing to attract wider international attention, producers often chose to mask the personality of their local varieties with a dash of Chardonnay or a splash of Cabernet. And because New World wines wrapped in a thick layer of oak were winning awards during this period, many Italians decided to give their wines the same treatment, with wildly varying degrees of success.

## ITALY IN THE 21st CENTURY

The international market's thirst for Chardonnay and Cabernet has reached a saturation point, with "ABC" (Anything But Chardonnay/Cabernet) now being the common battle cry among wine lovers. In this atmosphere of exploration and open-mindedness, Italy has the opportunity to take the wine world by storm, as no other country can offer the same wide variety of flavors and fragrances. Italian producers are now building their future on their unique and age-old viticultural heritage.

*Giotto:* La Vendemmia *(The Grape Harvest)*

# aglianico

Aglianico is often given the epithet: "The Barolo of the South". Certainly, its versatility makes it one of the most important Southern red grape varieties in terms of fine wine production. It lends body and character to lively rosés; to fruity quaffing wines; and to well-structured and velvety textured, long-lived reds. It is cultivated primarily in Campania, Basilicata, Puglia and Molise.

*Castel del Monte in Puglia*

Whatever its origins, the name Aglianico was first used in a letter dated 1559, in which Sante Lancerio, cellarmaster to Pope Paul III, describes the wines of Italy to Cardinal Guido Ascanio Sforza. He wrote, "Aglicanico wine comes from the mountain of Somma in the Kingdom of Naples, where good Greco is made."

Andrea Bacci, Pope Paul III's doctor, also had a word or two to say about this variety.

He wrote: "It is prepared from fairly dry grapes, and is rendered vigorous by ageing in oak and then stored in excellent vessels. It is therefore perfumed, savoury and attractively flavored. It is a very pleasing and stable wine with high nutritional properties: a tonic for the stomach and the limbs rather than an aperitif."

## TASTING NOTE
Ruby tending to brick red. The wine is generally full-bodied, with soft tannins. It is high in acidity. On the palate, there is a seductive blend of black cherry and blackberry fruit, with hints of violets and wild strawberries.

I also often find red licorice tones and bitter chocolate and black pepper notes.

## SYNONYMS
Aglianica, Agnanico, Gnanico, Gnanica, Glianico, Ellenico, Ellanico, Agliano, Gagliano.
Uva dei Cani, Uva di Castellaneta, Spriema, Cascavaglia, Fresella, Cerasole, Ruopolo.

## FOOD PAIRINGS
*Spaghetti alla chitarra*, goat or lamb casseroles, braised red meats in general and mature cheese.

The variety was most likely brought to Italy by Greek colonists during the 8th century B.C.

One theory suggests that the name Aglianico is a corruption of the word *Hellanic* or *Hellenic*, which is a general term for things of Greek origin. Noted ampelographer Professor Attilio Scienza theorizes that its change in spelling and pronunciation can be traced to the Spanish, who dominated parts of Southern Italy in the 15th and 16th centuries.

The double "l" ,when pronounced in Spanish fashion, sounds like the Italian "gli".

Others have speculated that its name is in fact derived from the Latin word *aglaia*, which means "splendor".

## CAMPANIA

The best-known Aglianico-based wine is Taurasi DOCG, whose production zone is centered around the ancient town of Taurasi, in the Campanian Province of Avellino. This town, originally called Taurasia, was a wine-production center long before the Romans conquered the area in 80 B.C. The local wines so impressed the Romans that they transferred thousands of colonists from Liguria to look after the vineyards. Taurasi is made from a minimum of 85% Aglianico. It has an alcohol

vals should be supported for their divine oddness. The Aglianico del Taburno (DOC since 1986) zone includes 12 communes in Benevento province. Its vineyards are planted at between 100 and 600 meters above sea level. The wine is made from a minimum of 85% Aglianico, to which may be added Piedirosso, Sciascinoso (also known as Olivella Nera) and Sangiovese. It has a minimum alcohol level of 11.5% and must be aged for two years before it is released on the market. With an alcohol level of 12.5% and three years ageing the wine

*Characteristic scenes from the coast of Campania.*

*Capri: the small port and the sea stacks*

level of 12% and must undergo three years of ageing. When the alcohol level is 12.5% and the wine has been aged for at least four years (18 months of which must be in wood), it is labelled *riserva*.

The variety also composes 85-90% of many Campanian reds from the province of Benevento. Each year this province hosts a grape festival in the town of Solopaca where models of such famous monuments as the Pisa Cathedral and Chiesa della Salute in Venice are decorated with grapes and presented to the public for viewing. These fast-fading festi-

may be labelled riserva. The refreshing rosé version should be drunk young.

Also in Benevento province is the hilly zone of Guardia Sanframondi (also called Guardiolo). Here, the Aglianico is made from a minimum of 90% of the named grape and has a minimum alcohol level of 11.5%.
When it has an alcohol level of at least 12.5% and is aged for two years, it may be labelled riserva.

The Aglianico produced in the vast Solopaca DOC zone is made from 85% of the named grape and is aged for one year. Aglianico also composes a portion of the blend of Solopaca Rosso and Rosato.

Aglianico is one of the varietals produced in the Sant'Agata dei Goti zone, which is also found in Benevento province.

The wine is made from a minimum 90% Aglianico and must be aged for a minimum of two years before being released to the market. When it has an additional year of bottle age and a minimum alcohol level of 12.5% it may be labelled riserva.

The variety is also blended with Piedirosso and small percentages of other red varieties to make Sant'Agata dei Goti Bianco. Yes, a white wine. The grapes used in its production are vinified off their skins.

The same basic blend is also used to produce a red and rosé.

The Sannio zone includes the entire province of Benevento. Its Aglianico is made in dry, passito and sparkling versions. Grapes for the passito style are left on the vine to dry or are collected and semi-dried on racks. This sweet wine has a minimum of 14.5% alcohol. The sparkling version also tends to be sweet.

In northern Campania, on the border with Lazio, Aglianico is either vinified on its own or with small percentages of Piedirosso to make the soft, and elegant Falerno del Massico Rosso DOC.

Tucked into a corner of northern Campania, between Lazio and Molise, is the Galluccio DOC zone. Here, Aglianico accounts for at least 70% of the zone's red and rosé. Both of these zones are found in the province of Caserta.

The large Cilento zone is located in the province of Salerno. Cilento Aglianico must be aged for one year. Aglianico is also part of the blend of the zone's red and rosé.

---

### CAPRETTO ALLA CAMPANA

SERVES 4
- 1¹/² kilos/3 lb 5 oz kid or lamb
- 1¹/² kilos/10 cups peas
- 4 eggs
- 1 onion
- 50 g/1/2 cup grated Parmesan cheese
- 150 ml/10 tbsp olive oil or pork fat
- salt • pepper
- the juice of one lemon

PREPARATION
Wash the meat and leave it to drain. Sauté the finely sliced onion over a medium heat. When the onion becomes transparent, add the meat. Lower the heat when the meat begins to brown and slowly add enough water to keep the meat from sticking. When the meat is almost done, add the peas (which have already been boiled) and leave them to cook for a few minutes. Just before serving, beat the eggs and add the grated cheese. Mix well, then season with salt and pepper. Spread egg and cheese mixture over the meat and peas. Then pour on the lemon juice. This dish is now ready to serve.

## MOLISE

The Molise DOC zone includes sites in the hills and foothills of around 70 communes in the provinces of Campobasso and Isernia.

Molise Aglianico is made from a minimum of 85% Aglianico, and has a minimum alcohol level of 11.5%.

When it has a minimum of 12.5% and has been aged for at least two years (six months of which must be in wood), it may be labelled riserva.

Aglianico is also included in the blend of Biferno Rosso.

## PUGLIA

The Castel Del Monte zone takes its name from one of Puglia's most impressive monuments, a massive octagonal castle which crowns an isolated peak in the province of Bari. Castel del Monte Aglianico is made from a minimum of 90% of the named grape, and has a minimum alcohol level of 12%. With a minimum alcohol level of 12.5% and at least two years ageing (one year of which must be in wood), the wine may be labelled riserva. It is also made in still and semi-sparkling rosé versions.

### GOAT MOLISE STYLE

SERVES 6
- 1 kilo/2 lb 3 oz goat meat
- 1000 ml/4 cups of red wine
- 2 bay leaves • 2 sage leaves
- 2 sprigs of rosemary • 1 chili pepper
- 80 ml/6 tbsp olive oil • 1 onion, finely chopped
- 500 g/1¾ cups of ripe tomatoes, peeled and chopped
- salt

PREPARATION
Wash the goat meat, dry it with a cloth and then cut it into pieces. Put the meat in a bowl along with the wine and the aromatic herbs, and let it marinate overnight in a cool place. The following day, brown the onions in olive oil. Add the meat to the onions and brown it over a high heat. Then, little by little, add the red wine marinade. When the wine has evaporated, add the peeled and diced tomatoes. Continue to cook, adding hot salted water as needed. Finish cooking over low heat until the meat is still firm and the sauce is dense.

### DOC AND DOCG

**BASILICATA**
Aglianico del Vulture

**CAMPANIA**
Taurasi, Aglianico del Taburno Rosso, Cilento Aglianico, Falerno del Massico Rosso, Galluccio Rosso and Galluccio Rosato, Guardia Sanframondi (or Guardiolo) Aglianico, Sannio Aglianico, Sant'Agata dei Goti Bianco, Sant'Agata dei Goti Aglianico, Sant'Agata dei Goti Rosso, Solopaca Aglianico

**PUGLIA**
Castel del Monte Rosso

**MOLISE**
Molise Aglianico

## BASILICATA

Basilicata's star wine – and its only DOC – is Aglianico del Vulture, whose production area lies on the foothills of Monte Vulture, an extinct volcano.

Its vineyards are planted on tufa-based soils, which are rich in mineral salts, at an average altitude of 500-600 meters above sea level (though some reach to 670 meters).

Aglianico del Vulture is made from 100% Aglianico, is aged for at least one year and has an alcohol level of 11.5%.

When it has a minimum alcohol level of 12.5% and is aged for three years it may be labelled "vecchio". If aged for at least five years, it can be called riserva.

Aglianico del Vulture tends to have a particularly rich, velvety texture. Near its production zone is the ancient town of Venosa (known originally as Venusia), the birthplace of Virgil, whose *Georgics* offer us a beautiful treatise on vine husbandy.

*Vineyard landscape and architecture
typical of the Basilica region.*

### LAMB LUCANA STYLE

SERVES 4
- 1/4 hindquarter of lamb
- 400 g/2½ cups potatoes
- 200 g/3/4 cup tomato sauce
- 200 g/1¾ cup small onions
- 50 g/1/2 cup grated Pecorino cheese
- 50 g/1/4 cup lard
- oregano
- 120 ml/10 tbsp olive oil
- salt and pepper

PREPARATION
Cut the lamb into pieces and put it in a baking pan along with a few tablespoons of olive oil. Then sprinkle the meat with salt, pepper, oregano and lard. Add the peeled, diced potatoes, the tomatoes and the whole onions. Mix well and add the grated Pecorino cheese. Put the pan in the oven and cook for an hour and a half at 200°C/360°F, stirring from time to time.

### MUTTON CHOPS "EN PAPILLOTE"

SERVES 4
- 8 mutton chops
- 16 green olives
- 16 small sweet-and-sour onions
- 40 ml/4 tbsp Puglian olive oil
- salt and pepper

PREPARATION
Carefully peel and wash the onions. If you wish to eliminate the bitter aftertaste of the onions, leave them in a pan of water for a day, changing the water frequently.
Place each chop, 2 olives and 2 onions on a piece of aluminium foil. Season with salt and pepper and drizzle with olive oil. Then tightly close the aluminium foil.
Place in a pre-heated oven for around 30 minutes. Serve at the table still wrapped in foil, so as to preserve the fragrance.

# albana

The Romans most likely brought
Albana to Romagna. There are
those who believe that the variety
takes its name from the Albani hills,
south of Rome. For others, the
name is derived from the Latin word
for white: *albana*.
This variety, a veritable sugar factory,
is relatively high in acidity and has
unusually high quantities of tannins
in the seeds and skins. It is
particularly suitable for wood ageing.

*Vineyard of Albana*

In 1987, Albana di Romagna earned the distinction of being the first white wine to receive the DOCG denomination.

The production zone for Albana di Romagna is concentrated on hillsides in the Romagnan provinces of Forli, Ravenna and Bologna on the southern edge of the Po Valley between the Apennines and the Adriatic. Here the fossil-rich soil is a mixture of clay, limestone, marl and sand.

The climate is continental, with cold winters and hot, dry summers.

Albana di Romagna is produced in four styles. Secco (dry), Amabile (semi-sweet), Dolce (sweet) and Passito.

Albana Secco tends to be a light, zippy white intended for drinking young. The Amabile is fresh, fruity and attractively sweet. It has a minimum alcohol level of 12%, as does the Dolce

version. It is the Passito, however, that has achieved the most important international recognition. When made from carefully selected grapes by a skilled winemaker, Albana Passito is rich, succulent and seductive. There is a great deal of leeway in the production of this wine.

Grapes may be left to over-ripen on the vine, or bunches can be picked and left to semi-dry on racks or mats in special, well-ventilated rooms. Vinification can be carried out in stainless steel tanks or barrels.

The wine's minimum alcohol level is 15.5%, and it must be aged for at least six months. Most winemakers, however, age their wines for two to four years. On average, less than 200,000 bottles of Albana Passito are made each year.

The producer who introduced the world to tru-

*Pressing of Albana grapes in specialized greenhouses*

ly classy Albana Passito is Cristina Geminiani of Fattoria Zerbina, an estate located in Faenza. Geminiani was the first to recognize the importance of selective harvesting of noble rot infected bunches and she was one of the first to vinify and mature Albana Passito in barrels, thereby creating her now legendary Scacco Matto (Checkmate) Albana di Romgagna DOCG.

A Romagna Albana Spumante is also produced.

To make this sweet, velvety sparkling wine (which has a minimum alcohol level of 15%), Albana grapes are left to semi-dry before pressing.

In the Colli Bolognesi, an area that includes the hills near the town of Bologna, Albana is blended with Trebbiano Romagnolo to make a light dry white called Colli Bolognesi Bianco.

## TASTING NOTES

Albana Secco: Straw, with pale golden highlights.

Imaginative tasters find subtle hints of peaches, roses, almonds and sage in the fragrance. There is a wide variation in the quality of these wines.

At its best, the wine's acidity adds to its overall appeal. But all too often the acidity dominates the palate.

Albana Passito: Golden yellow. On the nose one finds scents of peaches, apricot, candied fruit, acacia honey and, from the wood, spices and vanilla.

These fragrances are echoed in the rich palate and carry through the long, lingering finish. Well-made versions are often, and justly, compared to first-class Sauternes.

*Bologna: The Tower of the Asinelli*

## SYNONYMS
Albana di Romagna, Albana di Forli, Albana di Bertinoro, Albana Gentile, Forcella, Albana di Bertinoro, Riminese.

## FOOD PAIRINGS
Dry Albana: fish-based appetizers or prosciutto. Passito Albana: Foie Gras, or Gorgonzola, Castelmagno, Roquefort or Stilton cheese.

---

### MORTADELLA MOUSSE

SERVES 6
- 400 g/14 oz mortadella di Bologna
- 150 g/1/2 cup fresh whipped cream
- 1 tbsp of Parmesan cheese

PREPARATION
You may pound the mortadella and the cheese in a mortar and then pass it through a sieve or you may whizz the mortadella and cheese in a blender until a creamy consistency is obtained.
Then gently add the whipped cream, mixing well. Serve the mousse in goblets, and garnish with toast triangles.

---

### DOC AND DOCG

**EMILIA-ROMAGNA**
Albana di Romagna (dry, agreeable, sweet or passito)
Colli Bolognesi Bianco
Romagna Albana Spumante

# albarola

This vine may be of Tuscan origin.
It is still used as a lesser component
in some of that region's blended
whites, such as Candia dei Colli
Apuani and Montescudaio Bianco.
In Liguria it is a major component in
wines from the Cinque Terre zone,
and, under the name Bianchetta
Genovese, it is occasionally vinified
as a varietal. It also boosts the
alcohol level of other Ligurian
blended whites.

*Cable winch of an old-fashioned cart used for transporting casks.*

## TASTING NOTE
Pale yellow with green highlights. It has a light scent of wild herbs. On the palate it is slightly astringent.

## SYNONYMS
Bianchetta Genovese, Bianchetta, Gianchetta, Trebbiana, Trebbiano locale, Termosci, Trebbiana Bianca, Trebbianadi Sarzana.

## FOOD PAIRINGS
Aperitif, or with fish or snail-based dishes.

| DOC AND DOCG |
|---|
| **LIGURIA**<br>Bianco del Golfo del Tigullio, Bianchetta Genovese del Golfo del Tigullio, Bianco di Valpocevera, Bianchetta Genovese di Valpocevera |

### WHITEFISH PANCAKES

SERVES 4
- 500 g/1 lb 2 oz whitefish
- 75 g/5 tbsp of flour
- 1 handful of parsley
- 250 ml/1 cup olive oil
- salt and pepper

PREPARATION
Mix the flour with a tablespoon of olive oil and a little cold water to form a batter of medium consistency. Then mix in the cleaned whitefish, the finely chopped parsley, a pinch of salt and a dash of freshly ground pepper. Put the mixture in a cool place to rest for around half an hour. At this point, heat the olive oil in a pan and add enough batter to make a pancake.
When each pancake is finished, gently place it on absorbent paper towels. Lightly salt and serve piping hot.

# aleatico

This variety is most likely a mutation of Moscato Nero, which originated in Tuscany. Today, it is cultivated in Tuscany, Puglia, Lazio, Campania and Sicily, where it adds a gentle moscato-like sweetness to the perfumes of blended reds. It is the sole component in Elba Aleatico (Tuscany) and Aleatico di Gradoli (Lazio).

## TASTING NOTES
Ruby to garnet in colour. The wine is aromatic (hints of moscato) and has a fruity, soft texture.

## SYNONYMS
Uva Liatica, Agliano, Aleatico Nero della Toscana, Aliatico di Benevento.

## FOOD PAIRINGS
Simple desserts.

---

### DOC AND DOCG

**TUSCANY**
Elba Aleatico, Val di Cornia Aleatico

**LAZIO**
Aleatico di Gradoli

**PUGLIA**
Aleatico di Puglia, Gioia del Colle Aleatico Dolce, Gioia del Colle Aleatico Liquoroso, Salice Salentino Aleatico Dolce, Salice Salentino Aleatico Liquoroso Dolce

---

### MOSTACCIOLI (LAZIO)

SERVES 6
- 60 g/ 4 tbsp flour • 100 g/3/4 cup shelled walnuts
- pepper • 100 g/6 tbsp honey
- 2 egg whites • cinnamon

PREPARATION
Mix the flour with the honey, egg whites, walnuts, a dash of pepper and a dash of cinnamon. Knead the mixture, then spread it out on the work surface. Cut the dough into rectangular pieces. Put them on a baking sheet and bake at a moderate heat for around 20 minutes. Remove from the baking sheet when they are completely cool.

### WHEAT GRANOLA (PUGLIA)

SERVES 6
- 300 g/$1^{1/2}$ cup of wheat kernels • salt • 50 g/6 tbsp almond slivers • 50 g/6 tbsp chopped hazelnuts
- 100 g/1/2 cup chocolate chips • 1 tsp powdered cloves
- 1 tsp powdered cinnamon • 200 g/1 cup candied fruit

PREPARATION
Let the grains of wheat swell in water for 3 days, changing the water each day. Cook the wheat in abundant salted water, then drain. Let it cool, then put it in a pan. Mix in all the other ingredients and serve.

### GRAPE BREAD (TUSCANY)

SERVES 6
- 500 g/1 lb 2 oz bread dough • 500 g/$4^{1/4}$ cups of red grapes • 150 g/3/4 cup sugar • 50 ml/3 tbsp extra-virgin olive oil

PREPARATION
Mix the dough with some of the grapes and the oil. Knead well, then add the egg to the dough and knead it in. Put the dough in a baking pan and decorate with the remaining grapes and let rise. Sprinkle with sugar and bake for 35 minutes at 180°C/350°F.

# arneis

This variety is grown in Piedmont's Cuneo Province, with the greatest density of vineyards found on the left bank of the Tanaro River in the Roero DOC zone.

The first written record referring to this variety appeared in a document dated 1478, in which reference is made to a vineyard planted with *moscatelli and renexi* (the archaic name for Arneis).

Arneis is usually vinified to dryness, although some producers also make a sweet wine from semi-dried grapes. It is used in combination with other local varieties (Favorita, Cortese) as a base for sparkling wines.

The name Arneis is derived from a dialect word which refers to an odd person or a child who never listens to his parents.

In the old days, a row or two of this variety was often planted in red-grape vineyards and its anomalous nature probably explains its name.

## TASTING NOTE

This is a refreshing straw-yellow wine, with delicate apricot and green apple notes on the nose and palate.

## SYNONYMS

Bianchetto, Bianchetta (d'Alba), Nebbiolo Bianco.

## FOOD PAIRINGS

Flavorful antipasti, seafood, *vitello tonnato* and stuffed peppers.

| DOC AND DOCG |
|---|
| **PIEDMONT** |
| Roero Arneis (100% Arneis) |
| Langhe Arenis (100% Arneis) |

---

### ALBESE-STYLE RAW MEAT WITH ROYAL ARGARIC OR BOLETUS MUSHROOMS

SERVES 6
- 350 g/12 oz veal fillet
- 200 g/2¼ cups mushrooms
- 100 ml/1/2 cup extra-virgin olive oil
- 1 lemon • salt and pepper

PREPARATION

Choose freshly opened royal argaric mushrooms. Clean and slice them thinly, then cut the meat into thin slices and arrange them in a flower pattern and arrange it in petals around a plate. Sprinkle the mushrooms over the meat. In a bowl whisk together oil, salt and pepper. Use this sauce to dress the meat and serve immediately.

### RAINBOW TROUT FLAVORED WITH SAGE AND ONION

SERVES 8
- 1 rainbow trout weighing about 1500 g/3 lb 5 oz
- 1/2 onion • 10 sage leaves
- 50 g/3 tbsp butter
- 30 g/1tbsp flour
- 150 ml/1/2 cup white wine
- 50 g/3 tbsp red wine vinegar • salt

PREPARATION

Clean and fillet the trout and cut it into 8 steaks. Gently fry the sage and onion in the butter and, when golden, add the steaks, cooking them for two minutes on each side. Remove the trout steaks and keep them hot. Add the flour to the butter onions and sage, blending into a paste before adding the white wine and vinegar. Boil for 2-3 minutes until the sauce thickens, then pour it over the trout and decorate with raw cherry tomatoes and julienned artichokes.

# barbera

Barbera is found throughout Italy. In its native Piedmont, it is usually vinified as a single-variety wine, while in other regions it is more often part of a blend.

It is a vigorous variety that thrives on sand- or clay-based soils. However, many producers feel that it gives its most elegant results on limestone-rich soils in relatively cool sites.

Long considered a convenient, "workhorse" grape, Barbera was used for blending and supplied local tables with easy-drinking wines. With its medium to high acidity, deep color and medium to low tannins, it is extremely malleable and, in the past, producers readily turned out semi-sparkling, novello and even "white" versions.

While the variety can indeed be made into all of these styles, a good Barbera, when the grapes have been picked at optimum ripeness and great care has been taken in the cellar, is nothing short of magic.

The variety's name may derive from a cross between the word *barba* (beard) which was used to describe its complex root system and the dialect word *albéra* (which in turn is derived from the Latin *albuelis*). This term refers to the wooded sites where Barbera vines were first planted.

## PIEDMONT

The vine originated in the Monferrato hills of Piedmont, and it remains the most widely planted variety in the region, along with Moscato. It is the major component in eleven of Piedmont's DOC wines. The best-known of these are from the variety's home ground: the provinces of Asti, Alessandria and Cuneo.

## BARBERA D'ALBA DOC

The Barbera d'Alba production zone includes the areas of the Langhe and Roero in the province of Cuneo, where the grape is reputed to have been first introduced, in 1685, by Count Cotti of Neive.

The wine is made from 100% Barbera and has a minimum alcohol level of 12%. It may be labelled *superiore* when it has a minimum alcohol level of 12.5% and has been aged in wood for at least one year. When yields are reduced and when the grapes are harvested at optimum ripeness, Barbera produces deeply colored, robust yet refreshing wines, with luscious and appealing flavors of prunes and custard.

## BARBERA D'ASTI DOC

The Barbera d'Asti zone is centered on hillsides around the town of Asti, in the provinces of Asti itself and of Alessandria. The wines from Asti tend to be sumptuous and full-bodied and usually benefit from a little bottle-age. The wine is made from at least 85% Barbera, with the option of adding up to 15% Freisa, Grignolino and Dolcetto, either singly or in any combination. The wine must be aged until at least March 1st following the harvest. It has a minimum alcohol of 12%.

Wines labelled superiore have a minimum alcohol level of 12.5%, and have been aged for at least a year, six months of which must be in wood. The word "Nizza" on the label of a Barbera d'Asti Superiore means that the grapes used to produce the wine come from vineyards around the small town of Nizza Monferrato. Producers in this sub-zone have decided to carve out a special niche for themselves, with a particularly strict production code. Their goal is to produce wines with considerable structure that offer a consistently reliable level of quality in every vintage. Growers in the "Colli Astiani" (or "Astiano") and "Tinella" areas are also trying to follow suit.

## BARBERA DEL MONFERRATO DOC

The Barbera del Monferrato zone is also in the provinces of Asti and Alessandria.

The grape mix is the same as that of the Asti zone. Here the minimum alcohol level is 11.5%. With one year's ageing and a minimum alcohol level of 12.5%, the wine may be labelled superiore. In this zone, too, there has been a move away from producing light and lively (even often frothy) wines towards products with greater complexity and staying power.

## COLLI TORTONESI BARBERA DOC

The Colli Tortonesi zone, in the province of Grignolino, grown in the hills of the communes of Gabiano and Moncestino in the province of Alessandria. When the wines have been aged for at least two years and have a minimum alcohol level of 12.5%, they may be labelled riserva. Wines from the following zones tend to be of a lively and easy-drinking style: Collina di Torino (the entire province of Turin), Colline Novaresi (Novara province), Canavese (communes in Torino, Biella and Vercelli provinces) and Pinerolese (Torino and Cuneo provinces). This is also true of those bearing the basic regional Piedmont denomination.

## FURTHER PIEDMONTESE DOCS

*Grape harvesters on the steep slopes of Castagnole and San Giorgio Monferrato*

Alessandria, lies on the border with Lombardy's Olrepò Pavese zone. Barbera here is made from a minimum of 85% of the named grape. The minimum alcohol level is 11.5%. When it has 12.5% and at least one year ageing (six months of which must be in wood) it may be labelled superiore. Barberas from the zone's top producers have good structure and a creamy richness on the nose and palate.

## GABIANO DOC AND
## RUBINO DI CANTAVENNA DOC

Gabiano and the Rubino di Cantavenna DOCs are blends of 70-95% Barbera, with Freisa and

## BARBERA BASED

The first special, single-vineyard selection of Barbera was the Bricco dell'Ucellone from the 1982 vintage, released in 1985.

Its producer was Giacomo Bologna, founder of the Braida estate, which is located in the village of Rocchetta Tanaro in the province of Asti.

Bologna, who passed away in 1990, was one of the most dynamic, incisive and charming personalities on the Italian wine scene, and it is essentially thanks to his efforts in modifying the way Barbera is vinified that the variety has been brought into the international limelight.

*Old-fashioned vineyard shelters and winter work in the vineyards of the Langhe*

Michele Chiarlo, too, is a long-time proponent of Barbera. "You must remember," says Chiarlo, "that there are at least two major types of Barbera, the traditional one and the cru, and there are great differences between the two categories.

"The former tends to be a wine produced in large volumes, which should be drunk within five or six years. Then there are the Super Barberas which are grown in sites which are particularly suited to the variety, and where yields are reduced and the number of bunches is kept low.

"These wines are usually picked 10 to 20 days later than the regular harvest. Wines from such grapes are suitable for ageing in small barrels and have decidedly longer cellaring capacity: from 10 to 12 years. But to make such a wine takes more than just *terroir* and technology –

the producer must have the right mentality and strength of will to make a Super Barbera."

## LOMBARDY

Barberas from the Oltrepò Pavese zone, in the province of Pavia, tend to be lighter and more lively than those of Piedmont.

Barbera is the main variety in Oltrepò Pavese Rosso and Rosato, and in the fancifully named Buttafuoco, Barbacarlo and Sangue di Giuda. Barbera is mixed with Schiava Gentile, Marzemino and Sangiovese in the blend of Botticino DOC. The same group of varieties also form the basis for the DOCs of Cellatica and Capriano del Colle Rosso. Barbera usually takes a back seat to Cabernet Franc and Cabernet Sauvignon in the blend of Terre di Franciacorta Rosso.

## EMILIA-ROMAGNA

The Colli Piacentini zone lies on Emilia-Romagna's border with Lombardy. Here Barbera is blended with Croatina (often referred to locally as Bonarda) to make Gutturnio DOC. This wine can be light, fizzy and quaffable or it may be deeply colored, full and fruity, with the potential for long ageing: it depends entirely on the skills and the intentions of the producer.

A varietal Barbera is also made in the Colli Piacentini. This wine may be still or sparkling, and ranges from dry to sweet in style.

The Colli Bolognesi DOC zone is located in the Apennine foothills in the province of Bologna, on a mixture of limestone and clay soils. Within this district are seven sub-zones, five of which make a dry varietal Barbera. These are Colline di Riosto, Collie Marconiane, Serravalle, Terre di Montebudello and Monte San Pietro.

Their alcohol levels range between 11.5% and 12.5%. With three years' ageing, only Monte San Pietro may be labelled riserva. Barbera from the Colli di Imola zone (which is also in the province of Bologna) is made in both still and semi-sparkling styles. Barbera also makes up a good portion of the blend of Colli di Parma Rosso.

## SARDINIA

It is likely that Sardinian Barbera is descended from seeds brought to the island from the mainland, and the resulting vines vary slightly from their antecedents.

The variety is cultivated in the provinces of Cagliari, Oristano and Sassari. The styles local producers achieve with this grape vary widely, from simple and rather rough to velvety and full-bodied.

## CAMPANIA

In Campania, there are two DOCs containing Barbera: Castel San Lorenzo Barbera (85%) and Rosso (60-80%).

Castel San Lorenzo Barbera, when it has 12.5% and has been aged for at least two

*Work and vineyards in Monferrato*

*A landscape of the Roero: Montaldo and its ancient tower.*

years (of which six months must be in wood), may be labelled riserva.

## TASTING NOTE

Barbera-based wines are usually ruby-red in color, with purplish highlights when young. Their nose is fresh, with soft scents of ripe plum, sensations that are carried through onto the palate.

Well-made barriqued versions will be lush, dark, rich and creamy with warm spicy fruit which gracefully unfolds on the nose and palate.

## SYNONYMS

Barbera Amaro, Barberone, Barvesino, Barbin.

## FOOD PAIRINGS

Lighter styles make a fine accompaniment to pasta and rice dishes. In Piedmont it is the wine par excellence for accompanying *Bagna Càuda*.

The more firmly structured and barriqued styles are well suited to red meat dishes or mature cheeses.

| DOC AND DOCG | EMILIA-ROMAGNA |
|---|---|

**PIEDMONT**

Barbera d'Asti, Barbera d'Alba,
Barbera del Monferrato, Barbera Colli Tortonesi,
Barbera Collina Torinese, Barbera Colline Novaresi,
Rubino di Cantavenna, Gabiano,
Collina Torinese Rosso, Piemonte Barbera, Pinerolese
Barbera

**LOMBARDY**

Barbera Oltrepó Pavese, Oltrepó Pavese Rosso, Oltrepó
Pavese Rosato, Oltrepó Pavese Sangue di Giuda

**EMILIA-ROMAGNA**

Colli di Parma
Barbera Colli Bolognesi
Gutturino Colli Piacentini (Emilia-Romagna) 60%
Barbera, 40% Bondarda

**CAMPANIA**

Castel San Lorenzo Barbera
Castel San Lorenzo Rosso
Castel San Lorenzo Rosato

**SARDINIA**

Barbera di Sardegna

## BAGNA CÀUDA

SERVES 10
- 10 heads of garlic
- 1 litre/4 cups extra-virgin olive
- oil
- 20-25 salted Spanish anchovies
- 2500 ml/10 cups fresh milk
- VEGETABLES TO DIP: cardoons, raw peppers, baked peppers, peppers pickled with marc and vinegar, Savoy cabbage, celery, Jerusalem artichoke, baked beetroot, baked onions, boiled potatoes and boiled cauliflower.

PREPARATION

Break the garlic into cloves, peel them, remove the internal germ and lay them in a terracotta dish, covering them with milk. Leave overnight to mellow, this tames the garlic for sensitive palates. Then slice the garlic and cook in fresh milk over a low heat in a terracotta saucepan. After about an hour the garlic will become creamy. Wash red Spanish anchovies which have matured for at least a year in water and wine, remove the bones and dry the fish before adding them to the milk and garlic.
They too will dissolve, turning the cream brown and thickening it. Greater smoothness and creaminess can be achieved by blending briefly with a hand blender. At this point mix in very hot (but not fried) oil. The Bagna Càuda is ready to be served in specially made modern terracotta containers heated from below with a tea light. The traditional ritual of dipping the sliced raw vegetables can now begin.
When the Bagna Càuda is almost finished, a free-range hen's egg is cooked in the remaining oil, with an abundant sprinkling of white truffle of Alba.

## PHEASANT IN "SALMÌ"

SERVES 4
- 1 pheasant • 1 stick of celery
- 100 g/3½ oz bacon
- 1 carrot
- 1 onion
- oil and butter to cook in
- 1 sprig of rosemary
- 100 ml/1/2 cup dry white wine
- 50 ml/4 tbsp
- the pheasant's liver
- a small white truffle

PREPARATION

Pluck and clean the pheasant. Wash it and dry it, then slice the bacon and wrap the bird. Place the oil and butter in a copper saucepan and cook the pheasant in the oven at a medium heat until golden.
In the meantime chop the onion, carrot, celery, rosemary and pheasant's liver and add them to the pheasant. Add the wine, salt and pepper and cook for an hour and a half. When cooked, keep the pheasant hot. "Bind" the juices and vegetables with the cognac and cook for a minute. Now cut the pheasant into pieces and pour the "Salmì" sauce over it. As a final touch cover with petals of finely sliced truffle.

## STEWED OX

SERVES 8
- 1½ kilos/3 lb 5 oz ox blade
- 1 litre/4 cups Barolo wine
- 2 carrots
- 1 onion
- 1 stick of celery
- 1 bay leaf
- 1 clove
- 2 cloves of garlic

INGREDIENTS FOR COOKING AND SAUCE:
- 2 carrots
- 1 stick of celery
- 1 onion
- 100 ml/1/2 cup extra-virgin olive oil • 100 g/3½ oz sausage
- 100 g/3½ oz liver (veal or pig)
- 20 g/1 tbsp butter
- 500 ml/2 cups Barolo wine

PREPARATION

Twelve hours before cooking place the joint to marinate with all the finely chopped ingredients. Cover the meat completely with the wine and store in a cool place for the time indicated. When it is time to start cooking, discard the ingredients used for the marinade and prepare those for cooking. Finely chop the fresh carrot, celery and onion and fry gently in the butter.
Arrange the vegetables, the marinated meat, liver and sausage in a saucepan and add the oil. Cover and cook gently for an hour, then pour in the Barolo and cook for another two hours. Keep the meat hot and sieve the cooking liquid, creating the sauce. Serve slices of meat with very hot sauce.

# bombino

(white and black grape)

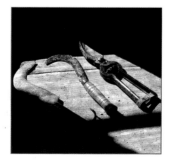

This variety is something of a mystery. No one has yet determined with certainty anything about its history. It occasionally turns up under the name Trebbiano in the blends of some excellent wines. It goes by the name Pagadebit (Debt Payer) and Stracciacambiali (Debt Settler) in Emilia-Romagna. These names refer to the variety's high yield, which allowed farmers to pay off their bills.

## BOMBINO BIANCO

Bombino Bianco is in the blends of many Puglian dry whites, as well as passito and late-harvest wines.

In the past, Bombino Bianco grapes were largely exported to Germany under the name Uva d'Oro or Gold Trauben.

## TASTING NOTE

Straw yellow to pale gold in color. Its flavors and fragrances are subdued. It has a velvety texture.

## SYNONYMS

Trebbiano d'Abruzzo, Pagadebit, Bonvino, Cola Tamburo, Trebbiano Campolese, Trivolese, Uva Castellana, Uva Romana.

## TASTING NOTE

Aperitif or with light white fish dishes.

## BOMBINO NERO

The origins and history of this southern Italian variety are unknown. It is found principally in Puglia, Basilicata, Lazio and Sardinia, where it is usually blended with such red varieties as Uva di Troia, Malvasia Nera, Aglianico and Motepulciano. It is the principal variety in Puglia's Castel del Monte Bombino Nero DOC, and may appear in the blend of Castel del Monte Rosato.

## FOOD PAIRINGS

Ruby red, aromatic, lightly tannic, high in extract.

## SYNONYMS

Bambino, Buonvino.

| DOC AND DOCG (BOMBINO BIANCO) |
| --- |
| **EMILIA-ROMAGNA** |
| Pagadebit di Romagna |
| **PUGLIA** |
| Castel del Monte Bombino Bianco |
| San Severo Bianco |
| Leverano Bianco |

| DOC AND DOCG (BOMBINO NERO) |
| --- |
| **PUGLIA** |
| Castel del Monte Rosato |
| Castel del Monte Bombino Nero |

# bonarda

Due to a string of misidentifications that stretches back hundreds of years, quite a bit of confusion surrounds the Bonarda, Croatina and Uva Rara varieties.
Bonarda originated in Piedmont and its cultivation is pretty much restricted to that region.

It is the main component in varietal wines, but it usually serves to add color and zest to such DOC blended wines as Sizzano, Boca, Lesona, Fara, Gattinara, Ghemme and Coste Della Sesia.

It is sometimes grown as a table grape.

## TASTING NOTE

Ruby with a purple sheen. It is lightly aromatic. On the palate, the wine is soft, with an amalgam of cherry and berry fruit flavors.

## SYNONYMS

Bondarda Piemontese, Banarda di Chieri, Bonarda del Monferrato, Bonarda dell'Astrigiano.

## FOOD PAIRINGS

Meat-filled ravioli, hot antipasti.

---

### DOC AND DOCG

**PIEDMONT**

Colline Torinesi Bonarda,
Colline Novaresi Uva Rara or Bonarda,
Piemonte Bonarda, Coste della Sesia Bonarda
or Uva Rara, Pinerolese Bonarda

**LOMBARDY**

Oltrepo Pavese Bonarda

**EMILIA-ROMAGNA**

Colli Piacentini Bonarda

---

### AGNOLOTTI AL PLIN

SERVES 6

FOR THE SAUCE: • 150 g/5 oz pork loin • 200 g/7 oz leg of veal • 200 g/7 oz rabbit • 200 g/7 oz escarole • 4 eggs • 20 g/1 tbsp Parmesan cheese • 20 g/1 tbsp butter • 50 ml/3 tbsp extra-virgin olive oil • 1 onion • 1 carrot • 1 sprig of rosemary • salt and pepper to taste

PREPARATION

Sauté the onion, carrot and the rosemary in oil and butter. Add the meat and brown it over a high heat. Once browned, lower the heat and continue to cook. Halfway through cooking add the lettuce, which has been washed under running water. Cook over a low heat for around 3 hours. Once cooked let the meat cool. Then cut it into small pieces and add 4 whole eggs and the Parmesan cheese and salt and pepper. Roll the pasta dough out into a very thin sheet. Cut into largish squares or rounds. In the center of each piece of pasta put a spoonful of the meat mixture. Cover with another piece of pasta and pinch the edges of the pasta together, so that no filling can escape during cooking. Cook them in abundant salted boiling water for 6 to 10 minutes, according to the thickness of the pasta. Traditionally in the Langa and Monferrato areas, agnolotti are served with meat sauce or with melted butter and sage leaves.

### SOUP PAVESE STYLE

SERVES 8

• 16 pieces of bread • 120 g/1/2 cup butter • 12 eggs • 60 g/1/4 cup grated Parmesan cheese • 1500 ml/3 lb 5 oz meat stock

PREPARATION

Heat the stock. Fry the bread in butter, taking care that the outside is golden but that the inside remains soft. Arrange two pieces of fried bread in each individual terracotta soup bowl and two eggs on top of the bread. Sprinkle with abundant grated Parmesan cheese and add a ladle of boiling stock, taking care not to pour the stock directly on top of the egg yolk.

*Vineyards around Gattinara*

## UVA RARA

The name "Uva Rara" is sometimes used to identify Bonarda in those areas where "Bonarda" is already being used to indicate Croatina.

Are you with me so far? An Uva Rara variety does exist in its own right, however. Its high level of sugars makes it a good table grape. It is rarely vinified on its own; rather it adds alcohol and a delicate fragrance of violets to blends.

### TASTING NOTE
Pale ruby with purple highlights. A lightly floral bouquet. Moderate acidity, minimal tannins and a lightly bitter aftertaste.

### SYNONYMS
Bonarda di Cavagliá, Bonarda di Gattinara, Balsamina, Oriola, Raione

# bosco

This is one of the most important varieties in Liguria; it is a component in the blend of practically all the region's white wines. Its name (*bosco* means "a wood") may be derived from the dense forests of its zone of origin, Cinque Terre.
From here, the variety spread to the area around Genoa.

It is rarely vinified on its own, but rather is blended with other local varieties, such as Albarola and Vermentino. Bosco is suitable for semi-drying, and is composed of at least 40% of Cinque Terre and Cinque Terre Sciacchetrà. The grapes for this latter wine are semi-dried to make a rich, golden to amber-colored dessert wine, which has a minimum alcohol level of 17%.

## TASTING NOTE
Straw yellow to pale gold. On the nose, one finds scents of wild herbs and chamomile flowers. Some tasters like to refer to "hints of the sea". On the palate the wine is soft and savory.

| DOC AND DOCG |
| --- |
| **LIGURIA** |
| Cinque Terre, Sciacchetrà delle Cinque Terre |

## SYNONYMS
Bosco Bianco, Bosco Bianco del Genovese, Uva Bosco.

## FOOD PAIRINGS
The dry version goes with fish dishes in general (whether baked or in a sauce). The passito version may be drunk on its own or with pastries.

*The Ligurian Coast around the "Cinque Terre"*

### CIUPPIN

SERVES 6
• 1½ kilos/3 lb 5 oz fish (eel, Conger eel, monk fish, octopus, cuttlefish, scorpion fish, etc.) • 1 onion, thinly sliced • 1 stalk of celery, chopped • 1 carrot, finely chopped • a handful of parsley, finely chopped • 2 cloves of garlic, finely chopped • a pinch of oregano • 75 ml/5 tbsp extra-virgin olive oil • 4 ripe tomatoes, de-seeded and peeled • 100 ml/1/2 cup white wine • salt and pepper

PREPARATION
Clean and fillet the fish and cut it into pieces. In an earthenware pot, fry the chopped vegetables and the seasonings in a little oil.
When they begin to brown, add a glass of wine and cook until the liquid evaporates. Then break up the tomato pulp with your fingers and add it to the earthenware pan. Mix well.
Cover the pan and leave to cook for around 30 minutes. Now add the fish pieces. Salt and pepper to taste. Cover and cook slowly for around 2 hours: until the mixture is reduced to a consistent textured sauce.
Put the fish and the sauce in a vegetable mill and then colander, collecting the liquid in a pan. Bring the "creamy" liquid thus obtained to a boil.
Put toasted croutons in the bottom of an individual earthenware soup bowls and pour the boiling liquid on top of them.
Add more croutons.
Just before serving sprinkle with freshly chopped parsley.

# brachetto

Brachetto is thought to have originated in the hills of Asti and Monferrato. Some believe that its use as a wine grape dates from Roman times. However, if this is so, its charms appear to have remained hidden until the 19th century, when the fashion for sweet, fizzy wines reached its peak.

This demand inspired local producers to set their sights on conquering international markets.

These hopes were dashed when *phylloxera vastatrix* arrived in the vineyards.

When time came to replant, this low-yielding variety lost ground to more prolific vines. During its heyday, Brachetto was planted in every province in Piedmont and even spilled over into the Oltrepó Pavese and Liguria. After World War I, its production zone became limited to the provinces of Asti, Alessandria and Cuneo, with its most highly esteemed vineyards lying in the hillsides around the commune of Acqui Terme.

Brachetto from this latter area received the coveted DOCG in 1996 under the name Brachetto d'Acqui. The slightly sparkling wine has a minimum alcohol level of 11.5%, while the fully sparkling version has a minimum alcohol level of 12%. A much larger area, consisting of hillsides in parts of the provinces of Alessandria, Asti and Cuneo produces the DOC wine: Piemonte Brachetto. This sweetish and often fizzy wine is made from a minimum of 85% Brachetto and has a minimum alcohol level of 11%. This variety is seldom vinified to complete dryness. There are, however, a few producers (particularly in the Roero) who are giving this style a try. With its low tannin level, good acidity and well-defined perfumes, it is ideal for sparkling wine production. Brachetto is best when drunk young.

---

### DOC AND DOCG

**PIEDMONT**

Brachetto d'Acqui
Piemonte Brachetto

---

### HAZELNUT CAKE

SERVES 4
- 200 g/3/4 cup ground roasted hazelnuts
- 200 g/3/4 cup powdered sugar
- 7 egg whites
- salt

PREPARATION

Whip the egg whites until firm. Then gently fold in the ground nuts, the sugar and a pinch of salt.
Spread the mixture on a baking sheet; it should be around 3 centimeters thick.
Bake at 150°C/300°F. for around 40 minutes. This in one of Piedmont's favorite desserts.

---

## TASTING NOTE

It is usually a bright pink-tinged red. On the nose are scents of strawberries and roses. It is supple and refreshing.

## SYNONYMS

Bracchetto, Borgogna.

## FOOD PAIRINGS

It is sometimes served as an aperitif. It goes well with non-acidic fruits like strawberries and peaches, and with nuts, particularly walnuts, hazelnuts and pistachios.

It is often served with plain sponge cakes or fruit tarts.

There are those who believe that this wine can even stand up to nut-based cakes drizzled with chocolate.

# canaiolo

Canaiolo, whose origins are uncertain, is cultivated mainly in Tuscany and, to a lesser degree, in the neighboring regions of Marche, Lazio, Umbria and Liguria. Its name may be derived from *dies caniculares* (dog days), the sultry period from late July through August when the grape changes color.

Canaiolo (along with Sangiovese, Malvasia and Trebbiano) was part of Baron Ricasoli's original formula for Chianti, and it is still an accepted part of the blend for DOCG Chianti and Chianti Classico.

It also may be included in the blends of the Tuscan DOC/DOCGs: Vino Nobile di Montepucliano, Carmignano, Colli Dell'Etruria Centrale, Colline Lucchesi, Montecarlo, Pomino, Rosso di Montepulciano, Sant'Antimo Rosso and Val di Cornia Rosso, and in the Umbrian DOC/DOCGs of Torgiano and Colli Amerini Rosso. Some producers are now experimenting with varietal Caniolo Nero.

## TASTING NOTE
Dark ruby red. On the nose one finds hints of black cherry fruit. As it matures, the wine develops lightly herbaceous top notes.

## SYNONYMS
Canaiolo Nero Comune, Canaiolo Nero Grosso, Canina, Cagnina, Uva dei Cani, Uva donna, Uva Merla, Uva fosca.

## FOOD PAIRINGS
It goes well with most vegetable-based dishes and is particularly nice with the following recipe for Beans "all'uccelletto".

### BEANS "ALL'UCCELLETTO"

SERVES 6
- 400 g/14 oz dried white Toscanelli beans
- 400 g/14 oz vine tomatoes
- 2 cloves of garlic • a sprig of sage
- 90 ml/6 tbsp oil • salt and pepper

PREPARATION
Leave the beans to soak in cold water overnight, then cook them in tepid water to soften them and drain them. Gently fry the garlic and sage in 6 spoonfuls of oil, add the beans and sprinkle with ground pepper. Add the peeled tomatoes and salt to taste. Cover and cook on a medium heat for about 15 minutes, until the tomato is completely dry. Eliminate the herbs and serve.

### CANAIOLO BIANCO

This indigenous variety is grown mainly in Tuscany and Umbria, where it is used to add weight to whites, such as Orvieto.

TASTING NOTE
Green-tinged yellow. Good body.
SYNONYMS
Canojolo, Caccione, Caccinella, Canina, Cacciumo, Uva Vecchia, Canajolo Bianco, Colomban, Tulopeccio, Drupeggio

# cannonau

Cannonau was probably brought to Sardinia by the Spanish in the 1400s. In Seville, the variety was known as Canonazo. Today it is more widely known in Spain as Ganache or Granaxa. In southern France, Valle d'Aosta, Algeria and Tunisia it goes by the name of Grenache.

The dry, windy climate of Sardinia is ideal for Cannonau.

After the phylloxera outbreak swept through Sardinia, Cannonau became a popular replacement variety. It emerged as a major player in the early 20th century, and is now the most widely planted vine on the island. It is used in the production of reds, rosés and fortified wines.

The Cannonau di Sardegna DOC zone includes the entire region. Within this area, are three sub-zones: Oliena (centered on the communes of Oliena and Orgosolo in the province of Nuoro), Capa Ferrato (which includes the communes of Castiadas, Muravera, San Vito, Villaputzu and Villasimius in the province of Cagliari) and Jerzu (centered on the communes of Jerzu and Cardedu in the province of Nuoro). Cannonau di Sardegna has a minimum alcohol level of 12.5% and is aged for at least six months. If it has an alcohol level of 13% and has been aged for at least two years is may be labelled riserva.

Liquoroso (or fortified) Cannonau is made in two styles: Dolce Naturale (a sweet version, a minimum alcohol level of 16%) and Secco (which is dry and has a minimum alcohol level of 18%). Both these styles must undergo at least six months of barrel ageing.

## TASTING NOTE

The wine is ruby red. It is usually well-structured with blackberry flavors. A wood-aged Cannonau can be powerful and long-lived, and its black-cherry fruit is shaped by a touch of chocolate.

## SYNONYMS

Granaccia, Grenache, Cannonao.

## FOOD PAIRINGS

Pasta dishes with very rich, meaty sauces, roast lamb, grilled meats and porcini mushroom-based dishes.

Its traditional Sardinian pairings are with *porceddu* (roast sucking pig) and land snails stewed in tomatoes

Cannonau Liquoros: This style is usually served with sweet biscuits after dinner, or as a *vino da meditazione*.

| DOC AND DOCG |
|---|
| **SARDINIA** |
| Cannonau di Sardegna |

### SPIT-ROASTED SUCKLING PIG

SERVES 8
• 1 suckling pig
• lard
• salt and pepper

PREPARATION

After you have gutted the pig, scrape the skin and burn off the bristles. Wash and dry the pig. Then put it on a spit in such a way that, when the pig revolves, its lowest part will be around $1^{1/2}$ feet from the fire.

When the meat begins to sweat, begin to turn the spit. Keep turning the animal until it is well cooked and a dark golden brown in color. While the pork is turning, put a few drops of lard on top of it. Be sure to salt and pepper the entire pig.

When done, slice the pork and place it on a serving tray and cover with myrtle leaves. Serve hot.

# carignano

Small amounts of Carignano are planted in Tuscany, Marche and Lazio, where the variety adds color to some blended reds and rosés. But it is in Sardinia that Carignano has made its strongest showing. It most likely arrived on the island with the Spanish in the 14th century. It found its ideal environment in the Sulcis area, in the province of Cagliari.

Here it is the main component in Carignano del Sulcis Rosso.

When this wine has a minimum alcohol level of 12.5% and has undergone three years of ageing, it may be labelled riserva.

Rosé and semi-sparkling versions are also produced.

## TASTING NOTE
Deep garnet red. It is round and full-bodied.

## SYNONYMS
Carignan, Uva di Spagna, Roussilloner.

| DOC AND DOCG |
|---|
| **SARDINIA** |
| Carignano, Carignano del Sulcis Rosso e Rosato |

## FOOD PAIRINGS
Good with lamb and goat-based dishes, as well as rich meaty pasta sauces.

*Orosei, Sardinia: the 7th -century "Church of the Souls"*

### CULUNGIONIS
### (Sardinian ravioli)
SERVES 6-8

FOR THE PASTA: • 300 g/2½ cups flour • 1 egg yolk • 120 ml/1/2 cup water
FOR THE SAUCE: • butter to taste • 8 sage leaves • 1 sachet of saffron dissolved in hot water • 100 g/1 cup grated Pecorino cheese
FOR THE FILLING: • 800 g/3½ cups mashed boiled potatoes • 200 g/1¾ cups fresh Pecorino cheese • 50 g/1/2 cup mature Pecorino or Grana Padano cheese • 50 ml/3 tbsp extra-virgin olive oil • 15g/1tbsp fresh mint

PREPARATION

To make the filling mix the fresh grated Pecorino cheese with the potatoes, oil and mint.

Set to one side and leave to rest. Pour the flour onto a pastry board and form a mound with a dip in the middle. Place the egg yolk in the dip and gradually pour in 6 tbsp of water.

Knead the dough thoroughly, adding a little water as needed. When the dough is smooth and elastic, roll it out into a thin sheet. Cut out discs measuring around 5 inches across.

Place the discs in turn on the palm of your hand and drop a spoonful of filling into the center. Close and seal the edges carefully.

The culungionis must look like little bags. In addition to the sauce suggested here, they can be served with tomato sauce.

Cook the culungionis until "al dente" in a large pot of salted boiling water.

In the meantime melt the butter in a frying pan before adding the sage and saffron dissolved in water.

Drain the culungionis and toss in the sauce before serving sprinkled with grated mature Pecorino cheese.

# carmenère

In the 18<sup>th</sup> century Carmenère was widely planted in the Médoc, where it helped add color and body to the zone's wines. Its name is said to be derived from the word "carmine", an obvious reference to its deep color. It is a low-yielding variety due to its susceptibility to coulure (failure of the vines to flower properly).

After phylloxera swept through Bordeaux, Carmenère lost ground to less vulnerable varieties. It made its way to northeastern Italy, mistakenly identified as Cabernet Franc, in the early 19th century. It is widely planted in Veneto, Trentino and Friuli, and, to a lesser degree, in Lombardy. Under the misnomer Cabernet Franc, Carmenère is a component in several DOCs. Because the correct name, "Carmenère", is not listed in the official DOC regulations, it cannot appear on the label of the DOC wines in which it plays a part. Innovative producers, whose faith in this variety is strong, have elected to create non-DOC wines which showcase the variety. Stefano Inama produces his award-winning Brandisimo, in the Colli Berici zone of Veneto, from a typical Bordeaux blend of a century ago: 65% Cabernet Sauvignon, 30% Carmenère and 5% Merlot. In the Latisana zone, the Masi company is semi-drying the grapes to add to their Grandarella, which is made from around 70%-75% Refosco, 15-20% Carmenère and 5-10% Corvina. Ca' del Bosco, the internationally acclaimed Franciacorta producer, has created a 100% varietal wine, whose label clearly depicts Carmenère's identity crisis: it shows a roguish, smiling wolf draped in a sheep's hide.

## TASTING NOTE
Ruby. Good body, with round mouth-filling flavor. It is slightly herbaceous when young. Its hints of green pepper, ripe black currant, cranberry and black pepper become fuller and more seductive with time.

## SYNONYMS
Cabernet Grande, Cabernet Italico, Uva Francese, Carbouet, Grand Vidure.

## PRODUCERS
Inama, Ca' del Bosco, Masi.

## FOOD PAIRINGS
Red meats, mature cheeses.

---

### DOC AND DOCG

With the wrong name of Cabernet Franc is one of DOCs

**LOMBARDY**
Garda Colli Mantovani, Terre di Franciacorta

**TRENTINO ALTO ADIGE**
Alto Adige, Trentino

**VENETO**
Bagnoli, Colli Berici, Colli Euganei, Lison Pramaggiore

**FRIULI VENEZIA-GIULIA**
Grave del Friuli, alone or with Cabernet Sauvignon and Merlot

# catarratto

This ancient vine is one of the most widely planted varieties in Sicily, adding body and alcohol to many local whites.

Before the introduction of Grillo, Catarratto was used on its own or was blended with Inzolia for the preparation of Marsala.

There are two important sub-varieties. Catarratto Comune, which is most heavily cultivated in the Trapani area, has a high sugar content, and is, therefore, most suitable for Marsala production.

Catarratto Lucido, which has a lower sugar level, is most widespread in the Alcamo zone.

## TASTING NOTE

Straw colored. On the nose, the wine is fresh, with touches of honeysuckle and lemon oil. It has good body and structure. On the palate, there is a light savory element that is reminiscent of wild herbs.

If picked on the green side it has a grassy note, which some tasters find similar to Sauvignon Blanc.

## SYNONYMS

Cataratto Bianco Nostrale, Cataratto Bianco Latino.

## FOOD PAIRINGS

Fish-based antipasti and soups, shellfish dishes, mature Pecorino.

*Sicily: vineyards facing the sea*

---

**DOC AND DOCG**

**SICILY**

Alcamo Bianco (also in "vendemmia tardiva"), Alcamo Catarratto, Contea di Sclafani Bianco, Contea di Sclafani Catarratto, Etna Bianco Melfi Vendemmia Tardiva (with Chardonnay and some more), Sambuca di Sicilia, Santa Margherita di Belice Bianco, Santa Margherita di Belice Catarratto, Sciacca Bianco

---

**SWORDFISH ROLLUPS**

SERVES 6

• 18 slices of swordfish • 30 g/1/4 cup grated Pecorino cheese • bread crumbs • capers • 50 g/1¾ oz boiled swordfish pulp • 10 green olives, finely chopped • parsley • 1 onion • 1 tablespoon tomato sauce • bay leaf • chili pepper • olive oil • salt

PREPARATION

Mix together the bread crumbs, the Pecorino, the boiled swordfish pulp, the capers, the finely chopped olives, the parsley, the tomato sauce, the oil, the salt and chili pepper. Put some of this mixture on each slice of swordfish. Roll the swordfish round the mixture and put it on a skewer, alternating the swordfish rollups with bay leaves and pieces of raw onion. Cook on the grill.

# cesanese

There are two main biotypes of Cesanese: Comune and d'Affile. As the names imply, Cesanese Comune is found at various sites around Lazio, while the production zone for Cesanese d'Affile is limited mainly to the province of Roma, with the variety being particularly prevalent in the commune of Affile.

Three DOC wines are based on these two bio-types: Cesanese del Piglio, Cesanese di Affile and Cesanese di Olevano Romano.
Their production zones are clustered together, and lie east of the Castelli Romani zone. These wines may be dry or sweet and are made in a variety of styles (still, semi- and fully sparkling).

## SYNONYMS
Cesanese di Affile: Cesanese del Piglio, Cesanese d'Olevano.
Cesanese Commune: Bonvino Nero, Nero Ferrigno, Sanginella.

## TASTING NOTE
Ruby with an orange sheen. On the nose one finds herbal notes of sage and rosemary. The wine is silky textured and has the slight astringency and flavor of plum skins.
Notes of wild plums and slightly under-ripe cherries soaked in brandy are also found on the palate.

## FOOD PAIRINGS
Rice with a light sauce. Light antipasti.

*The Abbey of St. Nilo at Grottaferrata.*

| DOC AND DOCG |
| --- |
| **LAZIO** |
| Cesanese del Piglio, Cesanese di Affile, Cesanese di Olevano Romano |

| **WILD CHICORY (PUNTARELLE) SALAD** | |
| --- | --- |
| SERVES 6 | |

- 1 kilo/2 lb 3 oz wild chicory
- 1 clove garlic
- 3 anchovies, de-boned and rinsed
- vinegar
- 50 ml/3 tbsp olive oil
- salt
- pepper

PREPARATION

Wash the wild chicory and discard the green outer leaves and the hard, woody bits.
Immerse the wild chicory in cold water for around an hour. Drain and dry the leaves and put them in a salad bowl.
Prepare a sauce by grinding (using a mortar and pestle) the anchovies, garlic, a little vinegar, oil, salt and pepper together.
Dress the wild chicory with this mixture and serve.

# ciliegiolo

This variety was probably introduced
by the Spanish.
The name derives from the aroma
and the color of cherries that are
characteristics of the grape.

Ciliegiolo is cultivated mainly in the south of Tuscany where it plays a marginal role in blends. Rather low in acidity, it is used to round out blends of wines that need softness.
Sometimes used in the Tuscany novellos.

## TASTING NOTE
Ruby red in color, full and soft.

## SYNONYMS
Cilgiegino, Ciliegiolo di Spagna

## FOOD PAIRINGS
First courses with light sauces and second courses of white meat; for example, roast rabbit and chicken "alla diavola".

| DOC AND DOCG |
|---|
| **TUSCANY** |
| Parrina, Colli Lucchesi, Chianti, Chianti classico, Val di Cornia Ciliegiolo |
| **LIGURIA** |
| Golfo del Tigullio Ciliegiolo, Colli di Luni Rosso |

## CHICKEN "ALLA DIAVOLA"

SERVES 4
- a chicken weighing about a little more than a kilo/2 lb 10 oz
- 60 ml/4 tbsp olive oil
- 1 lemon
- salt
- pepper

PREPARATION

Cut the chicken in half lengthways and flatten it with your hands. Coat it with oil, salt and pepper and cook it on a very hot grill, over the barbecue or in a cast iron pan, searing to color both sides and then continuing on a moderate heat to cook right through. If the chicken is very young it will take just half an hour. While cooking cover the chicken with a lid which is slightly smaller than the pan, so that it doesn't close, and weight it down: in this way it will cook more evenly.
Serve with wedges of lemon and fresh salad.

# coda di volpe

This is an ancient Campanian variety, whose name is derived from the fact that the shape and size of its bunches are thought, by some, to resemble a fox's (*volpe*) tail (*coda*). Two varietal Coda di Volpes are produced in Campania.
The Sannio zone encompasses the entire province of Benevento.

Here Code di Volpe is the primary grape in a still, dry varietal wine; in dry or sweet sparkling wines; and in a dessert wine made from semi-dried grapes. This Coda di Volpe Passito has a minimum alcohol level of 14.5%.

The Taburno zone, also located in the province of Benevento, lies in cool foothills and is surrounded by the Sannio zone.

The soil is clay on a stratum of volcanic limestone.

Taburno Coda de Volpe is a dry, still wine made from at least 85% of the named grape. In this zone, a zesty, easy-drinking sparkling wine is made from a blend based on Coda di Volpe and/or Falanghina.

Coda di Volpe is planted in vineyards on the slopes of Vesuvius, (the active volcano that overlooks the Bay of Naples), and plays a part in Vesuvio Bianco.

This variety is also included in the blends of the DOCs: Campi Flegrei Bianco, Greco di Tufo and Solopaca Bianco.

*Campania: the Paestum*

## FOOD PAIRINGS

Rice salad, seafood salad, grilled vegetables, spaghetti with garlic and oil, and soft cheeses.

## TASTING NOTE

Straw to pale golden in color. The wine has zippy acidity, a medium body and a savory, slightly tangy saltiness on the palate.

---

**DOC AND DOCG**

**CAMPANIA**

Taburno Coda di Volpe, Vesuvio Bianco, Sannio Coda di Volpe, Greco di tufo, Campi Flegrei

---

**VERMICELLI VESUVIUS STYLE**

SERVES 4

• 1 kilo/3$^{1/2}$ cups peeled tomatoes • 2 cloves of garlic, chopped • 1 hot chili pepper • 150 g/5 oz green olives, pitted and chopped • 50 g/1$^{3/4}$ oz capers • 125 ml/1/2 cup olive oil • parsley, finely chopped • 400 g/3/4 lb vermicelli

PREPARATION

Fry the garlic in oil. Add the peeled tomatoes and cook for around 15 minutes over a low heat. Add the capers, the olives and the chili pepper, and let cook for another 15 minutes. Cook the Vermicelli "al dente" and dress with the sauce. Then sprinkle with finely chopped parsley

# colorino

Colorino evolved from a wild Tuscan vine, and it is still cultivated primarily in the Tuscan provinces of Firenze, Siena, Arezzo and Pistoia. It is also found to a much lesser degree in Umbria, Marche, Lazio and Liguria.

As one may deduce from its name, Colorino was traditionally used to add a deep, satisfying color to blended wines. Producers are beginning to experiment with the variety and it could, in the future, play a bigger role in blended wines.

## TASTING NOTE
Deep beetroot-like red. It has an earthy note in its soft lindenberry-scented nose. On the palate, one finds hints of soft-fleshed apples, such as Golden Delicious.

## SYNONYMS
Abrostino, Colore, Raverusto.

## FOOD PAIRINGS
It goes very well with Tuscan first and second courses, in particular "parpardelle" with hare sauce.

*A view of Lucca*

### DOC AND DOCG

**TUSCANY**
Colli Lucchesi Montecarlo

### PAPPARDELLE WITH HARE

SERVES 4
• 1/4 hare • 125 ml/1/2 cup oil
• onion • red wine • rosemary
• garlic • thyme • marjoram • salt
• pepper • nutmeg
• 400 g/3/4 lb fresh pasta pappardelle

PREPARATION
Finely chop the herbs and place in a saucepan with the garlic. Add the hare chopped into pieces. Salt and pepper and cook over a medium heat, sprinkling with oil. When the hare is nicely browned, add a glass of red wine. Continue to add wine to the stewing meat until the meat is tender. Remove the bones. Pass the meat through a mincing machine. Crush the bones in a mortar. Fry the mince in the oil and sauce. Add nutmeg and a little pepper and the crushed bones and thicken the sauce. Boil the pappardelle in salted water; drain well and dress immediately with the very rich sauce.

# cortese

Cortese is believed to have originated in the Tortona and Alessandria zones of Piedmont. It then spread into the Oltrepó Pavese and to vineyards around Lake Garda. It has a high concentration of sugar, substantial acidity and relatively subdued alcohol. The best examples of Cortese are supple and have tenuous scents. When describing such wines, the fine line between delicate and insipid has occasionally been blurred.

## PIEDMONT

Cortese di Gavi is the best-known example of this variety. Its vineyards are planted on the hillsides around the ancient walled town of Gavi in the province of Alessandria. This wine was first championed by Vittorio Soldati in the early 1950s. It subsequently became Italy's second white DOCG (after Albana di Romagna). A furious spate of experimentation began with techniques such as cryo-maceration and the use of barrique. Today, many producers are coming to the conclusion that the wine shows at its best in its simpler, easy-drinking style. Oaked Cortese di Gavi, while often very well made and satisfying, tends toward anonymity. Such wines could, in fact, be substituted for oaked Chardonnays from anywhere in the world.

Before the outbreak of phylloxera at the end of the 19th century, Cortese was one of the most widely planted white varieties in the Novi Ligure and Tortona zones. The vineyards producing Colli Tortonesi Cortese lie on a band of hills in the province of Alessandria, on the border with Lombardy. Its wines, which may be still, semi- or fully sparkling, are made exclusively from Cortese. Cortese dell'Alto Monferrato and Piemonte Cortese are made from a minimum of 85% of the named grape, and they, too, are made in a variety of styles.

### WARM CAPON SALAD

SERVES 6
- 1 free-range capon weighing about 1½ kilos/3 lb 5 oz
- 1 capon liver
- 20 g/1 tbsp of butter • 1 onion • 1 leek
- 1 sprig of rosemary • salt and pepper
- 1 tbsp of chopped parsley
- salad leaves as preferred
- extra-virgin olive oil
- red wine vinegar

PREPARATION
Place a drizzle of oil, a knob of butter, the onion and rosemary in a saucepan. Fry gently until golden and add the whole capon. Gently fry until golden on both sides for about fifty minutes, then leave to cool slightly, remove the bones and leave in the oven at a temperature of 180°/350°F. Cook the liver in a knob of butter for three to four minutes on a high flame, adding the chopped parsley at the end of this time. Prepare the serving plates with a bed of seasonal salad leaves, equally distributing the capon after cutting it into fair-sized pieces, and dress with the gravy made from the liver and parsley. Add some finely sliced leek rings and a few drops of red wine vinegar.

### MARINATED TURKEY FILLET

SERVES 6
- 6 turkey fillets • 5 capers • 3 anchovies • 4 lemons
- 50 g/1/4 cup of black "Taggiasche" olives
- 200 ml/1 cup of olive oil

PREPARATION
Marinate the six fillets in oil and lemon juice for 10 hours. Then coat the fillets with white flour and fry for 4-5 minutes. Take the fillets out of the pan and place the other ingredients in the same pan and cook for one minute. Cut the turkey into slices and serve warm with the sauce made from the other ingredients.

*The fortress of Gavi with vineyards*

## LOMBARDY
Oltrepo Pavese Cortese is made from at least 85% of the named grape. Its alcohol level hovers at around 10.5%. It comes in still, semi- and fully sparkling versions.

## VENETO
Garda Cortese (minimum 85% Cortese) is fresh and slightly sweet. Its production zone lies on the hillsides around Lake Garda, and includes vineyards in the Veneto commune of Verona and the Lombardy communes of Mantova and Brescia.

## TASTING NOTE
Straw colored. The best Corteses are supple, and have very delicate perfumes of apples and apricot. On the palate, they have an attractive saline quality.

## SYNONYMS
Cortese Bianco Corteis, Courteis.

## FOOD PAIRINGS
Oysters, grilled vegetable-based dishes, sword fish carpaccio, seafood salad.

*Sprawling vineyards around Lake Garda*

---

### RISOTTO WITH PERCH

SERVES 6
- 800 g/1¾ lb perch filets and their skeletons
- 1 onion • 500 g/2½ cups rice • 1 sprig of sage
- 125 ml/½ cup glass of white wine • 140 g/½ cup butter • white flour • vegetable stock • salt

PREPARATION
Cook the fish bones in abundant salted water for around 20 minutes. Then strain the liquid to remove the bones, and bring to a boil. Fry the chopped onion in 3 tbsp of butter and add the rice. Stir it with a wooden spoon to make sure that each grain is toasted. Then add the wine. When this has evaporated, add the stock a ladle at a time until the rice is cooked. Meanwhile, flour the fish filets and fry them in 1/4 cup of butter, with the sage leaves. When the fish are golden, drain them on absorbent paper. Serve the rice covered with the filets, adding, if you like, the rest of the sage and melted butter.

---

### DOC AND DOCG

**PIEDMONT**
Cortese di Gavi o Gavi, Colli Tortonesi Cortese, Cortese dell'Alto Monferrato, Monferrato Casalese, Piemonte Cortese

**LOMBARDY**
Oltrepo Pavese Cortese

**VENETO**
Garda Cortese

# corvina (rondinella - molinara)

This variety seems to show at its best in the hillsides that form the Bardolino and Valpolicella zones in the Veneto region.

Here, a few producers make varietal Corvina, with varying degrees of success. The first, and certainly the most impressive of these wines thus far, is Allegrini's full-bodied yet supple La Poja.

Generally, however, (and this is certainly the case in the most famous reds of the Verona area), Corvina serves as the primary component of a blend. Its main partners are Rondinella and Molinara, along with the option of including small percentages of a vast array of other varieties (Barbera, Sangiovese and Cabernet among them).

As part of such blends, Corvina is found in charming, zesty rosés, medium-bodied reds, luscious dessert wines, and rich, powerful Amarones. Corvina is also the main component in a light and undistinguished yet quaffable red table wine, whose vineyards lie on the shores of Lake Garda.

## BARDOLINO

The Bardolino zone lies on the hillsides just to the east of Lake Garda, and is named after the small lakeside town of Bardolino. The wine is usually fresh, light and dry. Some producers are turning out fuller-bodied wines by semi-

*The grape harvest in crates in the Bardolino area*

drying some of the grapes before pressing. The differences between a fine Valpolicella and a "beefed up" Bardolino are blurring. Bardolino Superiore, which must have a minimum alcohol level of 11.5% and be aged for one year, has the distinction of being the Veneto's first red DOCG wine. It is well-structured and fruity but retains the zesty freshness which should be the hallmark of the wines of this zone. Bardolino Chiaretto (rosé) wines offer a vivacious accompaniment to summer meals, and Bardolino Novello claims the distinction of being Italy's first DOC "primeur" wine.

## VALPOLICELLA

The Valpolicella district begins to the east of the Bardolino zone, its vineyards fanning out around the city of Verona. Going from north to south, the zone reaches from the Lessini Mountains down to the Veronese plain. The Valpolicella area overlaps at points with the Soave zone to the east.

Before Amarone's rise to prominence, the mainstay of the zone was Valpolicella, a simple, refreshing red which did not aspire to anything higher than washing down your plate of bigoli or gnocchi. Now, with demand for Amarone far outstripping supply, some producers are finding ways to add muscle to Valpolicella in the hopes of getting a slice of the full-bodied wine market. Some are choosing to re-ferment Valpolicella on the lees of Amarone, while others are adding dried grapes to the fermenting wines. At this point, the only way of knowing which style is in any given bottle of Valpolicella is by tasting and keeping a note of the wine producer's name.

## AMARONE

Amarone is made from the same grape varieties as Valpolicella. The differences between the two wines begin with the harvest. The perfectly ripe bunches of grapes destined for Amarone are picked by hand a few days before those for Valpolicella. The bunches are then spread in a single layer on racks or in crates and are left in well-ventilated lofts to dry for around 100 days. This process concentrates the fruit and sugar contents. The resulting must is very rich and dense and it can take months to ferment to dryness. Majestically opulent Amarone is one of the only dry red wines to be made in viable quantities from semi-dried grapes. However, let the buyer beware. As a result of Amarone's newfound popularity (pre-1991, the wine was produced in very limited quantities and its true fans were limited to a few eccentrics keen on obscurities), some "new" producers have suddenly emerged who are turning out wines that just barely come up to DOC standards as they attempt to cash in on Amarone's considerable selling power. True Amarone, whether it be the dark, incense-tinged, velvety-textured traditional style or the fresher but no less powerful modern style, will always provide an exotically heady nose, whose luscious, almost sweetly ripe fruit is echoed on the palate.

Again, it is up to you, the wine lover, to keep track of the names of the producers who offer the type of wine you appreciate. Modern Amarones are ready to drink when they are released onto the market. The wine will also evolve in bottle: the spiciness of the oak will take on more intense notes of nutmeg, and

*Pressing the grapes*

the fruit flavors will expand beyond simple cherry tones to include hints of hazelnuts, leather and blackberries. Due to its substantial acidity, however, Amarone retains a distinct liveliness on the palate as it ages. A 1967 Bertani Amarone I tasted in 2000 still offered a youthful color and a fresh and satisfyingly rounded flavor.

## RECIOTO

Recioto della Valpolicella is also made from the same varieties as Valpolicella. Recioto differs from Amarone production in the following ways: 1) the grapes are usually dried from a week to several months longer and 2) the fermentation process is stopped before the wine has vinified to dryness.

Locally it is Recioto which is served at celebrations and offered to friends who drop by. Most Reciotos are best drunk within five years

of the vintage. That said, I have tasted a forty-year old Recioto (from the Tedeschi estate) which retained its precise dried-cherry fruit flavors during the hour the bottle remained open.

## TASTING NOTE
### CORVINA

A 100% Corvina wine is a fairly intense ruby. It is full-bodied and has a rich flavor and fresh, delicate perfumes. On the palate one finds hints of bitter cherries. Corvinas are often matured in oak barrels which, of course, add a spicy tone.

### BARDOLINO

It displays a paler ruby red color, with zesty and crisp cherry-like notes on the nose. Its taste is fairly dry with a hint of bitterness on the finish.

### AMARONE

Round, smooth, spicy, with ample weight and alcohol. Fresh, yet filled with dark, velvety cherry fruit. The finish should be long and filled with evolving fruit flavors.

### VALPOLICELLA

Medium to deep ruby. A whiff of bitter cherries on the nose. The wine's body can range from light and sprightly to full-bodied, depending on the intention of the producer.

### RECIOTO DELLA VALPOLICELLA

With all well-made Reciotos, there should be a fine balance between acidity and full, rich fruit. While the wine will be sweet, it should never be fat or cloying. Fragrances and flavors can include: dried cherries, cherries preserved under alcohol, blackberries, wild mint, nutmeg and incense.

### SYNONYMS

Corba, Corbina, Corgnola, Corvina Comune, Doppia, Nera, Reale and Rizza.

### FOOD PAIRINGS

Bardolino: Grilled trout, vegetable-based dishes, *bigoli con le agole* (thick spaghetti served with whitebait), *risotto alla tinca* (tench risotto) and *carne salada* (a starter of salted raw beef). Valpolicella: Soppressa (a local salami), or pasta and rice dishes served with meat or mushroom sauces. Fuller-bodied versions can be paired with *pastissada di caval* (horsemeat stew) and *bigoli con l'anatra* (thick spaghetti with duck ragout).

Recioto della Valpolicella: Plain pastries and sponge cakes.

Amarone: Brasato all'Amarone or mature Grana Padano or Parmesan cheeses. Some prefer to drink Amarone outside of mealtimes.

---

### BIGOLI WITH DUCK GIBLET SAUCE

SERVES 6
- 400 g/3 cups flour
- 50 g/1/4 cup butter
- 3 duck eggs
- milk
- duck giblets
- butter and olive oil

PREPARATION

Prepare a dough with the flour, eggs, butter and enough milk to obtain a firm and elastic dough. Prepare the bigolis, let them rest and the take care not to let dry them. Roll out the bigolis.
Clean the giblets.
Cut them into pieces and fry in butter or oil.
Add salt and continue to cook, adding water or stock to keep the pieces from sticking.
Cook the bigoli in abundant salted water. When the bigoli are done, dress them with the duck giblet sauce.

---

### BIGOLI COI ROVINAZZI

SERVES 6
- 350 g/3/4 lb bigoli
- 250 g/1/2 lb chicken giblets
- 100 g/1/2 cup butter
- sage leaves
- grated Parmesan cheese
- salt

PREPARATION

Cook the bigoli in abundant salted water. Meanwhile, clean the giblets and cut them into small pieces. Fry them in butter, then add some sage leaves.
Remove the chicken liver from the pan. Salt the remaining giblets and continue to cook for 20 minutes, adding a little water if needed.
Just before removing the pan from the heat put the chicken liver back into the pan. Drain the bigoli, dress them with the giblets and abundant Parmesan cheese.

---

### ANATRA COL PIEN (Duck with Stuffing)

SERVES 6
- 1 duck • 100 g/1/4 lb duck liver
- 70 g/2$^{1/2}$ oz soppressa • parsley
- garlic • 1/2 onion, sliced
- celery, chopped
- carrot, chopped
- bread crumbs
- grated Parmesan cheese
- 2 eggs • nutmeg • salt

PREPARATION

Clean the duck. Put the onion, a carrot, a celery stalk and a little salt in abundant boiling water. Clean and chop the duck liver and the soppressa. Then chop a good handful of parsley and a clove of garlic. Add all these ingredients into the pot. Mix together an egg, a good handful of Parmesan cheese, the breadcrumbs and a pinch of nutmeg. Fill the duck's cavity with this mixture. Sew up the cavity and put the duck in the pan of boiling water (in which the vegetables have been cooking). When the duck is cooked, open it. Remove the stuffing and slice the duck. Serve hot.

## OTHER GRAPES IN THE BLEND

The following varieties are all native to the area around Verona and may be used in the blend of Amarone, Valpolicella, Recioto della Valpolicella and Bardolino.

## CORVINONE

For decades this grape was thought to be a bio-type of Corvina but in 1993 DNA testing proved that it is a variety in its own right. When Corvinone is cultivated in the lower valley or on the plain, it gives high yields and its large berries absorb and retain water. These are not the attributes of a fine wine grape. However, when planted in hillside vineyards on meager soil and when yields are severely controlled, Corvinone can produce wines with good plummy fruit and velvety texture. The variety has a thick skin, which is essential in a grape destined for drying. It usually ripens a bit later than Corvina.
Synonym: Cruinon, Corvinon.

## RONDINELLA

Rondinella wines are ruby-colored. They have a light body and a faintly floral bouquet. To some they taste of slightly under-ripe persimmons; others find a vague echo of cherries.
This vine most likely arrived in the Veneto at the end of the 19th century.
Its name may have sprung from the fact that the dark color of its berries brings to mind the plumage of the rondine (swallow).
In the neighboring region of Lombardy, Rondinella composes up to 40% of the blend of Garda Colli Mantovani red and rosé.

## MOLINARA

100% Molinara wine is pink to pale ruby. There are hints of raspberry in its delicate perfume. It has crisp acidity, a supple body and medium alcohol.
Quintarelli makes a 100% Molinara which is an excellent partner for a dish of polenta and salami. Its name suggests the floury bloom (molino = mill) that covers the berries in the autumn.
Synonyms: Brepon, Breppion, Rossanella, Scolegno, Sola, Uva Salata, Vespone, Pola and Rossiccio Chiaro.

| DOC AND DOCG |
| --- |
| **VENETO** |
| Bardolino |
| Garda Orientale Corvina |
| Valpolicella |
| Amarone |
| Recioto della Valpolicella |

# croatina

The ancient Croatina vine may have originated in the Oltrepò Pavese of Lombardy. Due to its resistance to oidium (powdery mildew) it gained ground in the late 19th century. Today, it is most widely planted in Lombardy (in the Oltrepò Pavese zone), Piedmont (in the provinces of Alessandria, Vercelli and Novara) and Emilia-Romagna (in the Colli Piacentini area). In the Oltrepò Pavese and Piacentini zones, this variety is sometimes called Bonarda.

This creates no end of confusion for Italian wine lovers, as Bonarda is also the name of a separate variety. In Oltrepò Pavese, Croatina plays a part in the blend (along with Uva Rara, Barbera, Vespolina and Pinot Nero) of Oltrepò Pavese red and rosé, Buttafuoco and Sangue di Giuda. Croatina is also the primary grape in Oltrepò Pavese Bonarda, which is often slightly fizzy and Lambrusco-like. The hilly San Colombano area to the south of Milan is definitely a DOC zone to watch: here particularly lush and exciting wines come from Poderi di San Pietro. In the Colli Piacentini zone of Emilia-Romagna, Croatina is blended with Barbera to make a full-bodied wine called Gutturnio, and it is the sole component in Colli Piacentini Bonarda! In Piedmont it is usually blended with other grapes. However, this region also produces a varietal Croatina.

## TASTING NOTE

Deep, purply-ruby. It has the fresh, lightly fruity perfume of just-pressed grapes. The wine has a certain characteristic earthiness and slightly rustic tannins, good acidity and is medium-bodied.

## SYNONYMS

This variety is sometimes erroneously called Bonarda. (NOTE: there is a Piedmontese grape called Bonarda, which is not related to Croatina) Croata, Croattina, Crovattina, Crovettina, Croatino, Crovalmo, Crovattino, Neretto, Uva Vermiglia.

## FOOD PAIRINGS

Gnocchi with rabbit sauce, pork chops, cotechino, gnocchi with cheese.

---

### DOC AND DOCG

**EMILIA-ROMAGNA**
Colli Piacentini Gutturnio, Colli Piacentini Bonarda

**LOMBARDY**
Oltrepò Pavese Bonarda, San Colombano

**PIEDMONT**
Colline Novaresi Croatina, Cisterna d'Asti

---

### COTECHINO WRAPPED IN VEAL AND PROSCIUTTO

SERVES 4

• 1 cotechino (a large spiced Italian sausage), around 500 g/1 lb 2 oz • 1 large, thin slice of veal, around 400 g/ 14 oz • 1 slice of prosciutto crudo, around 100 g/1/4 lb • 1 onion • 500 ml/2 cups beef stock • 500 ml/2 cups Lambrusco • 60 ml/4 tbsp olive oil • a little salt

PREPARATION

Boil the cotechino. When it is half cooked, remove it from the cooking liquids, leave it to cool. Then carefully remove the sausage casing, leaving the cotechino in one piece. Beat the veal with a kitchen mallet until it is as thin as possible. Salt it lightly. Spread the piece of prosciutto onto the veal. Then put the cotechino on top of the prosciutto. Roll the veal and prosciutto around the cotechino and tie it with kitchen string. Pour olive oil in a high-sided frying pan and put it on the heat. Add the sliced onion to the pan and put the roll of meat on top of the onion. Cover with equal parts beef stock and Lambrusco. Lower the heat slightly, cover and leave to cook slowly, turning the meat from time to time. When the stock and wine are almost completely evaporated, the cotechino will be ready. Test it with a fork to be sure that it is cooked through. Leave it to cool, untie it and slice it. Strain the cooking sauce, then put it back in the pan along with the slices of meat. Heat through and serve.

# dolcetto

Some authorities believe that
Dolcetto originated in the Monferrato
hills. Others are of the opinion that
its home ground was Liguria, and
that it found its way to Piedmont as
a result of the many interregional
commercial exchanges which took
place during the Middle Ages.
Whatever its origins, this variety's
production zone today is still limited
to Piedmont and its neighboring
regions of Liguria and Valle d'Aosta.

This grape's name is usually said to derive from the particular sweetness (dolcezza) of its berries. Sweetness, however, is not a characteristic of the wines made from this variety.

Dolcetto cultivated in mountain and high hillside sites tends to produce elegant and delicately perfumed wines, while Dolcettos from the plains tend to be more robust and slightly higher in alcohol.

Most Dolcettos are fresh, fruity and intended for drinking two to four years from the vintage. Some producers, however, choose to make intensely concentrated, age-worthy wines. Both these styles share a dark, vivid color, lowish tannins and moderate to good acidity.

## PIEDMONT

Prior to the outbreak of the phylloxera epidemic, which tore through Europe's vineyards in the late 19th century, Dolcetto was considered one of Piedmont's most important varieties and its wines were held in high esteem. However, when post-phylloxera replanting began, Dolcetto vines were often replaced with those of the more productive Barbara variety. It is only in recent years that Dolcetto has begun to reclaim its former illustrious position.

There are no less than seven principal DOC production zones for Dolcetto: Dolcetto d'Alba, Dolcetto di Dogliani, Dolcetto di Diano d'Alba, Dolcetto delle Langhe Monregalesi, Dolcetto d'Asti, Dolcetto d'Acqui and Dolcetto d'Ovada. This grape also produces DOC varietals in the more extended Langhe, Colli Tortonesi, Monferrato and Pinerolese districts.

The Dolcetto d'Alba zone, in the province of Cuneo, is by far the largest, with around 1,660 hectares under vine in the hilly area around the town of Alba. Its wines have a big, juicy, mouth-filling blackberry fruit flavor. With one year of ageing and a minimum alcohol level of 12.5% they can be labelled superiore.

There are three other denominations located in Cuneo province.

Dolcetto di Diano d'Alba's territory (this wine may simply be labelled Diano d'Alba without specifying the variety) is limited to the hillsides in the single commune of Diano d'Alba. Its elegantly perfumed yet well-structured wines can carry the name of the vineyard (Sorì)on the label.

Dolcetto di Dogliani tends to have a very fruity fragrance and supple body. With one year of ageing and a minimum alcohol level of 12.5%, these wines may be labelled superiore.

*Piedmont: La Morra*

The Dolcetto delle Langhe Monregalesi is a small DOC that lies in the hills overlooking Mondovì. It has a bright ruby color, vinous nose, medium body and moderate acidity.

Dolcetto d'Asti, produced in twenty-four communes in the Monferrato hills, tends to be fruity, forward and quaffable. It, too, may be labelled superiore when it has undergone one year of ageing and has a minimum alcohol level of 12.5%.

The second largest zone in terms of surface under vine is that of Dolcetto di Ovada. Its territory lies on the border with Liguria and includes twenty-two communes in the province of Alessandria. Dolcetto d'Ovada is well-structured and suitable for ageing. Its perfumes include scents of violets and almonds.

Dolcetto d'Acqui is produced in twenty-three communes in the province of Alessandria. Its perfumes, too, include decidedly floral overtones. Both of the latter wines have a minimum alcohol level of 11.5%. With one year of ageing and an alcohol level of 12.5%, they may be labelled superiore.

## LIGURIA

In Liguria, the boomerang-shaped region south of Piedmont, the Dolcetto variety has a red stem and is known as Ormeasco. Due to differences in climate and terrain, its yields are lower than in Piedmont, and the resulting wine tends to be very dry and well-structured, with scents of wild berry fruits, bilberries, raspberries and even peachy notes.

The name Ormeasco comes from the village of Ormea, which lies in the DOC production zone of Riviera Ligure di Ponente, on the border with Piedmont. The superiore version has a minimum alcohol level of 12.5% and is aged for one year. In good vintages, this wine can continue to evolve for ten to twelve years. Ormeasco Sciac-trá is a fresh, perfumed, coral-colored wine, meant for drinking young. Its unusual name is really a description of the processes used in making a rosé: the grapes are pressed (schiacciare) and then the skins are taken away (tirare). Ormeasco Sciac-trá (also spelled Sciacchetrá) should not be confused with Cinqueterre's "Sciacchetrá", which is a sweet white wine made from semi-dried grapes.

Dolcetto is also part of the blend (20-70%) of Golfo del Tigullio Rosso. This zone, which also produces rosé, semi-sparkling and novello wines, lies on the hills around the port city of Genoa. Here Dolcetto is sometimes blended with Barbera and/or Ciliegiolo, to make supple, well-structured dry reds.

## VALLE D'AOSTA

Dolcetto is a lesser component in the blends of a number of Valle d'Aosta wines, including Chambave Rosso and Arnad-Montjovet.

## SYNONYMS

Beina, Bignola, Bignona, Bignonina, Cassolo, Dolcetta Nera, NibiòOrmeasco, Uva di Ovada, Uva d'Acqui, Uva del Monferrato.

## TASTING NOTE

There is a fuchsia sheen over deep, dark ruby. Dolcetto is noted for its supple body and its elegant perfumes, which can include scents of over-ripe cherries, blackberries, and, depending on the zone, either floral or chocolate tones.

## FOOD PAIRINGS

Dolcetto goes well with Bagna caôda, risottos and pasta dishes with meat, liver or mushroom sauces, as well as stewed and grilled meats or vegetables. The more robust and complex versions (such as the one from Ovada) are excellent with rich poultry or even game dishes such as jugged hare.

### TAJARIN WITH TRADITIONAL MEAT SAUCE

SERVES 6
- 1000 g/8¼ cups white flour
- 20 egg yolks
- a little warm water

FOR THE SAUCE
- 150 g/5 oz ground veal
- 150 g/5 oz ground pork
- 1 onion
- 1 carrot
- 1 clove garlic
- 1 sprig rosemary
- 125 ml/1/2 cup olive oil
- 200 ml/3/4 cup pulped tomatoes
- salt and pepper

TO MAKE THE TAJARIN

Make a mound of the flour. Then form a well in the middle of the flour and drop the egg yolks into this well. Knead until a smooth elastic dough is formed. Roll out the dough into a thin sheet using a rolling pin or a pasta maker. Fold the sheet over onto itself and cut it into narrow strips.
Leave the pasta to dry.
To cook the pasta, boil in abundant salted water for around 5 minutes.

TO MAKE THE SAUCE

Finely chop the vegetables and seasonings. Brown them in oil over a low heat. Add the veal and the pork. Brown the meat. After around 20 minutes add the pulped tomatoes. Salt and pepper to taste. Cook over a low heat, adding beef stock, if needed.

### CARDOONS WITH TRUFFLE FONDUE

SERVES 6
- 3 cardoons
- 50 g/3 tbsp butter
- the juice of 1 lemon
- 200 g/1¾ cups young fontina cheese, cubed
- 75 ml/5 tbsp whole milk
- 3 egg yolks
- white truffle to taste

PREPARATION

Boil the cardoons for 4 or 5 minutes with the lemon juice and salt in a large pan. Drain them and set aside. Now prepare the fondue. Heat the milk, then stir in the cubes of cheese. Be careful to keep the milk from boiling. Stir until the cheese is completely melted. Add the egg yolks and cook for another 3 or 4 minutes over a very low heat. Keep the fondue hot in a double boiler. Cut the cardoon into pieces. Fry them in butter for 2 minutes. Then put them on a plate and cover them with the cheese fondue, to which you have added fine truffle shavings.

### DOC AND DOCG

#### PIEDMONT

Dolcetto d'Acqui, Dolcetto d'Alba, Dolcetto d'Asti, Dolcetto delle Langhe Monregalesi, Dolcetto di Diano d'Alba (or Diano d'Alba), Dolcetto di Dogliani, Dolcetto di Ovada, Colli Tortonesi Dolcetto, Monferrato Dolcetto, Langhe Dolcetto, Pinerolese Dolcetto

#### LIGURIA

Golfo del Tigullio Rosso, Rosato e Novello, Ormeasco della Riviera Ligure di Ponente, Ormeasco Sciacchetrá della Riviera Ligure di Ponente, Valpolcèvera Rosso e Rosato

#### VALLE D'AOSTA

Chambave Rosso

# erbaluce

Erbaluce, which was known in Roman times as Alba Lux (dawn light), is an ancient Piedmontese vine. Some authorities think it may be a mutation of the Fiano variety brought to Piedmont by the Romans. Others believe that it is native to the pre-Alpine zone of the Canavese. Its high level of fixed acidity and its aromatic fragrance make it a good variety for both sparkling wine production and drying.

It is the sole variety in the fruity, refreshing wines of the Piedmontese DOC, Erbaluce di Caluso (also known as Caluso). This production zone is limited to a tiny area around the commune of Caluso in the province of Turin. A glass of sparkling Erbaluce makes a fine aperitif or, when sipped in the afternoon with a light nibble, it is a lively alternative to English teatime. The still version has a subtle yet satisfying flavor. Drink these wines young to fully enjoy their attractive freshness.

Caluso Passito, a luscious dessert wine, is perhaps the zone's best-known product. Grapes intended for its production are left to semi-dry until February or March. At that point, sugar levels are very high and the subsequent fermentation can take around a month to complete. The wine is then aged in oak barrels for four years.

From around 100 kilos of fresh grapes it is possible to make 30 litres of Caluso Passito. Only 25,000 to 30,000 bottles are produced each year. With its minimum alcohol level of 13.5% and its richness of flavor, this wine can easily continue to evolve for ten years or more. Caluso Passito Liquoroso, a fortified wine with an alcohol level of 17%, is also produced in the zone.

Erbaluce is also the sole variety in Canavese Bianco, whose production zone lies mainly in the province of Torino. This wine is dry and has a minimum alcohol level of 10%. However, some, such as Ferrando's attractively fragrant and fruity Castello di Loranzè Canavese Bianco, can reach 13%. The variety is also prominent in the Coste della Sesia Bianco and Colline Novaresi Bianco DOCs.

## TASTING NOTE

Dry Erbaluce: Pale golden yellow in color. On the nose, one finds fresh notes of wildflowers and hay. On the palate, it offers nicely weighted yet elegantly crisp fruit.

Its flavor is evocative rather than precise. One finds a mellowed citrus note and the extremely attractive sensation of honey without the sweetness.

Caluso Passito: Yellow-gold tending toward amber, full-bodied and velvety on the palate.

## SYNONYMS

Albaluce, Erbalucente Bianca, Greco Novarese.

## FOOD PAIRINGS

Dry: fish risotto; calamari; fried vegetables; stuffed mushrooms and artichokes; fried fish.
Caluso Passito: *vino da meditazione*; plain pastries or blue cheeses.

*The Castle of Pavone (province of Turin) with its classic vineyards*

| DOC AND DOCG | Caluso Passito |
|---|---|
| | Caluso Liquoroso |
| **PIEDMONT** | Colline Novaresi |
| Caluso o Erbaluce di Caluso | Coste della Sesia |
| Caluso Spumante | |

## PIEDMONTESE STYLE STUFFED PORCINI MUSHROOMS

SERVES 4

• 4 medium sized Porcini mushrooms
• 1 tbsp parsley, finely chopped
• 1 clove garlic
• 1 spring onion
• salt and pepper
• 70 ml/5 tbsp extra-virgin olive oil
FOR THE SAUCE
• 1 handful parsley
• 1 bunch of chervil
• 2 chive stems
• 100 ml/6 tbsp extra-virgin olive oil

PREPARATION

Thoroughly clean the mushrooms. Dig out the flesh from the stem and with this prepare the stuffing by finely chopping the flesh together with a slice of garlic and the scallions. Brown this mixture in olive oil.
Then cook over a very high heat for a minute. Salt and pepper to taste. Add the parsley. Refill the mushroom stems with this mixture. Now grease an oven-proof baking dish with olive oil.
Place the mushrooms in the dish and add salt and pepper to taste. Brush the mushroom caps with a little olive oil. Bake in a pre-heated oven at 180°C/350°F. for 10 minutes. In a blender, whizz the parsley, chervil and chives with a little oil. When the mushrooms are cooked, serve hot, drizzled with a little sauce.

## RICE AND FROG SOUP

SERVES 4

• 400 g/14 oz frog's legs • 600 g/1 lb 5 oz potatoes • 100 g/3/4 cups spring onions • 1 stick of green celery • 2 skinned, deseeded tomatoes cut into cubes • 10 g/2 tsp chopped parsley • 100 g/1/2 cup rice • 800 ml/3¼ cups meat stock • salt • extra-virgin olive oil

PREPARATION

Cook the rice in salted water until "al dente". Drain and leave to cool. Cook the frog's legs in the meat stock for five minutes, drain them, bone them and set aside. Cube the spring onion, potatoes and celery and boil them in the stock used to cook the frog's legs, cooking for about 20 minutes. Add the tomato and parsley, continuing to boil for a couple of minutes; add the rice and boned frog's legs. Divide into portions and drizzle with extra-virgin olive oil.

## MARINATED TROUT

SERVES 4

• 800 g/1¾ lb trout • 2 cloves of garlic • sage • carrots • onions
• celery • raisins
• zucchini • vinegar
• 750 ml/3 cups white wine

PREPARATION

Clean and fillet the trout. Cut it into medium-sized pieces. Prepare the sauce by gently frying the garlic and sage, adding finely sliced onion, half a carrot, the celery and zucchini, all cut into julienned strips. Gently fry all the vegetables and season to taste. When cooked, add the raisins soaked in white wine. Now add a bottle (3 cups) of white wine and 1 cup of white wine vinegar. Coat the trout in flour and cook in oil and sage. Lay it in a container and cover with the sauce you have prepared. Leave to soak for 10-12 hours and serve at room temperature.

## HAZELNUT CHOCOLATE PUDDINGS WITH HOT ZABAGLIONE

SERVES 4

• 80 g/3 oz dark hazelnut chocolate (gianduja) • 60 g/4 tbsp butter
• 30 g/1/4 cup white flour • 2 eggs
FOR THE ZABAGLIONE: • 3 egg yolks
• 50 g/3 tbsp sugar • 15 ml/1 tbsp Moscato

PREPARATION

Melt the chocolate with the butter. Add the egg yolks, one at a time, stirring continuously. Add the flour. Whip the egg whites until they are firm and gently add them to the chocolate mixture. Butter and flour 4 individual baking molds. Fill them with the chocolate mixture and bake at 200°C/390°F for 8 minutes. While it is baking, make the zabaglione. Mix all the ingredients together and whisk until frothy. Remove the baking molds from the oven, let cool and remove the chocolate from the mold. Arrange the puddings on a serving plate and serve with zabaglione and slices of seasonal fruit.

# falanghina

Falanghina is found principally in Campania, and may well have been a component in the famous wine of the Roman era, Falerno.
Its fortunes faded over time, however. It suffered during the phylloxera epidemic of the early 20th century, and it continued to lose ground after the World Wars, when many of its vineyards were abandoned.

Its rescue from extinction can be attributed, in large part, to Francesco Avallone. In the 1950s, Avallone, a lawyer with a profound interest in history, began researching the kinds of wines the Romans were likely to have drunk. In 1963 he founded his Villa Matilde estate with the express purpose of resuscitating ancient varieties of the Falerno zone.

"My father, a student of Roman law, always had a passion for the history of our zone," says Maria Ida Avallone.

"And he could not bear the thought that this great wine, one praised by poets and connoisseurs of the past, could be lost."

## SYNONYMS
Fallanghina, Falanchina, Uva Falerna (known locally as Bianca Zita).

## TASTING NOTES
Pale straw in color. The wine is supple.
A delicate vanilla tone – a characteristic of the grape, not a result of oak – runs through its fresh fruity flavor.

## FOOD PAIRINGS
Spaghetti with mussels, baked fish.

## FALANGHINA PASSITO
Plain sponge cake or as a vino da meditazione.

---

### SPAGHETTI WITH MUSSELS AND TOMATO SAUCE

SERVES 4
- 400 g/14 oz spaghetti
- 2 cloves garlic
- 1000 g/2 lb 3 oz mussels
- 500 g/1¾ cups peeled tomatoes
- 75 ml/5 tbsp olive oil
- salt and pepper
- a good handful of parsley

PREPARATION
Thoroughly clean the mussels. Rinse them under running water. Put them in a pan. Cover and cook them over a high heat. This will cause the mussel shells to open. Retain and filter any remaining cooking liquid. Fry the garlic in oil: when it has lost its color, remove it from the oil and add the crushed tomatoes. Cook the sauce, adding the cooking liquid. Add a twist of freshly ground pepper to taste. At the last moment add the mussels. Continue to cook for 2 or 3 minutes. Add plenty of chopped parsley and turn off the heat. Boil the spaghetti. Drain and dress with half the sauce. Put the remaining sauce in a tureen and serve it at table for those who enjoy more sauce on their spaghetti.

---

### DOC AND DOCG

**CAMPANIA**
Taburno or Aglianico del Taburno
Campi Flegrei Bianco
Falerno del Massico (100% Falanghina)
Penisola Sorrentina Bianco
Guardia Sanframondi (or Guardiolo)
Falanghina Sant'Agata de' Goti (or Sant'Agata dei Goti) (also Passito)
Sannio Falanghina (also Passito)
Capri
Solopaca

# favorita

Favorita, a biotype of Vermentino, is found in the Langhe region of Piedmont, and is the sole component in the delicate and refreshing Langhe Favorita.

*Panoramic view of vineyards in the Langhe (Piedmont)*

The first recorded mention of this variety dates from 1676 in the inventory of the Counts of Roero. Its origin is to be found in the practice of Ligurian oil merchants of giving vine cuttings as gifts when they traded their product.

## TASTING NOTE

Straw colored. A delicately aromatic bouquet and light almond note on the palate.

## FOOD PAIRINGS

Often served as an aperitif. It also goes well with mildly flavored antipasti and vegetable-based rice and pasta dishes.

| DOC AND DOCG |
| --- |
| **PIEDMONT** |
| Langhe Favorita |

### STUFFED PEPPER

SERVES 4
- 2 yellow peppers
- 100 g/1/4 lb tuna in oil
- 20 g/1 tbsp homemade mayonnaise
- 1 salted anchovy
- 1 tbsp parsley
- 1/2 tbsp of white wine vinegar
- 3 salted capers

PREPARATION

Put a little oil on the peppers and arrange them on a baking sheet and bake at 150°C/300°F for 30 minutes. While the peppers are baking, chop the parsley. Then fillet the anchovy and wash it under cold running water. Cut the tuna into pieces. Puree the fish and the capers in the blender. Now mix all the ingredients with mayonnaise and white wine vinegar, adding salt, if needed. When the peppers are cold, peel them and divide them into 4 pieces. On each piece put a heaping spoonful of the fish mixture and roll up the peppers around the filling. Make a dressing with extra-virgin olive oil, salt and vinegar and drizzle over the peppers.

# fiano

This ancient Southern Italian variety originated in the area around Lapia, a hamlet in the hills east of Avellino in Campania. Its structure makes it suitable for a certain amount of ageing, as well as for drying.
Like many indigenous (and low-yielding) grape varieties, Fiano faced extinction by the early 1970s.

Fortunately for wine lovers everywhere Dr. Antonio Mastroberardino, who has a passion for viticultural history, stepped in to rescue it. There are two varietal Fianos in Campania. The most well known is Fiano di Avellino. Small amounts of Greco, Coda di Volpe and Trebbiano Toscano may be added to the blend of this dry white. Sannio Fiano, whose production zone lies in the province of Benevento, is made in a dry, still style as well as a sparkling version, which may be either semi- or fully sweet. Fiano plays a part in the blends of the Campanian DOCs of Cilento Bianco, Penisola Sorretina Bianco and Vesuvio Bianco. In Puglia, it is in the blend of Gravina, whose production zone is in the province of Bari.

This wine may be dry or semi-sweet, and either still or sparkling.

## TASTING NOTE

Straw yellow in color. One finds scents of toasted hazelnuts on the nose. There is usually a mineral/salty note on the palate of this supple wine.

## SYNONYMS

Fiore Mendillo, Fiana, Latina Bianca, Minutolo, Cantina di Meo.

## FOOD PARING

Fish-based dishes.

| DOC AND DOCG |
| --- |
| **CAMPANIA** |
| Fiano di Avellino, Sannio Fiano, Penisola Sorrentina Bianco, Vesuvio Bianco |

*Fresco of libations at Pompei*

---

**FILLED CUTTLEFISH FISHERMAN STYLE**

SERVES 4
- 4 large cuttlefish • 500 g/1 lb 2 oz seafood (mussels, clams, tellinas) • soft bread
- 500 g/1$^{3/4}$ cups tomatoes • Parmesan cheese
- 2 cloves of garlic • 2 eggs • salt • chili pepper
- parsley • 50 ml/3 tbsp olive oil

PREPARATION

Fry one of the cloves of garlic in a little oil, add the seafood and cover. When it is done, remove it from the heat. Moisten the bread in water. Then squeeze it dry and put it, along with a beaten egg and the cheese, in a large bowl. Pour the fried seafood on top of it. Mix well. Stuff the cleaned cuttlefish with this mixture. Secure the opening of the cuttlefish by tying it with kitchen string. Brown the cuttlefish in oil along with a clove of garlic and the chili pepper. The dish is done, when the cuttlefish is golden and the tomatoes are cooked through. Serve the cuttlefish very hot, garnished with chopped parsley.

# franconia

This grape is of Austrian origin. Franconia's high yields and resistance to disease made it an ideal replacement vine after phylloxera wound its destructive course through Europe's vineyards. It was planted in France, Germany, Slovenia, and in the Italian regions of Friuli Venezia-Giulia (in 1879) and Lombardy (in 1929).

In Italy, up until the 1950s, Franconia was referred to as Blaufränkisch or Limberger.

*The characteristic "ronchi" (circular terraced plantations) that shape the vines of the eastern hills of Friuli.*

The name Franconia is derived from *frankisch*, a Medieval term used to designate German-language speaking foreigners.

## TASTING NOTE
Deep fuchsia-tinged ruby. It has broad perfumes which are reminiscent of black cherries, violets and rose petals. On the palate it has soft brambly fruit. It tends to be just a bit short on the finish.

## SYNONYMS
Blaufränkisch, Limberg, Frankovka Modrà, Kekfrank, Moravka, Franconien Bleu.

## FOOD PAIRINGS
Game and autumnal dishes, such as those featuring pumpkin and chestnuts. Also excellent with cheese-based specialties, such as the traditional "Frico" of Friuli.

### FRICO WITH POTATOES

SERVES 4
- 1 onion
- 4 medium-sized potatoes
- 1 tbsp butter
- 300 ml/1$^{1/4}$ cups stock
- 400 g/3$^{1/2}$ cups Montasio

PREPARATION
Finely chop the onion, peel the potatoes and cut them into thin slices. Heat the butter in a saucepan and gently fry the onion. Add the potatoes and toss lightly in the butter, add stock and cook slowly until the potatoes are soft. Add the cubed cheese and allow it to melt. Gently fry all the ingredients and eliminate the fat released by the cheese.

### DOC AND DOCG

**FRIULI VENEZIA-GIULIA**
Friuli Isonzo Franconia, Friuli Latisana Franconia

# frappato

This indigenous variety may have
originated in the commune of Vittoria
in the Sicilian province of Ragusa.
Other commentators, however,
believe that it arrived from Spain.
It may be vinified on its own or with
other Sicilian red varieties, such as
Nero d'Avola. It produces fresh,
fruity wines intended for drinking
young.

*Sicilian vineyards*

*Sicily: Mount Etna*

## TASTING NOTE
Cherry red in color. The wine is fresh and spicy on the nose, with strawberry and wild berry fruit notes that carry through on the palate.

## SYNONYMS
Frappato di Vittoira, Frappato Nero di Vittoria, Frappatu.

## FOOD PAIRINGS
Grilled meats.

| DOC AND DOCG |
| --- |
| **SICILY** |
| Cerasuolo di Vittoria |
| Eloro Frappato |

### CAPON SICILIAN STYLE

SERVES 6
- 1 whole capon
- 1 red onion
- 1 carrot
- 1 celery stalk
- 1 sprig of fresh rosemary
- 100 g/4 oz bacon
- 50 ml/1/4 cup dry Marsala
- 50 ml/3 tbsp olive oil
- salt and pepper

PREPARATION
Patiently de-bone the capon, retaining the bones, which will be used to make the stock. Sauté the finely chopped onion, carrot, celery and bacon. Add the bay leaf and the rosemary. When the vegetables are cooked, add the capon meat, which has been cut into pieces. Cook for a further 10 minutes. When the meat has browned, add the Marsala and cook on a high heat until the wine evaporates. Then add the tomatoes and the stock (which is obtained by cooking the capon bones with an onion and a carrot). Cook for around an hour, until the sauce is very dense. At this point, put the meat on a pre-heated serving platter and cover with the sauce. This dish may also be served with al dente spaghetti.

# freisa

At one time, Freisa was among the most important varieties in Piedmont and was widely planted in Lombardy and the Veneto as well.
It is now largely confined to the Asti and Casale areas of the Monferrato and to the Chieri and Alba zones.

Nowadays, commercially available Freisas tend to be lively, fresh and fruity dry wines, though the local Piedmontese tradition has always favored slightly sweet, sparkling or semi-sparkling products. Some producers are now also ageing Freisa in wood with excellent results. This barrel ageing concentrates the fruit and subdues the variety's natural exuberance. Each style is valid, though my personal preference is for the simpler, juicier dry version. Freisa is also used in small amounts to add zest to the blends of other Piedmontese reds.

## TASTING NOTE

It has a rich ruby color, sometimes with an almost fuchsia sheen. It is fresh and lively on the nose, with strawberry and wild berry scents which are echoed on the palate.

## SYNONYMS

Monferrina, Monfreisa, Fessietta, Freisa di Chieri, Fresa Fresia, Spannina.

## FOOD PAIRINGS

Veal, roast rabbit, and stewed poultry.
The sweeter style goes well with pastries in general, and particularly with the typical Carnival delicacies known as "bugie".

---

### DOC AND DOCG DA FREISA

**PIEMONT**

Piemonte, Freisa d'Asti, Freisa di Chieri (dry, sweet, sparkling), Langhe Freisa, Monferrato Freisa, Pinerolese Freisa

---

### BUGIE

SERVES 6
- 500 g/5 cups wheat flour
- 1 packet vanilla-flavored yeast
- 50 g/3 tbsp butter
- 2 egg yolks
- 2 tbsp sugar
- a pinch of salt
- 125 ml/1/2 cup milk
- 1000 ml/4 cups olive oil
- vanilla-flavored sugar
- 50 ml/3 tbsp grappa

PREPARATION
Place the flour in a mound on the work surface and form a deep well in the center of the mound. Into this well, put the vanilla-flavored yeast, the melted butter, 2 egg yolks, sugar, salt and milk. Knead the dough until it is smooth and elastic. Roll out the dough to a thickness of around 3 millimeters and cut with a diamond-shaped biscuit cutter. Put the oil in a large high-sided pan. When the oil is boiling, fry the small diamond-shaped pieces of dough until they puff up and turn golden. Remove them from the oil with a slotted spoon, and place them to drain on absorbent paper. Dust the fresh bugie with vanilla-flavored sugar and enjoy!

# fumin

Fumin is indigenous to Valle d'Aosta. Until a few years ago, it was used mainly to give color and zesty acidity to easy-drinking blends.

Now, thanks largely to the success of Costantino Charrère, Fumin is winning accolades and attracting the attention it deserves.

*Valle d'Aosta: the church of Introd with its vineyards.*

It was Charrère's father who, in the 1970s, first vinified the variety on its own.

This was a controversial idea at the time, as the vineyards in Valle D'Aosta were generally planted with an assortment of vines, making the concept of a varietal wine truly beyond local comprehension.

In addition, Fumin is very sensitive to microclimatic changes, meaning vineyard sites must be selected with care.

The variety has a genuine affinity for wood, and the potential to produce world-class wines. Fumin-based wines are definitely not meant to be drunk young; they need at least two years to mellow out.

## TASTING NOTE

Very dark ruby, with purple highlights. Good tannin and structure.

On the palate, spicy, lightly peppery notes mingle with those of wild berry fruits and greengage plums. Zesty acidity supports the alcohol.

## FOOD PAIRINGS

Red meats and mature cheese.

---

### CARBONADE

SERVES 4
- 800 g/1³/⁴ lb ox meat • 50 g/3 tbsp butter
- 1 onion, diced • 1 cup white flour
- 1 cup strong red wine • salt and pepper

PREPARATION

Cut the meat into pieces. Dredge the meat in flour and then brown it in butter. Remove the meat from the pan and place it on a plate. Brown the diced onion in the butter in which you have cooked the meat. Then put the meat back in the pan and cook it slowly, adding red wine a ladle at a time. Salt and pepper to taste.

---

### DOC AND DOCG

**VALLE D'AOSTA**

Valle d'Aosta Fumin

# gaglioppo

Gaglioppo is found in limited quantities in the Marche, Campania, Umbria and Sicily. But it is in Calabria that it thrives. It is the most widely planted variety in that region and it is a component in every one of Calabria's red DOC wines.

## CALABRIA

Gaglioppo most likely arrived on the Ionian coast of Calabria with the first Greek settlers. Its best known DOC is Cirò Rosso, whose production area is centered around the attractive town of Cirò Marina, located on the coast near Punta Alice, a southern promontory on the Gulf of Taranto.

Its location between the sea and the Sila Mountains creates extreme differences between day and night-time temperatures, which allow the grapes to ripen more slowly, thus achieving fuller development of aromas and flavors.

In Greek times, wines from this area were so highly prized that they were awarded to the winners of Olympic Games.

Cirò Rosso is made from 95% Gaglioppo, with the option of adding up to 5% Trebbiano Toscano and/or Greco Bianco. The wine must be aged for at least eight months and have a minimum alcohol level of 12.5%.

The word "classico" may be added to the label when the grapes used to make the wine are grown in the communes of Cirò and Cirò Marina. Both the red and rosé versions of Cirò Classico may be labelled *superiore* if they have a minimum alcohol level of 13.5%.

When the wine has been aged for at least two years, it may be called *riserva*.

Well-made Cirò Rosato is the color of blood-orange juice.

Its flavors are broad but elegant and on the palate it has mineral notes and hints of frozen strawberries.

For the region's other reds and rosés, Gaglioppo is blended with a number of red and white varieties, including Greco Nero, Nerello Cappuccio, Malvasia Nera, Malvasia Bianco and Greco.

## TASTING NOTE

Ruby to garnet in color. The wine is always refreshing on the nose, with an amalgam of scents that include tar, red licorice and rose hip tea. These sensations are carried through onto the palate. The wine is lightly tannic, with good body and medium-to-high alcohol.

## SYNONYMS

Arvino, Galloppo. Gaglioppa, Gaglioppa Nera, Galloffa, Uva Navarra, Lacrima Nera, Guarnaccia Nera

## FOOD PAIRINGS

Spicy pasta and vegetable dishes (roast red and yellow peppers), roast meats, spicy cheeses.

| DOC AND DOCG |
| --- |
| **CALABRIA** |
| Bivongi Rosso, also in rosé version |
| Cirò Rosso, also in rosé version |
| Donnici Rosso, also in rosé version |
| Melissa Rosso |
| Pollino |
| San Vito di Luzzi Rosso, also in rosé version |
| Sant'Anna di Isola Capo Rizzuto |
| Savuto Rosso |
| Scavigna Rosso, also in rosé version |
| Verbicaro Rosso, also in rosé version |

# garganega

Garganega is believed to be of Greek origin. While found in isolated pockets throughout Italy, it produces its most memorable results in the Veneto provinces of Vicenza, Padua and Verona. When grown in optimum sites, when yields are kept low and when the grapes are allowed to ripen fully, this variety is capable of producing whites with delicate flavors of pear, pineapple and apricot which become fuller and more luscious as the wine matures.

*The Veneto: typical sites and ancient monuments in the Soave production zone*

Garganega is especially the major component in Italy's most maligned wine: Soave.

## SOAVE

A real revolution has taken place in the Soave zone in the last ten years. The area's traditional top producers – Leonildo Pieropan and Roberto Anselmi – have been joined by a small but ever-increasing band of dedicated, quality-led winemakers, who are turning out elegant and flavorful Soaves.

The Soave production area, which received the DOC designation in 1968, is some thirty kilometers east of the northern Italian city of Verona. Most of its vineyards are on hillside sites, including the historic Classico zone, which lies between the quaint medieval town of Soave itself and that of Monteforte d'Alpone. The "Soave DOC" vineyards are situated on the foothills and plains surrounding the hilly area which the Soave regulations now refer to as "Colli Scaligeri".

The traditional blend for Soave is a minimum of 70% Garganega, with the optional addition of Chardonnay and/or Trebbiano di Soave. Some producers choose to make the wine using only Garganega. They are also free to use wood or use stainless steel. All these options mean that styles can vary considerably from producer to producer.

Simple Soave is designed to be drunk a year or two after the vintage. Soave that has spent some time in barrels can usually last a year or so longer. But it is with single-vineyard Soaves from quality-conscious producers that the Garganega variety is able to demonstrate its ageing potential. The first single-vineyard Soave was the 1971 Calvarino produced by Leonildo Pieropan. Today's crisp,

supple, floral-scented Calvarino is made from around 70% Garganega and 30% Trebbiano di Soave. In 1978 Pieropan launched his incomparable 100% Garganega Soave from the La Rocca vineyard. Now most quality-led producers make at least one single-vineyard wine. Well-made examples can be drunk from three to eight years after the harvest, and wines from top vintages and top producers can easily keep (and improve) for ten years or more.

Sandro and Claudio Gini stand out among the other winemakers producing age-worthy Soaves. In their cathedral-like cellar in Monteforte d'Alpone, the Ginis are setting aside cases of each vintage of their single-vineyard wines with the intention of doing periodic tastings to gauge the wines' evolution. A 1990 Salvarenza Soave Classico I tasted in 2001 continued to impress with its dried pineapple

fragrance and concentrated apricot sorbet-like freshness on the palate.

Some producers also make sparkling Soave. When made with care, this is a lovely wine for drinking with a light summer lunch or while watching the sun go down on a warm evening. It is, however, seldom found outside the zone.

## RECIOTO DI SOAVE

In 1998 Recioto di Soave, a sweet wine, became the Veneto's first DOCG. Grapes for Recioto are usually picked a bit earlier than the rest of the harvest, and are left to dry on racks or in wooden or plastic crates for several months before being pressed. The resulting must is very dense and rich and produces wines with an alcohol level of around 14%. When well-made, a Recioto di Soave is nothing short of magic: it achieves excellent balance between acidity and sweetness, with tantalizing fragrances of green tea and yellow fruits – peaches, apricots – mingling on the nose. Few Reciotos, however, live up to this ideal. Some producers also make a sparkling Recioto di Soave: it is an acquired taste.

## GAMBELLARA

A provincial border divides the Soave zone from the tiny (some 990 hectares in all) Gambellara area (DOC since 1970). The grape mix and wine styles are very much the same for both zones. Dry Gambellara is composed of a minimum of 80% Garganega. Gambellara Recioto is made from semi-dried grapes just as in Soave. The only difference is that here the grapes are sometimes draped onto screens which are hung from the ceiling, rather than dried on racks. Local producers are particularly proud of their sparkling Recioto. Gambellara Vin Santo is not made like Tuscan Vin Santo. Here the term simply applies to a wine made from semi-dried Garganega which is aged for a minimum of two years before being released onto the market.

## COLLI BERICI & COLLI EUGANEI

The Colli Berici zone, east of Gambellara and south of Vicenza, makes a DOC Garganega, to which small amounts of Trebbiano di Soave may be added. The Colli Euganei zone, south of the city of Padua, uses Garganega as a component in its Bianco. Both these zones are emerging as important areas for fine wine production, particularly with regard to Cabernet- and Merlot-based wines.

## TASTING NOTE

For a well-made dry Garganega: Fresh, citrusy fragrance with notes of elderflowers and acacia blossoms, and a creamy undertone. On the palate, elegant apricot flavors emerge.
For sweet Garganega: When good, it offers an exquisite balance between lively acidity and sweet, apricot-tinged fruit. I often find a light note of green tea on the nose.

## SYNONYMS

Garganega di Gambellara, Garganega Comune, Ora or D'Oro.

## FOOD PAIRINGS

Dry styles: Grilled freshwater fish or seafood.
Sweet styles: Dry pastries, sponge cakes or, for the adventurous, strongly flavored cheeses or foie gras.

---

### DOC AND DOCG

**VENETO**

Colli Berici Garganega with option of Trebbiano di Soave
Colli Berici Garganega sparkling, with Pinot bianco and other international white varieties
Colli Euganei Bianco Garganega with Prosecco, Tocai Friulano, Sauvignon and others
Gambellara
Gambellara Recioto
Gambellara Vin Santo
Garda Gambellara
Soave - Soave Recioto
Bianco di Custoza

## GRANSEOLE ALLA VENEZIANA
### (for the Garganega)

SERVES 4

• 4 medium-sized granseole (Adriatic crabs)
• lemon juice
• 8 tbsp of olive oil
• 2 tbsp spoons of chopped parsley pepper

PREPARATION

Wash the *granseole*, boil them in a large quantity of water for about 15 minutes and leave them to drain. Remove the claws from each carapace, break them using a claw opener and carefully remove the flesh. Place all the flesh in a bowl and season it with the olive oil, the lemon juice, the parsley, and the pepper. Place the seasoned meat into the shells and serve, decorating them with lemon slices.

## VENETIAN STYLE CUTTLEFISH

SERVES 4

• 8 black cuttlefish
• 1 small onion
• 2 tbsp chopped parsley
• 100 ml/1/2 cup dry white wine
• 1 clove of garlic
• 60 ml/4 tbsp tomato sauce
• 60 ml/4 tbsp stock
• 100 ml/6 tbsp oil

PREPARATION

Clean the cuttlefish, taking care to preserve the sack containing the ink, and cut it into strips. Gently fry the chopped onion and garlic in the oil and add the cuttlefish and parsley. Salt and cook on a low heat for about 15 minutes. Sprinkle with the wine and add the ink. Add the tomato sauce and cook for about 10 minutes. Serve with polenta.

## EEL VENETIAN STYLE

SERVES 4

• 1 eel • 1 onion
• 1 clove of garlic • flour
• 75 ml/5 tbsp olive oil
• 15 ml/1 tbsp vinegar • salt

PREPARATION

Clean the eel and rinse in running water. Then cut it into pieces and dredge in flour. Finely chop the onion and a clove of garlic, and put them in a frying pan with a little olive oil. Fry for a few minutes then add the eel. Brown the eel and then add a dash of vinegar and a bay leaf and salt to taste. Reduce the heat and cook slowly, adding warm water as needed to keep the meat from sticking.

## PANDOLI

SERVES 4

• 100 g/3/4 cup yeast
• 75 ml/5 tbsp milk
• 1000 g/10 cups flour
• 4 eggs • 100 g/1/2 cup sugar
• 200 g/7 oz lard or melted butter

PREPARATION

Put the yeast in a little warm milk and stir in a few spoonfuls of flour. Then put the rest of the flour (around 9 cups) in a mound on the work surface. Make a well in the center of the mound and put an egg in the well along with the sugar, a pinch of salt and the lard (or melted butter), and knead. Shape into "pandoli" (bread cakes) and place well apart on a buttered baking sheet and leave them to rise before baking at a moderate heat.

## SPONGE CAKE

SERVES 6

• 250 g/1$^{1/4}$ cups sugar
• 7 ml/1 tsp white wine vinegar
• fine salt
• 6 eggs
• 1 vanilla pod
• 10 g/2 tsp of lemon rind
• 150 g/5 oz egg yolks
• 160 g/1$^{1/4}$ cups plain flour
• 50 g/1/2 cup potato starch

PREPARATION

Whip the eggs, sugar, salt, vanilla and lemon rind with a whisk. Gradually add the egg yolks, as though making mayonnaise. Sieve the flour several times with the potato starch, and fold it gently into the mixture, working upwards. Cover baking trays with ovenproof paper and position aluminium rings measuring 9in across by 3.5in high and 0.2in thick on the baking tray and fill up to just over 3/4. Bake in a preheated oven at 180°C/350°F for about 35 minutes. Remove from the oven, place on a wire rack to cool and then remove the rings.

# grecanico

This Sicilian variety is part of the Greco family. In the bad old days, it is said, a good amount of Grecanico found its way to the Veneto, where it augmented the production of its not-too-distant cousin, Garganega. Today, the variety is coming into its own as a prominent ingredient in a variety of attractive dry white wines.

## TASTING NOTE
Straw to pale gold in color. Its bouquet is floral (particularly wild broom). The wine is of medium body, with a lemony note on the palate.

## SYNONYMS
Recanica, Grecanico Bianco, Grecanico Dorato, Grecanio, Grecanicu Bianco.

## FOOD PAIRINGS
A fine aperitif, good with Sicilian vegetable dishes (such as aubergine) or fish with onions.

### DOC AND DOCG

#### SICILY
Contessa Entellina Grecanico
Menfi Grecanico
Contessa di Sclafani Grecanico
Delia Nivoletti Grecanico
Santa Margherita di Belice Grecanico

### SICILIAN PEPPER AND ONION FLAN

SERVES 6
- 6 peppers
- 6 onions
- 4 eggs
- 50 g/1/2 cup grated Caciocavallo or Pecorino cheese
- bread crumbs
- olive oil
- oregano
- salt

PREPARATION
Grill the peppers and onions, then peel them and cut into strips. Mix beaten eggs, grated cheese, oregano and salt. Add the vegetable strips and pour into an ovenproof dish greased with oil and lined with bread crumbs. Bake for about 10 minutes. Serve hot or cold.

# grechetto

Grechetto is an off-shoot of the "Greco" family.
Within this sub-group one finds a great deal of variation in characteristics.

In Umbria (where it is cultivated principally in the province of Perugia), it is vinified as a varietal in the zones of Colli Martani, Assisi, Colli del Trasimeno and in the Colli Perugini, and it is a component in the blends of many of the region's dry whites, including Bianco di Torgiano, Montefalco Bianco and Orvieto.

In Tuscany, it produces varietal wines in the DOC zones of Cortona and Valdichiana, and is also a component in blended dry whites.

## TASTING NOTE

The wine is usually straw colored, with hints of elderflower and pears on the nose. On the palate it is usually fresh and undemanding.

## SYNONYMS

Grechetto Bianco, Grechetto di Orvieto.

## FOOD PAIRINGS

Seafood antipasti or freshwater fish dishes.

*Umbria: landscape around Orvieto*

| DOC AND DOCG |
| --- |
| **UMBRIA** |
| Colli Martani Grechetto |
| Todi Grechetto, Assisi Grechetto |
| Bianco di Torgiano |
| Colli del Trasimeno Grechetto |
| Colli Perugini Grechetto |
| Colli Amerini bianco |
| |
| **TUSCANY** |
| Vin santo di Montepulciano, Cortona Grechetto |
| Valdichiana Grechetto |

### BAKED TRASIMENO TENCH

SERVES 4
- 4 tench
- 2 tbsp bread crumbs
- 1/2 lemon
- 1 clove of garlic
- 1 sprig of parsley
- 1/2 tsp oregano
- oil
- salt
- black pepper

PREPARATION
Carefully clean the tench, open them along their backs and eliminate the heads and tails. Arrange the fish in an ovenproof dish, sprinkle with lemon juice, salt and pepper. Prepare an aromatic mixture of chopped parsley, garlic and bread crumbs and cover the fish with it evenly. Drizzle with oil and bake at 180°C/350°F for about 30 minutes. Serve hot.

# greco

In the 8th century B.C. a serious agricultural crisis, brought on in part by a swelling population, forced poorer Greeks to search for new territory across the sea. Some of these voyagers landed in what is now Calabria.

Among their precious possessions were seeds and vine cuttings. These were the antecedents of some of Italy's most important grape varieties.

During the Middle Ages, the Venetians, who traded throughout the Mediterranean Basin, created a popular market for "Greek Wines". To keep pace with the demand, vineyards of Greco vines were planted wherever the Venetians had ports.

Over time, the vines in these disparate areas subtly changed their characteristics based on the climate and the terrain in which they were planted. It is likely, for example, that Garganega (Soave's main grape) and Grechetto (the base of many Tuscan and Umbrian whites) are descended from Greco vines.

To further confuse the ampelographer, the perceived superiority of "Greek Wines" meant that any local variety of outstanding quality was likely to be called "Greco".

Two main sub-varieties have developed from the original Greco variety: Greco Bianco and Greco B (also known as Greco di Tufo). These are used in the composition of fine southern Italian white wines.

## CALABRIA
Greco Bianco is a part of the blend of every Calabrian DOC dry white, and it is an optional variety in many of the region's DOC reds and rosés.

It plays the major role in Cirò Bianco (at least 90%), Lamezia Greco (85%), and in the unusual sweet wine, Greco di Bianco. The production zone for this latter wine is limited to the commune of Bianco and part of the commune of Casignana in the province of Reggio Calabria. Grapes for Greco di Bianco are left to dry on racks before pressing. The resulting wine,

which has an alcohol level of at least 17%, can easily continue to evolve for 10 years.

## CAMPANIA
The sub-variety called Greco B found its perfect habitat in the volcanic soils of Campania, first on the slopes of Vesuvius, then spreading to the rest of the region. It featured in the blends of some of the Roman Empire's favorite wines. The best-known wine made from this variety is Greco di Tufo, whose production zone lies north of Avellino around the commune of Tufo, within an hour's drive from Naples. Greco di Tufo distinguishes itself from other Southern whites by its pronounced fruity character. This may be due to its cool vineyard sites, which lie at between 400 and 700 meters above sea level. The wine must be at least 85% Greco, with the option of adding Coda di Volpe to the blend. Greco di Tufo is best drunk young, within two to four years from the harvest.

The region's other DOC zones producing Greco-based wines are clustered east of Naples in the province of Benevento. They are Sant' Agata dei Goti (a minimum 90% Greco), Taburno Greco (minimum 85%) and Sannio Greco. A passito version of this latter wine is also made from grapes that are left to semi-dry on the vine or on racks in well-ventilated lofts. It reaches an alcohol level of around 14.5%. Sannio Greco is also made in sparkling styles of varying degrees of sweetness.

Greco B is grown on the Island of Capri in terraced vineyards that descend to the sea. It plays a part in the blend of Capri Bianco and it

may also be included in the blend of Penisola Sorrentina Bianco, whose production zone lies in hillsides in the province of Napoli.

## LAZIO

Both still and sparkling dry Grecos are produced in the province of Viterbo in the DOC zone of Vignanello.

These wines may be labelled as Greco di Vignanello or simply as Greco.

## TASTING NOTE

Dry: This wine is pale gold with amber highlights. It has hints of toasted almonds and figs on the nose and palate.

Sweet: Rich golden in color. This wine is fragrant with notes of orange blossoms, figs and honey. With age, the sweetness evolves into a richer, fuller sensation on the nose.

## SYNONYMS

Greco B, Greco di Napoli, Greco della Torre, Greco di Tufo, Greco del Vesuvio, Grieco, Grecula.

## FOOD PAIRINGS

Dry: Vegetable-based dishes, raw seafood, sautéed clams and mussels, fresh cheeses.

Passito: Dry pastries or as a *vino da meditazione*.

| DOC AND DOCG |
| --- |
| **LAZIO** |
| Vignanello Greco |
| **CAMPANIA** |
| Sant'Agata de' Goti (Sant'Agata dei Goti), Taburno Greco, Greco di Tufo |
| **CALABRIA** |
| Greco di Bianco, Bianco di Lamezia, Lamezia - Greco, Melissa Bianco, Verbicaro Bianco, Cirò, Bivongi, Donnici, San Vito di Luzzi, Scavigna |

## TASTY SQUID

SERVES 4
- 800 g/1³/⁴ lb baby squid
- 60 ml/4 tbsp olive oil
- 1-2 cloves of garlic
- salt
- chili pepper
- parsley
- lemon juice

PREPARATION

Clean, wash and dry the baby squid, then place half a glass of oil and 1 or 2 cloves of garlic in a frying pan.
Remove the garlic when golden, add the squid and cook after sprinkling with salt and chilli. When serving add chopped parsley and lemon juice.

## PEPPERY MUSSELS

SERVES 4
- 1500 g/3 lb 5 oz very fresh mussels
- 1 lemon cut into very small wedges
- a handful of parsley
- a clove of garlic
- peppercorns

PREPARATION

Carefully clean the mussels and wash thoroughly in running water, then place in a large saucepan with the garlic and a few spoonfuls of water. Cook until all the shells are completely open. Now transfer the mussels to a clean dish and leave them to rest for a few minutes in order to eliminate the sand. Season with freshly ground pepper and add the chopped parsley and lemon. Return to the heat for a few mints before serving.

## CAMPANIAN STYLE BABY OCTOPUS

SERVES 4
- 800 g/1³/⁴ lb fresh baby octopus
- 3 cloves of fresh garlic
- 100 ml/1/2 cup extra-virgin olive oil • 1 chili pepper
- 1 tbsp fresh bread crumbs
- 2 tbsp butter
- 1 sprig of fresh parsley
- 1 lemon
- salt and pepper

PREPARATION

Carefully wash the baby octopus and dry them with a clean cloth.
Heat the oil and crushed garlic in a frying pan and when golden add the baby octopus. Salt and add the chili pepper, frying on a high heat for 5 or 6 minutes before removing the garlic and chili pepper, and add the bread crumbs, butter and chopped parsley Mix thoroughly and leave to season for a few minutes. Serve hot with slices of lemon.

## SQUID IN STOCK

SERVES 4
- 1000 g/2 lb 3 oz squid
- garlic
- parsley
- ground red pepper
- salt
- 100 ml/1/2 cup oil
- 1/2 cup white wine

PREPARATION

Clean the squid and cut them into rings. Fry with garlic and oil. Add a little white wine and evaporate. Flavor with a small piece of stock cube and cook. Sprinkle with chopped parsley and red pepper and decorate with slices of lemon.

## GRECO NERO

The Greco Nero variety is thought to be among the grapes brought to Italy by the Greeks. It is grown in Calabria, where it is often blended with Greco Bianco to make rosés. It is also found in Lazio, Marche and Sardinia.

**SYNONYM**
Grecu niuru, Mazeigliano.

# grignolino

Grignolino is a Piedmontese vine, grown primarily in the zones of Asti and Monferrato Casalese. The name Grignolino (called Barbesino in Medieval times) may be derived from grignola, a dialect term for grape seed, as this variety has more pips (at least 3) than most. Grignolino is the main component in three DOC wines.

*Piedmont: the castle of Frassineto in Monferrato*

Grignolino d'Asti and Grignolino del Monferrato Casaleese are dry wines with a minimum alcohol level of 11%, which may include small percentages of Freisa in their makeup.

The third DOC comes from the vast Piemonte zone, which includes the provinces of Alessandria, Asti and Cuneo. Its dry Grignolino may include up to 15% of other red grapes in the blend. Grignolino is not an easy variety to work with, and the resulting wine usually has a tannin level that is at odds with its light color and body. The old-fashioned wine it yields was much appreciated back in the days when Piedmont was under the rule of the House of Savoy. Its acidity and structure were an ideal foil for the rich, buttery French-influenced foods of that period.

## TASTING NOTE

Pale garnet/ruby. There is often a floral tone (which some identify as dried roses) on the nose, and due to the wine's medium-to-high level of acidity, one can also find, at times, a pronounced grapefruit note. There is usually a soft tingle from the tannin in this supple-bodied wine.

On the palate there is a note of white pepper.

## SYNONYMS

Barbesino, Barbesinone, Verbesino, Balestra, Arlandino, Giordino, Rossetto, Nebbiolo Rosato.

## FOOD PAIRINGS

Fondue, or chicken served with cream, or cheese-based sauces.

---

### CHICKEN AND ASPARAGUS SOUP

SERVES 4
- 1500 ml/6 cups water
- 500 g/1 lb 2 oz mixed chicken meat
- 24 asparagus
- 1/2 onion • 1 carrot
- 1/2 stick of celery • salt

PREPARATION
Pour the water into a large saucepan and add carrot, celery, onion, diced chicken and the central part of the asparagus. Keep the tips for decorating the plate and eliminate the ends. Cook the stock and just blanch the asparagus tips so that they remain crisp. Blend the stock when cooked to make it creamy and velvety. Then decorate the plate with the asparagus tips.

---

### DOC AND DOCG

**PIEDMONT**
Grignolino d'Asti
Grignolino del Monferrato Casalese
Piemonte Grignolino

# grillo

This variety is probably of Puglian origin. It found its way to Sicily as a replacement vine in the aftermath of the late-19th century phylloxera epidemic. By the 1930s, it accounted for around 60% of the island's vines. This figure dropped to around 17,400 hectares by the 1950s. Today, it accounts for little more than 6,000 hectares, and its production area is largely confined to the seaboard between Trapani and Marsala.

Grillo is part of the grape mix for Marsala and is also blended with other varieties to make attractive dry whites.

The Grillo grape is high in sugar, and, like all successful Sicilian white varieties, it produces wines with good body, which can continue to evolve for three or four years.

## TASTING NOTE

Straw to pale gold. One finds light notes of hazelnuts, sweet corn and butterscotch on the nose. The wine has good body. A fresh almond note emerges on the finish.

## SYNONYMS

Riddu.

| DOC AND DOCG |
| --- |
| **SICILY** |
| Contea di Sclafani |
| Marsala |

## FOOD PAIRINGS

Sicilian antipasti. Eggplant-based casseroles.

| SICILIAN STUFFED EGGPLANTS |
| --- |
| SERVES 4 |
| • 1200 g/2$^{1/2}$ small eggplants |
| • 10 g/1 tbsp mint leaves |
| • 150 g/1$^{1/2}$ cups Caciocavallo cheese |
| • 150 g/1/2 cup olive oil |
| • 1 tbsp vinegar |
| • 1 tsp sugar |
| • onion |
| PREPARATION |
| Wash the eggplants and cut into the middle of the flesh. Sprinkle with salt and leave in a colander for the water to run out. Dice the cheese, slice the garlic and chop the mint and pepper. Use these ingredients to stuff the eggplants and fry gently in a pan. In another pan fry the onion in hot oil, add the sauce, the salt, the sugar and the vinegar. Add the eggplants and cook them. Serve hot or cold. |

# groppello

There are two main sub-varieties of Groppello. Groppello Gentile usually dominates the blends of rosés, while a preponderance of Gropello di Mocasina produces deeper, fuller-bodied wines. Often the two sub-varieties are blended together. The name Groppello stems from grop or groppo ("knot" in Veneto dialect), which refers to the variety's tightly packed bunches.

Groppello is believed to be indigenous to the northern tip of Lake Garda, and it is still found predominately in the Veneto (in the provinces of Vicenza, Verona and Treviso), in Trentino and in Lombardy (in the provinces of Brescia and Bergamo).

## TASTING NOTE

Bright ruby. The wine has medium acidity and good body. It is soft and round on the palate and has a lightly spicy flavor.

## SYNONYMS

For Groppello di Mocasina: Groppello S. Stefano, Grupel, Grupela Nera, Groppello Moliner, Mocasina.
For Groppello Gentile: Groppella, Grorello commune, Gropello fino, Groppello della Val di Non.

## FOOD PAIRINGS

Game, red meats and mature cheeses.

| DOC AND DOCG |
|---|
| **VENETO** |
| Garda Classico Groppello, Breganze rosso, Garda Classico Rosso |
| **LOMBARDY** |
| Riviera del Garda Bresciano Groppello, Riviera del Garda Bresciano Rosso |

### CASOEULA

SERVES 6
• 600 g/1 lb 5 oz pork ribs cut into pieces • 250 g/8 oz Luganega sausage • 100 g/4 oz fresh bacon rind • 1 pig's trotter • 2 small salamis suitable for cooking
• 1 Savoy cabbage • 200 g/7 oz celery • 180 g/6 oz carrots
• 1 onion • 20 g/1 tbsp butter
• 20 ml/1 tbsp extra-virgin olive oil
• 250 ml/1 cup dry white wine
• 1 tbsp tomato sauce
• 1 tbsp stock • salt and pepper

PREPARATION
Carefully wash the cabbage leaves and chop them roughly, leaving to dry in a saucepan over a low heat, making sure that they don't stick to the bottom of the pan. Flame the trotter and rind, cleaning them with a cloth. Split the trotter in half and cut the rind into strips, then boil them thoroughly in pan of salted water. They should be ready and degreased within about an hour. In the meantime fry the chopped onion in the butter and oil in a large saucepan. When it begins to color add the ribs, then the sausage cut into rounds and the salamis: leave them to mingle for a short while and then add the white wine and cook slowly until it evaporates. Take the meat out of the dish and add the sliced celery, carrots, and the tomato sauce dissolved in a little stock and season with salt and pepper. Cover and cook slowly, remembering to stir occasionally. Add the chopped cabbage, mix and lay the meat on top. Skim off any excess fat from the surface. Serve with slices of brown bread or, even better, polenta.

# inzolia (aka ansonica)

This variety is believed to be indigenous to Sicily, which remains its stronghold. In the past it was used mainly in the blend of Marsala, or else it was shipped in bulk to more northerly climes, where it added alcohol and body to blended wines. In recent years, Sicilian producers have begun to appreciate the variety's potential to make attractive dry whites.

Most producers now offer a varietal Inzolia or an Inzolia supported by small amounts of Chardonnay, Grillo, Catarratto, Grecanico or Sauvignon Blanc. Inzolia is very sensitive to climate, and those grown at high elevations tend to be distinctively grassy and herbaceous. In Tuscany this variety is known as Ansonica. Its arrival in that region is generally traced to the fact that, in former times, Tuscany was an avid importer of bulk Inzolia. In addition to dry whites, a passito style is also made on the island of Elba. Grapes for this wine are semi-dried for at least a week before being crushed and fermented.

## DOC AND DOCG

### SICILY
Contea di Sclafani Inzolia o Ansonica, Contessa Entellina Ansonica, Marsala, Menfi Inzolia, Sambuca di Sicilia Bianco, Santa Margherita del Belice Bianco
### TUSCANY
Ansonica Costa dell'Argentario, Elba Ansonica, Elba Ansonica Passito, Elba bianco, Spumante and Vin santo, Parrina Bianco

## TASTING NOTE
Straw to pale gold. Fresh and lightly floral (particularly elderflower).
A lightly saline note on the savory palate. Good body.

## SYNONYMS
Insolia, Ansonica, Ansora, Insora, Anzonica, Ansolica, Zolia Bianca, Ansolia.

## FOOD PAIRINGS
Bottarga (tuna fish roe) on fresh pasta, fish couscous, vegetable-based dishes, salt-baked fish, grilled swordfish, grilled shrimp.

## TUNA "ALLA MARINARA"

SERVES 4
- 4 fresh tuna fillets
- 75 ml/5 tbsp extra-virgin olive oil
- 400 g/1¼ cups ripe tomatoes
- 1 sprig of basil (chopped)
- 80 g/3 oz stoned black olives
- 30 g/1 oz capers
- salt • pepper

PREPARATION
Wash the slices of tuna, skin and dry them thoroughly. Grease an ovenproof dish with two spoonfuls of oil and arrange the fish pieces side by side. In the meantime blanch the tomatoes for a few seconds in boiling water, remove the seeds and cut them into little pieces. Dress the slices of tuna with the tomatoes, basil and stoned black olives, adding the capers and salt and pepper. Drizzle with oil and cook in the oven at 160°C/320°F for about 30 minutes. Serve hot.

# lacrima di morro
## (or lacrima nera)

This Lacrima is no relation to Campania's Lacryma Christi del Vesuvio (made from a blend of Piedirosso and Sciascinoso, with the option of adding Aglianico); rather it is a red variety peculiar to the hills around the town of Morro d'Alba (northwest of Ancona) in the Marche region.

It is called Lacrima ("tear" in Italian) because juice seeps from its berries as they ripen.

*Characteristic coastal landscapes and hills of the Marche*

The DOC, granted in 1985, virtually rescued this unusual grape from extinction and, indeed, gave it a new lease on life. From just 7 hectares (in 1985) its vineyard area has grown to around 102 hectares (2000) and the wine's small band of ardent producers continues to increase. They have tried carbonic maceration, late-harvesting, reducing skin contact and drying in pursuit of great Lacrima.

## TASTING NOTE

Lacrima di Morro is, generally speaking, light-bodied, with a fragrance that hovers between tea roses and violets.

However, carbonic maceration and other vinification and ageing techniques can deepen the color and broaden the body. Its particular rosy aroma, however, always remains.

## SYNONYMS

Lacryma Nera.

| DOC AND DOCG |
|---|
| **MARCHE** |
| Lacrima di Morro or Lacrima di Morro d'Alba |

## FOOD PAIRINGS

Roast pork with applesauce, chicken, duck with plum sauce, and even jam tarts.

| MACERATA STYLE CHICKEN |
|---|
| SERVES 4 |
| • 1 chicken |
| • 20 g/1 tbsp butter |
| • 3 eggs |
| • 50 ml/3 tbsp extra-virgin olive oil |
| • 1 lemon |
| • chicken giblets |
| • stock |
| • salt |
| PREPARATION |
| Prepare an entire chicken. Chop the giblets and place them in a saucepan with the oil and butter and the chicken, then add water and stock until a level of about 3 inches is reached. Cover the dish and cook over a low flame. When the chicken is ready the liquid will have almost all evaporated. Remove the chicken, cut it into pieces and arrange on a serving plate. Beat the eggs with the lemon juice and pour into the gravy. |

# lagrein

Lagrein flourishes in the Trentino-Alto Adige region, where it is the primary grape for Lagrein Dunkel (or Lagrein Scuro), a well-structured, deeply colored red with ageing potential, and Lagrein Kretzer (Lagrein Rosato), a delicate rosé intended for drinking young.

*Vipitena and Castle in Val Lagarina*

## TASTING NOTE

Deep ruby, with a slight fuchsia sheen. The wine has crisp acidity, and on the palate one finds an attractive blackberry flavor, which is reminiscent of fruit crumble.

## SYNONYMS

Lagarino.

## FOOD PAIRINGS

Meat lasagna, ravioli with duck sauce, roast pork.

When Lagrein Dunkel is aged for at least two years, it may be labelled as *riserva*.

When Lagrein is produced in the vineyards of the commune of Bolzano, it can be labelled as "Lagrein di Gries" (Grieser Lagrein or Lagrein aus Gries).

The name of this variety is thought to be derived from Lagara, a colony of Magna Graecia noted for the quality of its wines.

| DOC AND DOCG |
| --- |
| **TRENTINO - ALTOADIGE** |
| Alto Adige (Lagrein Kretzer) Lagrein Rosato |
| Alto Adige (Lagrein Dunkel) Lagrein Scuro |
| Alto Adige Cabernet-Lagrein |
| Alto Adige Merlot-Lagrein |
| Trentino Lagrein (Kretzer and Dunkel) |
| Vallagarina Lagrein |

## SPÄTZLE

SERVES 4
- 100 g/1 cup wheat meal
- 100 g/1 cup wheat flour
- 1000 ml/4 cups milk
- 100 ml/1/2 cup cream
- 3 eggs
- 70 g/ 3 oz smoked bacon
- 1 clove of garlic
- 30 ml/2 tbsp dry white wine
- chives
- potato starch
- salt
- 50 ml/3 tbsp oil

PREPARATION
Pour both types of flour into a bowl, add the eggs, oil, salt and several spoonfuls of water in order to obtain a smooth dough. Leave it to rest while you prepare the other ingredients.
Fry the bacon, cut into fine strips.

To it and the chopped garlic, add wine, milk and cream, bind with starch and add the chopped chives. Bring a pan of salted water to the boil. Press the dough through the special utensil into the boiling water.
Cook until the pieces float to the surface and lift out with a draining spoon. Add to the pan containing the condiment and toss before serving.

# lambrusco

The Romans called the wild vines growing at the edges (*labrum*) of cultivated fields (*bruscum*) labrusca vitis. The name evolved over time into Lambrusco, and refers to a family of vines cultivated principally in Northern Italy.

The most important of these vines in terms of wine production are Lambrusco di Sorbara, Lambrusco Salamino (so named because its bunches are said to resemble salami) and Lambrusco Grasparossa (named for the red – rosso – color of its stem – raspo). Lambrusco di Sorbara produces the lightest and zestiest wines of the three. It has a luscious, strawberry-juice hue. On the nose some find violets, and on the palate, it offers hints of frozen strawberries and cherries. Wine made from 100% Lambrusco Salamino has a dark, almost opaque purple color with violet froth. It has fruit flavor and medium body. Lambrusco Grasparossa is ruby with a cherry-colored froth. Its flavors are broader and the least precise of the three. Single-variety wines may be made from each of these grapes, or they may be blended with other Lambrusco sub-varieties, such as Lambrusco Marani, Lambrusco Maestri and Lambrusco Ruberti.

Andrea Bacci, Pope Sextus V's medical advisor and author of one of the major works on the topic of Italian wines, "De Naturali Vinorum Histoira dei Vinis Italiae", may well be the first to have noted the differences in the various Lambrusco zones. He states "On the hills in front of the city of Modena, Lambrusco vines are cultivated, whose white and red grapes yield delicious, spicy and fragrant wines which froth when poured into a glass." These vineyards within the province of Modena continue to yield the most prized wines. Among these, Lambrusco di Sorbara DOC, made from a blend of a minimum of 60% di Sorbara, and a maximum 40% Salamino, is usually designed for early drinking, while Lambrusco Grasparossa di Castelvetro (made from a minimum of 85% of the named grape), and the intensely aromatic and concentrated Lambrusco Salamino di Santa Croce (made from a minimum of 90% of the named grape) can have sufficient structure to allow them to keep for up to five years. All of these wines are made in both red and rosé versions. The Lambrusco Reggiano DOC is located in the province of Reggio Emilia and produces just about every style under the sun from various blends of Lambrusco grapes: sparkling white wines, reds and rosés.

The Lombardy region produces Lambrusco Mantovano DOC. This light and fruity blended Lambrusco wine is made in red and rosé styles. Traditional Lambrusco was a fairly dry wine whose sparkle was produced by a second fermentation in bottle – just like Champagne. Advances in technology in the 1960s radically changed Lambrusco's style. With the introduction of the Charmat method (which allowed the second fermentation to take place in large tanks rather than in bottle) it was possible for producers to dramatically increase volume and to make the wine sweet. It was this style – one defined by industrial-sized volume producers – which, in the late 1970s/early 1980s, literally flooded the United States market, where it was promoted as a kind of Italian Coca-Cola. During its heyday, Lambrusco accounted for around 50% of all Italian wine imported into the United States.

As a representative for a large Modena-based wine company told me: "We were addicted by the business in America in the 1980s – anything fizzy with the name Lambrusco on the label sold like crazy. Lambrusco was no longer thought of as a wine but rather as a beverage category."

But by the 1990s wine lovers had become more sophisticated and their motto became: "less but better". And "better", in the case of Lambrusco, means fresh fruit rather than simple sweetness and a definable structure rather than the amorphous softness of mass-production.

Producers in Emilia-Romagna have, in recent years, recognized the need to go back to their roots by producing drier, better structured wines.

These wines are satisfying and ideal for mealtimes.

cherry color, while those based on Salamino will be very dark purple with a lively violet froth. All Lambrusco will be low in alcohol (around 10.5%) and should have fresh, zippy acidity. On the palate its broad fruit flavors can include strawberry, raspberry and wild berry fruit. The finish should be clean.

## FOOD PAIRINGS

The zesty acidity and luscious fruit of dry Lambruscos makes them ideal partners for Emilian specialities, which are often rich in fats and flavor.

Unfortunately, most of the best Lambruscos are not as yet exported. They are, however, worth seeking out.

## TASTING NOTE

Sorbara-based wines will be a luscious pink, those with more Grasparossa will be a darker

The more substantial Lambruscos go perfectly with pork seasoned with juniper berries, roast lamb, pork salamis, sausages and ragouts, while the refreshing vivacity of the lighter, simpler style Lambruscos is exactly the right choice for setting off a steaming dish of zampone and lentils or a plate of mortadella.

## CLOVES-ROAST

SERVES 4
- 1200 g/2 lb 10 oz veal
- 100 g/4 oz sliced ham
- 4 cloves
- a sprig of rosemary
- 30 g/2 tbsp butter
- salt and pepper

PREPARATION
Melt the butter in a saucepan, flavoring with rosemary. Lay in the piece of veal wrapped in the very fine slices of ham aromatized with the cloves. Add salt and pepper to taste and leave to cook slowly in the covered saucepan, turning the meat occasionally to flavor it evenly.
Serve hot with boiled or roast beans.

## TAGLIATELLE WITH MEAT RAGOUT

SERVES 4
FOR THE PASTA:
- 400 g/3¼ cups flour
- 4 eggs
FOR THE SAUCE:
- 200 g/7 oz beef
- 50 g/2 oz bacon
- 50 g/3 tbsp butter
- 1 onion
- 1 carrot
- 1 stick of celery
- 100 ml/1/2 cup meat stock
- 3 cloves
- 20 g/1 tbsp tomato sauce
- 20 ml/2 tbsp of cream (optional)
- 50 g/1/2 cup grated Grana Padano
- cheese • salt and pepper

PREPARATION
Use the classic method to make the pasta. When the sheet of pasta is dry, dust it with flour, roll it up and cut into 0.2 inch thick strips.
Unravel the tagliatelle and lay them on a cloth lightly dusted with flour. Chop the beef, the bacon, the onion, carrot and celery.
Place the chopped ingredients in a saucepan with butter and a clove and fry for a few minutes, then add the stock.
Add the tomato sauce and season with salt and pepper.
Pour 2 cups water into the dish and cook for about 3/4 of an hour.
Drop the tagliatelle into a large pan of boiling salted water and take them out after a few minutes. Drain and dress with the hot ragout, adding a few spoonfuls of cream (optional) and the grated Grana Padano cheese.

## PIG'S FEET AND LENTILS

SERVES 4
- 1 pig's feet weighing about 1 kilo/2 lb 3 oz
- 300 g/1¾ cups lentils
- 4-5 sage leaves
- 1 sprig of rosemary
- several celery leaves
- 2 cloves of garlic
- 2 dried tomatoes cut in half
- 1 red chili pepper
- 50 ml/3 tbsp extra-virgin olive oil

PREPARATION
Soak the pig's feet in cold water for 10 hours, perforate the surface and place it in a pan full of cold water. Bring to the boil and cook for 3-4 hours. In the meantime place the lentils in a pan full of cold water with the aromatic herbs, celery leaves, garlic and chili. Add the tomatoes and cook for about 20 minutes on a medium heat until done. Remove the herbs and garlic and season the lentils with oil, salt and pepper. Remove the pig's feet and serve with the lentils.

| DOC AND DOCG | EMILIA-ROMAGNA |
|---|---|
| **LOMBARDY** | Lambrusco di Sorbara, Lambrusco Grasparossa di Castelvetro, Lambrusco Salamino di Santa Croce, Colli Piacentini Lambrusco Grasparossa, Colli Piacentini Lambrusco Montericco, Reggiano Lambrusco |
| Lambrusco Mantovano | |

# magliocco

Magliocco, an ancient Calabrian variety, is cultivated primarily in the provinces of Cosenza and Catanzaro. It is sometimes used to add body and structure to the blends of local wines. Magliocco was given new life by the Librandi company, which began researching and propagating ancient indigenous varieties in 1988.

*Calabria: the Castelle and the ruins of a Magna Grecia temple*

Their experimentation resulted in a 100% Magliocco wine, which they have named Magno Megonio.

This barrique-fermented red, whose first vintage was 1995, has true class and ageing potential.

## TASTING NOTE

Dark ruby. Fresh and clean on the nose, with scents of ripe plums, autumn leaves and newly polished leather. On the palate, one finds notes of damsons and berry fruits.

## SYNONYMS

Magliocco ovale, Magliuacculu.

## FOOD PAIRINGS

Roast lamb, game and mature cheeses.

### SICILIAN STYLE KID

SERVES 4

• 1 kilo/2 lb 3 oz young goat
• 1 onion • 350 g/2 cups potatoes
• 200 g/3/4 cup peeled plum tomatoes • 100 g/1 cup grated Pecorino cheese • salt • black pepper
• oregano • 125 ml/1/2 cup olive oil

PREPARATION

Cut the goat into pieces and lay them in a terracotta dish with the chopped onion, potato wedges and tomatoes. Add the Pecorino, salt, pepper, oregano and olive oil. Cook in the oven at a moderate heat for 1¹/² hours.

### "MILLE COSEDDE"

SERVES 6

• 350 g/3/4 lb pasta shapes • 150 g/3/4 cup dried broad beans • 150 g/3/4 cup dried chickpeas • 150 g/3/4 cup dried beans • 1/2 cabbage
• 1 onion • 1 carrot • 1 stick of celery
• 50 g/2 oz smoked bacon • 150 ml/3/4 cup extra-virgin olive oil
• 100 g/ 1 cup grated Pecorino cheese • salt • pepper • chili pepper

PREPARATION

Soak the beans in tepid water for about 24 hours. Drain them, pour them into a pan with boiling water and cook.

Clean the cabbage, chop it finely, and chop the carrot, onion and celery with the bacon and fry with oil on a low heat. Add the drained beans, cabbage and 8 cups of water, seasoning with salt, pepper and chili. When it begins to boil add the pasta and when it is cooked, serve with grated Pecorino cheese.

# maiolina

Maiolina is found in Lombardy's Franciacorta zone, where it is used to add color to fruity, easy-to-drink reds. Its name may be derived from the dialect word *majol* (bud), due to the high number of buds on each branch of this very vigorous vine, or it may be taken from the name of the hamlet of Maiolini (in the commune of Ome), where it is widely cultivated and where the surname Majolini is quite common.

This last theory has the most appeal for Simone Maiolini, whose family has been growing grapes in Franciacorta since the 14th century. He even went so far as to write his thesis on the Maiolina variety and has experimented with the grape at his family-owned estate in Ome. "It is not an easy variety," admits Maiolini. "To achieve the best results it is necessary to take drastic measures in the vineyards, both with pruning

and with thinning: the yield per vine must be reduced by more than half." When the grapes are treated in this way, Maiolini believes that it is possible to produce a wine suitable for ageing. With the 2001 harvest the company has chosen to produce a wine made exclusively from Maiolina, which they have decided to name, simply, Maiolina. "We decided to call it by the grape name because we figured we were the only ones in Italy to have it," explains Simone.

## TASTING NOTE

Deep ruby. Fresh, lightly floral fragrances mingle with soft red berry fruit notes, which are echoed on the palate.

## FOOD PAIRINGS

This wine is ideal for rich and tasty risottos, but also combines well with meats.

### MILANESE STYLE RISOTTO

SERVES 4
- 75 g/1/4 cup butter
- 50 g/2 oz bone marrow
- 1 small onion (chopped)
- 350 g/1¾ cups Carnaroli rice
- 100 ml/1/2 cup dry white wine
- a few saffron strands
- 1½ kilos/6 cups meat stock
- salt • pepper
- 50 g/3 tbsp Grana Padano cheese

PREPARATION
Melt 3 tbsp of butter in a pan with the beef and the bone marrow. Add the onion and fry until it is transparent. Add the rice and, using a wooden spoon, stir to toast the rice. Sprinkle with wine and cook, stirring continuously, adding more stock as needed. Add the saffron. When the rice has absorbed all the liquid, season with salt and pepper. Just before the rice is cooked add the Grana Padano and the remaining butter.

### MILANESE STYLE MARROW BONE

SERVES 4
- 6 one-inch thick veal marrow bone steaks • 100 g/1 cup flour
- chopped parsley • chopped garlic
- 80 g/1/4 cup butter

- a sliced onion
- 100 ml/1/2 cup dry white wine or stock • 1 lemon (only the rind)
- salt and freshly ground pepper

PREPARATION
Fry the sliced onion in butter in a large saucepan. Arrange the floured steaks in the pan and brown them on both sides. Cover the pan and leave the meat to cook slowly, sprinkling occasionally with wine. Salt and pepper to taste. In the meantime, prepare the condiment by chopping together the parsley, garlic and lemon peel. A few minutes before the steaks are ready, cover them with the condiment. Serve piping hot.

# malvasia (white and black grape)

The name Malvasia covers a large collection of vines, some of which are white, others red. Wines made from the various clones and biotypes tend to share similar characteristics: they usually have (in varying degrees of intensity) a musky, apricot-tinged fragrance as well as high residual sugar levels. These qualities make Malvasia particularly suitable for the production of both sparkling and passito wines.

The word Malvasia is derived from a corruption of Monemvasia, the name of a Byzantine fortified city built on a rock off the coast of the southeastern part of the Peloponnese.

The city is connected to the mainland by a single road leading to its main gate, and its name, Monemvasia, literally means "only one entry point". The Venetians landed here in 1248 and established a trading agreement with the locals, whereby they sold the sweet wines of the area throughout Europe under the name Monemvasia. The Venetians brought the "Monemvasia" vine first to Crete and later to Italy, where they encouraged its cultivation throughout the Mediterranean Basin.

Wine made from the variety was a very popular trading commodity, and during its heyday, Venice was filled with osterias devoted solely to Monemvasia/Malvasia.

## MALVASIA BIANCA

This biotype is found primarily in southern Italy, where it is usually blended with other varieties. It comes into its own in the Puglian DOC zone of Leverano, in the province of Lecce, where it is a major component in four very distinct types of wine. It makes up at least 85% of the blend of Leverano Bianco (a dry white) and of Leverano Bianco Passito (a velvety textured sweet white).

Grapes for this latter wine are left to semi-dry on the vine or on racks in well-ventilated lofts before pressing. There is also a late-harvest Malvasia made in this zone. The grapes for this wine are left on the vine until at least October 1st. This wine reaches a minimum alcohol level of 14.5%.

In Calabria, Malvasia Bianca can comprise up to 50% of Bivongi Bianco, a DOC zone located in the province of Reggio Calabria. It also provides a large part of the blend of the aperitif wine, San Vito di Luzzi Bianco.

## SYNONYMS
No known synonyms.

## MALVASIA DEL CHIANTI

This sub-variety has existed for centuries in Tuscany and was part of the original recipe for Chianti, perfected by Baron Bettino Ricasoli in 1870. Malvasia del Chianti is now also fairly widespread in the Veneto, Puglia and Lazio, and is often teamed up with its perennial partner, Trebbiano Toscano, in the blends of dry and sweet whites, the most famous of which is Orvieto.

## SYNONYMS

Malvasia Toscana, Malvasia Bianca Lunga, Malvasia Bianca di Bari, Malvasia Pugliese Bianco, Malvasia Trevigiana, Malvasia Cannilunga di Novoli.

## MALVASIA BIANCO DI CANDIA B.

This sub-variety is grown principally in Lazio, and to a lesser degree in Emilia-Romagna, Umbria, Tuscany and Liguria. In Lazio it is a major component (along with Trebbiano Toscano) in such DOC wines as Castelli Romani Bianco, Cerveteri Bianco, Circeo Bianco, Colli Albani, Colli della Sabina and Cori Bianco. It also makes up part of the blend for Lazio's most popular wine: Frascati. In addition to the dry version, this wine is made in a semi-sweet

*Sicily: the Basilica of Monreale and barrels for the maturation of wines*

(amabile) and a fully sweet style (called canellino). When Frascati has a minimum alcohol level of 11.5%, it can be labelled *superiore*. If the wine is bottled before December 31st of the vintage year, it is called *Novello*. And let's not forget sparkling Frascati!

## SYNONYMS
Malvasia rossa dei Castelli Romani, Malvasia Candida.

## MALVASIA DI CANDIA AROMATICA
To make things a tad more confusing, there also exists Malvasia di Candia Aromatica.
The Aromatica is said to have a finer perfume. This Malvasia is cultivated mainly in Emilia, particularly in the provinces of Piacenza, Parma and Reggio Emilia.
It is the primary component in a number of dry and semi-sweet wines, made in still, semi-sparkling, fully sparkling and passito styles.
It is also the major component in Lombardy's Oltrepò Pavese Malvasia.

This wine, too, can be dry, sweet, still, semi-sparkling or fully sparkling.

## SYNONYMS
Malvasia di Candia, Malvagia, Malvasia Bianca Aromatica, Malvasia di Alessandria.

## MALVASIA DEL LAZIO
This sub-variety is most widely planted in Lazio, where it is cultivated mainly in the DOC zones of Marino and Castelli Romani.
It is becoming ever more popular with Frascati producers, who are increasing its role in that wine.

## SYNONYMS
Malvasia nostrale, Malvasia Gentile, Malvasia Puntinata, Malvasia col puntino.

## MALVASIA ISTRIANA
The first documented reference to the variety istriana dates from around 1300.
This sub-variety is cultivated mainly in Friuli Venezia-Giulia, and dry varietal Malvasia is produced in every DOC zone in the region.
I often find a distinct note of mandarin oranges in wines made from this variety.

## SYNONYMS
Malvasia del Carso, Malvasia Friulana, Malvasia Weiss, Malvasia d'Istria.

## MALVASIA DI SARDEGNA
Malvasia is thought to have arrived in Sardinia during the island's Byzantine era. It is the major component in four wine styles: dry, sweet, sweet fortified and dry fortified.

It makes up at least 95% of Malvasia di Bosa and Malvasia di Cagliari.

## SYNONYMS
Avaréga, Malvagia, Marmaxia, Malmazia, Manusia, Uva Malvatica, Uva Greca.

## MALVASIA DI LIPARI
This Malvasia sub-variety was brought to the Lipari or Aeolian islands (a volcanic archipelago off the northeast coast of Sicily) by the Greeks.
The variety was in decline in 1963 when Carlo Hauner, a designer and painter, arrived on the island of Salina as a tourist. He was so struck by the beauty of the place that he moved there.
Mr. Hauner, who passed away in the 1990s, is considered largely responsible for resurrecting the vineyards and reputation of this vine.
A pleasant dry white wine is made from fresh grapes, but it is Malvasia delle Lipari Passito (made from semi-dried grapes) that has the more important reputation. This passito, which has a minimum alcohol level of 18%, has a crisp, appealing flavor which hovers between hazelnuts and wildflowers.
A fortified (liquoroso) style, which has a minimum alcohol level of 20%, is also made.

## SYNONYMS
No known synonyms.

## TASTING NOTE
Dry Malvasia: Straw yellow to pale gold. Fresh and fruity on the nose. Light almond and hazelnut notes, with distinct floral tones and

### DOC AND DOCG (MALVASIA BIANCO)

**LOMBARDY**
Oltrepo Pavese Malvasia

**FRIULI VENEZIA-GIULIA**
Carso Malvasia, Collio Goriziano (or Collio)
Malvasia Istriana, Colli Orientali del Friuli Malvasia
Istriana, Friuli Annia Malvasia, Malvasia Istriana,
Friuli Latisana Malvasia, Isonzo Malvasia Istriana

**SARDINIA**
Malvasia di Cagliari, Malvasia di Bosa

**EMILIA-ROMAGNA**
Colli di Parma Malvasia (also sparkling),
Colli Piacentini Valnure, Colli Piacentini Malvasia
(also Passito), Colli Piacentini Monterosso Val
d'Arda, Colli Piacentini Vin Santo,
Colli di Scandiano e di Canossa Malvasia, Colli di
Parma Malvasia (also sparkling)

**UMBRIA**
Colli Amerini Malvasia

**LAZIO**
Bianco Capena, Colli Albani, Colli Lanuvini, Cori
Bianco, Frascati, Genazzano bianco, Marino, Monte-
Compatri Colonna, Castelli Romani Bianco

**CAMPANIA**
Guardia Sanframondi (or Guardiolo) Bianco

**PUGLIA**
Gravina, Leverano Bianco

**CALABRIA**
San Vito di Luzzi Bianco

**SICILY**
Malvasia delle Lipari

more elusive apricot hints on the palate. The medium-to-high alcohol level results in good structure.

Not all producers are capable of achieving these clean, well-balanced results. They allow the alcohol to get the upper hand, thus negating any charm the fruit may have to offer.

Sweet Malvasia: Pale gold. Good structure.

Hazelnut and almond notes mingle with floral tones on the nose, and re-emerge on the palate. A rich texture and fine, clean finish.

### FOOD PAIRINGS
Dry Malvasia: light fish-based antipasti and soups. Due to its slight saline quality it also goes well with lobster, crabs and fatty fish.
Passito Malvasia: *vino da meditazione.*

## BARESE STYLE MACKEREL

SERVES 4
- 4 large mackerel
- 3 cloves of garlic
- 1 handful of parsley
- mint leaves
- 250 ml/1 cup white wine
- 125 ml/1/2 cup extra-virgin olive oil
- salt
- pepper

PREPARATION
Remove the fish innards and scales and boil the mackerel for a few minutes in salted water on a low heat. Drain and dry them, then fillet, trying not to break them. Make a marinade using vinegar, salt and pepper and soak the mackerel in it for 1/2 hour. In the meantime prepare another marinade with the oil, chopped parsley, garlic and mint. Add a little salt and immerse the mackerel. Marinate for about an hour and serve with black olives and cold boiled potatoes.

## POLENTA WITH PRAWNS
### (Friuli)

SERVES 4
- 250 g/1 cup maize semolina
- 50 g/3 tbsp butter
- 1000 g/2 lb 3 oz prawns
- 1 handful of fresh mushrooms
- 1 clove of garlic
- 15 g/1 tbsp chopped parsley
- 200 ml/1 cup white wine
- 1000 ml/4 cups vegetable stock
- pepper
- salt • nutmeg

PREPARATION
Make a quantity of soft polenta and leave to cool. Cut into slices and arrange in an ovenproof dish greased with butter. Peel the prawns and toss in a frying pan with a little butter. Add the mushrooms, garlic and chopped parsley. Sprinkle with the white wine, add the stock and bring to the boil. Season with freshly ground pepper and grated nutmeg and spread them over the slices of polenta. Bake in the oven for a few minutes and serve.

## SICILIAN STYLE CANNOLI WITH MALVASIA LIPARI

SERVES 4
- 150 g/1¼ cups flour
- 15 g/1 tbsp cocoa powder
- 20 g/1 tbsp butter
- 1 egg • 270 g/1¼ sugar
- 15 ml/1 tbsp Marsala
- 15 g/1 tbsp cornstarch
- 100 ml/6 tbsp milk
- 500 g/2 cups fresh Ricotta
- pieces of chocolate
- pistachio nuts • orange peel
- icing sugar • olive oil

PREPARATION
Prepare the cannoli by adding the butter, sugar, Marsala, cocoa powder and egg white to the flour. Knead to form an even ball. Leave it to rest wrapped in a cloth for two hours. Roll it out into a very thin sheet and cut out discs measuring about 5 inches across. Wrap them around special metal pipes (diameter 1 inch), wetting the ends with egg in order to stick them together, and fry in abundant oil. When golden, remove them and leave to dry and cool. When cool, carefully remove the pipes. Prepare the cream of Ricotta, sieving it with the cornstarch – dissolved earlier in a glass of milk – the sugar, pieces of pistachio nuts and chocolate. Fill every cannolo with the cream and decorate with icing sugar and orange peel.

## FLORENTINE STYLE "CASTAGNACCIO"
### with "MOSCADELLO"

SERVES 6
- 400 g/4 cups sweet chestnut flour
- 100 g/1/2 cup raisins
- 50 g/1/4 cup shelled pine nuts
- 50 g/1/4 cup shelled walnuts
- 30 g/2 tbsp sugar
- salt • 75 ml/5 tbsp olive oil
- 500 ml/2 cups water

PREPARATION
Sieve the chestnut flour into a large bowl, add the sugar and a pinch of salt and pour in 2 cups of cold water, stirring well to make a smooth liquid batter. Add two spoonfuls of oil and the raisins, soaked earlier; mix again and pour the batter into a greased ovenproof dish large enough for the "castagnaccio" to rise up to about 3/4 of an inch. Sprinkle the surface with pine nuts, crumbled walnuts and a few rosemary leaves. Before cooking it in an oven preheated to 200°C/390°F drizzle with oil. Bake for about 30 minutes until the surface is crunchy and cracked.

# MALVASIA NERA
## MALVASIA DI CASORZO

This variety is cultivated in the commune of Casorzo in the Piedmontese province of Asti. It makes up a minimum of 90% of a sweetish, aromatic red DOC wine called, not surprisingly, Malvasia di Casorzo. The rest of the blend may be made up of such varieties as Freisa, Grignolino and Barbera. The wine ranges from cherry to ruby red in color. It is also made in a sparkling version and a velvety textured passito style.

## SYNONYM

Moscatellina.

## MALVASIA DI SCHIERANO NERO

This variety is found mainly in Piedmont, with planting concentrated in the province of Turin. It is the main component in Malvasia Di Castelnuovo Don Bosco DOC. Small amounts of Freisa may be added to the blend. The wine tends to be cherry red and is generally on the sweet side. It is also made in semi-sparkling and fully sparkling styles.

## SYNONYMS

Malvasia di Castelnuovo del Bosco, Malvasia a grappolo corto.

## MALVASIER (MALVASIA NERA)

Malvasier has been planted in Trentino-Alto Adige for centuries. It is part of the DOC denomination Alto Adige (or Südtirol) Malvasia (Malvasier). It produces a dry, ruby red wine with orange highlights. It has good acidity and body.

*Piedmont: Vignale Monferrato*

## SYNONYMS

Malvasia Rossa, Roter Malvasier, Früher Roter Malvasier.

## MALVASIA NERA DI BRINDISI

As the name implies, this variety is found in Puglia, primarily in the provinces of Lecce, Taranto and Brindisi, and is used mainly as a component in rosés. It is part of the blend of such Puglian DOCs as Alezio, Leverano, Copertino, Lizzano, Nardó, Salice Salentino and Squinzano.

## SYNONYMS

Malvasia Nera di Lecce, Malvasia Negra, Malvasia Nera di Bari, Malvasia di Bitonto, Malvasia di Trani, Malvasia Nera di Candia.

| DOC AND DOCG (MALVASIA NERA) |
|---|
| **PIEDMONT** |
| Malvasia di Casorzo |
| Malvasia di Castelnuovo don Bosco |
| **TRENTINO ALTO ADIGE** |
| Alto Adige Malvasia (Malvasier) |

## MALVASIA NERA DI BASILICATA

This variety is thought to have arrived in Basilicata from Puglia as it shares many characteristics with Malvasia Nera di Brindisi.

## MALVASIA ROSA

This is believed to be a clonal mutation of the white variety, Malvasia di Candia Aromatica. It is found mainly in the province of Piacenza. It is usually used as a blending wine for sweetish, fizzy reds.

## SYNONYM

Malvasia rossa.

## FOOD PAIRINGS

Black Malvasia-based wines can be divided into sweet and dry styles. Sweet wines like Malvasia di Castelnuovo Don Bosco and that of Casorzo combine excellently with pastries. For dry wines one must distinguish between rosé wines and red ones. The former go well with grilled fish and vegetables, the reds with white meats with sauces.

---

### APPLE FRITTERS

SERVES 6
- 1000 g/5 cups flour
- 10 eggs
- 50 ml/1/4 cup dry white wine
- 2 lemons
- 1 pinch of salt
- 3 apples
- 15 g/1 tbsp natural yeast
- 1000 ml/4 cups extra-virgin olive oil for frying

PREPARATION
Mix the flour with the egg yolks, 10 tbsp of oil and enough dry white wine to obtain a smooth dough. Add a spoonful of yeast, the grated rind of two lemons, two pinches of salt and three spoonfuls of sugar. Whisk all the ingredients together for about 10 minutes. Leave to rest for at least two hours. Whisk the whites of the 10 eggs into stiff peaks and add these to the mixture along with the sliced apples. Drop spoonfuls of the mixture into boiling oil, fry until golden and serve piping hot.

### PIEDMONTESE NOUGAT

SERVES 6
- 200 g/3/4 cup honey
- 100 g/1/2 cup sugar
- 30 g/2 tbsp egg whites whisked into stiff peaks
- 150 g/1$^{1/4}$ cup toasted hazelnuts

PREPARATION
To make homemade nougat heat the honey in a small pan using the double boiler method, add the sugar and the whites whisked into stiff peaks, continuing to stir until the mixture is nicely whipped and shiny. Gradually add the toasted hazelnuts and continue cooking until it becomes difficult to mix. Line the bottom of a rectangular tin with a sheet of rice paper and pour in the mixture. Level and cut into strips while still warm.

### TYROLEAN STEW

SERVES 4
- 400 g/14 oz pork loin
- 300 g/10 oz sausage
- 50 g/2 oz bacon
- bay leaves • 3 cloves
- 100 ml/1/2 cup red wine • 75 ml/1/4 cup oil • 50 g/3 tbsp butter
- 1 onion • 300 g/1 cup tomatoes
- salt and pepper • 1/2 stock cube
- 3 potatoes

PREPARATION
Cut the pork into cubes and soak in a bowl with a glass of red wine, two spoonfuls of oil, salt, pepper, cloves and two bay leaves. Cover and leave at room temperature for an hour. Chop the bacon and the onion very finely and fry with a little butter and oil. After a few minutes add the sausage cut into pieces and fry until the fat dissolves a little. Add the pork and fry on a high heat, adding the marinade with the cloves and bay leaves and cooking until it evaporates. Add two cups of hot water and the tomatoes. Cover and cook on a moderate heat for about 1$^{1/2}$ hours. Halfway through the cooking time add the potatoes, after peeling and dicing them.

# marzemino

Marzemino seems to have emerged from the vineyards around the city of Padua, subsequently spreading throughout the Veneto and into Lombardy, Trentino, Friuli and Emilia. The variety is inevitably linked with Mozart, who is said to have had a great fondness for it. Certainly, the composer's librettist, Lorenzo da Ponte, enjoyed the wine to the point of including a reference to "excellent Marzemino" in the lyric of the opera *Don Giovanni*.

Marzemino is produced in dry, sparkling and passito versions.

The best example of this latter style is the Refrontolo Passito, which is made from a minimum of 95% Marzemino grapes grown in the Colli di Conegliano zone in the Veneto communes of Refrontolo, Pieve di Soligo and San Pietro di Feletto.

On the palate, this wine, which has a minimum alcohol level of 15%, is very soft, and is filled with ripe, sweet-cherry fruit.

Locally it is served on its own at the end of a meal.

The Veneto has two other Marzemino production zones: Breganze Marzemino has a relatively full body and Garda Marzemino is light and delicate. Trentino Marzemino is of medium body.

When it has a minimum alcohol level of 11.5% and has been aged for two years it can be labelled *riserva*. It is considered to show at its best two or three years after the harvest.

In the Emilia-Romagna zone of Colli di Scandiano e Canossa, Marzemino is treated in much the same way as Lambrusco, producing wines that are often slightly sweet and fizzy.

In Lombardy, Marzemino (here known as Berzamino) makes up a minimum 30% of the blend of Cellatica DOC.

## TASTING NOTE

Wine from this variety is ruby with purplish highlights. It has a tangy, fruity perfume, with hints of blackberries, walnuts and vanilla on the nose and palate.

## SYNONYMS

Barsemin, Bassanino, Berzemino and Marzemina, Bassamino.

## FOOD PAIRINGS

Roast and boiled meats or herb-flavored cheeses.

| DOC AND DOCG |
|---|
| **LOMBARDY** |
| Cellatica |
| Garda Marzemino |
| |
| **VENETO** |
| Breganze Marzemino |
| Passito di Refrontolo dei Colli di Conegliano |
| Garda Orientale Marzemino |
| |
| **TRENTINO ALTO ADIGE** |
| Trentino Marzemino |
| |
| **EMILIA-ROMAGNA** |
| Colli di Scandiano e Canossa, Marzemino |

## MARZEMINO BIANCO

The vine originated in Burgundy, and soon spread to Germany, Austria, Swizerland and Italy. In Vicenza, Trentino and Veneto it is a table grape.

## SYNONYMS

Chasselas Dorato, Edelweiss, Fendant, Queen Victoria.

## TASTING NOTE

Straw yellow.
Lightly aromatic, good acidity.

# monica

This variety is believed to have been brought to Sardinia by Spanish monks in the 11th century. From convent vineyards, Monica spread throughout the island. Monica is the major grape in the two DOCs.

Monica di Sargedna DOC, which has a minimum alcohol level of 11%, tends to be a round, full, easy drinking wine. Monica di Cagliari, on the other hand, produces wines of heftier alcohol content, which are intended for after-dinner consumption. The Dolce Naturale style has a minimum alcohol level of 14.5% and the Liquoroso reaches a minimum of 17.5%. Monica also enters into the DOC Mandrolisai, where it constitutes at least 35% of the blend.

## TASTING NOTE

Dark ruby color. One finds notes of damson plums and black pepper on the nose and palate. The wine is medium to full bodied.

## SYNONYMS

Monaca, Monica Nera, Munica, Munica niedda, Pascale Sardu, Miedda Mora.

## FOOD PAIRINGS

Grilled lamb and goat dishes, half-fat cheese.

| DOC AND DOCG |
| --- |
| **SARDINIA** |
| Monica di Sardegna, Monica di Cagliari, Madrolisai |

### "SA FREGULA"

SERVES 6
- 350 g/3/4 lb fregula (pasta granules made from durum wheat flour)
- 3 egg yolks
- 1 pinch of saffron
- salt

PREPARATION

Form a mound of flour on a terracotta plate, beat the eggs in a bowl with the saffron and salted water.
Pour a few drops into the middle of the flour and make tiny balls the size of pepper corns with your finger tips. Continue until all the flour has been used up. Leave to dry in a cool, dry place for 24 hours.

### BROAD BEANS AND BACON

SERVES 6
- 300 g/1³/⁴ cup dried broad beans
- 50 g/2 oz bacon
- 200 g/1/2 lb sausage
- 2 pig's feet
- 2 pork chops
- wild fennel
- wild chives
- Savoy cabbage
- tomatoes
- Pecorino cheese to dress
- 50 g/2 oz bacon fat
- onion
- garlic • basil • mint
- parsley • sage • oil
- croutons or Carasau (a special Sardinian bread)
- salt and pepper

PREPARATION

Admittedly some of these ingredients are very hard to find, but if you get the chance you really ought to try this dish, which is popular throughout Sardinia. Chop and fry the bacon fat, onion, garlic, basil, mint, parsley and sage in a terracotta saucepan. Leave the beans to soak over night. Chop and fry the onion, garlic, basil, mint, parsley and sage in bacon fat in a terracotta saucepan. Chop the sausages, pork chops and pig's feet into bite-sized pieces. Add the meat, beans, water and salt and pepper. Bring to a boil and let simmer for about an hour. Add the bacon, wild fennel, wild chives, cabbage and tomatoes and continue to cook over a low heat. Serve hot in large bowls garnished with croutons or Carasau.

# montepulciano

All right, let's get this out of the way at once: Montepulciano – the grape – has nothing to do with Montepulciano – the Tuscan town. The confusion began when early ampelographers took the easy path and linked the two. Montepulciano – the grape – is thought to have originated in Abruzzo and by the 19th century, spread to Puglia, Molise, Marche and Lazio.

This variety produces wines which have a full, lush fruitiness and naturally soft tannins, which give it an even bigger potential for making palate-pleasing wines than Sangiovese. It certainly is capable of producing some of Italy's finest reds.

## ABRUZZO

Montepulciano accounts for about half the total area under vine in Abruzzo, and is the basis for nearly all of the region's DOC red wines. The extremely large production area of Montepulciano d'Abruzzo includes hillside or upland plateaus in all four of the region's provinces. The landscape ranges from snowy peaks in the west and descends through hills to the Adriatic coast. Soils in the mountainous area consist mainly of calcareous rock, with those in the hilly eastern zone consisting mainly of clay-calcareous soils and sands. The climate is generally mild, with gentle breezes off the sea.

Montepulciano d'Abruzzo is made from at least 85% of the named grape, has a minimum alcohol level of 11.5% and must be aged for at least five months. With at least two-year ageing and a minimum of 12% alcohol, the wine may be labelled *riserva*. The rosé version of this wine is called Cerasuolo. Two of this zone's outstanding historic producers are Edoardo Valentini, one of the first to make estate-bottled wines, and Gianni Masciarelli, who was the first to experiment successfully with ageing Montepulciano in small barrels.

The Colline Teramane is a sub-zone of Montepulciano d'Abruzzo. Its vineyards are located in some thirty communes in the province of Teramo. The wine is produced from at least 90% Montepulciano and has a minimum alcohol level of 12.5%. With at least three years ageing it can be labelled *riserva*.

The vineyards of the Controguerra zone are located on hillsides in the province of Teramo. Montepulciano makes up at least 60% of Controgeurra Rosso, with the rest of the blend composed of Merlot and/or Cabernet (minimum 15%) plus other red grapes. When the wine has an alcohol level of 12.5% and at least one year of ageing (six months of which must be in bottle), it may be labelled *riserva*. The light and fruity nouveau-style Controguerra Novello is made from the same blend as the previous wine, but around 30% of its grapes undergo carbonic maceration.

The Contraguerra Passito Rosso, which is made from a minimum of 60% semi-dried Montepulciano grapes, is a dessert wine with an alcohol level of around 14%.

*Vineyards on outcrops of the Abruzzo Appennine*

## MOLISE

The Molise DOC zone comprises around 70 communes in the province of Campobasso and Isernia. Montepulciano Molise is made from at least 85% of the named grape and has a minimum alcohol level of 11%. With a minimum alcohol level of 12.5% and two years of ageing (six months of which must be in bottle), the wine may be labelled *riserva*. Molise Rosso and Biferno Rosso and Rosato are also Montepulciano-based. With a minimum alcohol level of 13% and at least three years of ageing Biferno Rosso may be labelled *riserva*.

## MARCHE

The most important red in the Marche is Rosso Conero, a Montepulciano-based wine whose vineyards lie on the seaside slopes of Mount Conero. The dynamic and well-nigh organic co-operative Terre Cortesi owns some 53% of the vineyards in this zone. Rosso Conero wines have a minimum alcohol level of 11.5%. With a minimum of 12.5% and two years ageing, it may be labelled *riserva*.

*Abruzzo: the church of St. Vito in the Chieti area*

*Marche: the vine-growing area of the Conero*

Rosso Piceno is the Marche's largest DOC zone. It stretches south to near the border with Abruzzo and includes the provinces of Ancona, Macerata and Ascoli Piceno. The primary grapes used for this DOC are Sangiovese (30%-50%) and Montepulciano (35%-70%). The word *superiore* on the label indicates that the grapes for the wine were grown in a small area in the southern part of the zone.

## PUGLIA
The San Servero zone is found in the province of Foggia. Dry red and rosé wines are made here from a blend of Montepulciano and Sangiovese. Both wines have a minimum alcohol level of 11.5%. Montepulciano is also a component in the blend of *Cacc'è mitte* di Lucera.

## LAZIO
In Lazio, Montepulicano plays a role in a number of reds, including sprightly novellos (the Italian equivalent of Beaujolais Nouveau); fizzy, slightly sweet wines; and satisfyingly fruity and full dry reds. Together with Sangiovese, Montepulciano comprises up to 60% of the blend of the various reds from the Cerverti zone, whose vineyards area is found in the provinces of Roma and Viterbo. Montepulciano makes up between 15% and 40% of the blend of the various reds produced in the Colli della Sabina zone, which straddles the border between the provinces of Roma and Rieti. The Colli Etruschi Viterbesi zone covers the entire province of Viterbo in northeastern Lazio. In this zone, which shares borders with Tuscany and Umbria, Montepulciano is known as Violone. The variety makes up at least 85% of the dry and fragrantly fruity Colli Etruschi Viterbesi Montepulciano. It comprises 20-45% of the zone's Rosso (both dry and semi-sweet styles), novello and rosé. It plays a minor role in the reds and rosés produced in the Castelli Romani zone, which lies in the province of Roma. The Tarquinia zone, which is located on the west coast of Lazio, produces a red based on Montepulciano and Sangiovese. Cori Rosso is a light, easy-drinking Montepulciano blend produced in the area around the communes of Cori and Cisterna in the province of Latina.

## TASTING NOTE
Very deep ruby color. Cherries, nutmeg/cinnamon and lightly roasted almond notes on the nose. On the palate, the wine has soft tannins and is satisfyingly full. A taster may find hints of plums, blackberries, raspberries, marasca cherries and wild strawberries.

## SYNONYMS
Violone Sangiovese Cardisco, Cordisco, Uva Abruzzese, Primaticcio, Morellone.

## FOOD PAIRINGS
Risotto with sausage, eggplant lasagna, roast lamb and spicy cheeses.

| DOC AND DOCG | |
|---|---|
| **ABRUZZO** | Violone dei Colli Etruschi Viterbesi |
| Montepulciano d'Abruzzo | Tarquinia Rosso |
| Montepulciano d'Abruzzo sub-zone Colline | Velletri Rosso |
| Teramane | Castelli Romani Rosso |
| Cerasuolo | Cerveteri |
| Controguerra Rosso | |
| Controguerra Passito Rosso | **MOLISE** |
| | Biferno Rosso |
| **MARCHE** | Pentro di Isernia (or Pentro) Rosso |
| Rosso Conero | Montepulciano del Molise (it will become Rosso del |
| Rosso Piceno | Molise) - Rosso del Molise |
| Esino Rosso | |
| | **PUGLIA** |
| **LAZIO** | Cacc'e mitte di Lucera (Montepulciano, Uva di Troia, |
| Cori Rosso (Montepulciano, Nero Buono di Cori and | Sangiovese, some more) |
| Cesanese) | San Severo Rosso (Montepulciano d'Abruzzo and |
| | Sangiovese) |
| | Castel del Monte Rosso |

## LAMB "CASCE E OVA"
### (Montepulciano d'Abruzzo and Sanviovese)

SERVES 4
- 1 kilo/2 lb 3 oz lamb
- 4 eggs
- 50 g/1/2 cup grated Pecorino cheese
- 50 g/1/2 cup Grana Padano cheese
- 2 sprigs of rosemary
- 2 cloves of garlic
- 75 ml/5 tbsp olive oil
- cayenne pepper

PREPARATION

Cut the lamb into about 16 pieces and cook in the oven with the oil, rosemary, garlic and pepper. Brown and turn the meat and continue to cook over a low heat, basting from time to time with hot water or stock. Beat the eggs and add the cheese. Pour this mixture over the cooked lamb and return the meat to the oven for a few minutes. Serve hot.

## ROMAN STYLE SPRING LAMB
### (Tarquinia rosso)

SERVES 4
- 1 kilo/ 2 lb 3 oz lamb
- 50 ml/3 tbsp extra-virgin olive oil
- 1 sprig of rosemary
- garlic
- 2 boned anchovies
- 60 ml/4 tbsp of vinegar
- salt
- pepper

PREPARATION

Cut the lamb into medium-sized pieces and put them in an ovenproof dish with the oil and two peeled and crushed cloves of garlic. Fry evenly, turning over the meat occasionally. Season with salt and pepper and cook, adding a little water if necessary. Crush the boned anchovies in a mortar with the rosemary and half a garlic clove. Dilute with vinegar and mix thoroughly to blend all the ingredients together. When the lamb is almost cooked, coat the lamb with the sauce and continue to cook until the vinegar has evaporated. Serve hot.

## RABBIT IN PORK
### (Rosso Conero)

SERVES 4
- 1 whole rabbit with innards
- wine vinegar
- 150 g/5 oz of fresh wild fennel
- 8 cloves of fresh garlic
- 70 g of bacon
- 70 g/2$^{1/2}$ oz sliced Parma ham
- 70 g/2$^{1/2}$ oz salami for cooking
- 4 slices of rolled bacon
- 100 ml/1 cup dry white wine
- salt
- pepper
- 60 ml/4 tbsp extra-virgin olive oil

PREPARATION

Wash the rabbit in water and vinegar. Remove the innards, clean them, and set them aside. Blanch the fennel with 2-3 cloves of garlic and save the cooking water. Finely chop and fry the bacon, Parma ham and salami on a low heat. Add the innards, cut into pieces, and the fennel, and continue cooking for a few minutes. Lay the rabbit on a cloth, sprinkle with salt and pepper and cover with rolled bacon. Spread the fried ingredients in the center along with the crushed garlic and ground pepper.
Roll up carefully to close in the filling, sew up the opening and tie the rabbit with string. Heat the oven to 170°C/340°F. Fry the rabbit in an ovenproof dish with a drizzle of oil. Add half of the wine and a glass of the water used to blanch the fennel. Transfer the dish to the oven and cook for about an hour, turning and frequently basting with the juices, adding wine and fennel water as needed. Remove the string and cut the rabbit into pieces, serving it with the stuffing cut into slices.

## MOLISANA STYLE PASTA SPIRALS
### (Biferno Rosso)

SERVES 4
- 400 g/3/4 lb pasta spirals
- 100 g/1/4 lb lean Parma ham
- 200 g/3/4 cup Ricotta
- salt
- pepper
- 50 ml/3 tbsp extra-virgin olive oil
- 70 g/1/2 cup Pecorino cheese

PREPARATION

Cook the pasta until "al dente". In the meantime prepare the sauce by frying the cubed ham and Ricotta in olive oil, adding salt and pepper. Pour the pasta into the pan and toss in the sauce. Serve with grated Pecorino cheese.

# moscato

The venerable and varied Moscato
family includes both white and red
varieties, all of which share an
attractive, grapey fragrance.
The name seems to be derived from
*muscum* or *muschio* (musk).

## MOSCATO BIANCO
It is likely that Moscato Bianco is the variety the Greeks called *Anathelicon moschaton* and the Romans called *Uva Apiana* (*ape zibibb*). It is a major component in DOC wines from Valle D'Aosta to Sicily, and is the primary variety in semi-sparkling, fully sparkling, fortified and passito wines.

## PIEDMONT
It is the most extensively cultivated white grape in Piedmont, where it is planted in around 100 communes of the provinces of Cuneo, Asti and Alessandria. Moscato Bianco produces the world's most famous sweet sparkling wine, Asti Spumante, as well as the splendid, lightly sweet and fizzy Moscato d'Asti. Both of these wines have been awarded the DOCG. These wines are usually served with very light sponge cakes or dry, sweet biscuits.

## TUSCANY
It is found in the Montalcino zone of Tuscany under the name Moscadello. Moscadello di Montalcino DOC is usually made from 100% of the named grape, though producers may add up to 15% of other varieties (such as Chardonnay and Pinot Bianco). A variety called Moscadello selvatica does exist, but very little survived the phylloxera epidemic of the late 19th century. Locally this variety was known as Zuccharina (sweety).

## PUGLIA
In Puglia, Moscato Bianco often goes by the name Moscato di Trani or Moscanto Reale, and is used to make naturally sweet and fortified wines.

## LOMBARDY
In Lombardy's Oltrepó Pavese zone, it is often blended with its favorite partner, Malvasia di Candia Aromatica, to make sweet semi- and fully sparkling wines; fortified wines and passito wines.

## SYNONYMS
Moscatella bianco, Moscadello, Moscatello di Montalcino, Moscato di Siracusa, Moscato di Canelli. In France it is known as: Muscat Blanc, Muscat Blanc à Petit Gains, Muscat de Frontignan. In Germany: Grüner Musckteller, Weisser Muscatel Traube, Moscato di Trani or Moscanto Reale.

## ZIBIBBO/SICILY
Some say that the name Zibibbo comes from the North African word *zibibb*, which means "dried grape". Another theory suggests that the name is taken from the nearby Tunisian port of Cape Zabibe. Hundreds of years ago the Arabs, who held sway over the island of Pantelleria, planted Zibibbo (also known as Moscato di Alessandria) as a table grape. Over the centuries, a thriving business in semi-dried grapes developed, with Pantelleria supplying bakers throughout Italy. All that came to an end some thirty years ago, when seedless varieties became more popular with confectioners.
From this economic crisis was born one of the world's finest dessert wines: Moscato di Pantelleria. Grapes for this passito wine are picked before the rest of the harvest and are left to dry for between 15 and 20 days. They are then pressed along with freshly picked grapes.

Fermentation can last up to two months. Well-made Moscato di Pantelleria tends to have a fresh, lively orange-blossom scented nose. On the palate, it is a seductive weave of flavors: candied orange peel, dried apricots and figs are laced with a rich, honeyed note. Gorgonzola and foie gras are the suggested partners for this wine.

## SYNONYMS
Moscatellone, Moscato di Pantelleria, Salamonica, Moscato di Alessandria.
In France: Muscat d'Alexandrie.

## MOSCATO GIALLO
This sub-variety, which is most often found in the Tri-Veneto area, may have been brought to Italy from Greece during the Middle Ages by Venetian traders. In the Colli Euganei area of Veneto, it is used to create exceptionally elegant dessert wines from semi-dried grapes. In Trentino-Alto Adige, where it usually goes under the name Goldenmuskateller, it is the main component in naturally sweet and fortified wines. Passito wines made from Moscato Giallo have lively acidity and a fresh, grapey nose, with distinct hints of orange blossoms. On the palate, one finds dried apri-

cots and candied orange peel. These sweet wines are fine partners for blue cheeses or foie gras. They are also very satisfying as *vini da meditazione*.

## TASTING NOTE
Generally speaking, wine made from Moscato grapes has lively acidity. There is often a touch of orange blossoms on the fruity nose. On the palate, one finds hints of dried apricots and orange zest.

**SYNONYMS**: Moscat, Moscato Sirio, Moscatel, Moscato Cipro.

**FOOD PAIRINGS**:
Gorgonzola.

## RED MOSCATO - *MOSCATO ROSA*
Some say the *rosa* in this variety's name is due to the delicate fragrance of roses found in the wines it produces. Moscato Rosa is cultivated in the regions of Trentino-Alto Adige (Rosenmuskteller) and, to a lesser degree in Piedmont and Friuli Venezia-Giulia, and in the province of Bologna in Emilia-Romagna. It is an excellent grape for semi-drying, and it is usually made in sweet or fortified styles.

## TASTING NOTE

Purple-tinged pink. There is a distinct scent of tea roses on the nose. The wine usually has good body.

## SYNONYMS

Rosen Muskateller, Muscat Rose, Uva Rosa, Moscato Rosato, Moscato delle rose nero, Rosenmuskateller Blauer, Moscata Rossa, Moscato rosa di Madera.

### MOSCATO DI SCANZO

Moscato di Scanzo's production zone is located in the hills of the commune of Scanzo in the province of Bergamo in Lombardy. Wines made from it were particularly popular in the mid-1800s when Russia and England's shared passion for sweet reds created a strong market for Moscato di Scanzo. In 1993 Moscato di Scanzo Passito from the Valcalepio area was awarded the DOC. This particular wine must be aged for 18 months and have a minimum alcohol level of 17%.

## TASTING NOTE

Ruby red tending toward cherry with garnet highlights. On the nose one finds distinct scents of roses. It has a delicate, almondy aftertaste.

## SYNONYMS

Moscatino di Scanzo.

## FOOD PAIRINGS

Passito: Plain sponge cakes, sweet biscuits, creamy puddings or blue cheese. Some believe that this wine also goes well with chocolate.

---

### DOC AND DOCG

**VALLE D'AOSTA**

Moscato (or Muscat), Moscato Passito (or Muscat Flétri)

**PIEDMONT**

Asti or Asti Spumante, Loazzolo, Moscato Bianco Passito, Piemonte Moscato, Piemonte moscato Passito

**LOMBARDY**

Valcalepio Moscato Passito, Valcalepio Moscato di Scanzo Passito, Oltrepo Pavese Moscato, Oltrepo Pavese Moscato Liquoroso (sweet or dry), Oltrepo Pavese Moscato Passito

**VENETO**

Colli Euganei Fior d'Arancio, Colli Euganei Fior d'Arancio Passito, Colli Euganei Moscato

**TRENTINO E ALTO ADIGE**

Moscato Rosa dell'Alto Adige (Rosenmuskateller), Alto Adige Moscato Giallo (Goldenmuskateller or Goldmuskateller), Trentino Moscato Giallo anche Liquoroso, Trentino Moscato Rosa anche Liquoroso

**SARDINIA**

Moscato di Sorso-Sennori anche Liquoroso, Moscato di Sardegna, Moscato di Cagliari

**TUSCANY**

Moscadello di Montalcino

**CAMPANIA**

Castel San Lorenzo Moscato, Castel San Lorenzo Moscato Spumante

**PUGLIA**

Moscato di Trani

**SICILY**

Moscato di Noto, Moscato di Pantelleria, Moscato Passito di Pantelleria, Moscato di Siracusa

## MARTINE PEARS IN MOSCATO AU GRATIN

SERVES 6
• 3 Martine pears
• 2 oranges peeled (removing the pith and membranes) and split into segments
• strawberries
• fresh berries
• grapes
• 300 ml/1¼ cups Moscato d'Asti
• 300 ml/1¼ cups water
• 300 g/1½ cups sugar
• the juice of a lemon
• 6 sponge fingers
• 100 ml/6 tbsp Amaretto or Grand Marnier liqueur
• 300 g/1¼ cups custard
• 300 g/10 oz Chantilly cream

FOR THE CUSTARD:
• 2 egg yolks
• 70 g/¼ cup sugar
• 1/2 vanilla pod
• 250 ml/1 cup milk

FOR THE CHANTILLY CREAM:
• 250/1 cup fresh single cream
• 30 g/2 tbsp icing sugar
• 1 sachet of vanillin

GARNISH:
• 100 g/3/4 cup sliced, toasted almonds

PREPARATION

Peel the pears, half them (leaving the stalk) and plunge them immediately into cold water and lemon to prevent them from turning brown. Pour the water into a saucepan with the sugar, wine, a few drops of lemon juice and the pears. Bring everything to the boil on a moderate heat. Turn off the heat and leave to cool in the syrup. For the custard: beat the yolks with the sugar. Add the hot milk and the vanilla pod. Place the mixture on the heat and stir constantly, cooking the custard without boiling it. It is ready when the spoon is covered with a creamy mixture. Remove the vanilla pod and leave to cool. For the Chantilly cream: whip the cream, add the icing sugar and the vanilla. Crumble a sponge finger for each person onto the serving plate and moisten with the chosen liqueur. Delicately lay the pear halves cut into fan shapes over the sponge crumbs. Surround with orange segments, strawberries and the other fruit. Mix the custard with the Chantilly cream and pour over the fruit. Garnish with the almonds and place under the grill to brown.

## APPLE STRUDEL

SERVES 6
• 250 g/2 cups white flour
• 1 fresh egg
• 1 pinch of fine salt
• 30 ml/2 tbsp olive oil
• 50 ml/3 tbsp water
• 2000 g/4½ lb apples
• 150 g/¾ cup bread crumbs
• 150 g/¾ cup fresh butter
• 100 g/½ cup sugar
• 50 g/¼ cup sultanas
• 75 ml/5 tbsp rum
• 50 g/¼ cup pine nuts
• powdered cinnamon
• lemon peel

PREPARATION

Sieve the flour and pour into a mound on the pastry board, adding the egg, salt and oil. Mix the ingredients thoroughly together, gradually adding the water. Knead energetically to obtain smooth, supple medium-consistency dough. Roll into a ball and grease it with oil and leave to rest for 1/2 an hour. In the meantime peel the apples, remove the core and slice finely. Place the apple slices in a dish and add the sugar, powdered cinnamon, grated lemon peel, sultanas, pine nuts and the rum. Mix everything together and leave to rest for a while.
Melt the butter in a saucepan, add the bread crumbs and cook until golden. Dust a clean cloth with flour and roll out the dough onto it using a rolling pin and your hands until you have a very fine layer of pastry (take care not to break it!). Grease the pastry with melted butter and sprinkle 2/3 of the pastry with the bread crumbs and arrange the apples. Lift the cloth at the side and slowly, carefully roll it up. Place the strudel in the buttered dish and grease the surface with the rest of the butter. Place it in the oven pre-heated to 220°C/420°F and cook for about 1/2 hour. Dust with icing sugar before serving. This dessert is best eaten when still warm and accompanied with cream.

# nebbiolo

Nebbiolo is Piedmont's premium red grape variety and is the primary component in four of the region's DOCG wines. It is believed to have originated in the hilly zones around the town of Alba, southeast of Turin, and it continues to have an affinity for hillside or even mountainous sites.

It is a late-ripening variety, with harvest often taking place in mid-October or even November, when autumn fog settles into the valleys. Some suggest that this may be the origin of Nebbiolo's name (*nebbia* = fog). Others think the name may be derived from the pale bloom on the grapes' skins which gives them a misty appearance.

Nebbiolo is a sensitive variety and is extremely demanding in terms of setting, terrain and climate.

It requires high altitude and not-too-arid sites with good exposure. Its successful cultivation zones lie in the most northern reaches of Italy, in the regions of Valle d'Aosta, Lombardy and Piedmont.

Its best-known vineyard sites remain in its birthplace: the Langhe hills. Here the soil is mostly limestone-based, with varying proportions of sand and clay. This is the area where Barolo, Barbaresco, Nebbiolo d'Alba and Roero are produced.

## BAROLO

It was a Frenchman who set Barolo on the road to becoming a great wine. At the beginning of the 1800s, eminent French oenologist Count Oudart came to the zone at the behest of Marchioness Falletti of Barolo. He suggested, in truly French manner, that the Italians should consider making wines from Nebbiolo "in the style of Bordeaux". This meant dry and with well-defined structures instead of the sweet, unfocused and often fizzy versions which existed as a result of lackadaisical winemaking practices. The Marchioness and Camillo Benso, Count of Cavour, who was to become Italy's first Prime Minister, threw themselves into creating a full-bodied, long-lived red, the ancestor of today's Barolo wine.

The Barolo zone, which was awarded the DOCG in 1980, lies to the south of the Tanaro River in the communes of Barolo, Castiglione Falletto, Serralunga d'Alba, and parts of those of La Morra, Monforte d'Alba, Verduno, Grinzane Cavour, Diano d'Alba, Roddi, Novello and Cherasco. Barolo is made from 100% Nebbiolo and undergoes a mini-

*Piedmont: Barbaresco vines in winter*

mum of three years ageing, two of which must be in cask.

Breathing in deeply over a glass of Barolo is a heady experience. Its perfume is of warming alcohol-drenched fruit, shot through with notes of licorice and yellow roses. On the palate, it is a potent mix of rich, brambly fruit – mulberries, sour cherries, blueberries – shaped and defined by zesty acidity and tannins. Most Barolos approach their peak at five or six years after the vintage. From certain producers in excellent years, the wine can continue to evolve for decades.

## BARBARESCO

In the late 1800s, Domizio Cavazza, the first director of Alba's oenology school, bought vineyards in Barbaresco and began experimenting with new techniques. Cavazza's passion for the zone led him to establish the Cantina Sociale del Barbaresco in 1893. For some, this marks the date of Barbaresco's

birth as an important wine. Still, for many years, Barbaresco continued to live in Barolo's shadow. Then, in the late 1970s, Angelo Gaja, with his exceptionally crafted wines and dynamic personality, brought Barbaresco to international attention. Now Barolo and Barbaresco can be considered as equals in the world of fine wine.

Barbaresco received the DOCG designation in 1980. Its vineyards are planted at 200-350 meters above sea level and lie to the east of Barolo. This zone is drier and warmer than Barolo. The wine is made from 100% Nebbiolo and is aged for two years, one of which must be in wood. Barbarescos are usually ready to drink four or five years after the vintage, although some can continue to evolve for ten years or more. Barbarescos are often said to be more elegant and supple than Barolo. I believe that this description largely depends on the skill of the producer. But when looking for differences between the two zones, I do consistently find a salty/savory quality in Barbaresco, which Italians refer to as *sapidità*.

## OTHER DOCGS

Piedmont's other DOCG Nebbiolo-based wines are Gattinara (DOCG since 1990) and Ghemme (since 1997). In these zones, located in the Novara-Vercelli hills, Nebbiolo is known as Spanna. Gattinara is made from Nebbiolo with the option of adding small percentages of Vespolina and Bonarda di Gattinara, and it must be aged for three years. When it is aged for more than four years and

*More Barbaresco vines, in the Langhe of Piedmont*

has a minimum alcohol level of 13%, the wine may be labelled *riserva*. Gattinara tends to be supple on the palate, with an elegant, floral nose. It is usually ready to drink upon its release onto the market, but well-made versions can continue to keep well for another ten years. Ghemme is made from a minimum of 75% Nebbiolo, with the option of adding Vespolina and/or Uva Rara. It is aged for three years, twenty months of which must be in barrel. If the wine has a minimum of four years ageing, 25 months of which are in barrel and a minimum alcohol level of 12.5%, the wine may be labelled *riserva*. Ghemme, too, presents real elegance when it comes from a talented producer.

## NEBBIOLO FROM ALBA AND ROERO

The Nebbiolo d'Alba zone covers a wide area in the province of Cuneo. The dry red versions of this wine, which must be aged for at least one year, are generally straightforward, soft and fruity. They are usually ready to drink within three or four years from the vintage. A sweetish sparkling version is also produced, although you are hardly likely to come across this wine outside of the zone.

The Roero DOC zone includes the entire communes of Canale, Corneliano d'Alba, Piobesi d'Alba and Vezza d'Alba and parts of another fifteen communes in the Province of Cuneo. Roero Rosso is made from 95-98% Nebbiolo, with the possibility of adding Arneis, a local white variety. This fruity style of Nebbiolo can be drunk within two years of the vintage.

## ALPINE WINES

Wines made from Nebbiolo grapes grown at high altitudes have extraordinary grace and elegance. These qualities are perhaps best expressed in Carema. This zone is composed of a narrow strip of well-exposed vineyards near the town of Carema in the province of Turin on the border with Valle d'Aosta. Carema is made from 100% Nebbiolo and is aged for three years in wood. When aged for an additional year it is labelled *riserva*. The wine has marked acidity and hints of alpine flowers, mint and tar on the nose. It should be drunk four to six years from the vintage.

Near the Swiss border in northern Lombardy, Nebbiolo is known as Chiavennasca, a name derived from the dialect term *ciu vinasca*, which can be translated as "most suitable for wine". Chiavennasca is the primary variety for Valtellina and Valtellina Superiore (DOCG since 1998), whose narrow ter-

*Lombardy: a vineyard setting in Valtellina*

raced vineyards are high up on Alpine slopes. Valtellina is best drunk within one to three years from the vintage, while Valtellina Superiore, which is aged in wood for at least a year, can continue to evolve for five to ten years. This latter designation has four sub-zones: Sassella, Grumello, Inferno (so called because of the high temperatures attained in its vineyards) and Valgella. The floral and herbal fragrances of Nebbiolo are highlighted in these wines and, with age, they develop attractive nuances of almond and hazelnut. A local speciality is Valtellina Sforzato or Sfursat. The grapes for this dry passito Nebbiolo are picked before the regular harvest and then semi-dried on racks. After three years in barrel, the wine is very concentrated and its alcohol level can reach around 14.5%.

The Valle d'Aosta, Italy's smallest region, lies between Piedmont and a range of snow capped peaks – Mont Blanc, the Matterhorn and Gran Paradiso – which separate the region from France and Switzerland. Here Nebbiolo is known as Picutener or Picotendro. Valle D'Aosta produces two Nebbiolo-based DOC wines. Arnad-Montjovet is made from a minimum of 70% Nebbiolo, to which the following varieties may be added alone or in combination: Dolcetto, Vien de Nus, Pinot Nero, Neyret and Freisa. This wine must be aged for at least eight months and have a minimum alcohol level of 11%. Arnad-Montjovet tends to be very fresh on the nose. Its attractive lifting acidity carries through onto the palate, which often displays a spicy note of black pepper over the brambly/blackberry fruit. When it has been aged

for one year and has a minimum alcohol level of 12% it can be labelled as *superiore* or *superiéur*. Donnas is primarily Nebbiolo, with the possible addition of Freisa and Nevret. The wine must have a minimum alcohol level of 11.5% and be aged for two years before being released onto the market. Donnas tends to be cherry-tinged ruby in color. A perfume of candied violets mingles with brambly/blackberry hints on the nose. On the palate, the soft, round fruit, with its attractive dash of freshly ground pepper, is buoyed by vivacious acidity.

## SYNONYMS
Brunenta, Chiavennasca, Marchesana, Martesana, Melasca, Nebiolo, Picotendre Picotener, Picoultener, Prunenta, Spanna.

## TASTING NOTE
Barolo/Barbaresco: Medium-deep ruby red with garnet to orange overtones. When Nebbiolo is aged in small, new oak barrels the color will be darker.

There should be an exhilarating rush of freshness on the nose, followed immediately by warming broader elements, which can include candied cherries, bitter cherries, plums, strawberries and raspberries. There are also darker tones of chocolate, hazelnuts, licorice, with herbs, cinnamon and vanilla as well.

With age, the wine develops a more pronounced orange tone, and suggestions of roses, dried violets, tar and freshly ground almonds and hazelnuts emerge on the nose and the texture on the palate becomes silkier.

*Piedmont: Carema with its terraced vines*

### DOC AND DOCG

**PIEDMONT**

Barbaresco
Barolo
Gattinara
Boca
Bramaterra
Carema
Colline Novaresi Rosso Nebbiolo
Vespolina e/o Croatina
Colline Novaresi Nebbiolo
Fara
Ghemme

Langhe Nebbiolo
Lessona
Nebbiolo d'Alba
Roero
Sizzano

**VALLE D'AOSTA**

Donnaz
Arnad-Montjovet

**LOMBARDY**

Valtellina
Valtellina Superiore
Valtellina Sforzato

## FOOD PAIRINGS

Barolo and Barbaresco: braised, stewed and roast red meats and game; aged cheeses.

## ALPINE NEBBIOLOS

Truffle fondue or roast veal.

## ALPINE NEBBIOLO

Medium cherry-tinged ruby in color. Their body is supple and their perfumes fresh and elegant. One finds violets, alpine flowers, blueberries, brambles, mint, and a touch of tar or black pepper on the nose and palate.

---

### BRASATO AL BAROLO

SERVES 8
- 1.2 kilos/2$^{1/2}$ lb leg of veal
- 750 ml/3 cups Barolo
- 250 ml/1 cup Barbera (to deepen the color)
- 2 carrots, peeled and chopped
- 2 white onions, peeled and chopped • 3 cloves of garlic
- 4 bay leaves
- a sprig of rosemary
- 6 cloves
- 1/2 inch stick of cinnamon
- 1000 ml/4 cups stock
- 10 g/1 tsp sugar • salt and pepper

PREPARATION
Put the meat in a large pan with the chopped vegetables, the wine and the spices and leave to marinate,

overnight. Drain the wine from the meat and vegetables, conserving the wine for use later. Fry the onions and garlic in a little oil. When the onion has browned, add the wine to the pan. Now add the meat and brown it over a moderate heat. Cover with the reserved wine and with meat stock, and continue to cook for 2$^{1/2}$ hours. Now remove the sauce from the pan and pass it through a sieve, then boil it without the meat, adding salt and pepper to taste. Pour the sauce over the meat and serve very hot with polenta and carmelized spring onions.

### VEAL SHANK

SERVES 4
- 1 veal shank
- 50 g/1/2 cup onion, finely chopped

- 25 g/1/4 cup carrot, finely chopped
- 25 g/1/4 cup celery, chopped
- 100 g/5 tbsp butter
- 1 handful of rosemary and sage
- 1 clove of garlic • 20 g/1 tbsp of thyme • salt and pepper

PREPARATION
Clean the meat. Melt the butter over a very low heat and then add the thyme and the pepper. Brown the meat on all sides in the butter. Meanwhile, spread a large piece of aluminium foil on a flat work surface and cover it with the chopped vegetables. Put the meat on top of this and drizzle on the melted thyme-flavored butter. Close the foil around the meat and put it in a baking pan. Bake in a pre-heated oven at 150° C/300°F. for around 2 hours.

# negroamaro

Negroamaro may have been brought to Italy by the Greeks, or it may indeed be indigenous to the coast of Puglia. It is certainly the most important vine in the region, and is a major component in many of Puglia's DOC zones. It is most densely planted around the towns of Lecce and Brindisi in the province of Taranto. It is usually blended with Malvasia Nera di Lecce, Sangiovese and Montepulciano to make appealing reds and rosés.

*Vineyards around Locorotondo in Puglia*

of Negroamaro and Uva di Troia. When the wine has a minimum alcohol level of 13% and has been aged for at least two years it may be labelled *riserva*.

Negroamaro is a lesser component in the wines of the Gioia del Colle and Ostuni zones.

## TASTING NOTE

Deep, dark ruby, with black highlights. Fresh with scents of apples, pears, plums and prunes. Very soft on the palate, with mouth-filling fruit flavor. Some tasters find notes of very ripe watermelon on the palate.

The Lizzano zone takes full advantage of Negroamaro's fruity, rounded character, using it in the blends of novellos, still and semi-sparkling reds and rosés and a fully sparkling rosé. The vineyards of the zone lie towards the northern part of the Gulf of Taranto and surround the town of Taranto itself. The attractive and full-bodied Rosso di Cerignola, whose production zone lies in the province of Foggia, is made from a blend

## SYNONYMS

Negro Amaro (alternate spelling), Albese, Jonico, Nero Leccese, Niuru Maru, Nicra amaron, Mangiaverde, Abruzzese, Uva Cane.

## FOOD PAIRINGS

This wine goes well with rich meats, such as roast pork or roast duck. It also makes a fine accompaniment for puréed greens.

---

### "CICERI E TRIA"

SERVES 6
- 200 g/1½ cups chickpeas
- 200 g/1/2 lb homemade tagliatelli
- celery
- onion
- salt • garlic clove
- 50 ml/3 tbsp olive oil

PREPARATION
Soak the chickpeas in cold water for 24 hours. Pour them into a pan and cover them with cold salted water. Add the celery, the onion (cut in half) and clove of garlic. Simmer over a low heat for three or four hours, until the chickpeas are cooked. Add the pasta and when this is cooked pour into bowls and drizzle with olive oil.

---

### DOC E DOCG

**PUGLIA**

Alezio Rosso and Rosato, Brindisi Rosso and Rosato, Copertino Rosso and Rosato, Leverano Rosso and Rosato,

Lizzano Rosso and Rosato, Lizzano Negroamaro Rosso and Rosato, Lizzano Rosato Spumante, Matino Rosso e Rosato, Nardò Rosso and Rosato, Rosso di Cerignola, Salice Salentino Rosso and Rosato, Squinzano Rosso and Rosato, Galatina Negramaro, Gioia del Colle Rosso and Rosato

# nerello mascalese

The Nerello designation refers to a large family of Sicilian vines. Nerello Mascalese is a sub-variety, which is believed to have originated on the volcanic slopes of Mount Etna, in northeastern Sicily.

*Sicily: Monreale, the Basilica*

In the 1950s, this vine's cultivation zone included the provinces of Catania and Messina. By the 1980s, it had spread across the island and had become Sicily's second most widely planted variety (after Nero d'Avola). It is seldom, if ever, vinified on its own. Rather, it is found in the blends of such Sicilian DOCs as Etna Rosso and Faro.

## TASTING NOTE

Ruby. The nose has a lively freshness along with notes of strawberry jam and Darjeeling tea. The wine is medium body, with brambly fruit emerging on the palate.

## FOOD PAIRINGS

Spicy casseroles, roasted meats with flavorful sauces.

---

### "FARSUMAGRU"

**SERVES 4**
- 800 g/1¾ lb rectangular slice of veal rump
- 200 g/1/2 lb ham • 200 g/1/2 lb pork sausage
- 4 hard-boiled eggs • 100 g/1/4 lb bacon fat
- 80 g/3 oz ground beef • 1 onion • 1 beaten egg
- 1 clove of garlic
- 100 g/1 cup spicy Caciocavallo cheese
- 60 g/1/2 cup grated Pecorino cheese
- pepper • 80 g/1/2 cup boiled peas
- tomato sauce • sugna (pork fat)
- 100 ml/1/2 cup red wine
- 75 ml/5 tbsp oil • salt and pepper

**PREPARATION**

Mix the ground meat with 1 egg and the Pecorino cheese. Add pepper. Arrange on the slice of veal rump a layer of ham, then add a layer of sliced boiled eggs, bacon fat and then Caciocavallo cheese. Sprinkle with the finely chopped garlic and onion. Then spread on a layer of the Pecorino and ground beef mixture, followed by a layer of peas and sausage slices. Roll up the slice of meat and fasten it with string. Fry in oil and pour over red wine, which has to evaporate, and the tomato sauce. Cover and cook for an hour. Remove the string, slice the roll and serve with the gravy.

---

### DOC AND DOCG

**SICILY**
Etna Rosso
Faro
Contea di Sclafani
Marsala
Sambuca

**CAMPANIA**
Lamezia Rosso and Rosato
Sant'Anna di Isola di Capo Rizzuto

# nero d'avola

There is a seductive wildness about certain red indigenous varieties that renders them infinitely more exciting than their "classic" counterparts. Their flavors are definite and consistent yet always in transition: suggestions and echoes of flavors overlap and shift on the palate with enticing elegance. Nero d'Avola is one of these varieties. Its fragrance is always refreshing, with blueberry hints melding into the brighter tones of wild berry fruits.

*Cellars and vineyards in Feudi di Butera*

Its tannins are soft and its body supple. Like all fine grape varieties, it has the ability to fulfil the wishes of its winemaker. If he or she wants a satisfyingly youthful style, then that is what Nero d'Avola will provide. If he or she dreams of making a graceful wine with ageing potential, Nero d'Avola will not disappoint. Giacomo Tachis, Italy's favorite winemaker and a passionate devotee of all things Sicilian, has described Nero d'Avola at various times as the Baron, the Prince, the King and the Emperor of Sicilian viticulture.

This grape is grown almost exclusively in Sicily, where it is vinified on its own or as part of a blend. It is increasingly partnered with Cabernet, Merlot, Pinot Nero, Sangiovese or Syrah to make exceptionally attractive wines. Nero d'Avola's potential has attracted the attention of producers from other regions who have started investing in Sicilian vineyards with the intention of turning out pleasant low-to-medium-priced wines.

The most famous 100% Nero d'Avola is Duca Enrico, the flagship wine of Duca di Salaparuta. The company commericialized this wine in 1988, and in 1989 it won one of Italy's top awards for fine wine, the Gambero Rosso's Tre Bicchieri. What sets Duca Enrico apart from other connoisseur classics is its elegance. There is a tendency today to think of great wines in terms of power, muscle, brawn and pungent aggressiveness. It is, therefore, a genuine pleasure to taste a wine like this, which brings to mind long-overlooked words like "breed" and "charm" and "class". It helps remind wine lovers that longevity and structure need not be weighed down by hard tannins and the overwhelming sensations of barrique. Duca Enrico opened the door to international acceptance for Sicily and for Nero d'Avola. To-

*A typical Sicilian cart in the cellars of the Pellegrino wine company business in Marsala*

day, many producers are also choosing to make supple yet long-lived wines from 100% Nero d'Avola. Indeed, viticulturalists throughout the region are exploring the differences that site, soil and training methods can make in the development of this grape, and winemakers are experimenting with every possible vinification and ageing technique.

## TASTING NOTE
Dark ruby. On the nose, it is fresh, with tar, red licorice, hazelnut, clove, blueberry and wild berry fruit tones. On the palate, it is supple and offers smokier, fleshier fruit sensations, with raspberry top notes and, often, a bitter chocolate tone.

## SYNONYMS
Calabrese, Calabrese d'Avola.

## FOOD PAIRINGS
Roast pork, spaghetti with pesto.

| DOC AND DOCG |
|---|
| **SICILIA** |
| Alcamo Rosso, Rosato and Novello |
| Alcamo Nero d'Avola |
| Cerasuolo di Vittoria |
| Contea di Sclafani Rosso |
| Contea di Scalfani Nero d'Avola |
| Contessa Entelliano Rosso (based on Nero d'Avola and/or Syrah) |
| Delia Nivorelli Rosso |
| Delia Nivorelli Nero d'Avola |
| Eloro Nero d'Avola |
| Eloro Rosso |
| Eloro Rosato |
| Eloro Pachino |
| Marsala Rubi |
| Menfi Rosso |
| Menfi Nero d'Avola |
| Menfi Bonera |
| Sambuca di Sicila Rosso and Rosato |
| Santa Margherita di Belice Rosso |
| Santa Margherita di Belice Nero d'Avola |
| Sciacca Rosso and Rosato |

# nosiola

Noisola is an indigenous variety, whose two original production zones are located in southern Trentino. The Valle dei Laghi zone lies along the Sarco River at the northern tip of Lake Garda (Italy's largest lake). The second area lies in the hills of Pressano, some ten kilometers from Trento.

*Alto Adige: vineyards*

Nosiola's name is derived from *nosela*, a local dialect word meaning "wild hazelnuts", which is the dominant flavor in wines made from this variety. Nosiola is very sensitive to climate and, as such, there is great variation in quality from vintage to vintage. The best wines are made from grapes grown in vineyards with exposures that allow for optimum ripening. Until recently the market for Nosiola was pretty much limited to local osterias and restaurants. In 1972, Giuseppe Fanti was the first to bottle Nosiola, and his small estate remains among the variety's best producers. Nosiola's zippy acidity makes it a candidate for sparkling wine production, and experiments with this process are taking place. Some producers are also choosing to ferment the variety in wood, with varying degrees of success. Trentino Vino Santo is a Nosiola-based passito, which is aged for at least three years and has an alcohol level of around 16%. The production area for this wine is limited to the communes of Arco, Calvino, Cavedine, Drena, Dro, Lasino, Nago-Torbole, Padergnone, Riva del Garda, Tenno and Vezzano. The variety may also play a part in the blend of Sorni Bianco, whose production zone includes the communes of Lavis, Giovo and San Michele all'Adige.

## TASTING NOTE
Pale straw. A muted nose, which occasionally has light notes of wildflowers. On the palate, it is zesty and has a saline element, alongside rather delicate sensations of wild hazelnuts. Vino Santo: Amber colored. On the nose and palate, the wine has an enticing nutty quality and an attractive note of candied orange peel. There is a crème brûlèe note on the finish.

## SYNONYM: Spargelen.

## FOOD PAIRINGS
Simple egg-based dishes and fresh cheese.

---

### "FRIGOLOTI" SOUP

SERVES 4
- 200 g/1¼ cups flour
- 1 egg
- a pinch of salt
- meat stock

PREPARATION
Mix the flour, egg and salt until the dough is compact. Grate it using a grater with large holes and lay it out to dry. Cook in the meat stock.

---

### DOC AND DOCG

**TRENTINO ALTO ADIGE**
Nosiola del Trentino, Vino Santo, Trentino Sorni

# ottavianello

This variety is perhaps better known by its French name, Cinsault. In Italy, it is cultivated in Puglia, where it is sometimes used to add complexity to the perfumes of blended reds. In the Ostuni DOC zone, in the province of Brindisi, it has its own varietal designation: Ostuni Ottavianello. It is the most widely planted variety on the island of Corsica.

*Puglia: Ostuni*

## TASTING NOTE
From medium to dark ruby. Delicate scents of almonds and hazelnuts on the nose. It often has good acidity, and good body.

## SYNONYMS
Cinsault, Hermitage, Ottaviano.

## FOOD PAIRINGS
Semi-soft cheese, cold rice salad, pastas with light sauces.

| DOC AND DOCG |
|---|
| **PUGLIA** |
| Ostuni Ottavianello |

### ORECCHIETTE WITH TURNIP TOPS

SERVES 4
- 400 g/ 1 lb orecchiette
- 400 g/1 lb of turnip tops
- cloves of garlic
- pieces of anchovy fillets
- 125 ml/1/2 cup extra-virgin olive oil and salt

PREPARATION

Boil the orecchiette in salted water. After a few minutes add the turnip tops (which take less time to cook). While they cook, dissolve the anchovy pieces in plenty of oil, taking care not to brown. Drain the orecchiette and place them in a serving bowl, dressed with the anchovy-flavored oil.

# pecorino

Pecorino, an early ripening variety, prefers cool, high hillside sites. The word "pecorino" in Italian refers to sheep and is, in fact, the name of a well-known cheese. Why this grape shares its name with a sheep's cheese is uncertain, but it may be connected to the seasonal movements of shepherds and their flocks. In the mid-1800s, Pecorino vines were cultivated throughout the Marche, Abruzzo, Umbria, Lazio and Puglia. However, this variety's low yields made it an unpopular choice for many producers, and it steadily lost ground.

Its comeback in the Marche region can be traced to Guido Cocci Grifoni, whose estate includes vineyards in the Falerio di Colli Ascolani DOC zone. The DOC regulations for this denomination include the addition of Pecorino. But back in 1983, few, if any, producers actually had Pecorino vines. Cocci Griffoni set about the task of finding and propagating this indigenous grape. Thanks to the success of Cocci Griffoni's 100% Pecorino, the variety was granted its own DOC in 2001: Offida Pecorino.

In Abruzzo, Pecorino is included in the blend of sparkling wines made in the Controguerra DOC zone. Producers here are also beginning to experiment with varietal Pecorinos. In Puglia, (where it sometimes goes by the name of Uva Piccoletta or Uvina), Umbria (where it is known as Uva delle Pecore or Uva Peconrina), and Lazio (where it is often identified as Trebbiano Vicio), Pecorino may be used as a lesser component in dry whites.

Pecorino-based wines have good alcohol and acidity levels, and seem to have the potential to age well.

## TASTING NOTE

Amber-tinged straw. Fresh, zippy acidity. A very light touch of cinnamon over Rennet apple and red licorice scents which are echoed on the palate. Some tasters find jasmine or broom on the nose.

| DOC AND DOCG |
| --- |
| **MARCHE** |
| Pecorino di Offida DOC |

## SYNONYMS

Dolcipappola, Iuvino, Forconese, Mosciolo, Moscianello, Norcino, Pecorina, Pecorino di Osimo, Promotico, Vecia, Trebbiano Vecio, Uvino, Vissanello.

## FOOD PAIRINGS

Hearty, meat-based antipasti: proscuitto, salami and raw fish. Highly seasoned pasta and rice dishes.

| DRUNKEN TUNA OF THE MARCHES |
| --- |
| SERVES 4 |
| • 500 g/1 lb large slice of fresh tuna |
| • 80 g/4 tbsp butter • 15 g/1/2 oz parsley |
| • 60 ml/4 tbsp white wine vinegar |
| • 1 onion • 1 bay leaf |
| • 200 ml/1 cup dry Marsala |
| • 500 ml/ 2 cups fish stock |
| • 4 salted anchovies • juice of one lemon |
| • 30 g/1 tbsp capers • 75 ml/4 tbsp oil |
| • 1 large slice of bread • salt • pepper |
| |
| PREPARATION |
| Boil the water and add the vinegar, then immerse the tuna and cook for two minutes. Drain the tuna and plunge it into cold water. Melt 3 tbsp of butter in a saucepan, fry the tuna and add the parsley (tied into a bunch), the bay leaf and thickly sliced onion. Season with salt and pepper. Pour Marsala over it, followed by the fish stock. Cook for 40 minutes with the lid on, moving the tuna occasionally and turning it over after the first twenty minutes. In a separate pan, heat the oil and fry the slice of bread, then arrange it on a serving plate. Dissolve the anchovies in the remaining butter and keep hot. Filter the juices of the tuna, add the dissolved anchovies, capers and lemon and simmer for a few minutes, then pour over the tuna and serve. |

# pelaverga

There has been much debate about how the Pelaverga variety of Verduno found itself in the Langhe: up until a short time ago some authorities maintained that it came from Saluzzo where there exists a cultivar of the same name, which is the major component in a DOC wine called Colline Saluzzesi Pelaverga. According to this thesis, it was the Blessed Valfrè who brought cuttings to the area in the 18th century. More recent studies tend to demonstrate that the Pelaverga piccolo biotype's presence in Verduno dates to a much earlier period.

Today its cultivation is limited to the communes of Verduno, La Morra and Roddi. The Pelaverga which grows on the foothills around the small town of Saluzzese has larger berries and was brought to the zone by the monks of Saint Columbo.

## TASTING NOTE

It has a fine ruby hue with cherry red and purple highlights. Its bouquet is intensely fruity and displays a peppery yet well balanced and velvety flavour. Colline Saluzzesi Pelaverga: pale ruby red with purplish reflections. It has a nose of currants and is moderately alcoholic and delicately spicy.

## SYNONYMS

Pelaverga piccolo: Pelaverga di Verduno.
Pelaverga N.: Caleura, Peilaverga, Uva Coussa.

## FOOD PAIRINGS

Pelaverga of Verduno: this wine goes well with meat dishes, but shows at its best with mushrooms. The Colline Saluzzesi Pelaverga is particularly good with tagliatelle or fettuccini with traditional Piedmontese sauces.

---

### FETTUCCINI WITH ANCHOVY SAUCE
#### (Colline Saluzzesi Doc Pelaverga)

SERVES 4

FOR THE PASTA:
- 200 g/1¾ cups soft white flour
- 4 egg yolks
- 50 ml/1/4 cup cold water

FOR THE SAUCE:
- 400 g/1½ cups tomato pulp
- 80 g/2½ oz salted anchovy fillets
- 25 g/2 tbsp butter
- 1 clove of garlic

PREPARATION

For the pasta: roll out a very thin layer of pasta and make a sausage-shaped roll, cutting it into 5mm strips. Lay the fettucini out on a pastry board so they don't stick together. For the sauce: fry the butter and when it sizzles add the garlic and anchovies. Cook over a moderate heat and allow the anchovies to dissolve completely. Add the tomato pulp and cook for about twenty minutes.

### MUSHROOM CAPS WITH VINE LEAVES
#### (Pelaverga Verduno)

SERVES 4
- 4 big, firm mushroom caps
- 4 vine or chestnut leaves
- crushed garlic, oregano
- salt and pepper

PREPARATION

Peel or clean the mushroom caps and arrange them on a vine leaf in a well-greased baking tray. Cover with the crushed garlic and oregano, and season with salt and pepper. Bake in the oven. Serve with the cooking juices.

# petit rouge

According to some studies Petit Rouge may belong to a group of vines known as "Oriou", which are indigenous to the Valle d'Aosta; others believe that Petit Rouge is of Burgundian origin. It is one of the most widely planted varieties in Valle d'Aosta and lends softness and elegant perfumes to that region's blended reds. It composes at least 60% of the blend of Chambave Rouge (the other varieties are Dolcetto, Gamay and Pinot Nero) and Torrette.

*Mountain vineyards in Valle d'Aosta*

raspberry and black currant, which are carried through on the palate. It has good body.

## SYNONYMS

Picciou oriou, Picciou rouge, Oriou Picciou, Oriou Gris, Picciourouzzo.

## FOOD PAIRINGS

Salami, hearty soups and stews.

## TASTING NOTE

Ruby colored. On the nose, it is fresh, with floral tones (particularly violets), and notes of

| DOC AND DOCG |
| --- |
| **VALLE D'AOSTA** |
| Chambave Rouge, Torrette, Valle d'Aosta Petit Rouge |

### VALPELLINESE SOUP

SERVES 4
- 150 g/5 oz Fontina cheese
- 100 g/3½ oz fatty Parma ham
- 50 g/1¾ oz bacon fat
- 50 g/3 tbsp butter
- meat gravy
- 1 kilo/4 cups meat stock
- slices of brown bread
- a Savoy cabbage
- spices

PREPARATION

Toast the slices of bread in the oven. Clean the cabbage, removing the hard center and the outer leaves. Place the remaining cabbage in a saucepan with the chopped bacon fat. Place the pan on a moderate heat and cook until the cabbage changes color. Line a terracotta dish with a layer of slices of bread,

drizzle with a few spoonfuls of gravy, cover with a little cabbage, dust with a pinch of spices, make a layer of ham and cover this with thin slices of Fontina. Add more bread, continuing in this order until all the ingredients have been used: the last layer will be of slices of Fontina, covered with pieces of butter. Pour over enough stock to cover the bread and place in the oven at 160°C/320°F. Cook for an hour and serve piping hot.

### VALDOSTANA STYLE TRIPE

SERVES 6
- 1 kilo/2 lb 3 oz cooked mixed tripe • 300 g/1 cup tomatoes
- 600 g/5 cups onions
- 100 ml/1/2 cup extra-virgin olive oil • 60 g/4 tbsp butter
- 150 g/5 oz Fontina cheese

- basil
- 1 stick of celery
- 1 carrot
- stock
- salt and pepper

PREPARATION

Carefully wash the tripe and cut it into thin strips. Roughly chop the onion, carrot, celery and basil leaves and fry everything in the olive oil. When the ingredients are golden, add the peeled and deseeded tomatoes and cook for about ten minutes. Add the tripe. Season with salt and pepper and cook on a low heat for about two hours, occasionally adding a cup of boiling stock. When cooked, add the cubed Fontina and butter and cook for a few more minutes, stirring to melt the Fontina. Serve the tripe piping hot with boiled potatoes.

# picolit

The origins of this vine, whose production zone is limited to the Friulian provinces of Gorizio and Udine, are uncertain. It seems to have arrived on the scene in a blaze of glory in the late 18th century, when Count Fabio Asquini created a market for a sweet wine made from this variety, which he considered an alternative to Hungarian Tokay.

He exported his Picolit to England, France, Germany and Austria, and his near-neighbors in Venice also showed a great liking for his wine. The name of the variety may be derived from the small (*piccolo*) size of its grapes and/or its low yields, the result of its vulnerability to floral abortion. Due to this tendency, Picolit vineyards are often planted with a small percentage of other varieties, principally Verduzzo Friulano, so as to encourage cross-pollination. The style of Picolit made from fresh grapes is fast disappearing. Most Picolit is made from grapes which have been semi-dried on racks as is customary with traditional drying. There is a tendency these days to vinify in barriques. Picolit made from semi-dried grapes and vinified in wood can easily continue to evolve for ten or more years. The Colli Orientali del Friuli zone is located in the hilly province of Udine. Its Picolit has a minimum alcohol level of 14%. It is labelled *superiore* when the alcohol is 14.5%. Within this DOC zone there are two sub-zones which may be named on the label: Cialla and Rosazzo. Picolit from the Collio Goriziano area (usually just known as Collio) has a minimum alcohol level of 14% and after two years ageing may be labelled *riserva*.

## TASTING NOTE
Bright gold in color. Zesty acidity balances its sweetness. Very delicate floral and white peach notes on the nose; these notes are echoed on the palate, alongside a touch of white chocolate, with honey and green tea on the lingering finish.

## SYNONYMS
Piccolit, Uva del Friuli, Piccolito, Piccolito del Friule.

## FOOD PAIRINGS
This is a *vino da meditazione* to enjoy on its own or you may pair it with foie gras, spicy cheese.

| DOC AND DOCG |
| --- |
| **FRIULI VENEZIA-GIULIA** |
| Colli Orientali del Friuli Picolit, Collio Goriziano Picolit |

### GUBANA

SERVES 6
- 2 sheets of frozen pastry dough
- 1 packet of vanilla-flavored sugar
- 30 g/2 tbsp butter to grease the pan
- 100 g/1/2 cup sultanas • 50 g/1/2 cup pine nuts • 125 g/1 cup walnuts
- 60 g/1/4 cup fresh butter • 1 egg and 1 egg yolk • 50 g/2 oz milk chocolate, in pieces • 25 g/4 tsp finely chopped dried figs • 4 prunes • the zest of 1 lemon • the zest of 1 orange
- 2 slices of pineapple • 125 ml/1/2 cup Picolit • 30 g/2 tbsp candied citrus fruit • 50 g/3 tbsp bread crumbs
- 100 g/4 oz zibibbo raisins

PREPARATION
Soak the sultanas and the zibibbo raisins in Picolit for around 20 minutes. Chop the nuts, figs, prunes and candied fruits, and put them in a bowl along with the pine nuts, raisins, pineapple, chocolate and the grated citrus peel. Sauté some bread crumbs in butter and add this to the bowl. Mix well. Separate the egg. Add the yolk to the mixture. Then beat the white until it is firm. Then add it and mix gently. Roll out the pastry sheet until it is very thin. Sprinkle with a little flour. Arrange the fruit and nuts in the center of the pastry. Carefully fold over the edges of the pastry to make a roll. Put the roll on a buttered baking sheet. Lightly beat the extra egg yolk and brush this over the top of the pastry. Bake in a hot oven at 180°C/350°F for around 45 minutes. Then dust the pastry roll with vanilla-flavored sugar. Serve warm.

# piedirosso

Piedirosso (red feet) is one of the ancient varieties of Campania. Some think this may be the variety Pliny the Elder referred to as "Colombina" in his *Naturalis Historiae*. This is due to the fact that the name Piedierosso is derived from the color the grape's rachis turns in autumn, which has been described as "red like the feet of a *colombina nera* (black dove)".

The variety, which is most widely planted on the foothills around Vesuvius in the province of Naples, features in the blend of many Campanian DOC reds. Perhaps the best known of these is Lacryma Christi Rosso and Rosato. In the past, the less tannic and lighter-bodied Piedirosso was used to soften the more potent Aglianico. However, with modern vinification techniques the need to use Piedirosso for this purpose has diminished.

## TASTING NOTE

Ruby colored. Its fragrance is an amalgam of balsamic and herbal notes (sage, rosemary, mint), as well as touches of black pepper, tar and white chocolate. It is supple bodied and has fresh acidity.

## SYNONYMS

Per 'd Palummo, Piede di Colombo, Palumbina nera, Strepparossa.

## FOOD PAIRINGS

Meatloaf and pasta and rice dishes with rich meaty sauces.

---

### DOC AND DOCG

#### CAMPANIA

Taburno Piedirosso, Campi Flegrei Rosso, Campi Flegrei Piedirosso, Capri Rosso, Cilento Rosso (also a rosé version), Costa d'Amalfi Rosso (also a rosé version), Falerno del Massico Rosso, Ischia Rosso, Ischia Piedirosso (also a passito version) Penisola Sorrentina Rosso (also a semisparkling version), Sant'Agata de' Goti Rosso (also as rosé and as Novello), Sant'Agata de' Goti Piedirosso, Sannio, Solopaca, Vesuvio Rosso (and rosé), Lacryma Christi del Vesuvio in Bianco, Rosato, Spumante (also a version at high alcoholic degree).

---

### RICE SARTÙ

**SERVES 6**

- 400 g/2 cups rice • 100 g/1 cup Parmesan cheese
- 2 eggs • salt

**FOR THE FILLING:** • 200 g/1/2 lb chopped meat
- 20 g/1 tbsp Parmesan cheese • 2 hard-boiled eggs
- 200 g/1/2 lb chicken liver • 1/2 onion
- 25 g/1/4 cup dried mushrooms
- 100 g/4 oz sliced cooked ham • bread crumbs
- 1 piece of stale bread • 1 fresh egg • 3 sausages
- 50 g/2 oz of pork bacon • 250 g/1³/⁴ cups peas
- 150 ml/1/2 cup soft young cheese
- pork fat • salt and pepper

**PREPARATION**

Make a tomato sauce, adding to it the sausages (cut into rounds). Prepare meatballs with ground meat, the stale bread (moistened in milk), the Parmesan cheese and the egg, seasoned with salt and pepper. Fry the meatballs in oil or pork fat. Cut the chicken livers into small pieces and fry in pork fat. Soak the mushrooms in warm water. Then cut them into small pieces. Boil the peas in the water in which the mushrooms have been soaking. Fry the onion until it becomes transparent. Combine the sausage rounds, meatballs, liver, peas and mushrooms in a pan along with a few spoonfuls of tomato sauce and cook over a low heat for around 10 minutes, stirring from time to time. Dice the fresh milk cheese. Julienne the cooked ham and slice the hard-boiled egg. Cook the rice in salted water, drain it and dress it with tomato sauce and Parmesan cheese. Then add the fresh egg to bind the mixture. Butter a deep-sided, medium-sized pan and sprinkle it with bread crumbs. Press around 3/4 of the rice mixture into the bottom and up the sides of the pan. Put on top a layer of the meat mixture, then add one of cheese, then one of the ham and egg slices. Cover with the remaining rice. Smooth the top with the back of a spoon, and sprinkle with bread crumbs and a few drops of pork fat. Bake in a pre-heated oven until the surface is golden. Then turn the sartú out onto a serving plate.

# pigato

Pigato is a biotype of Vermentino. It is found mainly in the Ligurian provinces of Savona, Imperia and Genova. It occasionally turns up as a lesser component in blended dry whites, and it composes at least 95% of the lively and refreshing Riviera Ligure di Ponete Pigato.

*Chests for the grape-harvest*

*Antique wine-measuring utensils*

## TASTING NOTE

Straw colored with scents of almonds on the nose and palate. Often has crisp acidity.

## FOOD PAIRINGS

Mushroom salad, oysters, stuffed zucchini flowers, onion soup, shrimp risotto.

---

### PANSOTTI DI MAGRO

SERVES 6

FOR THE DOUGH: • 450 g/3$^{1/2}$ cups flour
• 125 ml/1/2 cup dry white wine • 1 egg • salt
FOR THE FILLING: • 250 g/1/2 lb borage • 250 g/1/2 lb beet • 500 g/1 lb "preboggion"(a mixture of at least seven wild herbs, such as sow-thistle, pimpinella, dog's-tooth, parsley, rampion and nettles)
• 200 g/3/4 cup ricotta cheese (sheep cheese works best because it is smoother)
• 20 g/1 tbsp butter • 50 g/3 tbsp Parmesan cheese
• 2 eggs • nutmeg • salt
FOR THE SAUCE: You may use a commercially prepared walnut sauce

PREPARATION

Make the dough in the usual way, adding a few drops of water to obtain a compact and smooth consistency. Then roll out the dough to not more than 1/10 inch in thickness. Let the dough rest, covered with a cloth. For the filling: Carefully wash the vegetables and boil them in abundant salted water. Then drain and finely chop them. Mix them together with the egg, the ricotta (which has been strained through a sieve), the cheese, the melted butter (which has been flavored with nutmeg) and salt to taste. Cut the pastry sheet into squares of around 2 inches. In the center of each square put a spoonful of filling. Fold over the side of each square to form a triangle and seal the sides with your fingers. Boil abundant, lightly salted water. Drop in the triangles. After around 10 minutes they should be done. Remove them from the water with a slotted spoon. Put on a plate and dress with walnut sauce, sprinkle with grated cheese. Serve hot.

---

### DOC AND DOCG

**LIGURIA**

Riviera Ligure di Ponente Pigato

# pignoletto

Pignoletto is very likely the Grechetto variety. However, in Emlia-Romagna, under the name Pignoletto, it is used as the base for pleasant wines in a variety of styles (still, semi- and fully sparkling, and passito). The name "Pignoletto" is said to be derived from a wine called "Pino Lieto", which is described by Pliny the Elder in his *Naturalis Historia* as being "not sweet enough to be good".

## FOOD PAIRINGS
Cold rice salads, light anitpasti.

## PRODUCERS
Luigi Ognibene, Cantina dell'Abbazia, Vallone,

## TASTING NOTE
Green-tinged straw. On the nose, one finds delicate notes of ripe pears.

## SYNONYM
Grechetto.

| DOC AND DOCG |
|---|
| **EMILIA-ROMAGNA** |
| Colli Bolognesi Classico Pignoletto, Colli Bolognesi sub-zones of Colline Marconiane, Zola Predosa, Monte San Martino, Terre di Montebudello, Serravalle, Colline di Riosto, Colline di Oliveto, Pignoletto frizzante Colline di Riosto, Pignoletto frizzante Colline di Oliveto, Pignoletto passito Colline Marconiane, Pignoletto passito Colline di Oliveto, Pignoletto Spumante Colline Marconiane, Pignoletto Spumante Terre di Motebudello, Pignoletto superiore |

### TORTELLINI

SERVES 6

FOR THE DOUGH:
• 300 g/2¼ cups flour
• 3 eggs

FOR THE FILLING:
• 200 g/2 cups grated Parmesan cheese
• 100 g/1/4 lb pork loin
• 100 g/1/4 lb mortadella di Bologna
• 100 g/1/4 lb prosciutto
• 50 g/2 oz turkey breast
• 20 g/2 tbsp butter
• 2 eggs
• nutmeg
• salt and pepper
• 2 litres/8 cups beef stock

PREPARATION
Dice the pork and the turkey, and brown it in butter, letting the meat cook for around 10 minutes. Grind the meat along with the prosciutto and mortadella. Put it in a bowl. Add the two eggs, a dash of nutmeg, 1¾ cups of Parmesan cheese, and salt and pepper to taste. Mix well. Make the pasta dough in the usual way: make a mound of the flour and form a deep well in the center of the flour. Drop the eggs into this well and mix thoroughly with your hands. The dough should be firm. Roll out the dough until it is very thin, and then with a knife cut it into 1-inch squares or make disc-shapes using the lip of a drinking glass. In the center of each square (or round) of pastry put a little bit of the filling. Put another piece of pastry on top and tightly seal the edges. Bring the stock to a boil and drop in the tortellini, stirring gently, and cook for 2 or 3 minutes. Serve al dente, with grated Parmesan. If the tortellini are served dry (without the stock), they may be dressed with meat and tomato sauce.

# pignolo

The grape takes its name from its densely packed bunches which, to some, resemble pinecones (*pigna*). Its presence in Friuli Venezia-Giulia, and more particularly the sub-zone of Rosazzo, has been documented since Medieval times. But by the mid-20th century the variety had actually been reduced to a few vines growing near the walls of the Abbey of Rosazzo.

*Friuli: the Abbey of Rosazzo*

When Walter Filiputti decided to take the Abbey's vineyards in hand in 1981, his first thought was to pull up the old vines and replant with something better known. Fortunately, his enthusiasm for progress was held in check by an old friar who assured Filiputi that excellent wines could be made from Pignolo. The variety has high acidity and rich tannins and as such is a good candidate for barrel-ageing and cellaring. A 1985 Pignolo that I tasted in 2001 had a youthful vivacity and rich, spicy flavor that more than proved the variety's potential for longevity.

## TASTING NOTE

It is a medium-to-dark ruby in color. Its lively, fruity perfume has hints of black cherries and blackberries, together with a mulled wine spiciness. These qualities are carried through to the well-structured palate.

## SYNONYMS

Pignul, Pignola valtellinese, Pignolo spanna, Pignolo spanno.

## FOOD PAIRINGS

Roast meats, particularly pork, lamb, goat and game

---

### TOC DE PURCIT

SERVES 4

• 400 g/1 lb pork • 200 g/1/2 lb pork liver
• 125 g/1/4 lb bacon • 75 ml/5 tbsp oil
• 3 cloves • 1 pinch of cinnamon
• the zest of 1/4 lemon • 60 g/4 tbsp bread crumbs
• 40 g/2 tbsp flour • 250 ml/1 cup white wine
• salt and pepper

PREPARATION

Dice the pork and the liver. Chop the bacon and fry it in oil in a terracotta pan. Add the pork and brown it, add a glass of wine. When the wine is completely evaporated, add the liver. Cook over a relatively low heat, add the remaining wine and the seasonings. Salt to taste and continue to cook over a low heat with the pan covered for around 20 minutes.
Meanwhile, sieve the flour into a little cold water. Mix, then add the lemon zest and the bread crumbs. Mix well to obtain a creamy consistency. Add the meat and cook over a low heat for around an hour. Serve with soft polenta.

---

### DOC AND DOCG

**FRIULI VENEZIA-GIULIA**

Colli Orientali del Friuli Pignolo
Colli Orientali del Friuli sottozona Rosazzo Pignolo

# pinot grigio

Pinot Grigio has become the magic name in Italian restaurants around the world, and its subdued aromas and flavors allow it to move easily from the bar to the table. It is little wonder that it is now the biggest-selling Italian white wine in many export markets. Styles range from fresh and supple straw-colored wines; through barriqued versions; and on to the splendidly old-fashioned copper-colored wines still made by some artisan producers in Friuli Venezia-Giulia.

The differences in color and structure are determined by the length of time the juice remains in contact with the dark-colored skins of the grape. All of these wines share refreshing acidity, medium to high alcohol, and good body. Pinot Grigio is a genetic mutation of Pinot Nero, which most likely arrived in Friuli at the end of the 19th century and from there spread throughout the country. The

wine's transformation from rustic local tipple to international best-seller can be traced to the Santa Margherita company. They were the first (in 1961) to put the wine in clear bottles in an effort to convey the message that Pinot Grigio is a light, fresh, youthful wine. Santa Margherita now produces around 5,000,000 bottles a year of Pinot Grigio Valdadige DOC. Their marketing success opened the doors for other producers and other styles of Pinot Grigio. In the tiny northern region of Valle d'Aosta, there exists a particular clone of Pinot Grigio. Locally, this clone is called Malvoise. It is used to make a deeply colored dry wine from fresh grapes. A passito style (referred to locally as flétri) is also produced. This dessert wine (which has a minimum alcohol level of 16.5%) tends to range from golden to copper in color. On the nose one finds notes of chestnuts, hazelnuts and – at times – dried figs. There should be a touch of almond in the finish of this sweet wine.

## DOC AND DOCG

### FRIULI VENEZIA-GIULIA
Pinot Grigio di Aquileia, Pinot Grigio del Collio Goriziano (or del Collio), Pinot Grigio dell'Isonzo, Pinot Grigio di Latisana, Pinot Grigio della Valle Isarco, Pinot Grigio di Grave del Friuli, Pinot Grigio del Carso, Pinot Grigio dei Colli Orientali del Friuli, Annia Pinot Grigio

### TRENTINO ALTO ADIGE
Pinot Grigio dell'Alto Adige (or Südtirol), Pinot Grigio del Trentino, Pinot Grigio Valdadige (Etschtaler)

### LOMBARDY
Pinot Grigio dei Colli Mantovani del Garda
Pinot Grigio dell'Oltrepo Pavese

### VENETO
Pinot Grigio di Breganze, Pinot Grigio del Garda
Pinot Grigio di Lison-Pramaggiore
Pinot Grigio di Montello and dei Colli Asolani
Pinot Grigio Vini del Piave (or Piave)

### EMILIA-ROMAGNA
Pinot Grigio dei Colli piacentini

### UMBRIA
Pinot Grigio dei Colli Perugini, Pinot Grigio di Torgiano

### VALLE D'AOSTA
Nus Malvoisie, Nus Malvoisie Flétri

## TASTING NOTE
Straw to pale gold, or copper, depending on the length of skin contact. Fresh and clean on the nose, with faint scents of green apples, coriander, and fresh black pepper. Some also find the bitter-sweetness of chives. The faint scents one finds on the nose are echoed on the palate.

## SYNONYMS
Pinot Gris, Tokay d'Alsace, Malvoisie, Rulander, Grauer Burgunder, Grauer Riesling.

## FOOD PAIRINGS
Youthful styles: aperitif, with rice and pasta dishes, or chicken salad. With Barriqued or Copper-colored versions: bacalá Vicentina, rich fish soups.

# primitivo

Primitivo is believed to be of Dalmatian origin. Some researchers claim it was imported to Puglia (the Italian region in which it is most widely cultivated) over 2000 years ago. Others, including ampelographer Dr. Antonio Caló – who has vowed to track the variety to its source – maintain that Primitivo arrived in Puglia at the end of the 17th century and expanded its vineyard area widely in the 19th century, when it was planted in vineyards decimated by phylloxera.

Studies carried out by the University of California at Davis have determined that Primitivo and Zinfandel share the same DNA. As one Puglian producer put it, "They are like twins separated at birth – one growing up in Manhattan, the other in the Bronx." (He declined to say which was which.) The European Union considers Zinfandel and Primitivo identical varieties and allows either name to appear on labels. Dr. Caló says that the variety was probably brought to California in the mid-1800s by Agoston Haraszthy, the Hungarian entrepreneur who dabbled in, among other things, viticulture, farming, gold mining and politics. The success of Primitivo in foreign markets has gone a long way in establishing the quality image of Southern Puglia, where the variety thrives. Previously considered only suitable for blending, Primitivo is now a star on the international wine scene. The changes in the variety's fortunes are not solely due to its link with a familiar California variety. Major changes have taken place in processing the grapes – such as earlier harvesting and drastic reduction of yields – which have led to softer, fruitier, less alcoholic wines. Producers are also exploring the variety's affinity for oak. That said, Primitivo can certainly produce exciting, fruity, well-structured wines without resorting to barrel ageing.

## PUGLIA

The Primitivo di Manduria zone lies on the Salento Peninsula and is limited to the area around a few communes (one of them being Manduria) in the provinces of Taranto and Brindisi. The constant hot winds which sweep across the peninsula help maintain healthy vineyards by preventing the development of mold, and the extreme variance between day and night-time temperatures allows the grapes to ripen more slowly, thus achieving fuller development of aromas and flavors. The wine is made solely from Primitivo and is a firmly structured masterpiece of spicy blackberry fruit flavor. It has a minimum alcohol level of 14% and a mandatory ageing of nine months. In addition to this dry version, there are three sweet styles: Dolce Naturale (which has a minimum alcohol level of 16% and a mandatory ageing period of nine months), Liquoroso Dolce Natural (which has a minimum alcohol level of 17.5% and must be aged for at least two years) and Liquoroso Secco (which has a minimum alcohol level of 18% and mandatory ageing period of two years).

One theory holds that Primitivo was brought to the province of Bari by Benedictine monks in the Middle Ages. Be that as it may, the variety thrives here, where it has its own DOC denomination: Primitivo Gioia del Colle. The wine has a minimum alcohol level of 13%. With two years of ageing and a minimum alcohol level of 14% it can be labelled *riserva*. Primitivo is also the major variety (along with Montepulciano, Sangiovese, Negroamaro and Malvasi) in Gioia del Colle Rosso and Rosato.

Additionally, Primitivo plays a small part in the blends of the following Puglian DOCs: Aleatico di Puglia, Gioia del Colle Aleatico Dolce and Liquoroso Dolce, Salice Salentino Aleatico Dolce and Liquoros Dolce.

*Puglia: the "Trulli" and the vineyards*

## CAMPANIA

Falerno del Massico Primitivo is made from a minimum of 85% of the named grape, with the option of adding small percentages of Agliani-co, Piedirosso and Barbera. The wine has a minimum alcohol level of 13% and must be aged for at least one year before being released on the market. With two years of ageing the wine can be labelled *riserva* or *vecchio*. There is often a distinct mineral note in wines from this denomination.

Primitivo may be included in the blend of Cilento Rosato and Falerno del Massico Rosso.

## TASTING NOTE

Dark ruby with a luscious raspberry/fuchsia sheen when young. On the palate, one finds plum jam and blackberry and raspberry notes, along with hints of violets and an undertone of hay, tobacco and oriental spice.

## SYNONYMS

Primaticcio, Primativo, Primitivo di Gioia, Uva Olivetto, Zinfandel.

## FOOD PAIRINGS

Roast red meats, stews, game.

## POOR MAN'S CHOPS

SERVES 4
- 500 g/1 lb ground meat
- 200 g/1/2 lb stale bread
- 150 g/1¼ cup grated Parmesan cheese
- 1 clove garlic
- 20 g/2 tbsp pork fat or butter
- parsley
- marjoram
- salt and pepper
- olive oil
- 4 skewers

PREPARATION

Moisten the bread and put it in a bowl along with the ground meat, the parsley, the chopped garlic, the Parmesan cheese and the egg. Mix well. Add a pinch of salt, a dash of pepper, the pork fat and the marjoram. Mix well. Shape this mixture into crochettes of around 3 inches in length. Put the crochettes on a skewer, alternating them with pieces of stale bread, beginning and ending with bread. Put the skewers in an oven-safe dish which has been greased with oil. Add some knobs of butter, and bake in a pre-heated oven for around 30 minutes. When the crochettes ("chops") have browned, take them from the oven.

Slide the meat from the skewers and serve.

## STRASCINATI AND HORSE MEAT ROLL-UPS

SERVES 4
FOR THE DOUGH:
- 100 g/3/4 cup bran flour
- 250 g/2 cups white flour
- salt
FOR THE SAUCE:
- 4 slices of horse meat
- 300 g/1 cup of tomato sauce
- 150 g/5 oz bacon
- 100 g/1 cup Pecorino cheese
- 1 onion
- 4 cloves of garlic
- 1 bunch of parsley
- 125 ml/1/2 cup hearty red wine
- some tbsp olive oil
- salt and pepper

PREPARATION

Mix the white flour and the bran flour together and pass through a sieve. Put the flour in a mound and mix in a little warm, salted water. Knead until the dough has a firm, elastic consistency.
Then cut it into small pieces and roll them in the palm of your hand, forming small cylindrical ropes. Cut

the ropes into 1/2-inch pieces with a knife, and, with the blade of the knife, press down the pasta, forming in this way the classic strascinati shape.
Pound the slices of horse meat until they are thin. On each piece of meat arrange some slivers of bacon and of Pecorino, some parsley leaves and a piece of garlic (which has been thinly sliced). Roll up the meat around the filling and fix it in place with string. Fry the onion in olive oil and, after a few minutes add the meat rolls, and brown them. Add the wine and when it has evaporated, add the tomato sauce. Salt, pepper and cook for around 30 to 40 minutes.
Meanwhile cook the strascinati, drain them and dress them with the tomato sauce. Serve them along with the meat rolls, sprinkled with grated Pecorino cheese.

| DOC AND DOCG | |
|---|---|
| **PUGLIA** | Primitivo di Manduria (also in sweet and liquoroso versions) |
| Gioia del Colle Rosso | |
| Gioia del Colle Primitivo | **CAMPANIA** |
| | Primitivo di Falerno del Massico |

# prosecco

This variety may have originated around the Friulian town of Trieste, which lies on the border between northeastern Italy and Slovenia, where it is known as Glera. From there, it spread to the Venetian zone of Colli Euganei, where it is called Serprina. It then spread to northeastern Venetia, where it is most commonly known as Prosecco.

Its DOC production zone in this area includes 15 communes, of which Conegliano and Valdobbiadene are the best known. Prosecco can be extra dry (the most classic and widespread version), brut (more modern and of international taste) and dry (agreeable, whose most important production is Superiore di Cartizze). The sparkling version is made by a refermentation in autoclave, exalting its varietal aromas and freshness; so Prosecco is very drinkable and delightful. This method, named Italian, was introduced in the production of Prosecco Spumante at the end of the 19th century by the Scuola Enologica of Conegliano. Sparkling Prosecco is the aperitif of choice in the Venetia. Vineyards in the tiny area of Cartizze (near Valdobbiadene) constitute a premium sub-zone. Generally speaking, the wines of Cartizze are somewhat richer than other Proseccos. When have a minimum alcohol level of 11.5%, they may be labelled "Superiore di Cartizze", produced in the dry version. Prosecco is also the principal variety in the unusual Colli di Conegliano Torchiato di Fregona. This passito wine must have a minimum alcohol level of 16% and be aged for 13 months before being released on the market. The vineyards which produce grapes for this wine lie within the communes of Fregona, Sarmede and Cappella Maggiore.

## TASTING NOTE
Pale-greenish straw in color, with green apple and lightly floral perfumes, which carry through on the palate. The slightly sweeter style lends a depth and attractive complexity to the wine.

## SYNONYMS
Serprina, Glera.

## FOOD PAIRINGS
Aperitif; drier versions may be served with delicately flavored rice or pasta dishes.

## PRODUCERS
Vicenzo Toffoli, Bepin de Eto, Desiderio Bisol & Figli, F.lli Bortolin Spumanti, Bortolomiol, Canevel Spumanti, Col Vetoraz, Nino Franco, Le Colture, Angelo Ruggeri, Ruggeri & C., Stant'Eurosia, Tanoré, Adami, De Faveri, Carpené Malvolti, Sorelle Bronca, Miotti, Foss Marai, Case Bianche, Nino Franco, Bellussi, Gegoletto, La Loggia del Colle Carmina, Vincenzo Toffoli, Zardetto, Mionetto.

### RADICCHIO TREVISO STYLE

SERVES 6
- 4 large bunches red radicchio
- 100 ml/5 tbsp extra-virgin olive oil
- salt and pepper

PREPARATION
Carefully wash the radicchio bunches. Dry them and cut them into quarters lengthwise. Place them on a plate in a single layer and drizzle oil on them. Sprinkle with salt and pepper and leave to sit for around 20 minutes. Put them on a hot grill, turning occasionally to ensure that they are uniformly cooked through. Serve very hot.

### DOC AND DOCG

**VENETO**
Prosecco di Conegliano-Valdobbiadene, Colli di Conegliano Torchiato di Fregona Prosecco, vino passito, Colli Euganei Serprino, Montello and dei Colli Asolani Prosecco

# raboso

The name "Raboso" may be derived from *rabioso*, a dialect word used to describe fruit that is still a little acerbic. Raboso performs best in stony alluvial soils, and is most likely a descendant of a wild variety native to the Piave River Valley.

Due, perhaps, to its rustic genetic heritage, Raboso was one of the few varieties to make it through the phylloxera scourge relatively unscathed, although it did loose some ground to Cabernet and Chardonnay when vineyards were replanted in the early 20th century. There are two main sub-varieties: Raboso Piave and Raboso Veronese. Raboso Piave is cultivated in the Venetia, principally in the Piave river valley. Under the name Friularo, it composes up to 90% of Bagnoli di Sopra Friularo. When the wine is aged for at least two years (one of which must be in wood), it can be labelled *riserva*. The words "Vendemmia Tardiva" on the label indicate that at least 60% of the grapes used to make the wine were picked after November 11th. Raboso Piave and Raboso Veronese, either on their own or blended together, play a significant role in Bagnoli di Sopra's other wines. They comprise the base for the zone's red, rosé, and passito, as well as its white and rosé sparkling wines. The two sub-varieties are also used in combination for the production of Raboso from the Piave zone, which is located partly in the province of Treviso and partly in that of Venice. Raboso Veronese is cultivated principally in the Venetian provinces of Venice, Vicenza and Rovigo. It may comprise part of the Merlot-based blend of Colli Euganei Rosso. Raboso Veronese is also planted in the Emilia-Romagnan provinces of Ferrara and Ravenna, where it is used in small percentages in a variety of blended wines.

## TASTING NOTE

Ruby red, tending to garnet with age. A note of violet on the nose, which becomes more evident with age. Dry, austere and lightly acidic.

## SYNONYMS

Raboso Piave is also known locally as Raboso Nostrano, Friularo, Friularo di Bagnoli, Rabosa Friulara, Friulara.
Raboso Veronese: Rabosa, Raboso di Verona

## FOOD PAIRINGS

Pasta and rice with meat sauces; stuffed goose, goulash, and fowl.

---

### POLENTA AND LITTLE BIRDS

SERVES 6
- 500 g/4 cups corn flour
- 100 g/1/4 lb lard
- 100 g/1/2 cup butter
- 16 small birds (such as skylarks or thrushes)
- sage leaves
- salt

PREPARATION

Heat around 8 cups of salted water. When it begins to boil, slowly pour in the corn flour, stirring continuously, for 40 minutes. Meanwhile, clean the birds, removing their feathers. Do not clean out their innards, but only eliminate the eyes and the feet. Now wash and dry the birds and skewer them, alternating the birds with pieces of lard and sage leaves. Sauté the birds in butter until they are golden. Put the polenta on a plate. Place the birds on top of the polenta and add the cooking juices.

---

### DOC E DOCG DA RABOSO

**VENETO**

Bagnoli di Sopra Rosso e Rosato,
Bagnoli di Sopra Passito, Bagnoli Friularo,
Piave Raboso

# refosco

Refosco is the name of a family of vines which are found primarily in Friuli Venezia-Guilia and the Veneto, with smaller plantings in Sardinia and Puglia. The vine originated in Friuli, and was the most important red variety in the region until Merlot and Cabernet entered the picture at the end of the 19th century. The sub-variety which is most widely used for winemaking is Refosco dal Peduncolo Rosso. Its name is taken from its red (*rosso*) peduncle (*peduncolo*).

*Eastern hills in Friuli*

Another important member of the Refosco family goes by the name Terrano. Refosco Nostrano is also cultivated in Friuli (particularly the area around the commune of Faedis) and is used principally for blending with other local varieties. Nearly every Friulian zone has a varietal wine based on Refosco dal Peduncolo Rosso. The Veneto also produces a varietal wine in the Lison-Pramaggiore zone, which lies between the Livenza and Tagliamento Rivers.

### DOC AND DOCG

**VENETO**
Refosco dal Peduncolo Rosso di Lison-Pramaggiore

**FRIULI VENEZIA-GIULIA**
Colli Orientali del Friuli Refosco dal Peduncolo Rosso
Cialla Refosco dal Peduncolo Rosso
Annia del Friuli Refosco dal Peduncolo Rosso
Aquileia del Friuli Refosco dal Peduncolo Rosso
Grave del Friuli Refosco dal Peduncolo Rosso
Latisana del Friuli Refosco dal Peduncolo Rosso
Isonzo Refosco dal Peduncolo Rosso

### TASTING NOTE
Intense ruby, with deep rose overtones. On the nose one finds hints of ripe damson plums and raspberries, which are echoed on the palate. Notes of black pepper, fresh almonds and, occasionally, mint also emerge. Lightly tannic. A bitter chocolate note on the finish.

### SYNONYMS
Refosco.

### FOOD PAIRINGS
Flavorful rice and pasta dishes, such as meat-filled ravioli and lasagna; roast pork.

### PAPAZOI

SERVES 4
- 200 g/1 cup borlotti beans
- 200 g/1 cup pearl barley
- 100 g/1/2 cup wheat kernels
- 100 g/1/4 lb lard • 300 g/1$^{3/4}$ cups potatoes
- 1 bunch parsley, finely chopped
- 2 cloves garlic • 50 ml/4 tbsp olive oil
- salt and freshly ground pepper

PREPARATION
Leave the beans and the barley to soak for at least 24 hours, until they have softened. Chop the lard with the garlic. Fry them in oil in a large pan over a low heat. Then add abundant cold water, the beans and barley (which have been drained) and a little salt. Cook slowly for around 2 hours. Add the diced potatoes and continue to cook for around 45 minutes. Now add the chopped parsley and a good measure of freshly ground pepper. Do not stir during the cooking process.

# ribolla gialla

Ribolla Gialla is one of the oldest indigenous vines of Friuli, where it thrives on the windy hillsides of the Collio Goriziano and the Colli Orientali del Friuli zones. It may be the same as the ancient Rebula variety, which was brought to Italy by the Venetians from the Greek island of Cefalonia. In the 12th century, when Friuli was an important supplier of wines to the Republic of Venice, this variety enjoyed great popularity under the name of Rabiola del Collio.

Its importance declined radically in the 19th century when oidium (powdery mildew) infected great swathes of vineyards. Traditionally, Ribolla Gialla was used to produce Torbolino. This winemaking curiosity is essentially sweet, still-fermenting grape must, and is served during the autumn Festival of the Dead.

## TASTING NOTE
Straw yellow with green highlights. The nose is subdued but refreshing. This wine's defining characteristic is its full body and good structure, which, at first, seems at odds with its rather neutral nose and restrained flavor of Golden Delicious apples and cantaloupes.

## SYNONYMS
Ribuele, Ribuele Zale and Rebula.

## FOOD PAIRINGS
As an aperitif with a slice of prosciutto, or with delicately flavored vegetable, fish or white-meat dishes.

*Typical shapes of rows of vines on the eastern hills of Friuli*

---

### DOC AND DOCG

**FRIULI VENEZIA-GIULIA**

Collio Goriziano (or del Collio) Bianco
Ribolla Gialla Collio Goriziano
Colli Orientali del Friuli Ribolla Gialla

---

### GIAMBARS

SERVES 4
- 1 kilo/2 lb 3 oz shrimp • 3 or 4 cloves of garlic
- some basil leaves • 1 bunch of parsley
- some marjoram leaves • dry white wine
- paprika • olive oil • salt

PREPARATION
Carefully wash the shrimp and fry them in abundant olive oil (in which the garlic has already been fried). Finely chop the basil with the parsley and marjoram. Add these herbs to the shrimp and mix well. Then add the wine. Once the wine has evaporated, cover and cook over a low heat for around 15 minutes.

# rossese

*Rossese* is of French origin, and was most likely brought to Liguria by the soldiers of the Doria family. It spread from the Doria estate in Dolceacqua out along the Ligurian Riviera. The variety's name may refer to the color of the grape (*rossezza* means redness). Wines made from this variety can continue to age for three or four years.

Napoleon Bonaparte, it is said, was partial to Rossese wines, and in the Monregalesi hills (the source of his favorite examples) this fact is still regularly celebrated with sumptuously abundant Napoleonic feasts.

## TASTING NOTE

Ruby red tending to garnet with age. There are delicate hints of roses and black pepper on the nose, and delicate, soft fruit on the palate.

## SYNONYMS

Rossese Nericcio, Rossese di Dolceacqua, Rossese di Ventimiglia.

## FOOD PAIRINGS

*Spaghetti alla chitarra*, lamb, rabbit casserole, roast pork.

| DOC AND DOCG |
| --- |
| **LIGURIA** |
| Riviera Ligure di Ponente Rossese, Rossese di Dolceacqua |

### TRENETTE WITH PESTO

SERVES 6
- 500 g/1 lb trenette pasta (very similar to linguini in shape)
- 1 potato, diced
- 100 g/1/2 cup green beans, cut in pieces

FOR THE PESTO:
- 45 basil leaves
- 2 cloves of garlic
- a pinch of sea salt
- 40 g/1$^{1/2}$ tbsp grated Parmesan cheese • 40 g/1$^{1/2}$ tbsp grated Pecorino cheese
- 1 handful of fresh pine nuts
- extra-virgin olive oil

PREPARATION

For the pesto: put the basil, garlic and pine nuts in a marble mortar along with the sea salt and begin to grind it with a pestle, adding a little oil. Then add the cheese and continue to mix, adding more oil as needed. Blend well.

Boil abundant salted water. Put the green beans and the diced potato in the water. Then add the pasta. When the pasta is al dente, drain. Retain the cooking water and add a bit of it to the pesto to thin the sauce, if needed.

### RABBIT SANREMO STYLE

SERVES 4
- 1$^{1/2}$ kilos/3 lb 5 oz rabbit
- 60 ml/4 tbsp extra-virgin olive oil
- 2 bay leaves
- a pinch of thyme
- 1 onion, chopped
- 1/2 stalk of celery
- 1 tablespoon rosemary
- 30 g/2 tbsp pine nuts
- 2 walnuts
- 250 ml/1 cup stock (made from boiling down the head and the liver of the rabbit)
- 25 black olives
- 250 ml/1 cup Rossese di Dolceacqua
- salt

PREPARATION

Clean the rabbit, removing the head and liver. Cut the rabbit into pieces and leave under running water. Then put the rabbit in a strainer to drain. Put some oil in a terracotta pan and fry the onion along with the celery, pine nuts, walnuts, bay leaves, rosemary and thyme. When the onions have become transparent, add the pieces of rabbit, season with salt, and add the wine.
In a little water boil the head and liver of the rabbit. After around 30 minutes, remove the meat from the head. Cut the liver into pieces. Add the meat and liver pieces to the rabbit. Retain the rabbit stock, using it to moisten the rabbit meat and keep it from sticking as it continues to cook. Halfway through the cooking time, add the olives, and continue cooking. Serve the rabbit with the sauce in which it has been cooking and garnished with olives.

# ruché

This variety is found exclusively in its zone of origin in the Piedmontese province of Asti. The current interest in the variety derives from the efforts of a few determined small producers and also owes much to the Cantina Sociale di Castagnole Monferrato, which began experimenting with it in the 1950s.

The Cantina's successful results led to more plantings, and, in 1987, to the awarding of the DOC to Ruché produced in the Castagnole Monferrato zone. This wine may be either dry or slightly sweet (amabile).

## TASTING NOTE

Medium-to-light ruby in color. Hints of bitter cherries along with a citrus note are to be found on the fresh nose. On the palate, the wine is supple yet with a velvety undertone, and has hints of very ripe plums and black pepper.

## SYNONYMS

Roché, Rouchet.

## FOOD PAIRINGS

Pasta with meaty sauces, grilled and roast meats. Medium mature cheeses.

| DOC AND DOCG |
| --- |
| **PIEDMONT** |
| Ruché di Castagnole Monferrato |

---

### CAPONÉT

SERVES 6
- 1 small cabbage
- 200 g/1/2 lb steamed rabbit
- 400 g/1 lb roast veal
- 2 scallions
- 1/2 carrot
- 1 stalk celery
- 1/2 clove garlic
- 1 egg • 30 g/2 tbsp Parmesan cheese
- 30 g/2 tbsp cottage cheese
- 3 black truffles
- 30 g/2 tbsp butter
- salt and pepper

PREPARATION
Clean the cabbage leaves, then boil them in salted water. Chop the meat and add the egg, the Parmesan cheese and the cottage cheese. Finely chop the scallions, carrot, celery and garlic and fry in a little oil and butter. Then gently stir this in with the meat mixture. Add the diced black truffle.

Put the meat filling in the center of a cabbage leaf and fold the leaf over until it covers the meat. Place the stuffed cabbage leaves (Capunét) on a greased baking sheet. Put a dab of butter on each Capunét, and cook in a pre-heated oven for a few minutes.

# sagrantino

Sagrantino di Montefalco is one of Italy's greatest red wines. The Sagrantino variety may have been brought to the Umbrian town of Montefalco by Spanish Franciscan monks. There are even those who suggest that Saint Francis himself is responsible for its presence around the hilltop town. Others theorize that it was imported by Byzantine monks from Greece during the Middle Ages. Whatever the case, it is fairly certain that the vine did not exist in Montefalco before the 12th century.

During the Middle Ages the town was strictly a religious community, with wine playing an important role in its rites and ceremonies. Tending vines and working in the cellar were important duties for the monks and nuns assigned to the local orders. By the 14th century precise regulations concerning the care of the vineyards had been established and by 1540 there existed a communal ordinance setting out the date when harvesting could take place. Sagrantino's name, in fact, is most likely derived from *sagrestia* or *sacrestia* (vestry), and it should be remembered that *sacro* (holy) and *sagra* (celebration) share the same root. This variety tends to do best in south-facing vineyards where the soil is rich in calcium. The Montefalco Sagrantino DOCG (since 1992) zone is limited to well-exposed hillsides in the commune of Montefalco and parts of Bevagna, Gualdo Cattaneo, Castel Ritaldi and Giano dell'Umbria, all of which are in the province of Perugia. It is made exclusively from Sagrantino, has a minimum alcohol level of 13%, and must be aged for at least 30 months before being released onto the market. The zone's other DOCG wine is made from semi-dried grapes: Montefalco Sagrantino Passito. It has a minimum alcohol level of 14.5% and must be aged for at least 30 months before being released onto the market. This medium-sweet wine is best drunk between its fourth and sixth years, while it is at its peak. Sagrantino is partnered with Sangiovese in the DOC wine Montefalco Rosso. This wine is a rich, velvety mouthful ideally suited to such local specialities as roast goat or Pecorino cheese. It has a minimum alcohol level of 12% and must be aged for at least 18 months. When it has undergone a minimum of 30 months' ageing and has an alcohol level of 12.5%, the word *riserva* can be added to the label.

## TASTING NOTE

Dark ruby in color. The wine is full-bodied, with a rich, silky, spicy perfume reminiscent of blackberries. On the palate, it has a slight roughness, which I often find in indigenous varieties. This quality only adds to the wine's charm.

## FOOD PAIRINGS

Grilled and roasted meats, stews. Strongly flavored cheese.

---

### KABOBS SPOLETO STYLE

**SERVES 4**

- 100 g/1/4 lb pork loin, diced
- 4 lamb chops
- 150 g/5 oz breast of chicken
- 1/4 lb/4 slices of pork liver
- 1/4 lb/ 8 slices of bacon
- sage, rosemary, pepper, juniper berries
- 60 ml/4 tbsp olive oil • salt

**PREPARATION**

Take 4 long skewers and slide on pieces of pork, lamb, liver and chicken, alternating the meat with pieces of bacon and sage. Season with salt, pepper, rosemary and juniper berries. Drizzle 4 tbsp of oil over the meat and then leave them for 5 to 6 hours in a cool place. Cook them on the grill or in a frying pan over a moderate heat, for around 15 minutes. Serve them very hot.

---

### DOC AND DOCG

**UMBRIA**

Montefalco Sagrantino, Montefalco Sagrantino Passito, Rosso di Montefalco

# sangiovese

Sangiovese, which is believed to have been cultivated since Etruscan times in the area around Florence, is found throughout Italy and is responsible for some of the country's finest and most memorable wines. One popular theory suggests that Sangiovese's name may have come from a corruption of the phrase *sanguis Jovis* (the blood of Jove).

Sangiovese, like Pinot Nero, is subject to a great deal of clonal variation and as a result its color and structure vary dramatically. Basically, the different clones fall into two main groups: Sangiovese Grosso and Sangiovese Piccolo. Grosso is lower yielding and has smaller, thicker-skinned berries and therefore the wines made from it tend to have a darker color and better ageing potential.

It is likely that the Piccolo sub-variety was introduced into Tuscany in the 19th century. With its higher productivity it soon began to gain ground from the Grosso, and quickly spread into Emilia-Romagna, Umbria, Abruzzo, Lazio, Puglia and Campania.

## CHIANTI

The word "Chianti" was applied for the first time to indicate a geographical zone in 1100. In 1384 the word was extended to the wine from the zone (in a statute issued by the Chianti League for administrative purposes). The wine's modern history, however, begins with Baron Bettino Ricasoli (who became Prime Minister of Italy in 1870). The Baron established the recipe for Chianti that eventually became part of the DOC laws for the zone. This early version called for two red grapes (Sangiovese and Canaiolo) and two white grapes (Trebbiano and Malvasia). After World War II, changing economic realities practically put an end to activity in the vineyards. Rural poverty forced young people to move to the cities to find work. By the 1950s and 1960s farms could be bought for small change, and foreigners – particularly Americans, Germans, the British and Swiss – swarmed in to take advantage of bargain prices. Also, a great many Italian vineyard owners in the zone are originally from other parts of Italy.

In 1967 the DOC was granted to the Chianti and Chianti Classico zones, even if, in international markets, the name "Chianti" was most closely associated with cheap red wine. The Chianti Classico zone lies between the tourist-magnet cities of Sienna and Florence, while the larger area surrounding it is known simply as Chianti. This latter zone includes seven sub-zones. Each of these has its own particular terroir, history and style. In the 1970s a serious move was made to improve the quality and the reputation of Chianti in general, and in 1984 Chianti and Chianti Classico were rewarded with DOCG recognition. The approved formula for these wines changed: the amount of white grapes was drastically reduced and Cabernet was authorized as a possible component. In 1996 the DOCG laws changed, establishing separate DOCG regulations for the Chianti and Chianti Classico zones. From that time, it was possible for Chianti Classico to be made from up to 100% Sangiovese and the use of barriques was permitted.

The seven sub-zones of Chianti can be divided into two sets. The first group (Colli Aretini, Colli Senesi, Colline Pisane and Montalbano) tends to produce light, fresh, easy-drinking wines. The Colli Aretini, the most easterly area, lies between the Classico zone and the town of Arezzo. Wines from this sub-zone are medium to light-bodied and are usually intended for drinking young. The vineyards for the Colline Pisane (the most westerly sub-

zone) lie in the hills southeast of Pisa. The wines from this sub-zone tend to be soft and fruity and are also generally not suitable for ageing. The Colli Senesi, the largest sub-zone, includes a major part of the vineyards in the province of Sienna (excluding those in the Classico zone). Its borders reach to San Gimignano and descend to Montalcino and Montepulciano. Usually the wines from this area are fruity and youthful. However, age-worthy wines are sometimes also produced: the style depends on the microclimate and the skill and intention of the winemaker. The Montalbano sub-zone is located west of Florence and south of Pistoia, and is adjacent to the Carmignano zone. Its wines are lighter-bodied and best consumed within a few years from the vintage.

The second group of sub-zones – Colli Fiorentini, Montespertoli and Rùfina – tends to produce wines which have the structure to age well. The regulations governing their production require a minimum alcohol level of 12%, half a degree higher than the sub-zones mentioned earlier. With additional ageing and with a minimum alcohol level of 12.5%, the wines from these sub-zones can be labelled *riserva*.

The Colli Fiorentini sub-zone borders Chianti Rùfina at Pontassieve and descends to the outskirts of Florence, touching the northern border of Classico at the town of Strada in Chianti. From its 835 hectares of vineyards, the sub-zone's 171 producers turn out around 1.5 million bottles annually. Due to its size, a wide range of styles are produced: some are elegant and long-lived, others fresh and youth-

ful. Again, the style depends on the microclimate and the intentions of the producer.

The sub-zone of Montespertoli, which overlaps at points with the Colli Fiorentini, was awarded its own independent status in 1998. Until some years ago, this area was appreciated for its fresh easy-drinking wines. But recent replanting with new Sangiovese clones and drastically reduced yields have resulted in wines that are capable of ageing for three to five years. Many of Montespertoli's 15 producers tend to use 100% Sangiovese for their *riserva* wines, which have an obligatory ageing period of three years before they are released onto the market. Montespertoli Chiantis tend to have a velvety texture and that touch of violets on the nose that also distinguishes the elegant and long-lived wines of Chianti Rùfina, the coolest of the sub-zones. The wines from Chianti Rùfina are considered by many to rival the best Chianti Classico has to offer. Rùfina's territory includes the communes of Rùfina and Pelago and, in part, those of Dicomano, Londa and Pontassieve (this last borders the Colli Fiorentini area). Its vineyards are planted at between 200 and 600 meters above sea level on Apennine foothills northeast of Florence. The blend for Rùfina can include up to 10% Cabernet Sauvignon and/or Merlot. Local producers are currently giving more attention to Sangiovese and most replanting is with this variety. To be labelled *riserva* the wine must be aged for at least two years in wood. Rùfina wines, which are well-known for their ageing potential, are fuller and have higher acidity than wines from the other sub-zones.

*Chianti landscape*

## BRUNELLO DI MONTALCINO

Undistinguished wines had been produced on the hillsides surrounding the ancient Tuscan town of Montalcino since the Middle Ages. This might have remained the case had it not been for the Biondi-Santi clan, a family of winemakers, viticulturists and shrewd marketers. Popular legend says that in the mid-1800s, Clemente Santi produced a wine he called Vino Rosso Scelto, which won top honors at exhibitions in London and Paris, as well as in Italy. Some years later his grandson, Ferruccio Biondi Santi, succeeded in identifying and isolating the local mutation of the Sangiovese Grosso grape that gave his grandfather's Rosso Scelto its exceptional concentration of fruit. Ferruccio produced the first vintages made solely from this sub-variety in the 1870s and '80s, thereby creating the prototype for modern day Brunello di Montalcino. In 1964 Tancredi Biondi-Santi assisted in drawing up the DOC production regulations for the zone. In 1980 Brunello di Montalcino became one of the first wines to obtain the even more prestigious DOCG designation. Brunellos are aged for a total of four years, two of which must be in barrel. *Riservas* are aged for a total of five years. There are now many fine producers offering powerful and well-structured wines from this zone.

## ROSSO DI MONTALCINO

In 1984 DOC status was granted to Rosso di Montalcino. This wine is similar to Brunello in that it is made from the same sub-variety of Sangiovese Grosso. However, yields are usually higher and the wine has a lower alcohol level and is aged for only one year. In other words, it has a similar flavor but is more easily accessible, both in terms of structure and price.

---

### TUSCAN STEAK

INGREDIENTS
- 1 thick T-bone steak, not less than 800 g/1³/⁴ lb
- 30 ml/2 tbsp extra-virgin olive oil
- sea salt
- pepper

PREPARATION

Heat the grill and sprinkle the meat with salt.
Grill the steak for 6 minutes. Then turn it over and grill for another 6 minutes. Remove it from the grill. Salt and pepper to taste. Drizzle with good quality extra-virgin olive oil.

### WILD BOAR HUNTER STYLE

SERVES 6
- 2 onions • 2 new carrots
- 2 stalks of celery
- extra-virgin olive oil
- 1 leg of mutton
- 1 sprig of rosemary
- 65 ml/1/4 cup red wine
- 1 onion, chopped
- 1 clove of garlic, crushed
- 1 chili pepper
- 200 g/3/4 lb tomatoes, peeled and pulped • salt and pepper

PREPARATION

Brown the chopped onion, celery and carrots in olive oil. Put the meat in a pan which has a tightly fitting lid. Add the seasonings and brown the meat. Remove from heat and add the wine. Marinate the meat for at least 12 hours. In a large oven-safe pan, brown the onion, garlic and chili pepper in olive oil. Add the meat and its marinade, along with the tomatoes, to the pan and put it into the oven, which has been pre-heated at 200°C/390°F. Lower the temperature to 175°C/350°F and leave to cook for an hour, adding stock from time to time to prevent the meat from sticking. Remove the meat from the pan and keep it hot. Boil the cooking juices with 1/2 cup of water. Serve the meat with the freshly prepared sauce.

*The hills of Chianti with ancient castles*

## VINO NOBILE DI MONTEPULCIANO

Here Sangiovese is represented by the sub-variety known as Prugnolo Gentile. The name "Prugnolo" most likely refers to the plum (*prugna*) color of the grape. The "Gentile" was added to lend a touch of refinement to the name.

The wines from this small zone have long been appreciated. They were among Thomas Jeffer-

son's many favorites, and also ended up at the White House when Martin Van Buren was President. Alexandre Dumas mentioned Vino Nobile in *The Count of Montecristo* and Voltaire had Candide praise "macaroni, the partridges of Lombardy, sturgeon's eggs and the wine of Montepulciano." The wine became *nobile* in the 18th century. The designation *nobile* may have been used to indicate wine which was of exceptional quality and therefore suitable for noblemen who could pay a higher price.

Vino Nobile di Montepulciano is made from a minimum of 70% Sangiovese (Prugnolo Gentile), with Canaiolo Nero and the possible addition of lesser percentages of other varieties. The wine must be aged for two years before being released onto the market. Vino Nobile was among the first wines to receive the DOCG denomination. Some tasters detect a distinct note of violets on the nose of this wine.

## ROSSO DI MONTEPULCIANO

This wine comes from the same production zone as Vino Nobile. However, yields are usually high-

### WELL-COOKED BEEF TUSCAN STYLE

SERVES 4
- 1 kilo/2 lb 3 oz beef
- 500 g/1 lb 2 oz tomato sauce
- 2 carrots • 3 onions
- 2 cloves of garlic
- 2 stalks of celery
- 1 handful of rosemary
- 125 ml/1/2 cup red wine
- 50 ml/4 tbsp olive oil
- salt and pepper

PREPARATION

Sprinkle the meat with the chopped garlic and a touch of salt, pepper and the rosemary. Tie it up with kitchen string, and again add salt and pepper. Arrange the meat in a pan and slowly brown it in oil (for at least 15 minutes). Fry the chopped carrot, onion and celery, then add the wine and the tomatoes. Cook for around 15 minutes, then add the meat to the vegetables and cook over a very low heat for 3 to 4

hours. If the meat becomes dry, add a little warm stock or warm water. Before serving, take the meat from the pan. Let it cool and untie it. Then slice it thinly and arrange it on a serving platter. Put the hot sauce in which the meat has cooked in a serving bowl so that each guest can decide on the amount of sauce he or she desires.

er and the wine has a slightly lower alcohol level. It serves the same purpose as Rosso di Montalcino, offering a more immediate and cheaper version of the more important wine of the zone.

## MORELLINO DI SCANSANO

The Morellino di Scansano zone is a windswept collection of hills in the province of Grosseto between the Ombrone and Albegna rivers. For years, a few producers quietly turned out attractive if austere high quality reds. The zone's fortunes changed when the demand for Chianti began to outstrip the supply. For Chianti producers the Morellino di Scansano zone offered an ideal way to expand their production and keep their customers satisfied. Chianti producers (such as Antinori and Frescobaldi) began buying up land in the zone. This attracted the attention of outside investors and today land in the Morellino di Scansano area is hot property. New vineyards and state-of-the-art wineries are springing up daily. Morellino di Scansano is made from Sangiovese (known as Morellino in these parts), to which small amounts of other red grape varieties may be added. The wine may be labelled *riserva* when it has a minimum alcohol level of 11.5% and it has been aged for at least two years.

## CARMIGNANO

Carmignano's entire production zone lies within the communes of Carmignano and Poggio a Caiano in the province of Prato. The zone is dominated by the family-owned Capezzana estate, which is managed by Count Ugo Bonacossi. This elegant and scholarly gentleman was instrumental in establishing the Carmignano DOCG, which allows up to 20% Cabernet Sauvignon in the blend. The wines must be aged for a minimum of 18 months. When they are aged for three years they may be labelled as *riserva*. From top vintages, this wine can be very long-lived.

## BOLGHERI

This zone became DOC in 1994 and lies in the commune of Castagneto Carducci in the province of Livorno. Its most famous representative is the Cabernet Sauvignon-based Sassicaia. Sangiovese plays a part in Bolgheri Rosso and Rosato (rosé). It is also a major component (along with Malvasia Nera) in the unusual Vin Santo Occhio di Pernice. This medium-sweet pale red, which has a minimum alcohol level of 16%, is made from semi-dried grapes. It has more depth than most Vin Santos, with more seductive sensations of fruit preserves on the palate.

---

### DUCK WITH FENNEL SEEDS

SERVES 4
• 1 medium-sized duck • 100 ml/5 tbsp extra-virgin olive oil • 100 g/4 oz bacon, diced • 1 clove garlic • 2 tbsp fennel seeds • salt and pepper

PREPARATION
Clean the duck. Make sure that all the feathers are removed. Rub salt inside the duck and put in the diced bacon. Salt and pepper the outside of the duck and then smear with pork lard and sprinkle on fennel seeds and chopped garlic. Put the duck in an oval casserole, greased with olive oil. Brown the duck for around 15 minutes over a high heat, then continue to cook over a moderate heat for a good hour. Cut the duck in pieces. Put it back in the casserole, to heat through for a few more minutes and serve with the cooking sauce.

## MONTESCUDAIO

This hilly zone is located southeast of Livorno in the province of Pisa, and lies between the Chianti and Bolgheri zones. It was granted the DOC in 1977 for a Trebbiano Toscano-based white, Vin Santo, and a Sangiovese-based red. The DOC regulations allow for the inclusion of small percentages of Trebbiano and Malvasia to the red blend. Montescudaio reds tend to be similar to the lighter styles of Chianti. As with many emerging zones, there are producers of Montescudaio who are attempting to create more substantial, full-bodied wines.

## IMPORTANT SANGIOVESE-BASED WINES FROM OTHER REGIONS SANGIOVESE DI ROMAGNA (EMILIA-ROMAGNA)

A part of this zone lies in the foothills of the Apennines, which separate Romagna from Tuscany. The wine is made from Sangiovese with the possible addition of up to 15% other red grapes. It has a minimum alcohol level of 11.5%. When it has a minimum alcohol level of 12% and is aged for six months it can be labelled as *superiore*. If it is aged for at least two years it may be labelled *riserva*. This zone is capable of producing rich, plummy, silky-textured wines from Sangiovese Grosso. Three of this wine's top producers (Fattoria Zerbina, Drei Doná and San Patrignano) have joined together to form the Convito di Romagna, with the intention of promoting high quality Sangiovese di Romagna.

## ROSSO PICENO (MARCHE)

Rosso Piceno is the Marche's largest DOC zone. It stretches south to near the border with Abruzzo and includes the provinces of Ancona, Macerata and Ascoli Piceno. The primary grapes used for this DOC are Sangiovese and Montepulciano. The word *superiore* on the label indicates that the grapes for the wine were grown in a small area in the southern part of the zone. The best examples of Rosso Piceno are filled with raspberry and mulberry fruit and have a fresh, clean finish.

## TORGIANO ROSSO RISERVA (UMBRIA)

The zone lies in the hills overlooking the town of Torgiano in the province of Perugia. The wine, which became DOCG in 1990, is made primarily from a blend of Sangiovese and Canaiolo. The wine must have a minimum alcohol level of 12.5% and be aged for three years before being released onto the market.

## PAPPARDELLE WITH HARE SAUCE

SERVES 4
- 400 g/1 lb pappardelle (wide strips of fresh pasta)
- 1 saddle of hare
- 1/2 onion • 1 carrot
- 1/2 stalk of celery
- 1 bay leaf • 1 bunch of parsley
- 50 g/2 oz bacon
- 125 ml/1/2 cup red wine (such as Chianti dei Colli Fiorentini)
- 60 g/4 tbsp butter
- 50 ml/3 tbsp olive oil
- 20 g/1 tbsp tomato paste
- 1 cup stock
- 20 g/1 tbsp white flour
- 1 nutmeg
- freshly ground black pepper
- salt

PREPARATION
Put the oil and 2 tbsp of butter in a pan. Add the finely chopped onion, carrot, parsley and the celery. Then add the meat (which has been cut into small pieces), the chopped bacon and the bay leaf. Cook for around 10 minutes. When the onion begins to lose color, add the wine. Once the wine has evaporated, add the flour. Mix well with a wooden spoon. Dilute the tomato paste in a cup of hot stock and add this to the sauce. Mix well, then add salt, pepper and nutmeg and leave to simmer over a low heat until the liquid is completely evaporated. When done, add the pieces of hare to the sauce. Take the pieces of hare from the sauce when they have cooked through and keep them warm. Cook the pappardelle in abundant salted boiling water. Drain them and put them on a pre-heated serving platter, mix in the remaining butter. Then add the hare sauce, again mixing well. Place the hare on top of the pappardelle and serve.

## HEARTY LAMB SOUP

SERVES 4
- 1 kilo/2 lb 3 oz lamb, cut into pieces
FOR THE MARINADE:
- 1 kilo/4 cups wine
- 125 ml/1/2 cup vinegar
- 2 sage leaves
- 1 sprig of rosemary
- 4 basil leaves • 1 carrot, chopped
- 1 stalk of celery, chopped
- 1 onion, chopped
FOR THE SAUCE:
- 1 onion • 3 cloves of garlic
- 50 g/2 oz streaky bacon, chopped
- 1 chili pepper
- 60 ml/4 tbsp extra-virgin olive oil
- 125 ml/1/2 cup red wine
- 500 g/1$^{3/4}$ cups ripe tomatoes
- 1000 ml/4 cups meat stock
- 12 slices of stale bread
- 1 clove of garlic • salt

PREPARATION
Leave the lamb to marinate for at least 4 or 5 hours in the wine, vinegar, sage, rosemary, basil, carrot, celery and the onion. Finely chop the onion, garlic, the chili pepper and the bacon, and fry in olive oil in a high-sided frying pan. Remove the lamb from the marinade. Dry it and cook it over a very low heat. When the meat has browned, turn up the heat and add the glass of wine. When the wine has evaporated, add the pulped tomatoes and stir. Salt to taste. At the very last moment, slowly add a ladle of stock. Rub the bread with garlic and put in individual serving bowls. Cover the bread with the sauce and leave for a few minutes. Then add the pieces of lamb.

## LASAGNE FERRARA STYLE

SERVES 6

FOR THE PASTA:
- 400 g/3 cups white flour
- 4 eggs
- 150 g/1/2 cup boiled spinach
- salt

FOR THE SAUCE:
- 150 g/1/2 cup ground meat
- 150 g/1/2 cup prosciutto crudo, chopped
- 50 g/4 tbsp butter
- 80 g/3/4 cup grated Parmesan cheese
- 20 g/1 tbsp tomato paste
- 60 ml/1/4 cup of dry white wine
- 250 ml/1 cup stock
- 1 onion
- 1 carrot
- 1 stalk of celery
- 125 ml/1/2 cup milk
- salt and pepper

PREPARATION

To prepare the sauce:
thinly slice the onion, the carrot and the celery and put them in a terracotta casserole with 4 tbsp of butter and with the chopped prosciutto. Fry over a moderate heat for a few minutes, then add the ground meat and leave it to brown, adding the wine from time to time. Continue cooking over a high heat until the meat is golden brown. Dilute the tomato concentrate in a little hot stock and add it to the meat. Then add the milk. Lower the heat and let simmer for around an hour, adding more stock as needed.

To prepare the pasta:
Boil the spinach in a little salted water. Squeeze out the excess liquid and whirl in a blender. Make a mound of the lightly salted flour to which the spinach has been added. Make a well in the mound and put in an egg. Knead until a smooth and elastic dough has been formed. Shape the dough into a ball. Put the dough in a bowl. Cover and let it rest for around 30 minutes. Then divide the dough in half and spread it out to form two discs, using a rolling pin. Cut the dough to fit an oven-safe baking dish. Cook the lasagna for around a minute in boiling, salted water. Then remove it from the pot and place it under cold running water. Then drain it and lay it on absorbent paper. Cover the pasta with a tea towel.

To prepare the white sauce: melt the butter in a pan, slowly add the flour, mixing well. Before it begins to brown add the hot milk little by little. Continue to stir the sauce with a wooden spoon for 20 minutes, then add salt, pepper and nutmeg. The white sauce should be smooth, well cooked and not too dense.

Butter the ovenproof baking pan. Arrange the rectangles of lasagna on the bottom of the pan. Add a layer of sauce, then another sheet of pasta and cover that with sauce and Parmesan cheese. Continue to arrange the layers like this until all the ingredients are used up. On the top layer of pasta put a little white sauce, some knobs of butter and a sprinkling of grated Parmesan cheese. Bake in a pre-heated oven for 20-25 minutes, until a firm crust forms on the top of the lasagna. Serve hot.

## SYNONYMS

Brunello, Morellino, Morellino di Scansano, Prugnolo, Prugnolo Gentile, Sangiovese del Romagna, San Gioveto, San Roveto, Tignolo and Nielluccio (in Corsica).

## TASTING NOTE

Ruby-red, tending to garnet with age. Its perfumes should be rich and full. Some tasters find hints of leather, tobacco, truffles, figs, mulberries, raspberries, vanilla and cinnamon on the nose. Young Sangiovese has a ripe cherry fruit flavor, with a cherry stone bitterness on the finish.

## FOOD PAIRINGS

Braised or stewed red meats, game (particularly wild boar). Vegetarians need not despair, Sangioveses also go well with intensely flavored dishes based on mature and spicy cheeses, such as Gorgonzola or aged Pecorino or Parmesan.

## DOC AND DOCG

**LOMBARDY**

Capriano del Colle
(Sangiovese, Marzemino and Barbera)
Garda Rosso

**SARDINIA**

Arborea Sangiovese
Alghero Sangiovese

**LIGURIA**

Colli di Luni Rosso
Colline di Levanto Rosso

**EMILIA-ROMAGNA**

Sangiovese di Romagna

**TUSCANY**

Brunello di Montalcino
Carmignano
Chianti
Vino Nobile di Montepulciano
Bolgheri
Vin Santo Occhio di Pernice
Carmignano Vin Santo Occhio di Pernice
Barco Reale di Carmignano
Colline Lucchesi Rosso
Elba Rosso
Elba Vin Santo Occhio di Pernice
Montecarlo Rosso
Montecarlo Vin Santo Occhio di pernice
Monteregio di Massa Marittima Rosso
Monteregio di Massa Marittima Vin Santo Occhio di
Pernice
Pomino Rosso
Montescudaio Rosso

Morellino di Scansano
Parrina Rosso
Pomino Vin Santo Rosso
Rosso di Montalcino
Rosso dei Montepulciano
Sant'Antimo Vin Santo Occhio di Pernice
Rosso della Val di Cornia
Vin Santo del Chianti Occhio di Pernice

**LAZIO**

Aprilia Sangiovese
Cerveteri Rosso
Genazzano Rosso
Velletri Rosso
Vignanello Rosso

**CAMPANIA**

Taburno Rosso
Guardia Sanframondi (or Guardiolo) Rosso
Solopaca Rosso

**PUGLIA**

Orta Nova Rosso

**MARCHE**

Colli Pesaresi Focara Rosso
Esino Rosso
Rosso Piceno

**UMBRIA**

Torgiano Rosso Riserva
Colli Altotiberini Rosso
Colli Amerini Rosso
Colli del Trasimeno Rosso
Colli Martani
Rosso di Torgiano

# schiava

The name *schiava* literally means "slave" and refers to a Medieval training system that called for severely pruning the vine in order to produce good quality grapes. The variety is probably Slavic in origin and was brought to northern Italy with the arrival of the Longobards. Among the sub-varieties of Schiava are Schiava Gentile, Schiava Grossa and Schiava Grigio.

These cultivars are widespread throughout the Alto Adige, and are also found in Trentino and, to a lesser degree, in the province of Verona in the Veneto, and in the province of Brescia in Lombardy. In the Alto-Adige, Schiava often goes under the name Vernatsch, and is the primary grape in many dry reds. In this region the names of production zones and methods may also be written on the label in either Italian or German. The two best-known Schiava-based wines are Santa Maddalena (St. Magdalener) and Caldaro or Lago di Caldaro (Kalterer or Kalterersee). Santa Maddalena is produced from grapes grown in the hills surrounding the town of Bolzano and takes its name from one of the communes in the zone. Up to 10% of Lagrein and/or Pinot Nero may be added to the blend. The vineyards of the Caldaro zone are located near Lake Caldaro in the province of Bolzano. Here, too, small percentages of Pinot Nero and Lagrein may be added to the Schiava-based blend.

## TASTING NOTE

Lively ruby red in color. On the nose, one finds light notes of bacon and frozen strawberries. These notes are echoed on the palate.

| DOC AND DOCG |
| --- |
| **TRENTINO ALTO ADIGE** |
| Alto Adige Schiava |
| Alto Adige Santa Maddalena |
| Alto Adige Valle Venosta |
| Alto Adige Valle Isarco |
| Caldaro o Lago di Caldaro |
| Casteller Rosso, Schiava |
| Valdadige Rosso and Rosato |
| Valdadige Schiava |

## SYNONYMS

Schiava Grosso: Blauer Trollinger, Edelvernatsch, Frankenthal, Frankentahler, Grossvernatsch, Meraner Kurtraube, Schiavone, Trollinger, Uva Meranese, Bressana. Synonyms Schiava Gentile: Schiava piccola, Schiava media, Kleinvernatsch, Mittlervernatsch, Rother-Vernatsch. Synonyms Schiave Grigia: Grau-Vernatsch Grauer, Vernatsch.

## FOOD PAIRINGS

Gnocchi with a light sauce, risotto with chicken, white meats.

| RAVIOLI ATESINI |
| --- |
| SERVES 4 |
| • 250 g/1½ cups rye flour • 150 g/3/4 cup ricotta cheese • 250 g/2 cups wheat flour • 150 g/1/2 cup butter • 2 eggs • 1 slice of onion • milk as needed • 50 g/3 tbsp grated cheese • 500 g/1 cup spinach • salt and pepper • nutmeg |
| PREPARATION |
| To prepare the pasta: make a smooth firm pasta dough, mixing the 2 types of flour together with the egg (which has been beaten with a little salt) and enough warm milk to create a smooth, elastic dough. Let the dough rest under a damp cloth for at least an hour. Then, roll it out into a very thin sheet. Cut the pasta into discs of a little less than 2 inches in diameter. To prepare the filling: boil the spinach, drain it and squeeze out the excess moisture and put it in a pan with the butter and finely chopped onion. Mix in a tablespoon of grated cheese, salt, pepper and nutmeg. Sieve the ricotta and mix it with the spinach. Place a spoonful of the filling on each disc of pasta and fold it in half, forming a half-moon shape. Take care to seal the sides well. Then boil the pasta in abundant salted water. Cook it for a few minutes (4 or 5). Drain the pasta and dress it with butter and grated cheese. |

# schioppettino

This variety first appeared on the Friulian scene around 1300. It is primarily cultivated in the hills and foothills of the commune of Prepotto. The name Schioppettino originally referred to the lively effervescence (crackling = *scoppiettese*) of wines made from the grape (then known more commonly as Ribolla Nera).

*Eastern hills in Friuli: the Rocca Bernarda*

## TASTING NOTE

Deep, dark ruby red. On the nose, one finds dried flowers, particularly roses. On the palate, the wine is full-bodied, with a luscious, soft black pepper tone over richly textured fruit flavors, which include wild blackberries, raspberries and blackcurrants.

## SYNONYMS

Pocalza, Ribolla Nera, Schiopetino.

## FOOD PAIRINGS

Game and red meats, particularly roasts.

In the years following the outbreak of phylloxera, Schioppettino lost ground to heartier, high-yielding varieties. The 1970s and 1980s saw renewed interest in Schioppettino, and in 1992, it joined the list of varietal wines made in the Colli Orientali del Friuli DOC zone. Traditional Schioppettino wine was either sweet or semi-sweet. Today, it is generally dry, with good body and relatively high acidity.

| DOC AND DOCG |
| --- |
| **FRIULI VENEZIA-GIULIA** |
| Colli Orientali del Friuli Schioppettino |
| Colli Orientali del Friuli sottozona Cialla |
| Schioppettino |
| Isonzo del Friuli Schioppettino |

### EEL WITH TOMATO

SERVES 4
- 1 skinned eel
- 6 ripe tomatoes
- 1/2 an onion
- a soupçon of chili pepper oil
- 2 tbsp extra-virgin olive oil
- oregano • salt

PREPARATION

Slice the eel and place in a frying pan with olive oil. Cook over a moderate heat for 10 minutes, sprinkling with white wine. Separately, prepare a sauce with oil, sliced onion, diced tomatoes, salt, the chili pepper and oregano. Cook for 10 minutes and add the sauce to the eel, cooking for another 5 minutes. Serve on hot plates with polenta.

# tazzelenghe

Tazzelenghe originated in Friuli, and its production area remains limited to that region. Wines based on this variety have high levels of tannins and zesty acidity. These qualities most likely influenced the grape's name, which is derived from a combination of the dialect words for cut (*tazze*) and tongue (*lenghe*).

Tazzelenghe has a true affinity for wood age-ing, and, indeed, needs time to express its po-tential. It is approved under DOC regulations for use in blended wines from the provinces of Udine and Gorizia. A small, but growing num-ber of producers are creating robust, attractive and long-lived, single-variety wines from Tazzelenghe.

## TASTING NOTE
Deep ruby red. Lightly grassy and spicy notes on the nose. Firm tannins, zesty acidity and ro-bust body. On the palate there is an amalgam of wild berry fruits and bitter cherry flavours.

| DOC AND DOCG |
| --- |
| **FRIULI** |
| Colli Orientali del Friuli Tazzelenghe |

## SYNONYMS
Tazzalienge, Tazzalingua, Tacelenghe.

## FOOD PAIRINGS
Game, roast and stewed red meats.

| GULASCH TRIEST STYLE |
| --- |

SERVES 6
- 800 g/1³/⁴ lb ground beef
- 700 g/6 cups white onion
- 100 g/4 oz pork lard
- 1 bay leaf
- 1 sprig rosemary
- 1 pinch of thyme
- 1 tablespoon fresh marjoram
- 100 g/4 tbsp tomato sauce
- paprika
- salt and pepper

PREPARATION
Slice the lard and the onions. Melt the lard in a frying pan, then add the onions and leave them to slowly cook for 5 minutes.
Add the meat and cook covered over a medium heat for 20 minutes, stirring often. When the meat is browned, add salt and season with paprika and the aromatic herbs. Scoop off the fat during cooking. Add the tomato sauce, which has been diluted in an equal quantity of hot water, and continue to cook over a low heat for an hour and a half, stirring occasionally with a wooden spoon. When the meat has cooked through, remove the aromatic herbs and pass the meat through a sieve. Reheat for a few minutes. Serve in a soup bowl.

# teroldego

Some say the name Teroldego is derived from a corruption of *tiroler gold*. This was the name used in Vienna for wines made from this grape. Backing up this theory is the fact that Teroldego wine was extremely popular in Austria, Germany and Switzerland at the end of the 18th century.

Another version suggests that the name derives from *tirelle*, the trees or plants which originally supported the vines.

Today, Teroldego's production zone is essentially limited to the Rotaliano plain in the northern part of the province of Trentino, at the confluence of the Noce and Adige rivers. Teroldego Rotaliano DOC, which may be called either Rosso or Rubino on the label, has a minimum alcohol level of 11.5%. With an alcohol level of 12%, it may be labelled *superiore*. If it has at least two years of ageing, it may be called *riserva*.

## TASTING NOTE

Ruby with purple highlights. Zesty acidity. On the nose are scents of raspberry and black pepper. The wine has good body and is very lively on the palate. On the palate, it has a tart cherry flavor and an almondy note on the finish.

## SYNONYMS

Teroldego Rotaliano, Teroldigo, Teroldega, Teroldico, Tiroldico.

## FOOD PAIRINGS

Flavorful antipasti, vegetable casseroles (such as cauliflower au gratin) and roasts.

*Trentino: Castel Beseno in Vallagarina*

---

### DOC AND DOCG

**TRENTINO ALTO ADIGE**

Teroldego Rotaliano Rosso and Rosato
Teroldego Rotaliano Superiore

---

### VENISON WITH BLUEBERRIES

SERVER 4
- 1 kilo/2 lb 3 oz venison • 1 litre/4 cups red wine
- 1 onion • 100 g/4 oz lard
- bay leaf • juniper berries
- rosemary • 125 g/1 cup flour
- 100 ml/1/2 cup cream • blueberry jam

PREPARATION

Cut the venison into pieces and put them in a pan. Pour in the wine, add the spices (bay leaf, juniper berries, rosemary) and leave to rest for a day (or overnight). Chop the onion and the lard and fry. Take the meat from the wine and let it drain for a few minutes. Dredge the meat in flour and fry in the same pan in which the onions have been cooked. When the venison pieces are golden add part of the wine in which the meat was marinated. Let it cook through. Remove the venison from the pan. Add cream to the cooking juices left in the pan. Put the meat on a serving platter and cover it with the cooking juices and cream sauce. Serve hot accompanied by blueberry jam.

# terrano

Terrano is part of the Refosco family.
Its traditional home is in the iron-rich
soils of Friuli's Carso zone.
The Austrians, who controlled this
area for a time, prized Terrano-
based wines for their medicinal
properties, considering them an
excellent cure for anemia.

Terrano is blended with small percentages of Pinot Nero in the Carso Terrano DOC. In Emlia-Romagna, the variety is known as Cagnina. Its only DOC production zone in this region is located in the provinces of Forli-Cesena and Ravenna. At least 85% of Cagnina di Romagna is composed of the named grape.

## TASTING NOTE
Very deep ruby. Zesty acidity. Good body. On the palate it is an amalgam of wild berry fruits.

## SYNONYMS
Refosco del Carso, Refosco d'Istria, Cagnina.

## FOOD PAIRINGS
Pork-based dishes

| DOC AND DOCG |
| --- |
| **FRIULI VENEZIA-GIULIA** |
| Terrano del Carso |
| **EMILIA-ROMAGNA** |
| Cagnina di Romagna |

| SAUSAGES AND WINE |
| --- |
| SERVES 4 |
| • 4 sausages |
| • 1 tbsp vinegar |
| • 125 ml/1/2 cup red wine |
| PREPARATION |
| Pierce the sausage skins. Brown the sausage, with a dash of vinegar. When the vinegar has evaporated add the red wine and finish cooking. Serve hot accompanied by polenta (mush). |

# tocai friulano

Tocai Friulano is grown in the regions of Friuli, Veneto and the eastern zones of Lombardy. It is used in the blend of several Veneto wines, notably Bianco di Custoza and Lugana, but it is in Friuli that the variety is allowed to take center stage as a 100% varietal wine.

Italian producers added the "Friuliano" to the variety's name fairly recently in order to satisfy a complaint lodged with the European Union by Hungary, whose most famous wine is Tokay. Hungarian Tokay is not made from Tocai grapes and its style is at the opposite end of the spectrum from Italian Tocai. Nonetheless, Italian Tocai Friulano will become known simply as Friulano in 2008 when the Friuli producer's time limit to appeal to the European Court runs out. This confusion between Tocai and Tokay essentially arose from the to-ing and fro-ing of either 11th-century Italian missionaries or 17th-century noblemen, depending on whose version of events you choose to follow. The most widely accepted story in Friuli has the Countessa Aurora Formentini Batthyány bringing cuttings from the Friulian vine to Hungary as part of her dowry in 1632. Whatever the case, it was most likely Hungarian Tokay's historic reputation as a fabulous medicinal elixir, capable of giving life to those on the verge of death, which encouraged its name to be linked with important wines in other regions. Outside of Italy, this variety is most commonly known as Sauvignon Vert or Sauvignonasse.

## TASTING NOTE

Pale yellow/gold. There is a slight saline note on the nose alongside the subtle scents of wildflowers. Some find hints of geranium leaf or hay. The wine has a definite structure and a creamy texture and flavor (crème pâtissière). Some find ghosts of apricots on the palate. The slightly saline note on the nose carries on through the finish.

## SYNONYMS

Cinquien, Malaga, Tocai Bianco, Tocai Italiano, Brebbianello, Sauvignon à gros grain, Sauvignon de la Corrèze, Sauvignon Vert, Sauvignonasse.

## FOOD PAIRINGS

It is ideal with a plate of thinly sliced cooked ham or proscuitto or barley and bean soup, and it is one of the few wines suggested as an accompaniment for boiled asparagus.

### CIALZONS DE TIMAO

SERVES 6

FOR THE PASTA:
- 450 g/3 cups flour • 5 eggs • salt

FOR THE FILLING:
- 500 g/3 cups potatoes
- 25 g/1 tbsp sugar • 150 g/1/2 cup butter
- 30 g/2 tbsp grated Parmesan cheese
- 1 bunch of parsley • some mint leaves
- 1 onion • 2 litres/8 cups stock
- 30 ml/2 tbsp cognac • nutmeg
- cinnamon • salt and pepper

PREPARATION

Mix the flour with the egg and a pinch of salt, and knead for around 15 minutes. Form the dough into a ball and leave to rest. Meanwhile prepare the stuffing by boiling the potatoes in their skins. Then peel them and pass them through a sieve. Put the potatoes in a baking pan. Add the finely chopped parsley, the mint, the sugar and the cognac. Then add salt, pepper and a pinch of nutmeg and cinnamon. Fry the onion in 1/4 cup of butter. Then gently add it to the potato mixture. Roll out the dough into a thin sheet. Cut small disc-shapes from the dough. Put a bit of filling on each disc. Fold over the pasta and firmly close the sides so that no filling can escape. Cook the pasta in boiling stock. When the pasta is done, drain it and dress it with the remaining melted butter and grated cheese.

| DOC AND DOCG | Colli Berici Tocai Italico, Colli Euganei Tocai Italico |
|---|---|
| **LOMBARDY**<br>San Martino della Battaglia also in the liqueur version | **FRIULI VENEZIA-GIULIA**<br>Collio Goriziano Tocai Friulano, Colli Orientale del Friuli Tocai Friulano, Annia Tocai Friulano, Aquileia Tocai Friulano, Grave Tocai Friulano, Latisana Tocai Friulano, Isonzo Tocai Friulano |
| **VENETO**<br>Breganze Bianco (Tocai Friulano 85%), | |

# traminer aromatico
## gewürztraminer

Traminer Aromatico is the name
Gewürztraminer is best known by in
Italy. The variety is popularly believed
to have originated in vineyards
around the town of Termeno in the
Alto Adige. In this bilingual region,
Termeno is also known as Tramin.

That the word "Traminer" means "from Tramin", is often played as the trump card when discussing Gewürztraminer's origins. Italian Gewürztraminer has a very different style from those made in other countries. This wide divergence in fragrance and flavor can be attributed to the way the wild vine evolved over the centuries in the different microclimates of Europe, and to the various clones now used in each producing country. Generally speaking, Italian Traminer Aromatico has a softer, gentler, more floral style than its Alsatian counterpart. When the wine is well-made, it has exceptionally elegant perfumes, and its high alcohol level is balanced by concentrated fruity flavors.

## TASTING NOTE

Pale gold, often with a pea-green sheen. Crisp acidity. Medium body. A subtle note of tinned lichees mingles with wildflower scents and an earthy/mineral tone. On the palate, the wine is fresh and lively.

## SYNONYMS

Gewürztraminer, Roter Traminer, Traminer Rosa, Termeno Aromatico, Savagnin rosé, Clevener.

## FOOD PAIRINGS

Aperitif, or smoked speck or salmon.

### DOC AND DOCG

**TRENTINO**
Trentino Traminer

**ALTO ADIGE**
Alto Adige (Südtirol) Traminer Aromatico
Valle Isarco Traminer Aromatico
Valle Venosta (Vinschgau) Traminer Aromatico

**FRIULI VENEZIA-GIULIA**
Carso Traminer
Colli Orientali del Friuli Traminer
Collio Traminer
Friuli Annia Traminer
Friuli Grave Traminer

### LIVER DUMPLINGS

SERVER 4
- 4 slices of stale bread
- 30 g/2 tbsp flour
- 125 ml/1/2 cup milk
- 1 egg
- 200 g/1/2 lb beef or pork liver
- marjoram
- 100 g/1/2 cup pork fat or olive oil
- parsley
- 1 clove of garlic
- 50 g/3 tbsp butter
- 1 lemon
- grated cheese
- 1 1/2 onion
- salt and pepper

PREPARATION
Finely chop the onion and brown it with a little oil or pork fat. Add the bread (which has been soaked in milk and cut in pieces). Let the bread fry for a few minutes. Then remove the pan from the heat. Chop the liver and dredge it in a mixture of flour, egg, parsley, marjoram, chopped garlic, lemon zest and salt and pepper. Blend the liver mixture with the onion and bread mixture. Form into small dumplings. Cook them in salted boiling water. Drain them and dress them with butter and grated cheese.

# trebbiano

The name Trebbiano refers to a very large family of vines. The most important of these in terms of Italian winemaking are Trebbiano Toscano (which is found throughout Italy and is known in France as Ugni Blanc), Trebbiano di Soave (also known as Verdicchio), and Trebbiano Romagnolo.

*A view of Florence*

The name "Trebbiano" may be derived from the Trebbia river, a tributary of the Po, or it could be connected to any of the scores of similarly named hamlets throughout Italy. In Roman times wines from villages with such names were called Trebulani.

Trebbiano has endured a spotty reputation and has been wrongly accused of producing neutral wines. Its image problem is directly linked to overproduction and lax vinification methods. As with many Italian varieties, when the vine is treated with respect and intelligent winemaking practices are employed, the resulting wines can be exceptionally attractive. The winemaking techniques that are changing the taste-profile of Trebbiano include de-stemming and de-seeding before pressing, maceration on the skins to allow for a more complete extraction of the grape's polyphenolic components and fermentation and/or maturation in wood.

## TREBBIANO TOSCANO

Trebbiano Toscano, along with its favorite partner Malvasia, is part of the blend used to produce most Vin Santos. It makes up 40-60% of Umbria's most well-known white, Orvieto, and it is a major part of the blend for Lazio's Frascati and Est! Est!! Est!!! It is part of practically all Tuscan and Umbrian DOC dry whites, and it plays a lesser role in those of Emilia-Romagna, Campania, Molise, Calabrai, Puglia, Venetia and Sardinia.

In Abruzzo, this variety is used on its own or in conjunction with a variety known locally as Trebbiano d'Aburzzo. This latter grape is also known as Bombino Bianco. The production zone for the Trebbiano d'Abruzzo DOC denomination includes practically the whole of the region, and its wines are among the best of Italy's dry whites. They are well-structured, flavorful and have the potential for a certain amount of ageing. Edoardo Valentini was the first great champion of Trebbiano d'Abruzzo. He began studying the techniques for producing great wines from this variety (and from Montepulciano) back in the 1950s. His Trebbianos, which he releases four or five years after the harvest, can easily evolve for eight to ten years. Gianni Masciarelli is another top producer of Trebbiano (and Montepulciano). Masciarelli has chosen to ferment his Trebbiano in small barrels as he feels that the wood enhances the wine's richness on the palate. There are few others who achieve the same high-quality results.

## SYNONYMS

Biancame, Albano, Albanella, Biancone, Procanico, Trebbiano Fiorentino, Coda di Caballo, Ugni Blanc.

*Umbria: Orvieto*

## PIKE IN ANCHOVY SAUCE

SERVES 4
- 1½ kilos/ 3½ lb pike
- 1 celery stalk, chopped
- 1 carrot, chopped
- 1 onion, chopped
- 120 g/1/2 cup peppers conserved in vinegar
- 60 g/1/4 cup salted capers
- 1 clove garlic
- 1 bay leaf
- 125 ml/1/2 cup white wine
- salt
- 2 tbsp parsley, chopped
- 6 salted anchovies
- olive oil

PREPARATION
Wash the capers and the filleted anchovies under running water. Put 1 liter of water in a kettle. Add the celery, carrot, onion, garlic, bay leaf, white wine and a pinch of salt. Put the pike in the kettle when the water begins to boil. Cover and reduce the heat, simmering until the fish is cooked. Prepare the sauce by chopping the peppers, the capers, the anchovies, the parsley and the garlic clove. Then fry these ingredients in abundant oil. Now remove the pike from the water. Remove its skin and arrange the pike in pieces on a serving platter. Cover the pike with sauce and leave it to rest for a few hours in the refrigerator.

## FRIED OCTOPUS

SERVER 6
- 800 g/1¾ lb octopus
- 125 ml/1/2 cup extra-virgin olive oil
- 2 cloves garlic
- parsley • salt and pepper

PREPARATION
Clean the octopus and skin it. Wash it thoroughly and cut it into pieces. Fry the garlic and chopped parsley in oil and add the octopus. Cover the pan and shift it from time to time to keep the octopus from sticking to the bottom of the pan. The cooking time should not exceed 30 minutes. Serve hot.

## BACCALA MOLLICATO

SERVES 4
- 400 g/1 lb dried salt cod
- 200 g/1/2 lb stale bread crumbs
- 2 cloves garlic
- 100 ml/1/2 cup olive oil
- 1 bunch of parsley, chopped
- 1 pinch of oregano
- paprika
- salt

PREPARATION
Leave the dried salt cod to soak for 2 or 3 days, changing the water often. Then put the cod in a little boiling, lightly salted water and cook for around an hour. Remove the bones and skin from the fish and crumble the flesh into a bowl. Dress with half the oil, the chopped parsley, the chopped garlic, the oregano, the paprika and salt. Arrange the cod in an oven-proof dish and sprinkle with bread crumbs. Salt again and add the remaining oil. Bake at a moderate heat for around 40 minutes.

## TREBBIANO DI SOAVE

Trebbiano di Soave is widespread throughout the Venetian provinces of Verona and Vicenza, and the Lombardy provinces of Brescia and Mantova. It may comprise up to 30% of the Soave blend and 90% of that of Lugana, a dry white whose zone lies at the southern end of Lake Garda. Here, the variety is known as Trebbiano di Lugana. In the Marche the variety is known as Verdicchio.

## SYNONYMS

Verdicchio, Trebbiano di Lugana.

## TREBBIANO ROMAGNOLO

In Emilia-Romagna, Trebbiano Romagnolo is the primary variety in a number of DOC still and fizzy whites, which include both sweet and dry styles. Trebbiano di Romagna is composed of 85% to 100% Trebbiano Romagnolo. The variety makes up at least 85% of Colli Di Imola Trebbiano. It is blended with Albana to produce Colli Bolognesi Bianco. It comprises 50-70% of the blend of the light-bodied Colli di Rimini Bianco. It is teamed up with Sauvignon and Malvasia Bianco di Candia to make Bosco Eliceo Bianco. Trebbiano Romagnolo plays a part in Trebbinano Val Trebbia, and Valnure and in the Vin Santos of Emilia-Romagna.

Trebbiano Romagnolo and/or Trebbiano Toscano feature in Sardinia's Arborea Trebbiano. This wine, too, is made in a variety of sweet and dry styles and may be either still or fizzy.

It is also cultivated in Lazio and Puglia.

## TASTING NOTE

Straw yellow. Delicately aromatic, with scents of dried wildflowers. On the palate, it is soft. Simple versions verge toward neutrality. Faint notes of white peaches emerge on the palates of more complex styles.

## SYNONYMS

Trebbiano della fiamma, Trebbiano di Romagna.

## FOOD PAIRINGS

Well-made examples are suited to smoked salmon, smoked fish. Pink-fleshed fish. Delicate antipasti, seafood risotto, mussels marinara, fish soup.

## DOC AND DOCG

The Trebbiano grapes are used for more than 80 DOCs

**LOMBARDY**
Capriano del Colle Trebbiano, Garda Colli Mantovani Bianco, Lugana

**VENETO**
Bianco di Custoza

**SARDINIA**
Trebbiano di Arborea

**EMILIA-ROMAGNA**
Bosco Eliceo Bianco, Trebbiano di Romagna, Colli Bolognesi Bianco, Colli di Faenza Bianco, Colli Piacentini Bianco, Colli di Imola, Colli di Rimini, Reno

**TUSCANY**
Bianco della Valdinievole, Bianco dell'Empolese, Bianco dell'Empolese Vino Santo, Bianco di Pitigliano, Bianco Pisano di San Torpè, Valdichiana Bianco, Vergine, Bolgheri Bianco, Carmignano Vin Santo, Colli dell'Etruria Centrale Bianco, Colli dell'Etruria, Centrale Vin Santo, Colline Lucchesi Bianco, Elba Bianco, Elba Vin Santo, Montecarlo Bianco, Montecarlo Vin Santo, Montecucco Bianco, Monteregio di Massa Marittima Bianco, Monteregio di Massa Marittima Vin Santo, Montescudaio Bianco, Montescudaio Vin Santo, Parrina Bianco, Pomino Vin Santo Bianco, Sant'Antimo Vin Santo, Val d'Arbia Bianco, Val di Carnia Bianco, Vin Santo del Chianti

**MARCHE**
Bianco dei Colli Pesaresi, Falerio dei Colli Ascolani

**UMBRIA**
Colli Altotiberini Bianco, Colli Amerini Bianco, Colli Martani Trebbiano, Colli Perugini Bianco, Orvieto, Torgiano Bianco

**LAZIO**
Aprilia Trebbiano, Cerveteri Bianco, Est! Est! Est!

**ABRUZZO**
Trebbiano d'Abruzzo

**MOLISE**
Biferno Bianco, Pentro di Isernia (or Pentro) Bianco

**CAMPANIA**
Taburno Bianco, Castel San Lorenzo Bianco, Solopaca Bianco

**PUGLIA**
Gioia del Colle Bianco, Lizzano Bianco

**CALABRIA**
Scavigna Bianco

# uva di troia

This grape's origins, like those of many indigenous varieties, are murky. One theory is that it originated in Asia Minor and was brought to Puglia by the Greeks. What is known, is that the variety only seems to thrive in Puglia, particularly in the provinces of Bari and Foggia. The commune of Troia is found in this area and it may well be this town which gives its name to the variety.

ried out on vinification methods which may lead to a change in the resulting wine's profile. Micro-oxygenation, for example, a technique Rivera is exploring, seems to make wine made from Uva di Troia softer, and brings out the variety's fresh scents of violets.

## TASTING NOTE

Deep ruby color with violet highlights. It has decent acidity and distinct tannins.
Tasters find violets and licorice on the nose.

## SYNONYMS

Nero di Troia, Vitigno di Troia, Uva Barlettana e Canosa.

## FOOD PAIRINGS

Suited to fowl, lamb and young goat.

There are two types of Uva di Troia. One has big clusters and large berries; the other, referred to locally as Carnosina, has smaller clusters and smaller berries. It is this latter type which may yield the most interesting results in the future. As with a great many of Italy's indigenous varieties, experiments are being car-

---

### DOC AND DOCG

**PUGLIA**

Cacc'e mmitte di Lucera, Castel del Monte Rosso, Castel del Monte Uva di Troia, Rosso Barletta, Rosso Canosa, Rosso di Cerignola

---

### LAMB AL VERDETTO

SERVES 4
- 1 kilo/2 lb 3 oz lamb pieces • 1 onion
- 400 g/3 cups fresh peas
- 1/2 cup extra-virgin olive oil
- parsley • salt and pepper

PREPARATION
Peel and slice the onion. Fry the onion in about 1/2 cup of olive oil until it becomes transparent. Add the lamb and fry it for 15 minutes. Then add the peas, a dash of pepper, salt and parsley and continue to cook (with the lid on) over a low heat for around 30 minutes.

# verdicchio

DNA testing has proved that Verdicchio, Trebbiano di Soave and Trebbiano di Lugana are one and the same. Under these last two names it is widespread throughout the Veneto, where it may be a component in the blends of Soave, Gambellara and Bianco di Custoza. It can also be a part of the blends of the Lombardy DOCs of Capriano del Collie Trebbiano, Colli Morenici Mantovani del Garda Bianco and Lugana.

*Marche: Urbino*

These wines are discussed in more detail in the Trebbiano chapter.

In the Marche, the variety is known as Verdicchio, a name which is likely derived from the greenish (verde) highlights found in the wine. Verdicchio can attain 13% alcohol with ease, and, when yields are controlled and harvesting is carried out with care, wines made from the variety have good structure, high extract and a luscious strain of apricot-like fruit, which fills out the mineral/salty note that is its hallmark. Its malleable character - which is not unlike Chardonnay – allows it to be used in a variety of styles: from dry sparklers, to fresh and zesty quaffing wines, to weightier (at times oaked) versions and even passito dessert wines. Not surprisingly it accounts for around two-thirds of the Marche's DOC production

Its two major vineyard areas surround the medieval town of Jesi and the hamlet of Matelica. The Esino River, which has its source in the Apennines, runs through the centers of these two towns on its way to the sea. In the distant past, this area was the basin of a lagoon, and its clay/sandy soil is extremely rich in minerals, particularly iron and magnesium. Some authorities say the variety was already established here by the 8th century B.C. The vineyards of the Matelica zone lie southwest of Jesi, and are planted at higher elevations on the foothills of the Apennines. There is a distinct difference in the styles of the two zones. The wines of Jesi tend to have elder flower aromas and broader fruit tones. Verdicchio from the Matelica zone is more restrained and elegant, with a delicate but persistent note of apricot fruit.

When the wine is made from grapes grown in mature vineyards, which have naturally restricted yields and a deep and complex root system, Verdicchio can develop an intensity of flavor and true ageing capacity.

## TASTING NOTE

Zippy acidity. Apricot and elder flower notes on the nose and palate.

## SYNONYMS

Trebbiano di Soave, Verdicchio verde, Verdone, Verdicchio Dolce, Verdicchio Vero, Terbiana, Trebbiano di Lugana, Trebbiano Veronese, Peloso and Verzello.

## FOOD PAIRINGS

This is a great wine for sushi, seafood antipasti and risotto and grilled white-fleshed fish.

| DOC AND DOCG |
| --- |
| **MARCHE** |
| Esino Bianco, Verdicchio dei Castelli di Jesi, Verdicchio di Matelica |

## FISH SOUP ANCONA STYLE

SERVES 8

• 1500 g/3 lb 5 oz of assorted fish (red mullet, mackerel, flounder, prawns, mullet, lobster, bass, hake, squid, cuttlefish, scorpion fish, sole, gurnard)
• 700 g/2¹ᐟ² cups tomatoes
• 125 ml/1/2 cup olive oil
• 50 g/5 tbsp parsley
• 2 cloves
• 1 onion
• 125 ml/1/2 cup vinegar
• 125 ml/1/2 cup white wine
• 8 pieces of whole wheat bread
salt and pepper

PREPARATION

Clean the fish. In a terracotta casserole brown the sliced onion in olive oil. Add the parsley, the finely chopped garlic and tomatoes (which have been peeled and de-seeded). Add wine and simmer. Salt and pepper the scorpion fish and cook over a low heat for 20 to 30 minutes. Remove the flesh from the fish and pass it through a sieve directly into the casserole. Add the other fish in this order: first the shellfish, then the crustaceans, and finally the hake and sole. Simmer for a few minutes. Then add the vinegar and cook uncovered for another 15 minutes. Serve the soup over a piece of bread.

## PUGLIESE

SERVES 4/6

• 1000 g/2 lb 3 oz of Taranto mussels • 400 g/ 2 cups rice (a variety which doesn't overcook)
• 5 or 6 medium potatoes
• 3 medium onions
• 6 or 7 medium red tomatoes
• 50 g/3 tbsp grated Pecorino cheese
• a clove of garlic
• a sprig of parsley • celery
• 50 ml/4 tbsp extra-virgin olive oil
• salt and pepper

PREPARATION

Wash the mussels thoroughly (in running water) scrubbing the shells with steel wool and open them using a special knife (throw away any empty shells). Peel the potatoes and cut them into thick slices. Peel and slice the onions. Chop the parsley with garlic and celery. Grease a high-sided round ovenproof dish measuring about 10 inches across. Arrange the onions, potatoes, chopped celery, parsley and garlic, the rice and mussels (with the mollusk facing downwards), dust with Pecorino and season with salt and pepper. Repeat until the dish is full and arrange the tomatoes (cut into wedges) on the last layer and dress with the Pecorino, salt, pepper and oil. Fill the dish with water and bake at about 180°C/350°F for 40 minutes. While cooking check that there is enough water, adding more when necessary so that the dish remains damp.

## ANCONA STYLE DRIED COD

SERVES 4

• 400 g/1 lb dried cod
• 300 g/1 cup peeled plum tomatoes
• 50 g/1/4 cup of medium potatoes
• 125 ml/1/2 cup full fat milk
• 125 ml/1/2 cup dry white wine
• 1 sprig of fresh rosemary
• 1 medium carrot
• 1 sprig of fresh parsley
• 250 ml/1 cup extra-virgin olive oil
• 30 g/2 tbsp fresh butter

PREPARATION

Open the dried cod, fillet it and cut into even-sized pieces measuring about 4 inches per side. Soak in milk for 3-4 hours, drain it and keep the milk. Fry the garlic, carrot and half of the chopped parsley in butter and 3 tbsp of oil. Arrange a layer of dried cod (skin downwards) on a grid or crossed canes in the bottom of a saucepan to prevent the fish from sticking. Spread it with part of the fried ingredients, a pinch of rosemary and chopped parsley with strips of tomato. Cover with more fish and continue to alternate the layers until all the ingredients have been used up. Season every layer with salt and pepper. Cover with the peeled potato wedges and pour over the remaining oil, the wine and the milk. Cover and cook on a low heat for about 3 hours, shaking the saucepan but never stirring. Remove the dish from the heat and place some paper towels between the pan and the lid. Leave to rest for 10-15 minutes before serving.

# verduzzo (friulano)

There are two distinct types of Verduzzo. Verduzzo Friulano is cultivated primarily in the plain and thrives on clay soils and rocky terrain, such as those of Grave del Friuli. It is usually vinified dry and produces a wine with fresh, broad perfumes of apples and pears.

When cultivated in hilly zones in marly soils, such as those of the Colli Orientali, it is used to make sweet, full-bodied wines, which have good potential for ageing. Within the Colli Orientali is the sub-zone of Ramandolo, whose vineyards are located around the communes of Nimis, Tarcento and Ramandolo. This sub-zone lends its name to a fruity sweet or semi-sweet wine made from Verduzzo. The wine's richness is the result of either late harvesting or a light drying. Ramandolos are often matured in oak. The great variation in style – from light and elegant to opulent and rich – depends upon the intentions of the winemaker.

## TASTING NOTE

Dry: Straw yellow with green highlights. Light scents of apples, pears, apricots and almonds. Sweet: Yellow gold. Floral and creamy notes on the nose. Full-bodied. Good acidity balances the broad, honeyed fruit. Some tasters find hints of candied orange peel on the nose.

## FOOD PAIRINGS

Dry: Fish, seafood, vegetable risotto, mature cheese. Sweet: Plain pastry, strudel. Some Friulani suggest that it is an excellent teatime alternative.

### GNOCCHI ALL'ANTICA CARNIA

SERVES 6
- 1 kilo/ 4 cups potatoes
- 250 g/2 cups flour
- 75 g/1/2 cup aged Carnico cheese
- 50 g/3 tbsp butter
- 70 g/3 tbsp sugar
- 2 eggs
- cinnamon
- nutmeg
- salt

PREPARATION

Boil and mash the potatoes. Then mix them with the flour, 2 tbsp of cheese, the egg, 1 tbsp of sugar, a little nutmeg and a pinch of salt. Knead well, until a smooth elastic dough is attained. Then form the gnocchi from the dough. Boil the gnocchi in a large pan of boiling water for around 15 minutes. Drain the gnocchi and dress it with melted butter and sprinkle with the remaining sugar and the cinnamon.

### DOC AND DOCG

**VENETO**

Lison-Pramaggiore Verduzzo, Piave Verduzzo

**FRIULI VENEZIA-GIULIA**

Colli Orientali del Friuli Verduzzo friulano, Colli Orientali del Friuli Ramandolo, Annia Verduzzo friulano, Aquileia Verduzzo friulano, Latisana Verduzzo friulano, Isonzo Verduzzo friulano

# vermentino

This Malvasian sub-variety came to Italy from Spain, by way of Corsica, during the late 14th century. It most likely arrived in Liguria before spreading south to Sardinia. It is a problematic variety: when it is good it is refreshing and flavorful. The variety tends to show at its best when grown in seaside zones, where it makes wines intended for early drinking.

## LIGURIA

Ligurian viticulture is characterized by terraces carved from the cliffs that descend vertiginously toward the sea. Here, Vermentino is a component in a number of elegant and aromatic dry whites, including those from the Cinque Terre, Colli di Luni, Riviera Liguri di Ponente, Golfo del Tigullio and Colline di Levanto zones. It is also a component in Cinque Terre Schiacchetrá. This wine is made from semi-dried grapes, has a minimum alcohol level of 17%, and must be aged for at least one year before being released on the market. It varies from lightly to fully sweet in style. A fortified version is also produced.

## SARDINIA

Vermentino arrived in Sardinia at the end of the 19th century, and seems to have found its ideal habitat in the Gallura zone on the northern part of the island. The granite-based soil found in this area gives local Vermentino a decidedly steely, attractively bitter note. The DOCG production zone includes the entire province of Sassari and part of the province of Nuoro. Vermentino di Gallura, an aromatic dry wine, is made from a minimum of 95% Vermentino and has a minimum alcohol level of 12%. With 13% alcohol, it can be labelled *superiore*. The Vermentino di Sardegna production zone includes the entire island. Within this denomination are dry, sweet and sparkling wines composed of at least 85% Vermentino. These wines usually have a minimum alcohol level of 12%. When they have a minimum alcohol level of 14%, they may be labelled *superiore*. The Alghero DOC makes a semi-sparkling Vermentino in both dry and sweet versions.

## TUSCANY

In Tuscany, Vermentino is in the blends of a number of dry whites, including those of Bolgheri, Val di Cornai, Candia dei Colli Apuani, Montescudaio and Montergio di Massaa Marittima.

## TASTING NOTE

The ideal Vermentino is pale gold with pea-green highlights. On the refreshing, mildly aromatic nose, one often finds notes of wild herbs, which a friend once described as "a haunting touch of marijuana." On the palate, there is a lightly saline element as well as very slight peachy tones. There is often a bracing lemon sorbet-like acidity on the bitter-sweet finish. The slightly grainy texture of Vermentino reminds me of that found in Chenin Blanc.

## SYNONYMS

Uva Sapaiola, Formentino, Malvasia Grossa, Malvasie Précoce d'Espagna, Malvoisie à Gros Grains.

## FOOD PAIRINGS

Seafood, grilled fish, fish mousse, grilled vegetables.

---

### VERMENTINO NERO

This is considered to be a variation of white Vermentino. It is found principally in Tuscany and Liguria, where it may play a small role in the blend of Colli Luni Red.

| DOC AND DOCG | TUSCANY |
|---|---|

**TUSCANY**

Bolgheri Vermentino, Candia dei Colli Apuani, Monteregio di Massa Marittima Vermentino

**LIGURIA**

Colli di Luni Bianco, Colli di Luni Vermentino, Colline di Levanto Bianco, Riviera Ligure di Ponente Vermentino

**SARDINIA**

Vermentino di Sardegna (also sparkling), Vermentino di Gallura, Alghero Vermentino

## CACCIUCCO

SERVES 6

• Assorted fish: 2 kilos/4¹/² lb palombo, monkfish, angler fish, moray eel, scorfano, gurnard, gronco
• 500 g/1 lb 2 oz octopus and squid
• 12 prawns
• 1 kilo/3³/⁴ cups ripe tomatoes
• 150 ml/3/4 cup extra virgin olive oil
• 4 garlic cloves
• onion, chopped
• carrot, chopped
• celery, chopped
• parsley
• 1 chili pepper
• 125 ml/1/2 cup dry white wine
• pieces of bread
• salt and pepper

PREPARATION

Clean the large fish, removing their heads, which will be used later. Clean the smaller fish, keeping them whole. Fry the onion, carrot, celery, parsley, the chili pepper and three cloves of garlic in oil. Salt and pepper. When the vegetables have softened, add the octopus and squid, which have been cut into pieces. When all the liquid has evaporated from the pan, add the white wine. When the wine has evaporated, add the tomatoes (which have been peeled and de-seeded). When the octopus and squid have cooked remove them from the pan and set aside. To the heated pan add the fish heads and the smaller fish. Cook for around 25 minutes, adding a little hot water from time to time. Remove the fish heads from the sauce. If the sauce is too dense dilute it with a little water. Put the large fish, which have been cut into pieces, and the small fish into the tomato sauce mixture and cook them over a low heat for around 15 minutes, adding a little hot water as needed. At this point, put the octopus and squid back in the pan and add the prawns. Bring to a boil for around 15 minutes. Serve in individual soup bowls on top of a piece of toasted bread, which has been rubbed with garlic.

## BURIDDA OF CUTTLEFISH

SERVES 6

• 1¹/² kilos/3 lb 5 oz cuttlefish
• 6 ripe pulped tomatoes
• 400 g/3 cups fresh peas
• 1 onion, finely chopped
• 2 cloves garlic
• 20 g/ 2 tbsp of parsley, chopped
• 25 g/1 tbsp capers
• 125 ml/1/2 cup dry white wine
• 125 ml/1/2 cup extra-virgin olive oil
• salt and pepper

PREPARATION

Clean the cuttlefish, removing the mouth, bones, eyes and ink sack. Wash with care and cut the cuttlefish into strips or pieces. Then sauté the pieces in a drop or two of oil along with the chopped garlic. When the cuttlefish begins to turn golden, add the tomato pulp, the capers, 1/2 cup of wine and season with salt and pepper. Cover and cook for around an hour over a low heat. If necessary, add a ladle of stock to keep the fish from sticking to the pan. Halfway through the cooking time, add the peas, and a few minutes before serving, sprinkle with chopped parsley.

## BAKED MULLET

SERVES 4

• 350 g/3/4 lb mullet
• 60 ml/4 tbsp extra-virgin olive oil
• salt
• 60 ml/4 tbsp red wine vinegar
• 125 ml/1/2 cup dry white wine
• freshly ground pepper
• salt

PREPARATION

Clean the fish under running water. Dry them and put them in a greased ovenproof pan. Salt the fish and dress them with oil and vinegar. Bake for 15 minutes at 160°/320°F. Then add the white wine and let it cook for a further 15 minutes. Remove the fish from the oven, filet them and serve with their cooking juices and a dash of freshly ground pepper.

# vernaccia (white and black grape)

The name Vernaccia may be derived from *vermaculus*, a Latin term used to define all that comes from a given place. Other etymologists believe the name stems from Vernazza, a town in Liguria's Cinque Terre zone. Whatever the case, Vernaccia is the name of three completely distinct varieties. Two are white, one is red.

## VERNACCIA DI SAN GIMIGNANO

This Vernaccia is believed to have been planted around the town of San Gimignano in the 13th century by Vieri de' Bardi, a native of Liguria. Wines made from this variety soon found their way to London shops, where they were offered for sale under the name of Vernage. Vernaccia proved so popular, that during the late 15th century cuttings of the vine were taken to Lombardy and to the Marche. However, Vernaccia did not thrive when planted beyond the temperate hillsides around San Gimignano. Vernaccia di San Gimignano added to its long and well-documented history by becoming one of Italy's very first DOC wines. Thirty years later it earned the even more esteemed DOCG denomination. It is one of the smallest zones in Tuscany, with around 850 hectares (2,099 acres) under vine. Its vineyards are planted at around 280 meters (919 feet) above sea level on a mix of yellow sand, clay and volcanic rock.

### TASTING NOTE

Straw yellow. It is lightly aromatic, with notes of sage, dried flowers and broom. On the palate it is subdued.

### SYNONYMS

Vernaccia.

### FOOD PAIRINGS

Ribollita (dry soup), fricasseed rabbit. The traditional pairing is with eels from the Bolsena.

## VERNACCIA DI ORISTANO

This Vernaccia was most likely introduced to Sardinia by the Phoenicians, although some believe that the Spanish brought it to the island toward the end of the 14th century. It is one of Sardina's most important varieties, even though its cultivation is limited to the lower Tirso valley in the province of Oristano. Vernaccia di Oristano has a minimum alcohol level of 15%. When the wine has a minimum of 15.5% and has been aged for at least three years it can be labelled *superiore*. The *riserva* undergoes four years of ageing. The *liquoroso dolce* version undergoes 2 years of ageing and has an alcohol level of 16.5%, while the *liquorosi secco* has an alcohol level of 18%.

### TASTING NOTE

Amber to gold. On the nose, one finds notes of toasted hazelnuts and faint peachy tones. It is rich and full-bodied, with a nutty aftertaste.

### FOOD PAIRINGS

Locally it is used as an aperitif (served with the *bottarga*) or as an after-dinner drink. It may also be paired with marzipan-based desserts or blue cheeses.

### SYNONYMS

Vernaccia bianca, Varnaccia, Garnaccia, Cranaccia, Granazza, Vernaccia Austera.

| DOC AND DOCG |
|---|
| **TUSCANY** |
| Vernaccia di San Giminiano |
| Colli dell'Etruria Centrale |
| **SARDINIA** |
| Vernaccia di Oristano |

*Tuscany: San Gimignano*

## RIBOLLITA

SERVES 6

- 300 g/1¹ᐟ² cup dried broad beans
- 1/2 red cabbage
- 1/2 green cabbage
- 200 g/1 cup spinach
- 250 g/1 cup ripe tomatoes
- 400 g/1 lb stale bread
- 1 ham bone or bacon rind
- 1 potato
- 1 handful of parsley
- 1 celery stalk
- 1 carrot
- 1/2 large onion
- 2 cloves of garlic
- thyme
- grated pecorino cheese
- 2000 ml/8 cups stock
- 150 ml/1/2 cup extra virgin olive oil
- salt and pepper

PREPARATION

Cook the beans with bacon rind (or a ham bone). Meanwhile, fry the onion, garlic, celery, carrot and parsley. When the onion changes color, add the chopped vegetables and the thyme. Then the tomatoes and salt and pepper. Cook for a few minutes. Then add the liquid in which the beans have cooked and the bacon rind (ham bone). Puree half of the beans and add them to cooking liquid. Boil the soup for a few minutes. Then pour into serving bowls in which a piece of bread has been placed. Garnish with the remaining whole beans.

If you like, you can serve the soup "re-boiled" (ribolitta) by leaving it until the following day. Pour a little olive oil in the center of the cooking pan and slowly (re) boil the soup, taking care that it does not stick to the bottom of the pan.

## SPAGHETTI "ALLA BUTTARIGA"

SERVES 4

- 280 g/10 oz spaghetti
- 50 g/3 tbsp sliced salted mullet roe
- 1 clove of garlic
- 30 g/2 tbsp chopped parsley
- 1 pinch of chili pepper
- 100 ml/ 8 tbsp oil • salt

PREPARATION

Boil water in a large saucepan and only add a little salt as the mullet roe used in the sauce is very salty. Cook the spaghetti until "al dente" (firm). In the meantime, pour the oil into a frying pan and gently fry the garlic, add the parsley and chili pepper and cook on a high flame. Then add 3/4 of the mullet roe cut into slices. Drain the spaghetti and toss in the frying pan with the sauce. Serve on individual plates, decorating with the remaining mullet roe.

## VERNACCIA NERA

This variety is found in Umbria and the Marche. Its best-known DOC is Vernaccia di Serrapetrona, whose 40 hectares of vineyards are found around the tiny town of Serrapetrona (population under 1000) in the province of Macerata, some 19 miles (30 kilometers) from Ancona in the Marche. The vineyards are on average 500 meters (1,640 feet) above sea level. In this zone the winters are cold and summers are mild. A portion of the grapes used to make this naturally sparkling red are hung up to dry for a few months after harvest. These grapes are usually pressed in January, and the resulting rich, dense must is then blended with wine made from fresh grapes from the same vintage. This wine's greatest proponent is Alberto Quacquarini, whose family has been producing Vernaccia di Serrapetrona for four generations. The wine is made in both dry and sweet versions.

## TASTING NOTE

Ruby red. Its perfume is vaguely reminiscent of raspberries and dried flowers. It ranges from dry to lightly sweet, according to the intentions of the producer.

## SYNONYMS

Vernaccia di Cerreto, Morone, Vernaccia Selvatica.

## FOOD PAIRINGS

*Crescia fogliata*: this strudel made with apples, dried figs, raisins and walnuts is a specialty of Macerata province. Also sponge cake soaked in Vernaccia and served with cream and red berry fruits.

### RICE CAKE

SERVES 6
- 500 g/2¹ᐟ² cups rice • 1 liter/4 cups milk
- 300 g/1¹ᐟ² cups sugar • the zest of one orange
- the zest of one lemon • 300 g/1¹ᐟ² cups bread crumbs • 200 g/1 cup raisins • 125 ml/1/2 cup rum
- 6 espresso cups/150 ml/1/2 cup coffee
- 150 g/1/2 cup dried figs • 150 g/1¹ᐟ⁴ cups corn flour
- 80 g/3 oz powdered bitter chocolate
- 50 ml/3 tbsp extra-virgin olive oil
- 150 g/1 cup flour
- 1000 g/6¹ᐟ² cups apples and pears, sliced
- 50 g/1/4 cup powdered sugar

PREPARATION
Cook the rice in abundant salted water. Drain the rice and put it in a large saucepan. Add all the other ingredients – except the powdered sugar – and cook over a low heat for a few minutes, mixing continuously. Pour this mixture into a greased baking pan and bake at a medium temperature for around 1 hour. Sprinkle with powdered sugar and serve.

### DOC AND DOCG

**MARCHE**
Vernaccia di Serrapetrona DOC

# vespaiolo

Vespaiolo's name is most likely
derived from the fact that its ripe
berries attract large numbers of
wasps (*vespe*). This variety is found
mainly in the hillsides of Veneto's
Breganze zone, which lies south of
Vicenza. There are two Vespaiolo-
based DOC wines. Breganze
Vespaiolo is a light dry white, which
is, for the most part, consumed
locally.

The second is Torcolato, the opulent dessert wine made famous by Fausto Maculan. This wine is made from semi-dried grapes and has a minimum alcohol level of 14%. According to Maculan it takes around five years for Torcolato to reach its peak, and it can continue to improve for at least another five years. In great vintages, the wine can last twenty years or more.

## TASTING NOTE

Dry Vespaiola: Medium-straw. On the nose, one finds scents of apples and straw. Often a very slight hint of honey emerges on the nose and palate.

Torcolato: Deep golden yellow. On the nose, one finds floral and honeyed tones. On the palate the wine is opulent.

## SYNONYMS

Bresparola Bianco, Vespaia, Vesparola, Uva vespera, Bespaia, Vespera, Vespaiola.

## FOOD PAIRINGS

Dry: Locally this wine is often paired with a dish of asparagus and egg drizzled with mimosa sauce. Another favorite partner is polenta and bacalá.

Torcolato: Panettone and other plain sponge cakes, sweet biscuits, or even with blue cheeses or foie gras.

| DOC AND DOCG |
| --- |
| **VENETO** |
| Breganze Vespaiolo, Breganze Bianco, Breganze Torcolato |

## BACCALÀ ALLA VICENTINA

SERVES 12
- 1 kilo/2 lb 3 oz dried salt cod
- 500 g/4 cups onion
- 1 litre/4 cups extra-virgin olive oil
- 3 to 4 anchovies
- 500 ml/2 cups fresh milk
- 100 g/1 cup flour
- 50 g/1/2 cup grated Parmesan cheese
- 1 bunch of parsley, finely chopped
- salt and pepper

PREPARATION

Soak the well-beaten dried salt cod in cold water, changing the water every 4 hours, for 2 to 3 days. Open the fish lengthwise, remove the guts and bones. Cut it into square pieces, equal in size. Finely slice the onion and fry it in oil. Add the anchovies, which have been gutted and cut into pieces. Turn off the heat, add the parsley. Spread this mixture on the bottom of an ovenproof dish. Dredge the cod in flour; put it in the ovenproof pan with the onion. Cover the fish with the rest of the fried onions, adding the milk, the grated cheese and salt and pepper. Add the oil, until the fish is covered. Cook over a very low heat for around 4$^{1/2}$ hours, shaking the pan every now and then. The cooking time for dried salt cod varies dramatically.

Serve hot with a slice of polenta. Baccala is great after 12-24 hours.

# Other Emerging Varieties

# casetta

Legend has it that this variety originated in the small San Valentino valley in Trentino, and spread to the parallel valley of Lagarina. Today, it is cultivated in the province of Trento and that of Verona. Casetta, which takes its name from a family who lived in the hamlet of Marani, had all but disappeared by 1990 when Albino Armani (of the estate which bears his name) and Tiziano Tomasi (whose family estate is La Ca' Da Lora) set up a project to study the variety with the Istituto Agrario di San Michele all'Adige, where Tomasi works as a researcher. Casetta is rich in polyphenols, has high acidity and relatively high tannins. Casetta-based wines can easily continue to evolve for ten years or more. "This is not a modern wine," warns Tomasi.

## SYNONYMS
Maranela, Foja, Tonda, Lambrusco a Folgia Tonda.

## TASTING NOTE
Very deeply concentrated ruby. Zippy acidity. On the nose, one finds tar, earthy and mineral notes. On the palate, the wine combines herbaceous (grassy) notes with plum, raspberries, and wild cherry notes.

## FOOD PAIRINGS
Spicy stews (goulash) and braised meats, game.

# dindarella

This variety is indigenous to the area around Verona, and is often found in the blends of local DOCs, such as Valdadige, Garda Orientale and Valpolicella. The relatively small size of the production zone, however, does not guarantee straightforward nomenclature: Dindarella is also widely known as Pelara. The variety's relatively thick skin makes it ideal for semi-drying. Recently it has been regaining ground in Valpolicella. It is occasionally vinified on its own.

## SYNONYMS
Pelara, Dindarela, Bindarela and Bigolona.

## TASTING NOTE
Pale ruby. On the nose, it is lightly aromatic, with hints of red pepper. Lively on the palate.

## FOOD PAIRINGS
Delicately flavored antipasti.

# durello

The name of this very vigorous vine is derived from its tough (*dura*) skin. Its most important DOC zone lies in the Lessini mountains in the provinces of Verona and Vicenza, not far from the Soave zone. Lessini Durello is a light dry white with a minimum alcohol level of 10%. When it has an alcohol level of 11% it can be labelled *superiore*. This grape's high acidity makes it ideal for sparkling wine production, and Lessini Durello Spumante is rapidly becoming the aperitif of choice in Soave and Verona. Durello may be used as a lesser component in such DOC wines as Breganze Bianco, Gambellara and Lugana.

## SYNONYMS
Durella, Durelo, Durola, Rabbiosa, Cagnina.

## TASTING NOTE
Its color is pale straw with green highlights. It has extremely crisp acidity and very light, lemony fruit, with some floral notes.

## FOOD PAIRINGS
Very delicate antipasti. Locally, sparkling versions are often offered as aperitifs.

# longanesi

This variety's name is linked to that of the Longanesi brothers, whose estate is at Bagnacavallo near Ravenna. In the 1950s Antonio Longanesi discovered the variety planted in a vineyard among Trebbiano, Uva d'Oro and Cagnina, and decided to cultivate. The Longanesi grape, which the local producers continue to call *Bursòn* (Antonio's own nickname), eventually became the principal component in a wine that bears the grape name, and obtained IGT recognition. This variety is believed to have been planted by the Romans in the pine forest of Classe, with the first recorded citation of it growing in the current area of production dating to the 17th century. It is cultivated especially in the communes of Bagnacavallo, Lugo, Fusignano, Costignola and Russi. Sometimes vinified as a varietal, it also gives interesting results when blended with other varieties, such as Sangiovese, Merlot and Cabernet Sauvignon.

## SYNONYMS
Bursòn.

## TASTING NOTE
Red with purplish highlights. One finds notes of violets, plums, spices and caramel on the nose, which carry through onto the palate.

## FOOD PAIRINGS
At its best with strongly flavored dishes, roasts and mature cheeses.

# oseleta

Oseleta is a rare and precious gem. It has everything: excellent structure, full flavor and silky elegance. Yet it was on the verge of extinction in the early 1970s. Why? Because in those days in its home ground, the Veneto's Valpolicella zone, the emphasis was on quantity, and Oseleta is a notoriously low yielder. Fortunately the grape was rescued by enlightened viticulturists in the province of Verona. For years, The Masi Technical Group, which is responsible for the oenology and experiments conducted by the Masi Wine Company, examined Oseleta's potential and worked to establish new vineyard sites for the variety. The result of their experimentation is the Oseleta-based wine, Osar. The success this wine has achieved has led to plantings by other wine estates in the zone. According to the DOC regulations Oseleta may be used in small percentages in the blends of Valpolicella and Amarone, although this is seldom acted upon.

## SYNONYMS
Oselina.

## TASTING NOTE
Deep, near opaque ruby. Good structure. Zippy acidity adds zest to the rich, ripe-plum fruit flavors. Full-bodied and satisfying.

## FOOD PAIRINGS
Sautéed red meats and mature cheese.

# passerina

The origins of this vine are uncertain. It does, however, share many genetic factors with Trebbiano Toscano, from which it may be derived. It is found in Marche, Umbria and Lazio, where it is used in small percentages in blended whites. The variety's high level of acidity makes it a candidate for sparkling wine production. Tenuta Cocci Grifoni makes a Passerina Brut.

## SYNONYMS
Cacciadebiti, Caccione, Camplese, Pagadebit Gentile, Sciacciadebito, Uva d'oro, Trebbiano di Teramo, Uva Passa, Uva Passera.

## TASTING NOTE
Straw colored. It has zesty acidity. Earthy notes of green apple and straw on the nose. On the palate, one finds mineral notes.

## FOOD PAIRINGS
Lightly flavored fish-based antipasti or rice dishes.

# perricone

This vine is native to western Sicily and adds body and alcohol as a minor component in many of the region's reds. As Jadid, Rapitalá's attractive and fruity *novello*, demonstrates, Perricone is well suited to carbonic maceration. Other producers will most certainly follow this example and increase the variety's participation in their own *novello* wines.

## SYNONYMS
Perricone Nero, Pignatello, Niuru, Pignateddu, Quaraccia, Nieddara.

## TASTING NOTE
Ruby. Soft, lightly floral perfumes as well as a touch of anise on the nose. Good body. Medium to good tannins.

## FOOD PAIRINGS
Very delicate antipasti. Locally, sparkling versions are often offered as an aperitif.

# timorasso

Timorasso originated in Piedmont's Novi Ligure and Tortona zones. Before phylloxera infestation struck the region in the late 19th century, Timorasso was among Piedmont's most widely planted white varieties, and it was cultivated as far away as Genova, where it was used as a table grape. Post-pylloxera, many of its vineyards were replanted with other varieties. Timorasso's fortunes were again diminished by the international success of Cortese di Gavi in the 1960s and 1970s, when it became easier for producers to market the already established Cortese variety. Fortunately, there were winemakers who believed in Timorasso's potential. This variety's greatest supporter is Walter Massa, who makes elegant, age-worthy Timorassos at his estate, Vigneti Massa, in Piedmont's Colli Tortonesi area.

## SYNONYMS
Timoraccio, Timorazze, Morasso

## TASTING NOTE
Pale golden-straw. A restrained nose of almond and hazelnut notes, along with a seductive touch of honey. An Italian friend defines this wine as being reminiscent of Torrone di Cremona, a soft, creamy hazelnut-filled nougat. The wine is dry with good body and firm structured. With age, it becomes richer on the palate and slightly spicy notes emerge.

## FOOD PAIRINGS
White meats, spaghetti with an onion-based sauce.

# tocai rosso

Tocai Rosso is principally grown in the Berici hills, south of the Veneto city of Vicenza. Popular legend suggests that the progenitor of this variety was brought to this area from Hungary during the reign of Maria Theresa by a carpenter returning to his home in Barbarano Vicenza after fulfilling his military service. Be that as it may, Tocai Rosso has nothing to do with Hungarian Tokay. It is, in fact, none other than Garnacha Nero, a variety widely planted in Spain, France and Australia. As Grenache Noir, it is the main component in Provence's most celebrated rosé, Tavel.

Tocai Rosso's production zone is centered on the commune of Babarano, which has its own DOC denomination.

| DOC AND DOCG |
|---|
| **VENETIA** |
| Colli Berici Tocai Rosso |

## TASTING NOTE

A strawberry-juice red, tinged with rose. Fresh on the nose, with an amalgam of wild blueberry and raspberry fruit on the palate.

## SYNONYMS

Grenache, Garnacha, Cannonau.

## FOOD PAIRINGS

Ideal with the Vicenza specialities of *bacalá* (dried salt cod) and *coniglio farcito* (stuffed rabbit). Turkey with pomegranate sauce has also been suggested.

# The Festival of Taste

*compiled by Mario Busso and Carlo Vischi*

The selection presented here is the summary of an extraordinary festival of taste; an easy and accessible guide to the best national oenological production of Italian grape varieties. The wines and producers that we have selected satisfy, with their offer of quality, the entirely spiritual need of those who, like us, love to find in wine the gesture of the research and tradition of a location; of those who, like us, love to receive confirmation from things which are well known but, above all, face the search for all things new, which is often nothing more than the rediscovery of things which have gone before, presented with experimental and innovative criterion.

We have been supported by a brilliant team of professional tasters and wine enthusiasts.

The confrontation of this "professionalism" has made it possible to taste the wines with the scientific methodology of experts and with the criteria of pleasure of hedonists.

The long list that follows contains no "excommunications", just the clear addresses of those producers who seem to have been struck by the incurable human ambition of taking their commitment further, focusing on continued improvement.

In this list we have followed three assessment criteria and used them to indicate several producers.

- The wines which made a positive impression in their category are marked with a heart, the symbol of seduction and enjoyment.

- We thought it was a good idea to mark some producers with the sign of the new moon, as they are emerging in the market with a symbiotic combination that binds the personality and strength of the wine produced with the grape variety and the territory.

- The third criterion was that of indicating some wineries which combine quality and quantity with a price policy that encourages the general consumer and young people to approach wine without economic fears. They honor Italian oenology, offering an approach to wine which quenches the thirst for everyday drinking but also that of whetting the appetite for the recipes presented when entertaining at home.

# key

The following list includes the wines in alphabetical order, region by region from North to South. Those highlighted in fuchsia are red wines, while those in yellow are white. The rosé wines are highlighted in pink.

The abbreviations next to the individual wines should be read as follows:
DOC: wine with denomination of controlled origin
DOCG: wine with denomination of controlled and guaranteed origin
IGT: territorial geographical indication
VDT: table wines
a/o: and/or

Wine particularly appreciated within its category

Emerging producer

Excellent quality/price ratio and easy to find on the market

Member of the Wine Tourism Movement

## VALLE D'AOSTA

### VALLE D'AOSTA ARNAD-MONTJOVET doc

*Vines: Nebbiolo (minimo 70%), Dolcetto a/o Vien de Nus a/o Pinot Nero a/o Neyret a/o Freisa (max 30%)*

Cooperativa La Kiuva
frazione Pied de Ville 42
11020 Arnad AO
tel. 0125/966351

### VALLE D'AOSTA CHAMBAVE MOSCATO doc

*Vines: Moscato bianco*

Coop. La Crotta di Vegneron
piazza Roncas 2
11023 Chambave AO
tel. 0166/46670

### VALLE D'AOSTA CHAMBAVE MOSCATO PASSITO doc

*Vines: Moscato bianco*

Coop. La Crotta di Vegneron
piazza Roncas 2
11023 Chambave AO
tel. 0166/46670

### VALLE D'AOSTA DONNAS doc

*Vines: Nebbiolo (min. 85%), Freisa a/o Neyret (Max 15%)*

Caves Cooperatives de Donnas
via Roma 97 - 11020 Donnas AO
tel. 0125/807098

### VALLE D'AOSTA ENFER D'ARVIER doc

*Vines: Petit Rouge (min. 85%), Vien de Nus a/o Neyret a/o Dolcetto a/o Pinot Nero a/o Gamey (Max 15%)*

Coop Co- Enfer
via Corrado Gex
11010 Arvier AO
tel. 0165/99238

### VALLE D'AOSTA FUMIN doc

*Vines: Fumin (min. 90%)*

Caves de Onze Commmunes
località Urbains 14
11010 Aymavilles AO
tel. 0165/902912

Coop. La Crotta di Vegneron
piazza Roncas 2
11023 Chambave AO
tel. 0166/46670

Ferres Grosjean
frazione Ollignan
11020 Quart AO
tel. 0165/765283

Les Cretes
località Villetos 50
11010 Aymavilles AO
tel. 0165/902274 cuore

### VALLE D'AOSTA PETIT ROUGE doc

*Vines: Petit Rouge (min. 90%)*

Istitut Agricole Regional
regione La Rochère 1/a
11100 Aosta AO
tel. 0165/215811

### VALLE D'AOSTA TORRETTE doc

*Vines: Petit Rouge (min. 70%), Pinot Nero a/o Gamey a/o Fumin a/o Vien de Nus a/o Dolcetto a/o Mayolet a/o Premetta (Max 30%)*

Caves de Onze Commmunes
località Urbains 14
11010 Aymavilles AO
tel. 0165/902912

Costantino Charrere
Les Moulin 28
11010 Aymavilles AO
tel. 0165/902135

Ferres Grosjean
frazione Ollignan
11020 Quart AO
tel. 0165/765283

Les Cretes
località Villetos 50
11010 Aymavilles AO
tel. 0165/902274

### VDT BIANCHI

Ezio Voyat
via Arberaz 31
11023 Chambave AO
tel. 0166/46139
*Le Gazzelle Bianco (Moscato)*

### VDT ROSSI

Costantino Charrere
Les Moulin 28
11010 Aymavilles AO
tel. 0165/902135
*Vin de La Sabla (Petit Rouge+Barbera+Fumin)*

Ezio Voyat
via Arberaz 31
11023 Chambave AO
tel. 0166/46139
*Rosso Le Muraglie (Petit Rouge+altre)*

## PIEDMONT

### ALBUGNANO doc

*Vines: Nebbiolo (min. 85%), Freisa a/o Barbera a/o Bonarda (max 15%)*

Cantina Sociale del Freisa
via San Giovanni 6
14022 Castelnuovo
Don Bosco AT
tel. 011/9876117

Pianfiorito
Loc. S. Stefano 6
14020 Albugnano AT
tel. 011/9920665

### ASTI docg

*Vines: Moscato bianco*

Banfi
Via V. Veneto 22
15019 Strevi AL
tel. 0144/363485

Cantina Sociale di Canelli
Via Luigi Bosca 30
14053 Canelli AT
tel. 0141/823347

Cascina Fonda
Loc. Cascina Fonda 45
12056 Mango CN
tel. 0173/677156

Cascina Pian d'Or.
Fraz. Bosi 15
12056 Mango d'Alba CN
tel. 0141/89440

Nuova Perlino
Via Valgera 94
14100 Asti
tel. 0141/446811

Enrico Serafino
Frazione Valpone 79
12043 Canale CN
tel. 0173/967111

Martini & Rossi
C.so V. Emanuele 42
10123 Torino TO
tel. 011/81081

### BARBARESCO docg
*Vines: Nebbiolo*

Albino Rocca
Via Rabajà 15
12050 Barbaresco CN
tel. 0173/635145

Bruno Rocca
Via Rabajà 29
12050 Barbaresco CN
tel. 0173/635112

Castello di Neive
Via Castelborgo 1
12057 Neive CN
tel. 0173/67171

Gaja
Via Torino 36/a
12050 Barbaresco CN
tel. 0173/635158

La Spinetta
frazione Annunziata 17
14054 Castagnole Lanze AT
tel. 0141/877396

Molino
Via Ausario 5
12050 Treiso CN
tel. 0173/638384

Poderi Colla
Fraz. S. Rocco Seno d'Elvio 82
12051 Alba CN
tel. 0173/290148

Produttori del Barbaresco
Via Torino 52
12050 Barbaresco CN
tel. 0173/635139

Sottimano
Loc. Cottà 21
12057 Neive CN
tel. 0173/635186

Tenute Cisa Asinari-Marchesi
di Gresy
Via Rabajà 43
12050 Barbaresco CN
tel. 0173/635222

Varaldo
Via Secondine 2
12050 Barbaresco CN
tel. 0173/635160

Vignaioli Elvio Pertinace
Loc. Pertinace 2
12050 Treiso CN
tel. 0173/442238

### BARBERA D'ALBA doc
*Vines: Barbera*

Altare
Cascina Nuova 51
Fraz. Annunziata
12064 La Morra CN
tel. 0173/50835

Azelia
Via Alba-Barolo 53
12060 Castiglione Falletto CN
tel. 0173/62859

Cascina Cà Rossa
Loc. Case Sparse 56
12043 Canale CN
tel. 0173/98348

Cascina Luisin
Loc. Rabajà 23
12050 Barbaresco CN
tel. 0173/635154

Collina Serragrilli
Via Serragrilli 30
12057 Neive CN
tel. 0173/677010

Commendator G.B. Burlotto
via V. Emanuele 28
12060 Verduno CN
tel. 0171/470122

Cordero di Montezemolo
Fraz. Annunziata 67/b
12064 La Morra CN
tel. 0173/50344

Enzo Boglietti
Via Roma 37
12064 La Morra CN
tel. 0173/50330

Funtanin
Via Torino 191
12043 Canale CN
tel. 0173/979488

Gianni Voerzio
S. da Loreto 1/bis
12064 La Morra CN
tel. 0173/509194

Hilberg - Pasquero
Via Bricco Gatti 16
12040 Priocca CN
tel. 0173/616197

La Cerretta
P.zza Cappellano 9
12050 Serralunga d'Alba CN
tel. 0173/613108

Livia Fontana
Via Pugnane 12
12060 Castiglione Falletto CN
tel. 0173/62844

Marcarini
P.zza Martiri 2
12064 La Morra CN
tel. 0173/50222

Marsaglia
Via Mussone 2
12050 Castellinaldo CN
tel. 0173/213048

Matteo Correggia
Via S. Stefano Roero 124
12043 Canale CN
tel. 0173/97009

Monchiero - Carbone
Via S. Stefano Roero 2
12043 Canale CN
tel. 0173/95568

Negro
Cascina Riveri
Fraz. S. Anna 1
12040 Monteu Roero CN
tel. 0173/90252

Principiano
Via Alba 19
12065 Monforte d'Alba CN
tel. 0173/787158

Podere Ruggeri Corsini
Via Garibaldi 14
12065 Monforte d'Alba CN
tel. 0173/78625

Taliano
Corso A. Manzoni 24
12046 Montà CN
tel. 0173/976512

Teo Costa
Via. San Salvario 1
12050 Castellinaldo CN
tel. 0173/213066

Terre da Vino
Via Bergesia 6
12060 Barolo CN
tel. 0173/564611

Terre del Barolo
Via Alba-Barolo 5
12060 Castiglione Falletto CN
tel. 0173/262053

 Vajra
Via delle Viole 25
Loc. Vergne
12060 Barolo CN
tel. 0173/56257

Vigna Rionda - Massolino
P.zza Cappellano 8
12050 Serralunga d'Alba CN
tel. 0173/613138

## BARBERA D'ASTI doc

*Vines: Barbera min. 85%;*
*Grignolino a/o Freisa a/o*
*Dolcetto min 15%*

Bava
S. da Monferrato 2
14023 Cocconato d'Asti AT
tel. 0141/907083

Bersano & Riccadonna
P.zza Dante 21
14049 Nizza Monferrato AT
tel. 0141/720211

Braida
Via Roma 94
14030 Rocchetta Tanaro AT
tel. 0141/644113

Cà Bianca Gruppo
Italiani Vini
Reg. Spagna 58
15010 Alice Bel Colle AL
tel. 0144/745420

Cà d' Carussin
Reg. Mariano 27
14050 S. Marzano Oliveto AT
tel. 0141/831358

Cantina Sociale di Nizza
Strada Alessandria 57
14049 Nizza Monferrato
tel. 0141/721348

Cantine Sant'Agata
Reg. Mezzena 19
14030 Scurzolengo AT
tel. 0141/203186

Castello del Poggio
Loc. Il Poggio 9
14038 Portacomaro AT
tel. 0141/202543

Dezzani
C.so Pinin Giachino 140
14023 Cocconato d'Asti AT
tel. 0141/907044

Franco e Mario Scrimaglio
Via Alessandria 67
14049 Nizza Monferrato AT
tel. 0141/721385

Franco M. Martinetti
Via S. Francesco da Paola 18
10123 Torino TO
tel. 011/8395937

Hastae
Piazza Italia 1/bis
14030 Rocchetta Tanaro AT
tel. 0141/644113

Icardi
Via Balbi 30
12053 Castiglione Tinella CN
tel. 0141/855159

l'Post dal Vin
Terre del Barbera
Via Salie 19
14030 Rocchetta Tanaro AT
tel. 0141/644143

Luigi Coppo
Via Alba 66
14053 Canelli AT
tel. 0141/823146

Malgrà
Via Nizza 8
14046 Mombaruzzo AT
tel. 0141/725055

Marchesi Alfieri
Castello Alfieri
14010 S. Martino Alfieri AT
tel. 0141/976288

Michele Chiarlo
S.da Nizza-Canelli 99
14042 Calamandrana AT
tel. 01421/769030

Scarpa
Via Montegrappa 6
14049 Nizza Monferrato AT
tel. 0141/721331

Tenuta La Meridiana
Fraz. Tana Bassa 5
14048 Montegrosso d'Asti AT
tel. 0141/956250

Terre da Vino
Via Bergesia 6
12060 Barolo CN
tel. 0173/564611

Tre Roveri-Maccario
Via Cordara 61
14046 Mombaruzzo AT
tel. 0141/774522

## BARBERA MONFERRATO doc

*Vines: Barbera (min. 85%).*
*Freisa a/o Dolcetto a/o*
*Grignolino (max 15%)*

Accornero
Ca' Cima 1
15049 Vignale Monferrato AL
tel. 0142/933317

Bava
S.da Monferrato 2
14023 Cocconato d'Asti AT
tel. 0141/907083

Cantina Sociale 6 Castelli
frazione Salere 41 n. 3
14041 Agliano AT
tel. 0141/964004

Cantina Sociale di Nizza
Strada Alessandria 57
14049 Nizza Monferrato AT
tel. 0141/721348

Cantina Sociale
Maranzana
Via San Giovanni 20
14040 Maranzana AT
tel. 0141/77927

Cantina Vignaioli
Astibarbera
fraz. San Marzanotto
Loc. Tagliata 314
Asti
tel. 0141/597863

Colle Manora
Via Bozzole 4
15044 Quargnento AL
tel. 0131/219252

F.lli Castino
Via Spessa 40
14041 Agliano Terme AT
tel. 0141/954502

Franco Mondo
Reg. Mariano 33
14050 S. Marzano Oliveto AT
tel. 0141/834096

l'Post dal Vin
Terre del Barbera
Via Salie 19
14030 Rocchetta Tanaro AT
tel. 0141/644143

Valpane
Cascina Valpane 10/I
15039 Ozzano Monferrato AL
tel. 0142/486713

Vicara
Casc. Madonna delle Grazie 5
15030 Rosignano M.to AL
tel. 0141/488054

**BAROLO** docg
*Vines: Nebbiolo*

Aldo Vajra
Via delle Viole 25
Loc. Vergne
12060 Barolo CN
tel. 0173/56257

Altare
Cascina Nuova 51
Fraz. Annunziata
12064 La Morra CN
tel. 0173/50835

Anselma
Loc. S. Giuseppe 38
12065 Monforte d'Alba CN
tel. 0173/787217

Armando Parusso
Loc. Bussia 55
12065 Monforte d'Alba CN
tel. 0173/78257

Azelia
Via Alba-Barolo 53
12060 Castiglione Falletto CN
tel. 0173/62859

Batasiolo
Fraz. Annunziata 87
12064 La Morra CN
tel. 0173/50131

Cascina Ballarin
Fraz. Annunziata
12064 La Morra CN
tel. 0173/50365

Commendator G.B. Burlotto
Via V. Emanuele 28
12060 Verduno CN
tel. 0171/470122

Conterno - Fantino
Via Ginestra 1
Loc. Bricco Bastia
12065 Monforte d'Alba CN
tel. 0173/78204

Cordero di Montezemolo
Fraz. Annunziata 67/b
12064 La Morra CN
tel. 0173/50344

Costa di Bussia
Loc. Bussia 26
12065 Monforte d'Alba CN
tel. 0173/77017

Domenico Clerico
Loc. Manzoni 67
12065 Monforte d'Alba CN
tel. 0173/78171

Franco M. Martinetti
Via S. Francesco da Paola 18
10123 Torino TO
tel. 011/8395937

Giacomo Conterno
Loc. Ornati 2
12065 Monforte d'Alba CN
tel. 0173/78221

Gianfranco Alessandria
Località Manzoni 13
12065 Monforte d'Alba CN
tel. 0173/78576

Gianni Voerzio
S.da Loreto 1/bis
12064 La Morra CN
tel. 0173/509194

Gigi Rosso
Via Alba Barolo 20
12060 Castiglione Falletto CN
tel. 0173/262369

La Cerretta
P.zza Cappellano 9
12050 Serralunga d'Alba CN
tel. 0173/613108

Marcarini
P.zza Martiri 2
12064 La Morra CN
tel. 0173/50222

Marchesi di Barolo
Via Alba 12 - 12060 Barolo CN
tel. 0173/564400

Palladino
P.zza Cappellano 9
12050 Serralunga d'Alba CN
tel. 0173/613108

E. Pira
Via V. Emanuele 1
12060 Barolo CN
tel. 0173/56247

Podere Rocche dei Manzoni
Loc. Manzoni Soprani 3
12065 Monforte d'Alba CN
tel. 0173/78421

Poderi Aldo Conterno
Loc. Bussia 48
12065 Monforte d'Alba CN
tel. 0173/78150

Giuseppe Rinaldi
Via Manforte 3
12060 Barolo CN
tel. 0173/56156

Roberto Voerzio
Loc. Cerreto 1
12064 La Morra CN
tel. 0173/509196

Sandrone
Via Pugnane 4
12060 Barolo CN
tel. 0173/560023

Sylla Sebaste
Via S. Pietro delle Viole 4
12060 Barolo CN
tel. 0173/56266

Terre da Vino
Via Bergesia 6
12060 Barolo CN
tel. 0173/564611

Terre del Barolo
Via Alba-Barolo 5
12060 Castiglione Falletto CN
tel. 0173/262053

**BOCA** doc
*Vines: Nebbiolo (dal 40 al 70%),
Vespolina (dal 20 al 40%),
Bonarda novarese (max 20%)*

Le Piane
Strada delle Piane
28010 Boca NO
tel. 0041/81/4165510

Podere ai Valloni
Via Reg. Traversagna
28010 Boca NO
tel. 011/505911

## BRACHETTO D'ACQUI docg
*Vines: Brachetto*

 Banfi
Via V. Veneto 22
15019 Strevi AL
tel. 0144/363485

 Cà dei Mandorli
Via IV Novembre 5
14040 Castel Rocchero AL
tel. 0141/760131

Castello del Poggio
Loc. Il Poggio 9
14038 Portacomaro AT
tel. 0141/202543

Enrico Serafino
Frazione Valpone 79
12043 Canale CN
tel. 0173/967111

Giorgio Carnevale
Via G. Trombetta 157
14030 Cerro Tanaro AT
tel. 0141/409115

La Dogliola
Reg. Infermiera 226
14051 Bubbio AT
tel. 0144/83557

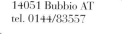 Marenco
P.zza V. Emanuele 10
15019 Strevi AL
tel. 0144/363133

Servetti
Strada Giaccaria 1/A
15061 Cassine AL
tel. 0144/767800

Vecchia Cantina Sociale di
Alice Bel Colle e Sessame
Via Stazione 157
15010 Alice Bel Colle AL
tel. 0144/74114

Viticoltori dell'Acquese
Via IV Novembre 14
15011 Acqui Terme AL
tel. 0144/322008

## BRAMATERRA doc
*Vines: Nebbiolo, localmente
detto Spanna (dal 50 al
70%), Croatina (dal 20 al
30%), Bonarda a/oVespolina
(dal 10 al 20%)*

Barboni Lodovico
Via Pietro Micca
frazione Santa Maria 75
13060 Roasio VC
tel. 0163/860012

Sella
Via IV Novembre 110
13853 Lessona BI
tel. 015/99455

## CAREMA doc
*Vines: Nebbiolo (min. 85%)*

Cantina Produttori Nebbiolo
di Carema
Via Nazionale 28
10010 Carema TO
tel. 0125/811160

Ferrando
Via Torino 599/a
10015 Ivrea TO
tel. 0125/641176

## COLLI TORTONESI
## BARBERA doc
*Vines: Barbera (min. 85%)*

 Cascina Montagnola
S.da Montagnola 1
15058 Viguzzolo AL
tel. 0131/898558

 Mutti
Loc. S. Ruffino 49
15050 Sarezzano AL
tel. 0131/884119

Paolo Poggio
Via Roma 67
15050 Brignano Frascata AL
tel. 0131/784650

 Vigneti Massa
P.zza G. Capsoni 10
15059 Monleale AL
tel. 0131/80302

Volpi
S.S. 10 N° 72
15057 Tortona AL
tel. 0131/821917

## COLLI TORTONESI
## CORTESE doc
*Vines: Cortese (min. 85%)*

Cantina Sociale di Tortona
Via Muraglie Rosse 5
15057 Tortona AL
tel. 0131/861265

Coop. Valli Unite
15057 Cascina Montesoro
Costa Vescovado AL
tel. 0131/838100

 Volpi
S.S. 10 n. 72
15057 Tortona AL
tel. 0131/821917

## COLLINE NOVARESI
## BIANCO doc
*Vines: Erbaluce*

 Rovellotti
Via Tamiotti 3
28074 Ghemme NO
tel. 0163/840478

## COLLINE NOVARESI
## NEBBIOLO doc
*Vines: Nebbiolo (min. 85%)*

Il Roccolo di Mezzomerico
Cascina Roccolo Bellini 4
28040 Mezzomerico NO
tel. 0321/920407

 Lorenzo Zanetta
C.so Italia 64/c
28070 Sizzano NO
tel. 0321/820621

## COLLINE NOVARESI
## ROSSO doc
*Vines: Nebbiolo, localmente
chiamato Spanna (min. 30%),
Bonarda, localmnte chiamata
Uva Rara (max 40%), Vespolina
a/o Croatina (max. 30%)*

Antichi Vigneti di Cantalupo
Via M. Buonarroti 5
28074 Ghemme NO
tel. 0163/840041

Rovellotti
Via Tamiotti 3
28074 Ghemme NO
tel. 0163/840478

## COLLINE SALUZZESI
## PELAVERGA doc
*Vines: Pelaverga*

Fratelli Casetta
Via Castellero 5
12040 Vezza d'Alba CN
tel. 0173/65010

Maero
Via Villa 7 - 12030 Brondello CN
tel. 0175/76115

## CORTESE DELL'ALTO
## MONFERRATO doc
*Vines: Cortese (min. 85%)*

Cantina Sociale Maranzana
Via San Giovanni 20
14040 Maranzana
tel. 0141/77927

 282

Cantine Sant'Agata
Reg. Mezzena 19
14030 Scurzolengo AT
tel. 0141/203186

Marenco
P.zza V. Emanuele 10
15019 Strevi AL
tel. 0144/363133

Neirano
Via S. Michele 39
Fraz. Casalotto
14046 Mombaruzzo AT
tel. 0141/739382

Villa Montoggia
S.da Parasio 16
17076 Ovada AL
tel. 0143/81412

## DOLCETTO D'ACQUI doc
*Vines: Dolcetto*

Banfi
Via V. Veneto 22
15019 Strevi AL
tel. 0144/363485

Campazzo
Fraz. Costa 36
15010 Morbello AL
tel. 0144/768975

Cantina Sociale di Ricaldone
Via Roma 3
15011 Ricaldone AL
tel. 0144/74119

Cascina Bertolotto
Via Pietro Porro 70
15018 Spigno Monferrato AL
tel. 0144/91223

Marenco
P.zza V. Emanuele 10
15019 Strevi AL
tel. 0144/363133

Servetti
Strada Giaccaria 1/A
15061 Cassine AL
tel. 0144/767800

Viticoltori dell'Acquese
Via IV Novembre 14
15011 Acqui Terme AL
tel. 0144/322008

## DOLCETTO D'ALBA doc
*Vines: Dolcetto*

Aldo Vajra
Via delle Viole 25
Loc. Vergne
12060 Barolo CN
tel. 0173/56257

Batasiolo
Fraz. Annunziata 87
12064 La Morra CN
tel. 0173/50131

Brezza
Via Lomondo 4
12060 Barolo CN
tel. 0173/56354

Brovia
Via Alba-Barolo 54
12060 Castiglione Falletto CN
tel. 0173/62852

Cà Viola
Lia Langa 17
12050 Montelupo Albese CN
tel. 0173/617570

Cadia
Via Roddi-Verduno 62
12060 Roddi CN
tel. 0173/615398

Fratelli Casetta
Via Castellero 5
12040 Vezza d'Alba CN
tel. 0173/65010

Cavallotto
Via Alba Monforte 40
Loc. Bricco Boschis
12060 Castiglione Falletto CN
tel. 0173/62814

Ceretto
Loc. S. Cassiano 34
12051 Alba CN
tel. 0173/282582

F.lli Mossio
Via Montà 12
12050 Rodello CN
tel. 0173/617149

F.lli Oddero
Via S. Maria 28
12064 La Morra CN
tel. 0173/50618M

Gigi Rosso
Via Alba Barolo 20
12060 Castiglione Falletto CN
tel. 0173/262369

Giovanni Rosso
Via Foglio 18
Loc. Baudana
12050 Serralunga d'Alba CN
tel. 0173/613142

Fratelli Manzone
Loc. Manzoni 33
12065 Monforte d'Alba CN
tel. 0173/78110

Marcarini
P.zza Martiri 2
12064 La Morra CN
tel. 0173/50222

Marchesi di Barolo
Via Alba 12
12060 Barolo CN
tel. 0173/564400

Molino
Via Ausario 5
12050 Treiso CN
tel. 0173/638384

Rizzi
Loc. Rizzi 13
12050 Treiso CN
tel. 0173/638161

Sandrone
Via Pugnane 4
12060 Barolo CN
tel. 0173/560023

Terre del Barolo
Via Alba-Barolo 5
12060 Castiglione Falletto CN
tel. 0173/262053

Vignaioli Elvio Pertinace
Loc. Pertinace 2
12050 Treiso CN
tel. 0173/442238

Terrenostre Cantina
Dolcetto e Moscato
Loc. San Martino
12054 Cossano Belbo CN
tel. 0141/88137

**DOLCETTO ASTI** doc
*Vines: Dolcetto*

Bava
S.da Monferrato 2
14023 Cocconato d'Asti AT
tel. 0141/907083

Brema
Via Pozzomagna 9
14045 Incisa Scapaccino AT
tel. 0141/74019

Cà del Grifone
Re. Boschi 5 - 14044 Fontanile AT
tel. 02/90756346

Cantina di Monbaruzzo
Via Stazione 15
14046 Mombaruzzo AT
tel. 0141/77019

Cerutti
Via canelli 205
14050 Cassinasco AT
tel. 0141/851286

La Torre di Castelrocchero
S.da Acqui Terme 7
14040 Castel Rocchero AT
tel. 0141/760139

Torelli
Reg. S. Grato 142
14051 Bubbio AT
tel. 0144/83380

**DOLCETTO DI DIANO D'ALBA** doc
*Vines: Dolcetto*

Abrigo Giovanni
Via S. Croce 9
12055 Diano d'Alba CN
tel. 0173/69345

Alario
Via Santa Croce 23
12055 Diano d'Alba
tel. 0173/231808

Bricco Maiolica
Via Bolangino 7 - Fraz. Ricca
12055 Diano d'Alba CN
tel. 0173/612049

F.lli Savigliano
Via Guido Cane 43
12055 Diano d'Alba CN
tel. 0173/231803

Massimo Oddero
Via San Sebastiano 1
12055 Diano d'Alba CN
tel. 0173/69169

Porta Rossa
Piazza Trento e Trieste 5
12055 Diano d'Alba CN
tel. 0173/69210

Gigi Rosso
Via Alba Barolo 20
12060 Castiglione Falletto CN
tel. 0173/262369

Terre del Barolo
Via Alba-Barolo 5
12060 Castiglione Falletto CN
tel. 0173/262053

**DOLCETTO DI DOGLIANI** doc
*Vines: Dolcetto*

Aldo Marenco
Fraz. Pamparato Pironi 25
12063 Dogliani CN
tel. 0173/721090

Anna Maria Abbona
Fraz. Moncucco 21
12060 Farigliano CN
tel. 0173/797228

Boschis
Fraz. S. Martino
di Pianezza 57
12063 Dogliani CN
tel. 0173/70574

Cantina di Clavesana
Via Madonna della Neve 19
12060 Clavesana CN
tel. 0173/790451

Cozzo Mario
Fraz. Madonna delle Grazie
12063 Dogliani CN
tel. 0173/70571

Luzi Donadei-Fabiani
Borgo Chicchi Soprani 3
12060 Clavesana CN
tel. 0173/790387

Marziano ed Enrico Abbona
Via Torino 242
12063 Dogliani CN
tel. 0173/70484

Pecchenino
B.ta Valdiberti 59
12063 Dogliani CN
tel. 0173/70686

Pira
B.ta Valdiberti 69
12063 Dogliani CN
tel. 0173/78538

Poderi Einaudi
B.ta Gombe 31/32
12063 Dogliani CN
tel. 0173/70191

Poderi La Collina
Via Dante Alighieri 42
12063 Dogliani CN
tel. 0173/70155

Quinto Chionetti
B.ta Valdiberti 44
12063 Dogliani CN
tel. 0173/71179

Romana Carlo
Frazione Gombe
12063 Dogliani CN
tel. 0173/76315

**DOLCETTO DELLE LANGHE MONREGALESI** doc
*Vines: Dolcetto*

Cantina Clavesana
Via Madonna della Neve 19
12060 Clavesana CN
tel. 0173/790451

Cascina Monsignore
Via S. Giovanni 22
12080 Vicoforte CN
tel. 0174/563187

Luzi Donadei-Fabiani
Borgo Chicchi Soprani 3
12060 Clavesana CN
tel. 0173/790387

**DOLCETTO DI OVADA** doc
*Vines: Dolcetto*

Cantina Tre Castelli
Via De Gasperi 90
15010 Montaldo Bormida AL
tel. 0143/85136

Castello di Tagliolo
Via Castello 1
15070 Tagliolo Monferrato AL
tel. 0143/89195

La Guardia
Reg. La Guardia
15010 Morsasco AL
tel. 0144/73076

**La Slina**
Loc. Madonnina 29
15060 Castelletto d'Orba AL
tel. 0143/830542cuore

**Montobbio**
Via Lavagello 29/a
15060 Castelletto d'Orba AL
tel. 0143/830147

**Villa Montoggia**
S.da Parasio 16
17076 Ovada AL
tel. 0143/81412M

## ERBALUCE DI CALUSO doc
*Vines: Erbaluce*

**Bersano & Riccadonna**
P.zza Dante 21
14049 Nizza Monferrato AT
tel. 0141/720211

**Cantina della Serra**
Via Strada Nuova 12
10010 Piverone TO
tel. 0125/72166

**Cantina Produttori Erbaluce di Caluso**
Piazza Mazzini 4
10014 Caluso TO
tel. 011/9831447

**Cieck**
S.da Bardesono
Fraz. S. Grato
10011 Agliè TO
tel. 0124/330522

**Ferrando**
Via Torino 599/a
10015 Ivrea TO
tel. 0125/641176

**La Cella di San Michele**
Via Cascine di Ponente 21
13886 Viverone BI
tel. 0161/98245

**Orsolani**
Via Michele Chiesa
10090 S. Giorgio Canavese TO
tel. 0124/32386

## ERBALUCE DI CALUSO PASSITO doc
*Vines: Erbaluce*

**Cantina della Serra**
Via Strada Nuova 12
10010 Piverone TO
tel. 0125/72166

**Cieck**
S.da Bardesono
Fraz. S. Grato
10011 Agliè TO
tel. 0124/ 330522

**Enrico Serafino**
Frazione Valpone 79
12043 Canale CN
tel. 0173/967111

**Ferrando**
Via Torino 599/a
10015 Ivrea TO
tel. 0125/641176

**Orsolani**
Via Michele Chiesa 12
10090 S. Giorgio Canavese TO
tel. 0124/32386

## ERBALUCE DI CALUSO SPUMANTE doc
*Vines: Erbaluce*

**Cieck**
S.da Bardesono
Fraz. S. Grato
10011 Agliè TO
tel. 0124/330522

**La Cella di San Michele**
Via Cascine di Ponente 21
13886 Viverone BI
tel. 0161/98245

## FARA doc
*Vines: Nebbiolo (dal 30 al 50%), Vespolina (dal 10 al 30%), Bonarda (max 40%)*

**Dessilani**
Via Cesare Battisti 21
28073 Fara Novarese NO
tel. 0321/829252

## FREISA D'ASTI doc
*Vines: Freisa*

**Cantina del Freisa**
via S. Giovanni 6
14022 Castelnuovo Don Bosco AT
tel. 011/9876117

**Cascina Gilli**
Via Nevissano 36
14022 Castelnuovo Don Bosco AT
tel. 011/9876984

**Graglia**
Fraz. Bardella 67
14022 Castelnuovo Don Bosco AT
tel. 011/9874708

**La Montagnetta**
Bricco Cappello, 4
14022 Roatto AT
tel. 0141/938343

## FREISA DI CHIERI doc
*Vines: Freisa*

**Cantina del Freisa**
via S. Giovanni 6
14022 Castelnuovo Don Bosco AT
tel. 011/9876117

## GATTINARA docg
*Vines: Nebbiolo, localmente detto Spanna (min. 96%)*

**Antichi Vigneti di Cantalupo**
Via M. Buonarroti 5
28074 Ghemme NO
tel. 0163/840041

**Antoniolo**
C.so Valsesia 277
13045 Gattinara VC
tel. 0163/833612

**Giancarlo Travaglini**
S.da delle Vigne 36
13045 Gattinara VC
tel. 0163/833588

**Lorenzo Zanetta**
C.so Italia 64/c
28070 Sizzano NO
tel. 0321/820621

**Sergio Gattinara**
Piazza Monsignor Francese
13045 Gattinara VC
tel. 0163/832704

**Torraccia del Piantavigna**
Via Romagnano 69/a
28074 Ghemme NO
tel. 0163/840040

## GAVI docg
*Vines: Cortese*

Broglia
Tenuta La Meirana
Loc. Lomellina 14
15066 Gavi AL
tel. 0143/642998M

Cantina Produttori del Gavi
Via Cavalieri di V. Veneto 45
15066 Gavi AL
tel. 0143/642786

Castellari Bergaglio
Fraz. Rovereto 136
15066 Gavi AL
tel. 0143/644000

Domini Villae Lanata
Reg. S. Bovo 6
12054 Cossano Belbo CN
tel. 0141/88551

Franco M. Martinetti
Via S. Francesco da Paola 18
10123 Torino TO
tel. 011/8395937

La Chiara
Loc. Vallegge 24/2
15066 Gavi AL
tel. 0143/642293

La Giustiniana
Fraz. Rovereto 5
15066 Gavi AL
tel. 0143/682132

La Scolca
Fraz. Rovereto 170
15066 Gavi AL
tel. 0143/682176

Marco Bonfante
Strada Vaglio Serra 72
14049 Nizza Monferrato AT
tel. 0141/725012

Podere Saulino
Via Gavi 85
15067 Novi Ligure AL
tel. 0143/743174

Santa Seraffa
Loc. Colombara - 15066 Gavi AL
tel. 0143/643600

Terre da Vino
Via Bergesia 6 - 12060 Barolo CN
tel. 0173/564611

Villa Sparina
Fraz. Monte Rotondo 56
15066 Gavi AL
tel. 0143/633835

## GHEMME docg
*Vines: Nebbiolo, localmente detto Spanna (min 75%), Vespolina a/o Uva Rara (max 25%)*

Antichi Vigneti di Cantalupo
Via M. Buonarroti 5
28074 Ghemme
tel. 0163/840041

Ioppa
Via Ottavio Trinchieri 12
28078 Romagnano Sesia
tel. 0163/833079

Mirù
Piazza Antonelli 24
28074 Ghemme
tel. 0163/840032

Rovellotti
Via Tamiotti 3
28074 Ghemme
tel. 0163/840478

## GRIGNOLINO D'ASTI doc
*Vines: Grignolino (min 90%)*

Cantina Sociale 6 Castelli
frazione Salere 41 n. 3
14041 Agliano AT
tel. 0141/964004

F.lli Castino
Via Spessa 40
14041 Agliano Terme AT
tel. 0141/954502

Guasti Clemente
Via IV Novembre 80
14049 Nizza Monferrato AT
tel. 0141/721350

Spertino
S.da Lea 505
14047 Mombercelli AT
tel. 0141/959098

## GRIGNOLINO DEL MONFERRATO CASALESE doc
*Vines: Grignolino (min. 90%), Freisa*

Accornero
Ca' Cima 1
15049 Vignale Monferrato AL
tel. 0142/933317

Bricco Mondalino
Reg. Mondalino 5
15049 Vignale Monferrato AL
tel. 0142/933204

Cantina Terre di Vignale
via B. Mazzucco 2
15049 Vignale Monferrato AL
tel. 0142/93393

Castello di Lignano
Reg. Lignano
15035 Frassinello M.to AL
tel. 0142/334529

La Scamuzza
Cascina Pomina 17
15049 Vignale Monferrato AL
tel. 0142/926214

Tenuta Castello di Razzano
Fraz. Casarello 2
15021 Alfiano Natta AL
tel. 0141/922124

Tenuta La Tenaglia
S.da Santuario di Crea 6
15020 Serralunga di Crea AL
tel. 0142/940252

Vicara
Casc. Madonna delle Grazie 5
15030 Rosignano M.to AL
tel. 0142/488054M

## LANGHE ARNEIS doc
*Vines: Arneis*

Castello di Neive
Via Castelborgo 1
12057 Neive CN
tel. 0173/67171

Cordero di Montezemolo
Fraz. Annunziata 67/b
12064 La Morra CN
tel. 0173/50344

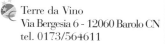

Ceretto
Loc. S. Cassiano 34
12051 Alba CN
tel. 0173/282582

Terre da Vino
Via Bergesia 6
12060 Barolo CN
tel. 0173/564611

### LANGHE FAVORITA doc
*Vines: Favorita*

Cantina del Nebbiolo
Via Torino 17
12040 Vezza d'Alba CN
tel. 0173/65040

Fratelli Casetta
Via Castellero 5
12040 Vezza d'Alba CN
tel. 0173/65010

Deltetto
C.so Alba 33
12043 Canale CN
tel. 0173/979383

Gianni Gagliardo
B.ta Serra dei Turchi 88
Fraz. S. Maria
12064 La Morra CN
tel. 0173/50829

Valdinera
Via Cavour 1
12040 Corneliano d'Alba CN
tel. 0173/619881

### LANGHE FREISA doc
*Vines: Freisa*

Aldo Vajra
Via delle Viole 25, Loc. Vergne
12060 Barolo CN
tel. 0173/56257

Cavallotto
Via Alba Monforte 40
Loc. Bricco Boschis
12060 Castiglione Falletto CN
tel. 0173/62814

Gianni Voerzio
S.da Loreto 1/bis
12064 La Morra CN
tel. 0173/509194

Gigi Rosso
Via Alba Barolo 20
12060 Castiglione Falletto CN
tel. 0173/262369

### LANGHE NEBBIOLO doc
*Vines: Nebbiolo*

F.lli Bera
Cascina Palazzo 12
12050 Neviglie CN
tel. 0173/630194

Gaja
Via Torino 36/a
12050 Barbaresco CN
tel. 0173/635158

Gianni Voerzio
S.da Loreto 1/bis
12064 La Morra CN
tel. 0173/509194

Marcarini
P.zza Martiri 2
12064 La Morra CN
tel. 0173/50222

### LANGHE ROSSO doc

Poderi Colla
Fraz. S. Rocco Seno d'Elvio 82
12051 Alba CN
tel. 0173/290148
*Bricco del Drago* (Dolcetto+
Nebbiolo)

### LESSONA doc
*Vines: Nebbiolo, localmente
detto Spanna (min. 75%),
Vespolina a/o Bonarda (max
25%)*

Sella
Via IV Novembre 110
13853 Lessona BI
tel. 015/99455

### LOAZZOLO doc
*Vines: Moscato bianco*

Borgo Maragliano
Regione San Sebastiano 2
14050 Loazzolo AT
tel. 0144/87132

Forteto della Luja
Casa Rosso 4
Reg. Bricco
14050 Loazzolo AT
tel. 0141/831596

### MALVASIA
### DI CASORZO
### D'ASTI doc
*Vines: Malvasia di Casorzo
(min 90%), Freisa,
Grignoilino, Barbera*

Accornero
Ca' Cima 1
15049 Vignale Monferrato AL
tel. 0142/933317

Cantina Sociale di Casorzo
Via S. Lodovico 1
14032 Casorzo AT
tel. 0141/929229

Guasti Clemente
Via IV Novembre 80
14049 Nizza Monferrato AT
tel. 0141/721350

Antonella Natta
Via San Rocco 26
14020 Pino d'Asti AT
tel. 011/9925454

### MALVASIA
### DI CASTELNUOVO
### DON BOSCO doc
*Vines: Malvasia di Schierano.
Freisa (max 15%)*

Bava
S.da Monferrato 2
14023 Cocconato d'Asti AT
tel. 0141/907083

Cantina Sociale del Freisa
via San Giovanni 6
14022 Castelnuovo Don Bosco AT
tel. 011/9876117

Cascina Gilli
Via Nevissano 36
14022 Castelnuovo Don Bosco AT
tel. 011/9876984

### MONFERRATO
### ROSSO doc

Forteto della Luja
Casa Rosso 4 - Reg. Bricco
14050 Loazzolo AT
tel. 0141/87197
*Le Grive* (Barbera +
Pinot Nero)

### MOSCATO D'ASTI docg
*Vines: Moscato bianco*

Ariano & Ariano
Via Stazione 37/A
12058 Santo Stefano Belbo CN
tel. 0144/844112

Tenuta Bompè Silvano Boroli
Borgata Como 34
12051 Alba CN
tel. 0173/286977

Cà d'Gal
S.da Vecchia 108
Fraz. Valdivilla
12058 S.Stefano Belbo CN
tel. 0141/847103

Cascina Fonda
Loc. Cascina Fonda 45
12056 Mango CN
tel. 0173/677156cuore

Caudrina
S.da Brosia 20
12053 Castiglione Tinella CN
tel. 0141/855126

Elio Perrone
S.da S. Martino 3/bis
12053 Castiglione Tinella CN
tel. 0141/855803

Forteto della Luja
Casa Rosso 4 - Reg. Bricco
14050 Loazzolo AT
tel. 0141/87197

La Badia
Via Castiglione 9
14052 Calosso AT
tel. 0141/853319

La Morandina
Via Morandini 11
12053 Castiglione Tinella CN
tel. 0141/855261

La Spinetta
Via Annunziata 17
14054 Castagnole Lanze AT
tel. 0141/877396

Marenco
P.zza V. Emanuele 10
15019 Strevi AL
tel. 0144/363133

Paolo Saracco
Via Circonvallazione 6
12053 Castiglione Tinella CN
tel. 0141/855113

Terre da Vino
Via Bergesia 6
12060 Barolo CN
tel. 0173/564611

Volpi
S.da Statale 10
15057 Tortona AL
tel. 0131/821917

Fratelli Bera
Via Castellero 12
12050 Neviglie CN
tel. 0173/630194

**NEBBIOLO D'ALBA** doc
*Vines: Nebbiolo*

Bricco Maiolica
Via Bolangino 7
Fraz. Ricca
12055 Diano d'Alba CN
tel. 0173/612049

Cantina del Nebbiolo
Via Torino 17
12040 Vezza d'Alba CN
tel. 0173/65040

Cascina Val Del Prete
Strada Santuario 2
12040 Priocca CN
tel. 0173/616534

Gili
Località Pautasso 7
12050 Castellinaldo CN
tel. 0173/639011

Penna Luigi e Figli
Fraz. S. Rocco Seno d'Elvio 96
12051 Alba CN
tel. 0173/286991

Poderi Colla
Fraz. S. Rocco Seno d'Elvio 82
12051 Alba CN
tel. 0173/290148

Renato Ratti
Fraz. Annunziata 7
12064 La Morra CN
tel. 0173/50185

Sandrone
Via Pugnane 4
12060 Barolo CN
tel. 0173/560023

Teo Costa
Via. San Salvario 1
12050 Castellinaldo CN
tel. 0173/213066

Valdinera
Via Cavour 1
12040 Corneliano
d'Alba CN
tel. 0173/619881

**PIEMONTE
MOSCATO** doc
*Vines: Moscato bianco*

Bersano Cav. Dario
Reg. Marziano 12
14050 S.Marzano
Oliveto AT
tel. 0141/856154

Volpi
S.da Statale 10
15057 Tortona AL
tel. 0131/821917

**PIEMONTE
MOSCATO
PASSITO** doc
*Vines: Moscato bianco*

Marenco
P.zza V. Emanuele 10
15019 Strevi AL
tel. 0144/363133

Tenuta Olim Bauda
Strada Prata 22
14045 Incisa Scapaccino AT
0141/74266

Terre da Vino
Via Bergesia 6
12060 Barolo CN
tel. 0173/564611

**ROERO** doc
*Vines: Nebbiolo*

Delletto
C.so Alba 33 - 12043 Canale CN
tel. 0173/979383

Enrico Serafino
Frazione Valpone 79
12043 Canale CN
tel. 0173/967111

Funtanin
Via Torino 191
12043 Canale CN
tel. 0173/979488

Giovanni Almondo
Via S. Rocco 26
12052 Montà d'Alba CN
tel. 0173/975256

Malvirà
Via S. Stefano Roero 144
12043 Canale CN
tel. 0173/978145

Marsaglia
Via Mussone 2
12050 Castellinaldo CN
tel. 0173/213048

Matteo Correggia
Via S. Stefano Roero 124
12043 Canale CN
tel. 0173/97009

Taliano
Corso A. Manzoni 24
12046 Montà CN
tel. 0173/976512

Teo Costa
Via. San Salvario 1
12050 Castellinaldo CN
tel. 0173/213066

### ROERO ARNEIS doc
*Vines: Arneis*

Cà du Russ-Sergio Marchisio
Via Silvio Pellico 7
Castellinaldo 12050 CN
tel. 0173/213069

 Cascina Pellerino
Loc. S.Anna
12040 Monteu Roero CN
tel. 0173/978171

Cornarea
Via Valentino 150
12043 Canale CN
tel. 0173/65636

 Deltetto
C.so Alba 33 - 12043 Canale CN
tel. 0173/979383

 Funtanin
Via Torino 191
12043 Canale CN
tel. 0173/979488

Malvirà
Via S. Stefano Roero 144
12043 Canale CN
tel. 0173/978145

Pescaja
località San Matteo 59
Cisterna d'Asti AT
tel. 0141/979711

Terre da Vino
Via Bergesia 6
12060 Barolo CN
tel. 0173/564611

### RUCHÉ DI CASTAGNOLE MONFERRATO doc
*Vines: Ruché (min. 90%)*

Cantina Sociale
di Castagnole Monferrato
Via XX Settembre 64
14030 Castagnole M.to AT
tel. 0141/292131

Cantine Sant'Agata
Reg. Mezzena 19
14030 Scurzolengo AT
tel. 0141/203186

Cascina Terra Felice
S.da Com. Montià
14030 Castagnole M.to AT
tel. 0041/796945851

Crivelli
Via Castello 20
14030 Castagnole M.to AT
tel. 0141/292357

Dezzani
C.so Pinin Giachino 140
14023 Cocconato d'Asti AT
tel. 0141/907044

### SIZZANO doc
*Vines: Nebbiolo (dal 40 al 60%), Vespolina (dal 15 al 40%), Bonarda (max 25%)*

Lorenzo Zanetta
C.so Italia 64/c
28070 Sizzano NO
tel. 0321/820621

### VERDUNO PELAVERGA doc
*Vines: Pelaverga piccolo (min 85%)*

Bel Colle
Fraz. Castagni 56
12060 Verduno CN
tel. 0172/470196

Cadia
Via Roddi-Verduno 62
12060 Roddi CN
tel. 0173/615398

Castello di Verduno
Via Umberto I 9
12060 Verduno CN
tel. 0172/470125

Commendator G.B. Burlotto
Via V. Emanuele 28
12060 Verduno CN
tel. 0172/470122

F.lli Alessandria
Via Beato Valfrè 59
12060 Verduno CN
tel. 0172/470113

Terre del Barolo
Via Alba-Barolo 5
12060 Castiglione Falletto CN
tel. 0173/262053

### VDT BIRBET
*Vitigno: Brachettone*

Cantina del Nebbiolo
Via Torino 17
12040 Vezza d'Alba CN
tel. 0173/65040

Malabaila di Canale
Cascina Pradvaj
Fraz. Madonna Cavalli
12043 Canale CN
tel. 0173/98381

Teo Costa
Via. San Salvario 1
12050 Castellinaldo CN
tel. 0173/213066

### VDT ROSSO

 La Dogliola
reg. Infermiera 226
14051 Bubbio AT
tel. 0144/83557
*Angulus Ridet (Brachetto)*

## LIGURIA

### CINQUE TERRE doc
*Vines: Bosco (min. 40%), Vermentino a/o Albarola (max 40%)*

Cooperativa Agricoltura di Riomaggiore
loc. Groppo - fraz. Manarola
19010 Riomaggiore SP
tel. 0187/920435

Forlini e Cappellini
via Riccaboni 45
19010 Manarola SP
tel. 0187/920496

Walter De Batté
via Trarcantu 25
19017 Riomaggiore SP
tel. 0187/920127

### CINQUE TERRE SCIACCHETRÀ doc
*Vines: Bosco (min. 40%), Vermentino a/o Albarola (max 40%)*

Cooperativa Agricoltura di Riomaggiore
loc. Groppo - fraz. Manarola
19010 Riomaggiore SP
tel. 0187/920435

Walter De Batté
via Trarcantu 25
19017 Riomaggiore SP
tel. 0187/920127

**COLLI DI LUNI ROSSO** doc
*Vines: Sangiovese (dal 60 al
70%), Cigliegiolo a/o Canaiolo
a/o Pollera Nera (min.15%)*

Cantine Lunae Bosoni
via Bozzi 63
19034 Ortonovo SP
tel. 0187/660187

Il Monticello
Via Groppolo 7
19038 Sarzana SP
tel. 0187/621432

Il Torchio
via Provinciale 202
19030 Castelnuovo Magra SP
tel. 0187/674075

Ottaviano Lambruschi
via Olmarello 28
19030 Castelnuovo Magra SP
tel. 0187/674261

**COLLI DI LUNI
VERMENTINO** doc
*Vines: Vermentino (min. 90%)*

Cantine Lunae Bosoni
via Bozzi 63
19034 Ortonovo SP
tel. 0187/660187

Conte Picedi Benedettini
via Mazzini 57
19038 Sarzana SP
tel. 0187/625147

Il Monticello
via Groppolo 7
19038 Sarzana SP
tel. 0187/621432

Il Torchio
via Provinciale 202
19030 Castelnuovo Magra SP
tel. 0187/674075

La Pietra del Focolare
via Dogana 209
19034 Ortonovo SP
tel. 0187/662129

Ottaviano Lambruschi
via Olmarello 28
19030 Castelnuovo Magra SP
tel. 0187/674261

Podere Terenzuola
via Vercalda 14 54035
Fosdinovo MS
0187/680030

Santa Caterina
via Santa Caterina
19038 Sarzana SP
tel. 0187/629429

**GOLFO DEL TIGULLIO
BIANCHETTA
GENOVESE** doc
*Vines: Bianchetta Genovese , é
un sinonimo dell'Albarola
(min. 85%)*

Enoteca Bisson
Corso Gianelli 28
16043 Chiavari GE
tel. 0185/314462

Fratelli Parma
via Garibaldi 8 - 16040 Né GE
tel. 0185/337073

**GOLFO DEL TIGULLIO
CIGLIEGIOLO** doc
*Vines: Cigliegiolo (min. 85%)*

Enoteca Bisson
corso Gianelli 28
16043 Chiavari GE
tel. 0185/314462

Fratelli Parma
via Garibaldi 8
16040 Né GE
tel. 0185/337073

**GOLFO DEL TIGULLIO
VERMENTINO** doc
*Vines: Vermentino (min. 85%)*

Enoteca Bisson
corso Gianelli 28
16043 Chiavari GE
tel. 0185/314462

Fratelli Parma
via Garibaldi 8
16040 Né GE
tel. 0185/337073

**GOLFO DEL TIGULLIO
PASSITO** doc

Enoteca Bisson
corso Gianelli 28
16043 Chiavari GE
tel. 0185/314462
*Acinirari* (Vermentino)

**GOLFO DEL TIGULLIO
ROSSO** doc
*Vines: Dolcetto (dal 20 al
70%), Cigliegiolo (dal 20 al
70%)*

Enoteca Bisson
corso Gianelli 28
16043 Chiavari GE
tel. 0185/314462

**RIVIERA LIGURE DI
PONENTE ORMEASCO** doc
*Vines: Dolcetto (min. 95%)*

Durin
via Roma 92
17037 Ortovero SV
tel. 0182/547007

Foresti
via Braje 223
18013 Camporosso IM
tel. 0184/292377

Lupi
via Mazzini 9
18026 Pieve di Teco IM
tel. 0183/36161

**RIVIERA LIGURE DI
PONENTE PIGATO** doc
*Vines: Pigato (min. 95%)*

Bruna
via Umberto I 81
18028 Ranzo IM
tel. 0183/318082

Cantine Calleri
Regione Fratti 2
17031 Salea di Albenga IM
tel. 0182/20085

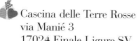 Cascina delle Terre Rosse
via Manié 3
17024 Finale Ligure SV
tel. 0196/98782

Cascina Feipu dei Massaretti
regione Massaretti 7 - Bastia
17030 Albenga SV
tel. 0182/20131

Claudio Vio
frazione Crosa 19
17030 Vendone SV
tel. 0182/76338

Durin
via Roma 92
17037 Ortovero SV
tel. 0182/547007

Foresti
via Braje 223
18013 Camporosso IM
tel. 0184/292377

Lupi
via Mazzini 9
18026 Pieve di Teco IM
tel. 0183/36161

Maria Donata Bianchi
via delle Torri 16
18010 Diano Castello IM
tel. 0183/498233

Tenuta Giuncheo
località Giuncheo
18033 Camporosso IM
tel. 0184/288639

Terre Bianche
località Arcagna
18035 Dolceacqua IM
tel. 0184/31426

### RIVIERA LIGURE DI PONENTE VERMENTINO doc
*Vines: Vermentino (min. 95%)*

Cascina delle Terre Rosse
via Manié 3
17024 Finale Ligure SV
tel. 0196/98782

Terre Bianche
località Arcagna
18035 Dolceacqua IM
tel. 0184/31426

Foresti
via Braje 223
18013 Camporosso IM
tel. 0184/292377

Cantine Calleri
Regione Fratti 2
17100 Salea di Albenga IM
tel. 0182/20085

Claudio Vio
frazione Crosa 19
17030 Vendone SV
tel. 0182/76338

Lupi
via Mazzini 9
18026 Pieve di Teco IM
tel. 0183/36161

Colle dei Bardellini
via Fontanarosa 12
18100 Imperia IM
tel. 0183/21370

Tenuta Giuncheo
località Giuncheo
18033 Camporosso IM
tel. 0184/288639

### ROSSESE DI DOLCEACQUA doc
*Vines: Rossese (min. 95%)*

Cantine Calleri
Regione Fratti 2
17100 Salea di Albenga IM
tel. 0182/20085

Foresti
via Braje 223
18013 Camporosso IM
tel. 0184/292377

Lupi
via Mazzini 9
18026 Pieve di Teco IM
tel. 0183/36161

Tenuta Giuncheo
località Giuncheo
18033 Camporosso IM
tel. 0184/288639

### VDT

Enoteca Bisson
corso Gianelli 28
16043 Chiavari GE
tel. 0185/314462
*Il Müsaico (Dolcetto + Barbera)*

## LOMBARDY

### OLTREPÒ PAVESE BUTTAFUOCO doc
*Vines: Barbera (dal 25 al 65%), Croatina (dal 25 al 65%). Uva Rara, Vespolina e Pinot Nero (max 45%)*

Fiamberti Giuseppe & Figli
via Chiesa 17
27044 Canneto Pavese PV
tel. 0385/88019

Il Montù
via Marconi 10
27040 Montù Beccaria PV
tel. 0385/262252

Picchioni Andrea
località Camponoce 4
27044 Canneto Pavese PV
tel. 0385/262138

Quaquarini Francesco
via Casa Zambianchi 26
27044 Canneto Pavese PV
tel. 0385/60152

Tenuta La Costa
via Costa 68
27040 Castana PV
tel. 0385/241527

Verdi Bruno
via Vergomberra 5
27044 Canneto Pavese PV
tel. 0385/88023

### CAPRIANO DEL COLLE BIANCO doc
*Vines: Trebbiano di Soave, localmente chiamato Trebbiano di Lugana o Trebbiano veronese (min. 85%)*

La Cascina Nuova
Via Cascina Nuova 10
25020 Poncarale BS
tel. 030/2540058

### CAPRIANO DEL COLLE ROSSO doc
*Vines: Sangiorese (min. 40%), Barbera (min. 3%), Marzemino, localmente chiamato Berzamino, (min. 35%), Merlot a/o Incrocio Terzi n. 1 (max 15%)*

La Cascina Nuova
via Cascina Nuova 10
25020 Poncarale BS
tel. 030/2540058

La Vigna
via Torrazza
25020 Capriano del Colle BS
tel. 030/9748061

### GARDA CLASSICO CHIARETTO doc
*Vines: Groppello (min. 30%), Barbera (min. 5%), Marzemino (min. 5%), Sangiovese (min. 5%)*

Avanzi Giovanni
via Risorgimento 32
25080 Manerba sul Garda BS
tel. 0365/551013

291

Ca' dei Frati
via Frati 22
25010 Lugana di Sirmione BS
tel. 030/919468

Costaripa
via Cialdini 12
25080 Moniga del Garda BS
tel. 0365/502010

Pasini Fratelli
via Videlle 2
25080 Raffa di Puegnago BS
tel. 0365/651419

Provenza
via Colli Storici
25015 Desenzano del Garda BS
tel. 030/9910006

Visconti
via Battisti 139
25015 Desenzano del Garda BS
tel. 030/9120681

### GARDA CLASSICO GROPPELLO doc

*Vines: Groppello (min 85%)*

Avanzi Giovanni
via Risorgimento 32
25080 Manerba sul Garda BS
tel. 036/5551013

Cantine Berardi
viale Brescia 83
25080 Molinetto di Mazzano BS
tel. 030/2620152

Cascina La Pertica
via Picedo 24
25080 Polpenazza del Garda BS
tel. 0365/651471

Costaripa
via Cialdini 12
25080 Moniga del Garda BS
tel. 0365/502010

La Torre
via Torre 3 - 25080 Moncasina
di Calvagese Riviera BS
tel. 030/601034

Monte Cicogna
via delle Vigne 6
25080 Moniga del Garda BS
tel. 0365/503200

Pasini Fratelli
via Videlle 2
25080 Raffa di Puegnago BS
tel. 0365/651419

Redaelli De Zinis
via Nobile Redaelli De Zinis 10
25080 Cavalgese
della Riviera BS
tel. 030/601001

### GARDA CLASSICO MARZEMINO doc

*Vines: Marzemino (min. 85%)*

Averoldi
via Cantrina 1
25081 Bedizzole BS
tel. 030/674451

Cantine Valtenesi e della Lugana
via Pergola 21
25080 Moniga del Garda BS
tel. 0365/502002

Masserino
via Masserino 2
25080 Puegnago BS
tel. 0365/651757

### GARDA CLASSICO ROSSO doc

*Vines: Groppello (min. 30%),
Barbera (min. 5%),
Marzemino (min. 5%),
Sangiovese (min. 5%)*

Ca' dei Frati
via Frati 22
25010 Lugana di Sirmione BS
tel. 030/919468

Cantina Marangona
c/o Antica Corte Ialidy
25010 Pozzolengo BS
tel. 030/919379
*Antica Corte Ialidy*

Cantine Berardi
viale Brescia 83
25080 Molinetto di Mazzano BS
tel. 030/2620152

Costaripa
via Cialdini 12
25080 Moniga del Garda BS
tel. 0365/502010

La Guarda
via Zanardelli 49
25080 Castrezzone di
Muscolina BS
tel. 0365/372948
*Sabbioso*

La Torre
via Torre 3
25080 Moncasina di
Calvagese Riviera BS
tel. 030/601034
*Il Torrione*

Pasini Fratelli
via Videlle 2
25080 Raffa di Puegnago BS
tel. 0365/651419

Provenza
via Colli Storici
25015 Desenzano del Garda BS
tel. 030/9910006

Redaelli De Zinis
via Nobile Redaelli
De Zinis 10
25080 Cavalgese
della Riviera BS
tel. 030/601001

Tenuta Roveglia
località Roveglia 1
25010 Pozzolengo BS
tel. 030/918663

### GARDA COLLI MANTOVANI BIANCO doc

*Vines: Trebbiano Garganega*

Azienda Agricola Gozzi
Fattoria Colombara
via Ortaglia 16
46040 Monzambano MN
tel. 0376/800377

### LAMBRUSCO MANTOVANO doc

*Vines: Lambrusco varie
varietà, Lambrusco di
Sorbara, Lambrusco
Grasparossa, Ancellotta e
Fortana*

Ca' de Medici
via Della Stazione 34
42040 Loc. Cadè
Reggio Emilia
tel. 0522/942141

Cantina Sociale e Cooperativa
di Quistello
via Roma 46
4606 Quistello MN
tel. 0376/618118

Cantine Lebovitz
viale Rimembranze 4
46034 Governolo di
Roncoferraro MN
tel. 0376/668115

### LUGANA doc

*Vines: Trebbiano di Soave,
localmente chiamato
Trebbiano di Lugana
(min. 90%)*

Avanzi Giovanni
via Risorgimento 32
25080 Manerba sul Garda BS
tel. 036/5551013

Bulgarini Bruno
località Vaibò 1
25010 Pozzolengo BS
tel. 030/918224

Ca' dei Frati
via Frati 22
25010 Lugana di Sirmione BS
tel. 030/919468

Ca' Lojera
località Rovizza
25019 Sirmione BS
tel. 045/7551901

Cantine Valtenesi e della
Lugana
via Pergola 21
25080 Moniga del Garda BS
tel. 0365/502002

Casa Vinicola Zenato
fraz. San Benedetto di Lugana
37010 Peschiera del Garda VE
tel. 045/7550300

Fratelli Fabiano
Via Verona 6 - S.S. 11
37060 Sona VR
tel. 045/6081111

Monte Cicogna
via delle Vigne 6
25080 Moniga del Garda BS
tel. 0365/503200

Provenza
via Colli Storici
25015 Desenzano del Garda BS
tel. 030/9910006

Sartori
via Casette 2
37024 Negrar VR
tel. 045/6028011

Tenuta Roveglia
località Roveglia 1
25010 Pozzolengo BS
tel. 030/918663

Valerio Zenato
viale Indipendenza
Loc. San Benedetto di Lugana
37019 Peschiera del Garda VR
tel. 045/7552724

Visconti
via Battisti 139
25015 Desenzano del Garda BS
tel. 030/9120681

## LUGANA SPUMANTE doc

*Vines: Trebbiano di Soave,
localmente chiamato
Trebbiano di Lugana (min.
90%)*

Ca' dei Frati
via Frati 22
25010 Lugana di Sirmione BS
tel. 030/919468

Provenza
via Colli Storici - 25015
Desenzano del Garda BS
tel. 030/9910006

Valerio Zenato
viale Indipendenza
Loc. San Benedetto di Lugana
37019 Peschiera del Garda VR
tel. 045/7552724

Visconti
via Battisti 139
25015 Desenzano del Garda BS
tel. 030/9120681

## VALCALEPIO MOSCATO
## DI SCANZO doc
*Vines: Moscato di Scanzo*

La Brugherata
via Medolago 47
24020 Scanzorosciate BG
tel. 035/655202

Monzio Compagnoni
via degli Alpini 3
24069 Cenate di Sotto BG
tel. 030/9884157

Tenuta Castello di Grumello
via Fosse 11
24064 Grumello del Monte BG
tel. 035/4420817

## OLTREPÒ PAVESE
## BARBERA doc
*Vines: Barbera (min 85%)*

Bellaria
via Castel del Lupo 28
frazione Mairano
27045 Casteggio PV
tel. 0383/83203

Fattoria Cabanon
località Cabanon 1
27052 Godiasco PV
tel. 0383/940912

La Costaiola
via Costaiola 11
27054 Montebello della
Battaglia PV
tel. 0383/83169

Marco Vercesi
frazione Crosia 1
27040 Montù Beccarla PV
tel. 0385/61330

Martilde
frazione Croce 4/a/1
27040 Rovescala PV
tel. 0385/756280

Podere San Giorgio
località Castello
27046 Santa Giulietta PV
tel. 0383/899168

Tenimenti Castelrotto
frazione Castelrotto 6
27047 Montecalvo Versiggia PV
tel. 0385/98162

Tenuta Pegazzera
via Vigorelli 151
27045 Casteggio PV
tel. 0389/804646

Travaglino
località Travaglino 6
27045 Calvignano PV
tel. 0383/872222

Vanzini
frazione Barbaleone 7
27040 S. Damiano al Colle PV
tel. 0385/75019

Vercesi del Castellazzo
via Aureliano 36
27040 Montù Becaria PV
tel. 0385/60067

Verdi Bruno
via Vergomberra 5
27044 Canneto Pavese PV
tel. 0385/88023

## OLTREPÒ PAVESE BARBERA VIVACE doc

*Vines: Barbera (min 85%)*

Ca' Montebello
località Montebello 10
27040 Cigognola PV
tel. 0385/85182

Fattoria Cabanon
località Cabanon 1
27052 Godiasco PV
tel. 0383/940912

Isimbarda
località Castello
27046 Santa Giulietta PV
tel. 0383/899256

Monsupello
via San Lazzaro 5
27050 Torricella Verzate PV
tel. 0383/896043

Monterucco
valle Cima 38
27040 Cigognola PV
tel. 0385/85151

Pietro Torti
frazione Castelrotto 9
27047 Montecalvo Versiggia PV
tel. 0385/99763

Tenuta Pegazzera
via Vigorelli 151
27045 Casteggio PV
tel. 0389/804646

Vanzini
frazione Barbaleone 7
27040 S. Damiano al Colle PV
tel. 0385/75019

## OLTREPÒ PAVESE BONARDA doc

*Vines: Croatina, detta Bonarda localmente (min 85%)*

Ca' di Frara
località casa Ferrari 1
27040 Mornico Losana PV
tel. 0383/892299

Cantine Coop. di Casteggio
via Torino 96
27045 Casteggio PV
tel. 0383/806311

Fratelli Agnes Di Giovanni
via Campo del Monte 1
27040 Rovescala PV
tel. 0385/75206

Il Montù
via Marconi 10
27040 Montù Beccaria PV
tel. 0385/262252

Martilde
frazione Croce 4/a/1
27040 Rovescala PV
tel. 0385/756280

Tenuta Mazzolino
via Mazzolino 26
27050 Corvino S. Quirico PV
tel. 0383/876122

Travaglino
località Travaglino 6
27045 Calvignano PV
tel. 0383/872222

Vanzini
frazione Barbaleone 7
27040 S. Damiano al Colle PV
tel. 0385/75019

Vercesi del Castellazzo
via Aureliano 36
27040 Montù Becaria PV
tel. 0385/60067

## OLTREPÒ PAVESE BONARDA VIVACE doc

*Vines: Croatina, detta Bonarda localmente (min 85%)*

Anteo
località Chiesa
27043 Rocca de' Giorgi PV
tel. 0385/48583

Ca' del Gé
via Ca' del Gé 3
27040 Montalto Pavese PV
tel. 0383/870179

Ca' Montebello
località Montebello 10
27040 Cigognola PV
tel. 0383/85182

Cantina Sociale La Versa
via Crispi 15
27047 Santa Maria della Versa PV
tel. 0385/798411

Caseo
Frazione Caseo 9
27040 Canevino PV
tel. 0385/99937

Castello di Luzzano
frazione Luzzano 5
27040 Rovescala PV
tel. 0523/863277

Clastidio
via San Biagio 32
27045 Casteggio PV
0383/82566

Doria
via Casa Tacconi 3
27040 Montalto Pavese PV
tel. 0383/870143

Fratelli Agnes Di Giovanni
via Campo del Monte 1
27040 Rovescala PV
tel. 0385/75206

Isimbarda
località Castello
27046 Santa Giulietta PV
tel. 0383/899256

Le Fracce
via Castel del Lupo 5
27045 Casteggio PV
tel. 0383/82526

Monsupello
via San Lazzaro 5
27050 Torricella Verzate PV
tel. 0383/896043

Pietro Torti
frazione Castelrotto 9
27047 Montecalvo Versiggia PV
tel. 0385/99763

Riccardo Albani
strada San Biagio 46
27045 Casteggio PV
tel. 0383/383622

Tenuta il Bosco
località il Bosco
27049 Zenevredo PV
tel. 0385/245326

Vanzini
frazione Barbaleone 7
27040 S. Damiano al Colle PV
tel. 0385/75019

Vercesi del Castellazzo
via Aureliano 36
27040 Montù Beccaria PV
tel. 0385/60067

Verdi Bruno
via Vergomberra 5
27044 Canneto Pavese PV
tel. 0385/88023

### OLTREPÒ PAVESE MALVASIA doc

*Vines: Malvasia bianca di Candia (min 85%)*

Ca' di Frara
località casa Ferrari 1
27040 Mornico Losana PV
tel. 0383/892299

Cantine Coop. di Casteggio
via Torino 96
27045 Casteggio PV
tel. 0383/806311

Tenuta il Bosco
località il Bosco
27049 Zenevredo PV
tel. 0385/245326

### OLTREPÒ PAVESE ROSSO doc

*Vines: Barbera (dal 25 al 65%), Croatina (dal 25 al 65%). Uva Rara a/o Vespolina a/o Pinot Nero (max 45%)*

Cantina Sociale La Versa
via Crispi 15
27047 S. Maria della Versa PV
tel. 385/798452
*Donelasco*

Isimbarda
loc. Castello - 27046 S. Giulietta PV
tel. 0383/899256
*Monplò e Montezavo*

Le Fracce
via Castel del Lupo 5
27045 Casteggio PV
tel. 0383/82526
*Il Garboso e Bohemi*

Monsupello
via San Lazzaro 5
27050 Torricella Verzate PV
tel. 0383/896043
*La Borla*

Montelio
via Domenico Mazza 1
27050 Codevilla PV
tel. 0383/37090
*Vigna Solarolo*

Riccardo Albani
strada San Biagio 46
27045 Casteggio PV
tel. 0383/383622
*Vigna della Casona*

Tenuta Frecciarossa
via Vigorelli 141
27045 Casteggio PV
tel. 0383/804465
*Villa Odero*

Travaglino
località Travaglino 6
27045 Calvignano PV
tel. 0383/872222
*Marc'Antonio*

Vercesi del Castellazzo
via Aureliano 36
27040 Montù Becaria PV
tel. 0385/60067
*Orto di San Giacomo*

Verdi Bruno
via Vergomberra 5
27044 Canneto Pavese PV
tel. 0385/88023
*Cavariola*

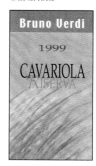

### OLTREPÒ PAVESE MOSCATO doc

*Vines: Moscato bianco (min 85%), Malvasia bianca di Candia (max 15%)*

Anteo
località Chiesa
27043 Rocca de Giorgi PV
tel. 0385/48583

Cantine Coop. di Casteggio
via Torino 96
27045 Casteggio PV
tel. 0383/806311

Vanzini
frazione Barbaleone 7
27040 S. Damiano
al Colle PV
tel. 0385/75019

Verdi Bruno
via Vergomberra 5
27044 Canneto Pavese PV
tel. 0385/88023

### OLTREPÒ PAVESE MOSCATO PASSITO doc

*Vines: Moscato bianco (min 85%), Malvasia bianca di Candia (max 15%)*

Cantina Sociale La Versa
via Crispi 15
27047 Santa Maria della
Versa PV
tel. 0385/798411

Litubium
via Roccasusella 13
27050 Retorbido PV
tel. 0383/374485

Montini
via Emilia 21
27046 Santa Giulietta PV
tel. 0383/899231

### SAN COLOMBANO doc

*Vines: Croatina (dal 30 al 45%), Barbera (dal 25 al 40%), Uva Rara (dal 5 al 15%), altre raccomandate a/o autorizzate dalle provincie di Milano e Pavia (max 15%)*

Antonio Panigada - Bannino
via della Vittoria 13
20078 San Colombano al
Lambro MI
tel. 0371/189103

Pietrasanta
via Sforza 55/57
20078 San Colombano al
Lambro MI
tel. 0371/897540

Poderi San Pietro
via Monti 37
20078 San Colombano al
Lambro MI
tel. 0371/208054

### SAN MARTINO DELLA BATTAGLIA doc

*Vines: Tocai friulano (min 85%)*

Cascina Spia d'Italia
via M. Cerutti 61
25017 Lonato BS
tel. 030/9130233

## SAN MARTINO DELLA BATTAGLIA LIQUOROSO
*Vines: Tocai friulano (min 85%)*

Cascina Spia d'Italia
via M. Cerutti 61
25017 Lonato BS
tel. 030/9130233

## SFORZATO DI VALTELLINA docg
*Vines: Nebbiolo, detto localmente Chiavennasca (min 80%)*

 Aldo Rainoldi
via Stelvio 128
23030 Chiuro SO
tel. 0342/482225

Casa Vinicola Fratelli Bettini
via Nazionale 68
23030 S. Giacomo di Teglio SO
tel. 0342/786068

Casa Vinicola Pietro Nera
via IV Novembre 43
23030 Chiuro SO
tel. 0342/482631

 Casa Vinicola Triacca
via Nazionale 121
23030 Villa di Tirano SO
tel. 0342/701352

Memete Prevostini
via Lucchinetti 65
23020 Mese SO
tel. 0343/41003

Nino Negri
via Ghibellini 3
23030 Chiuro SO
tel. 0342/482521

Salis 1637 - Conti Sertoli Salis
piazza Salis 3
23037 Tirano SO
tel. 0342/710404

Sandro Fay
via Pila Caselli 1
23030 S. Giacomo di Teglio SO
tel. 0342/786071

## VALTELLINA SUPERIORE docg
*Vines: Nebbiolo, detto localmente Chiavennasca (min 90%)*

Aldo Rainoldi
via Stelvio 128
23030 Chiuro SO
tel. 0342/482225

Casa Vinicola Pietro Nera
via IV Novembre 43
23030 Chiuro SO
tel. 0342/482631

 Casa Vinicola Triacca
via Nazionale 121
23030 Villa di Tirano SO
tel. 0342/701352

Memete Prevostini
via Lucchinetti 65
23020 Mese SO
tel. 0343/41003

Nino Negri
via Ghibellini 3
23030 Chiuro SO
tel. 0342/482521

Sandro Fay
via Pila Caselli 1
23030 S. Giacomo di Teglio SO
tel. 0342/786071

Salis 1637
Conti Sertoli Salis
piazza Salis 3
23037 Tirano SO
tel. 0342/710404

## BENACO BRESCIANO IGT MARZEMINO

Costaripa
via Cialdini 12
25080 Moniga del Garda BS
tel. 0365/502010
*Mazane*

## BERGAMASCA IGT FRANCONIA

Podere della Cavaga
via Gafforelli 1
24060 Foresto Sparso BG
tel. 035/930939
*Ol Giopì*

## PAVIA IGT UVA RARA

Frecciarossa
via Vigorelli 141
27045 Casteggio PV
tel. 0383/804465

## PAVIA IGT ROSSO

Cantine di Casteggio
via Torino 96
27045 Casteggio PV
tel. 0383/896311
*Il Longobardo (Barbera + Bonarda + altri)*

## VDT

Ca' del Bosco
via Case Sparse 20
25030 Erbusco BS
tel. 030/7766111
*Carmenero (Carmenère)*

Majolini
località Valle via Manzoni 10
25050 Ome BS
tel. 030/6527378
*Maiolina (Maiolina)*

## TRENTINO

### TRENTINO MOSCATO GIALLO doc
*Vines: Moscato Giallo (min. 85%)*

Cantina d'Isera
via al Ponte 1
38060 Isera TN
tel. 0464/433795

Gaierhof
via IV Novembre 51
38030 Roveré della Luna TN
tel. 0461/658527

Vinicola Aldeno
V. Roma 76 - 38060 Aldeno TN
tel. 0461/842511

### TRENTINO MOSCATO ROSA doc

*Vines: Moscato Rosa (min. 85%)*

Endrizzi
località Masetto 2
38010 S. Michele all'Adige TN
tel. 0461/650129

Letrari
via Monte Baldo 13/15
38068 Rovereto TN
tel. 0464/480200

Maso Bergamini
località Bergamini 3
38050 Cognola TN
tel. 0461/983079

Roberto Zeni
via Stretta 2 - frazione Grumo
38010 S. Michele all'Adige TN
tel. 0461/650456

### TEROLDEGO ROTALIANO doc

*Vines: Teroldego*

Cantina Endrizzi
località Masetto 2 TN
38010 San Michele all'Adige
tel. 0461/650129

---

Cantina Mezzacorona
via IV Novembre 127
38016 Mezzocorona TN
tel. 0461/605163

Cantina Rotaliana
corso del Popolo 6
38017 Mezzolombardo TN
tel. 0461/601010

Casata Monfort
via Carlo Sette 21
38015 Lavis TN
tel. 0461/241484

Cavit
via Del Ponte 31
38100 Ravina di Trento TN
tel. 0461/381711

Concilio
zona Industriale 2
38060 Volano TN
tel. 0464/411000

Conti Bossi Fedrigotti
via Unione 43
38068 Rovereto TN
tel. 0464/439250

Fedrizzi Cipriani
via IV Novembre 1
38017 Mezzolombardo TN
tel. 0461/602328

Foradori
via della Chiesa 1
38017 Mezzolombardo TN
tel. 0461/601046

Fratelli Dorigati
via Dante 5
38016 Mezzocorona TN
tel. 0461/605313

---

Gaierhof
via IV Novembre, 51
38030 Roveré della Luna TN
tel. 0461/658527

La Vis
via del Carmine, 7
38015 Lavis TN
tel. 0461/246325

Marco Donati
via Battisti 41
38016 Mezzocorona TN
tel. 0461/604141

Roberto Zeni
via Stretta 2 - frazione Grumo
38010 S. Michele all'Adige TN
tel. 0461/650456

### TRENTINO LAGREIN doc

Cavit
via Del Ponte 31
38100 Ravina di Trento TN
tel. 0461/381711

Gaierhof
via IV Novembre 51
38030 Roveré della Luna TN
tel. 0461/658527

Graziano Fontana
via Case Sparse 9
38010 Faedo TN
tel. 0461/650400

Letrari
via Monte Baldo 13/15
38068 Rovereto TN
tel. 0464/480200

---

Maso Bergamini
località Bergamini 3
38050 Cognola TN
tel. 0461/983079

### TRENTINO MARZEMINO doc

*Vines: Marzemino (min. 85%)*

Battistotti Riccardo
via IV Novembre 21
38060 Nomi TN
tel. 0464/834145

Cantina di Nomi
via Roma 1
38060 Nomi TN
tel. 0464/834195

Cantina d'Isera
via al Ponte 1
38060 Isera TN
tel. 0464/433795

Cantina Mezzacorona
via IV Novembre 127
38016 Mezzocorona TN
tel. 0461/605163

Casata Monfort
via Carlo Sette 21
38015 Lavis TN
tel. 0461/241484

Cavit
via Del Ponte 31
38100 Ravina di Trento TN
tel. 0461/381711

Conti Bossi Fedrigotti
via Unione 43
38068 Rovereto TN
tel. 0464/439250

De Tarczal
via G.B. Miori 4
38060 Marano di Isera TN
tel. 0464/409134

Letrari
via Monte Baldo, 13/15
38068 Rovereto TN
tel. 0464/480200

Longariva
via Zandonai 6
38068 Rovereto TN
tel. 0464/437200

Vallarom
via Masi 21
38063 Avio TN
tel. 0464/684297

### TRENTINO NOSIOLA doc
*Vines: Nosiola (min 85%)*

Cantina di Toblino
fraz. Sarche
via Ponte Oliveti 1
38070 Calavino TN
tel. 0461/564168

Cavit
via Del Ponte 31
38100 Ravina di Trento TN
tel. 0461/381758

Cesconi
via Marconi 39
38015 Pressano Lavis TN
tel. 0461/240355

Concilio
zona Industriale 2
38060 Volano TN
tel. 0464/411000

La Vis
via del Carmine, 7
38015 Lavis TN
tel. 0461/246325

Pojer e Sandri
località Molini 6
38010 Faedo TN
tel. 0461/650342

Pravis
via Lagolo 26
38076 Lasino TN
tel. 0461/564305

Roberto Zeni
via Stretta 2 - fraz. Grumo
38010 S. Michele
all'Adige TN
tel. 0461/650456

Spagnolli Enrico
via G.B. Rosina
38060 Isera TN
tel. 0464/409054

Vallis Agri
via Valentini 37
38060 Calliano TN
tel. 0464/834113

### TRENTINO TRAMINER AROMATICO doc
*Vines: Traminer (min. 85%)*

Balter
via Vallunga II 24
38068 Rovereto TN
tel. 0464/430101

Cantina Mezzacorona
via IV Novembre 127
38016 Mezzocorona TN
tel. 0461/605163

Cesconi
via Marconi 39
38015 Pressano Lavis TN
tel. 0461/240355

Conti Bossi Fedrigotti
via Unione 43
38068 Rovereto TN
tel. 0464/439250

Graziano Fontana
via Case Sparse 9
38010 Faedo TN
tel. 0461/650400

Maso Furli
via Maso Furli 32
38015 Lavis TN
tel. 0461/240667

Pojer e Sandri
località Molini 6
38010 Faedo TN
tel. 0461/650342

### VALDADIGE PINOT GRIGIO doc
*Vitigno: Pinot grigio*

Santa Margherita
via Ita Marzotto 8
30025 Fossalta di
Portogruaro VE
tel. 0421/246111

### TRENTINO VINO SANTO doc
*Vines: Nosiola (min. 85%)*

Cantina di Toblino
fraz. Sarche
via Ponte Oliveti 1
38070 Calavino TN
tel. 0461/564168

Cavit
via Del Ponte 31
38100 Ravina di Trento TN
tel. 0461/381711

Distilleria Giovanni Poli
via Vezzano
38070 S. Massenza TN
tel. 0461/864119

Fratelli Pisoni
via San Siro 7/a
38076 Porgolese di Lasino TN
tel. 0461/563216

Pedrotti Gino
Loc. Lago di Cavedine -
Pietramurata
38070 Cavedine TN
tel. 0461/564123

### DOLOMITI E VALLAGARINA IGT BIANCO

La Vis
via del Carmine 7
38015 Lavis TN
tel. 0461/246325
*Sorni Bianco (Nosiola +
Chardonnay e Pinot Bianco)*

### DOLOMITI E VALLAGARINA IGT ROSSO

La Vis
via del Carmine 7
38015 Lavis TN
tel. 0461/246325
*Sorni Rosso (Lagrein +
Teroldego)*

Foradori
via della Chiesa 1
38017 Mezzolombardo TN
tel. 0461/601046
*Granato*

## VIGNETI DELLE DOLOMITI IGT NOSIOLA

Castel Noarna
via Castelnuovo 1
38068 Noarna di Rovereto TN
tel. 0464/413295

## ALTO ADIGE

### ALTO ADIGE GEWURZTRAMINER doc
*Vines: Gewurztraminer (min 95%)*

Cantina di Termeno
strada del Vino 144
39040 Termeno BZ
tel. 0471/860126

Cantina Produttori Cortaccia
Strada del Vino 2
39040 Cortaccia BZ
tel. 0471/880115

Cantina Produttori San
Michele Appiano
via Circonvallazione 17/19
39057 S. Michele Appiano BZ
tel. 0471/664466

Cantina Viticoltori di Caldaro
via Cantine 12
39052 Caldaro BZ
tel. 0471/963149

Elena Walch
via A. Hofer 1
39040 Termeno BZ
tel. 0471/860172

Franz Haas
via Villa 6
39040 Montagnana BZ
tel. 0471/812280

Hofstatter
piazza Municipio 5
39040 Termeno BZ
tel. 0471/860161

K. Martini & Sohn
via Lamm Weg 28
39050 Cornaiano BZ
tel. 0471/663156

Tiefenbrunner
via Castello 4
Frazione Miclara
39040 Cortaccia BZ
tel. 0471/880122

### ALTO ADIGE GEWURZTRAMINER PASSITO doc
*Vines: Gewurztraminer (min 95%)*

Cantina di Termeno
strada del Vino 144
39040 Termeno BZ
tel. 0471/860126

Elena Walch
Via A. Hofer 1
39040 Termeno BZ
tel. 0471/860172

### ALTO ADIGE LAGREIN DUNKEL doc
*Vines: Lagrein (min 95%)*

Cantina Benedettina
Muri-Gries
piazza Gries 21
39100 Bolzano BZ
tel. 0471/273448

Cantina di Termeno
strada del Vino 144
39040 Termeno BZ
tel. 0471/860126

Cantina Produttori Colterenzio
Strada del Vino, 8
39050 Cornaiano BZ
tel. 0471/660633

Cantina Produttori Cornaiano
via San Martino 24
39050 Cornaiano BZ
tel. 0471/662654

Cantina Produttori di Andriano
via della Chiesa 2
39010 Andriano BZ
tel. 0471/510227

Cantina Produttori di Merano
via San Marco 11
39012 Merano BZ
tel. 0473/235544

Cantina Vini H. Lun
via Villa 22/24
39044 Egna BZ
tel. 0471/813256

Franz Gojer - Glögglhof
via Rivellone 1
frazione Santa Maddalena
39100 Bolzano BZ
tel. 0471/978775

Hofstatter
piazza Municipio 5
39040 Termeno BZ
tel. 0471/860161

Ignaz Niedrist
località Cornaniano
via Ronco 5
39050 Appiano BZ
tel. 0471/664494

K. Martini
via Lamm 28
39050 Cornaiano BZ
tel. 0471/663156

Loaker Tenuta Schwarhof
località Santa Giustina 3
39100 Bolzano BZ
tel. 0471/365125

Thomas Mayr & Söhne
via Mendola 56
39100 Bolzano BZ
tel. 0471/281030

### ALTO ADIGE MOSCATO GIALLO doc
*Vines: Moscato Giallo*

Alois Lageder Tenuta
Löwengang
via dei Conti 9
39040 Magré BZ
tel. 0471/809500

Manincor - Tenuta Graf
Enzenberg
piazza Morandelli 6
39052 Caldaro BZ
tel. 0471/960230

### ALTO ADIGE MOSCATO PASSITO doc

Cantina Produttori di Merano
via San Marco 11
39012 Merano BZ
tel. 0473/235544

## ALTO ADIGE MOSCATO ROSA doc

*Vines: Moscato Rosa*

 Franz Haas
via Villa 6
39040 Montagnana BZ
tel. 0471/812280

 Laimburg
via Laimburg 6
39040 Ora BZ
tel. 0471/969700

Heinrich Plattner
via Santa Giustina, 2
39100 Bolzano BZ
tel. 0471/973245

## ALTO ADIGE SCHIAVA doc

*Vines: Schiava (min 85%)*

Cantina di Andriano
via della Chiesa 2
39010 Andriano BZ
tel. 0471/510137

Cantina di Cornaiano
via Lamm 28
39050 Cornaiano BZ
tel. 0471/663156

Cantina di Termeno
strada del Vino 144
39040 Termeno BZ
tel. 0471/860126

Thomas Mayr & Söhne
via Mendola 56
39100 Bolzano BZ
tel. 0471/281030

 Cantina di Termeno
strada del Vino 144
39040 Termeno BZ
tel. 0471/860126

Elena Walch
via A. Hofer, 1
39040 Termeno BZ
tel. 0471/860172

## LAGO DI CALDARO doc

*Vines: Schiava (min 85%),
Lagrein a/o Pinot Nero
(max 15%)*

Cantina Vini Josef Brigl
via San Floriano 8
39050 Cornaiano BZ
tel. 0471/662419

 Cantina Viticoltori
di Caldaro
via Cantine 12
39052 Caldaro BZ
tel. 0471/963149

Conte Kuenburg
Castell Salleg
vicolo di Sotto 15
39052 Caldaro BZ
tel. 0471/974140

K. Martini
via Lamm 28
39050 Cornaiano BZ
tel. 0471/663156

Manincor
Tenuta Graf Enzenberg
piazza Morandelli 6
39052 Caldaro BZ
tel. 0471/962080

## ALTO ADIGE SANTA MADDALENA doc

*Vines: Schiava (min 90%),
Pinot Nero a/o Lagrein
(max 10%)*

 Cantina Produttori di Bolzano
Santa Maddalena
via Brennero 15
39100 Bolzano BZ
tel. 0471/972944

Cantina Sociale di Terlano
via Colle d'Argento 7
39018 Terlano BZ
tel. 0471/257135

 Cantina Vini H. Lun
via Villa 22/24
39044 Egna BZ
tel. 0471/813256

Hans Rottensteiner
via Sarentino 1/a
39100 Bolzano BZ
tel. 0471/282015

Heinrich Plattner
Via Santa Giustina
239100 Bolzano BZ
tel. 0471/973245

Josef Nidermayer
via Casa di Gesù 15
39050 Cornaiano BZ
tel. 0471/662451

## ALTO ADIGE VALLE ISARCO GEWÜRZTRAMINER doc

*Vines: Gewürztraminer*

 Abbazia di Novacella
Via Abbazia 1
39040 Varna BZ
tel. 0472/836189

 Cantina Produttori Valle Isarco
via Coste 50
39043 Chiusa BZ
tel. 0472/847553

## VENETO

## AMARONE DELLA VALPOLICELLA doc

*Vines: Corvina veronese (dal
40 al 70%), Rondinella (dal
20 al 40%), Molinara (dal 5
al 25%), Negrara a/o
Rossignola a/o Barbera a/o
Sangiovese a/o Garganega
(max 15%)*

Accordini
via Bolla 9
frazione Pedemonte
37020 Pedemonte di
Valpolicella VR
tel. 045/7701733

Allegrini
via Giare 9/11
37022 Fumane
di Valpolicella VR
tel. 045/6832011

Bolla
piazza Cittadella 3
37122 Verona VR
tel. 045/8670911

Campagnola
via Agnella 9
37020 Valgatara di
Valpolicella VR
tel. 045/7703900

Cantina Sociale della
Valpolicella
via Ca' Salgari 2
37024 Negrar
di Valpolicella VR
tel. 045/7500070

Casa Vinicola Gerardo Cesari
via Luigi Ciocca 35
25027 Quinzano BS
tel. 030/9925811

Casa Vinicola Santi
via Ungheria 33
37031 Illasi VR
tel. 045/6520077

Castellani Michele
via Granda 1
frazione Valgatara
37020 Marano
di Valpolicella VR
tel. 045/7701253

---

Cavaliere G.B. Bertani
località Novare
frazione Arbizzano
37024 Negrar
di Valpolicella VR
tel. 045/6011211

Cecilia Beretta
via Sant'Eurosia
frazione Mizzole
37030 Verona VR
tel. 045/8402021

Conti Guerrieri Rizzardi
via Verdi 4
37011 Bardolino VR
tel. 045/7210028

Corte Sant'Alda
località Fioi - via Capovilla 28
37030 Mezzane di Sotto VR
tel. 045/8880006

Dal Forno Romano
via Lodoletta 1
37030 Cellore d'Illasi VR
tel. 045/7834923

Fratelli Nicolis
via Villa Girardi 29
37029 San Pietro
in Cariano VR
tel. 045/7701261

---

Fratelli Tedeschi
via Verdi 4/a
37020 Pedemonte di
Valpolicella VR
tel. 045/7701487

Le Salette
via Pio Brugnoli 11/c
37022 Fumane
di Valpolicella VR
tel. 045/7701027

Luigi Brunelli
via Cariano 10
37029 San Pietro
in Cariano VR
tel. 045/7701118

Masi Agricola
via Monteleone
37020 Gargagnago di
Valpolicella VR
tel. 045/6832511

Montresor
via Ca' di Cozzi 16
37124 Verona VR
tel. 045/913399

Pasqua
via Belviglieri 30
37131 Verona VR
tel. 045/8402111

Quintarelli
via Cerè 1
37024 Negrar
di Valpolicella VR
tel. 045/7500016

Roccolo Grassi
via San Giovanni di Dio 19
37030 Mezzane di Sotto VR
tel. 045/8880089

San Rustico
frazione Valgatara via Pozzo 2
37020 Marano
di Valpolicella VR
tel. 045/7703348

---

Santa Sofia
via Ca' Dede' 61
37020 Pedemonte di
Valpolicella VR
tel. 045/7701074

Sartori
via Casette 2 - 37024 Negrar VR
tel. 045/6028011

Serego Alighieri
via Stazione 2
37020 Gargagnago di
Valpolicella VR
tel. 045/7703622

Tenuta Musella
località Monte del Drago
37036 San Martino Buon
Albergo VR
tel. 045/973385

Tenuta Sant'Antonio
via Ceriani 23
37037 San Zeno di Colognola
ai Colli VR
tel. 045/7650383

Venturini
via Semonte 20
37029 S. Pietro in Cariano VR
tel. 045/7701331

Viviani
via Mazzano 8
37024 Negrar
di Valpolicella VR
tel. 045/7500286

Zenato
via San Benedetto 8 - frazione
San Benedetto di Lugana
37010 Peschiera del Garda VR
tel. 045/7550300

### BARDOLINO CHIARETTO docg

*Vines: Corvina veronese (dal 35 al 65%), Rondinella (dal 10 al 40%), Molinara (dal 10 al 20%), Negrara (max 10%), Rossignola a/o Barbera a/o Sangiovese a/o Garganega (max 15%)*

Bolla
piazza Cittadella 3
37122 Verona VR
tel. 045/8670911

Cantine Eugenio Tinazzi
località Polinchia
37010 Cavaion Veronese VR
tel. 045/7235394

Fratelli Zeni
via Costabella 9
37011 Bardolino VR
tel. 045/7210022

Lamberti
Gruppo Italiano Vini
via Gardesana
37010 Lazise VR
tel. 045/7580034

Le Fraghe
località La Colombara 37
37010 Cavaion Veronese VR
tel. 045/7236832

Le Vigne di San Pietro
via San Pietro 23
37066 Sommacampagna VR
tel. 045/510016

Montresor
via Ca' di Cozzi 16
37124 Verona
tel. 045/913399

### BARDOLINO CLASSICO docg

*Vines: Corvina veronese (dal 35 al 65%), Rondinella (dal 10 al 40%), Molinara (dal 10 al 20%), Negrara (max 10%), Rossignola a/o Barbera a/o Sangiovese a/o Garganega (max 15%)*

Bolla
piazza Cittadella 3
37122 Verona VR
tel. 045/8670911

Boscaini Paolo & Figli
via Ca'de Loi
37020 Marano
di Valpolicella VR
tel. 045/6832411

Cavaliere G.B. Bertani
località Novare
frazione Arbizzano
37024 Negrar VR
tel. 045/6011211

Corte Gardoni
via Gardoni 5
37067 Valeggio sul Mincio VR
tel. 045/7950382

Fratelli Zeni
via Costabella 9
37011 Bardolino VR
tel. 045/7210022

Le Fraghe
località La Colombara 37
37010 Cavaion Veronese VR
tel. 045/7236832

Le Tende
località Le Tende 6/a
37017 Colà di Lazise VR
tel. 045/7590748

Le Vigne di San Pietro
via San Pietro 23
37066 Sommacampagna VR
tel. 045/510016

Santa Sofia
via Ca' Dedè 61
37020 Pedemonte di
Valpolicella VR
tel. 045/7701074

### BARDOLINO SUPERIORE docg

*Vines: Corvina veronese (dal 35 al 65%), Rondinella (dal 10 al 40%), Molinara (dal 10 al 20%), Negrara (max 10%), Rossignola a/o Barbera a/o Sangiovese a/o Garganega (max 15%)*

Cantine Eugenio Tinazzi
località Polinchia
37010 Cavaion Veronese VR
tel. 045/7235394

Cantine Lenotti
via Santa Cristina 1
37011 Bardolino VR
tel. 045/7210484

Cavalchina
località Cavalchina
37060 Custoza VR
tel. 045/516002

Conti Guerrieri Rizzardi
via Verdi 4
37011 Bardolino VR
tel. 045/7210028

### BIANCO DI CUSTOZA doc

*Vines: Trebbiano Toscano, localmente noto come Castelli romani, (dal 20 al 45%), Garganega (dal 20 al 40%), Tocai Friulano, localmente noto come Trebianello (dal 5 al 30%), Cortese, localmente noto come Bianca Fernanda a/o Malvasia toscana a/o Riesling italico a/o Pinot Bianco a/o Chardonnay (dal 20 al 30%)*

Campagnola
via Agnella 9
37020 Valgatara di
Valpolicella VR
tel. 045/7703900

Corte Sant'Arcadio
Località Cà Brusà 12
37014 Castelnuovo
del Garda VR
tel. 045/7575331

Cavalchina
località Cavalchina
37060 Custoza VR
tel. 045/516002

Lamberti-Gruppo Italiano Vini
via Gardesana
37010 Lazise VR
tel. 045/7580034

Le Tende
località Le Tende 6/a
37017 Colà di Lazise VR
tel. 045/7590748

Le Vigne di San Pietro
via San Pietro 23
37066 Sommacampagna VR
tel. 045/510016

Montresor
via Ca' di Cozzi 16
37124 Verona
tel. 045/913399

*Vitigno: Vespaiola (min. 85%)*

 Maculan
via Castelletto 3
36042 Breganze VI
tel. 0445/873733

**COLLI BERICI
TOCAI ROSSO** doc

*Vines: Tocai Rosso (min. 85%),
Garganega (max 15%)*

Cantina Sociale Colli Vicentini
viale Europa 107
36041 Alte di
Montecchio M. VI
tel. 0444/491360

Marcato
via Prandi 10 - 37030 Roncà VR
tel. 045/7460070

Piovene Porto Godi
via Villa 14
36020 Toara di Villaga VI
tel. 0444/885142

*Vines: Moscato giallo
(min. 95%)*

Borin
via dei Colli 5
35043 Monticelli
di Monselice PD
tel. 0429/74384

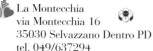 La Montecchia
via Montecchia 16
35030 Selvazzano Dentro PD
tel. 049/637294

 Vignalta
via Marlunghe 7
35032 Arquà Petrarca PD
tel. 0429/777225

Villa Sceriman
v. dei Colli 68 - 35030 Vò PD
tel. 0499/940123

*Vines: Moscato giallo (min. 95%)*

Borin
via dei Colli 5
35043 Monticelli
di Monselice PD
tel. 0429/74384

Ca' Lustra
via San Pietro 50
35030 Faedo di Cinto
Euganeo PD
tel. 0429/94128

San Nazario
via Monte Versa 9
35030 Vò PD
tel. 0499/940194

*Vines: Moscato Giallo
(min. 95%)*

Vignalta
via Marlunghe 7
35032 Arquà Petrarca PD
tel. 0429/777225

Villa Sceriman
v. dei Colli 68 - 35030 Vò PD
tel. 0499/940123

*Vines: Moscato Giallo (min.
95%)*

Villa Sceriman
via dei Colli 68
35030 Vò PD
tel. 0499/940123

*Vines: Garganega (min. 80%)*

Cantina Sociale di Gambellara
via Mazzini 2
36053 Gambellara VI
tel. 0444/444012

Cavazza
via Selva 22
36054 Montebello Vicentino VI
tel. 0444/649166

Dal Maso
via Selva 62
36054 Montebello Vicentino VI
tel. 0444/649104

La Biancara
contrà Biancara 8
36053 Gambellara VI
tel. 0444/444244

Zonin-Podere Il Giangio
via Borgolecco 9
36053 Gambellara VI
tel. 0444/640111

*Vines: Garganega (min. 80%)*

Cavazza
via Selva 22
36054 Montebello Vicentino VI
tel. 0444/649166

Dal Maso
via Selva 62
36054 Montebello Vicentino VI
tel. 0444/649104

La Biancara
contrà Biancara 8
36053 Gambellara VI
tel. 0444/444244

Zonin
via Borgolecco 9
36053 Gambellara VI
tel. 0444/640111

*Vines: Garganega
(min. 80%)*

Cantina Sociale Colli Vicentini
viale Europa 107
36041 Alte di Montecchio
Maggiore VI
tel. 0444/491360

Cantina Sociale di Gambellara
via Mazzini 2
36053 Gambellara VI
tel. 0444/444012

Zonin
via Borgolecco 9
36053 Gambellara VI
tel. 0444/640111

*Vines: Garganega
(min. 80%)*

Cantina Sociale
Colli Vicentini
viale Europa 107
36041 Alte di Montecchio
Maggiore VI
tel. 0444/491360

Cantina Sociale
di Gambellara
via Mazzini 2
36053 Gambellara VI
tel. 0444/444012

**LISON PRAMAGGIORE
REFOSCO
DAL PEDUNCOLO
ROSSO** doc

*Vines: Refosco dal Peduncolo
Rosso (min. 85%)*

Cantina Sant'Osvaldo
via Monsignor Zovatto 81
30020 Locon di Annone
Veneto VE
tel. 0422/864012

Paladin & Paladin-Bosco
del Merlo
via Postumia 12
30020 Annone Veneto VE
tel. 0422/768767

 Santa Margherita
via Ita Marzotto
30025 Fossalta di
Portogruaro VE
tel. 0421/246268

Tenuta Sant'Anna
via Zovatto 71
30020 Locon di Annone
Veneto VE
tel. 0422/864511

**LISON
PRAMAGGIORE
TOCAI** doc
*Vines: Tocai italico
(min. 85%)*

Principi di Porcia
Brugnera
via Zumano 29
33082 Azzano Decimo PN
tel. 0434/631001

 Santa Margherita
via Ita Marzotto
30025 Fossalta di
Portogruaro VE
tel. 0421/246268

Tenuta Sant'Anna
via Zovatto 71
30020 Locon di Annone
Veneto VE
tel. 0422/864511

**MONTI LESSINI
DURELLO SPUMANTE
METODO CLASSICO** doc
*Vines: Durello (min 85%),
Garganega a/o Pinot Bianco
a/o Chardonnay a/o
Trebbiano di Soave a/o Pinot
Nero (max 15%)*

Cantina Sociale Colli Vicentini
viale Europa 107
36041 Alte di Montecchio
Maggiore VI
tel. 0444/491360

Fongaro
località Motta Piane 6
37030 Roncà VR
tel. 045/7460240

Marcato
via Prandi 10
37030 Roncà VR
tel. 045/7460070

**PIAVE RABOSO** doc
*Vines: Raboso (min. 95%)*

Cecchetto
via Piave 67
31620 Tezze di Piave TV
tel. 0438/28598

Le Rive
via Grave Di Sopra 50
31047 Ponte di Piave TV
tel. 0422/754137

Moletto
via Moletto 19
31045 Motta di Livenza TV
tel. 0422/860576

Molon Traverso
via Risorgimento 40
31040 Campodipietra di
Salgareda TV
tel. 0422/804807

Rechsteiner
via Frassenè 2
31040 Piavon di Oderzo TV
tel. 0422/752074

**PROSECCO PASSITO
VINO DA TAVOLA**

Bisol
via Fol 33
31049 Valdobbiadene TV
tel. 0423/900138

**PROSECCO DI
CONEGLIANO
VALDOBBIADENE
BRUT** doc
*Vines: Prosecco (min. 85%)*

Andreola Orsola
via Cal Longa 52
31010 Farra di Soligo TV
tel. 0438/989379

Dea
via Garibaldi 309
31049 Valdobbiadene TV
tel. 0423/971017

Bellenda
via Giardino 90
31029 Carpensica di Vittorio
Veneto TV
tel. 0438/920025

Bisol
via Fol 33
31049 Valdobbiadene TV
tel. 0423/900138

Cantina Produttori di
Valdobbiadene
via San Giovanni 65
31049 Valdobbiadene TV
tel. 0423/982070

Carpenè Malvolti
via Carpenè 1
31015 Conegliano TV
tel. 0438/364611

Col de' Salici
Borgo degli Albizzi 14
50123 Firenze
tel. 055/243101

Col Vetoraz Spumanti
strada delle Treziese 1
31040 Santo Stefano di
Valdobbiadene TV
tel. 0423/975291

Consorzio Cantine Sociali
della Marca Trevigiana
via Baite 14
31046 Oderzo TV
tel. 0422/814681

De Faveri Spumanti
via Sartori 21
31020 Bosco di Vidor TV
tel. 0423/987673

Foss Marai
strada Giulia 75
31040 Giulia in
Valdobbiadene TV
tel. 0423/900560

Mionetto
via Colderove 2
31049 Valdobbiadene TV
tel. 0423/9707

Nino Franco
via Garibaldi 147
31049 Valdobbiadene TV
tel. 0423/972051

Ruggeri
via Prà Fontana
31049 Valdobbiadene TV
tel. 0423/9092

**Sorelle Bronca**
via Martini 20
31020 Colbertaldo di Vidor TV
tel. 0423/987201

**Zardetto Spumanti**
via Marcorà 15/a
31020 Ogliano
di Conegliano TV
tel. 0438/208909

**PROSECCO DI
CONEGLIANO VALDOB-
BIADENE DRY** doc
*Vines: Prosecco (min. 85%)*

**Adami Adriano**
via Rovede 27
31020 Colbertaldo di Vidor TV
tel. 0423/982110

**Astoria Vini**
viale Antonini 9
31020 Crocetta
del Montello TV
tel. 0423/665042

**Belussi Spumanti**
via Erizzo 215
31049 Valdobbiadene TV
tel. 0423/982147

**Bisol**
via Fol 33
31049 Valdobbiadene TV
tel. 0423/900138

**Bortolomiol**
via Garibaldi 142
31049 Valdobbiadene TV
tel. 0423/975794

**Col Vetoraz Spumanti**
strada delle Tresiese 1
31040 Santo Stefano di
Valdobbiadene TV
tel. 0423/975291

**De Faveri Spumanti**
via Sartori 21
31020 Bosco di Vidor TV
tel. 0423/987673

**Il Colle**
via Colle 15
31020 S. Pietro di Feletto TV
tel. 0438/486926

**Masottina**
via Bradolini 54
31010 Castello
di Roganzuolo TV
tel. 0438/400775

**PROSECCO DI
CONEGLIANO
VALDOBBIADENE
EXTRA DRY** doc
*Vines: Prosecco (min. 85%)*

**Adami Adriano**
via Rovede 27
31020 Colbertaldo di Vidor TV
tel. 0423/982110

**Andreola Orsola**
via Cal Longa 52
31010 Farra di Soligo TV
tel. 0438/989379

**Bepin de Eto**
via Colle 32/a
31020 S. Pietro di Feletto TV
tel. 0438/486877

**Bortolin**
via Menegazzi 5
31040 Santo Stefano di
Valdobbiadene TV
tel. 0423/900135

**Canevel**
via Cal Piandre 25
31049 Valdobbiadene TV
tel. 0423/975940

**Cantina Produttori di**
**Valdobbiadene**
via San Giovanni 65
31049 Valdobbiadene TV
tel. 0423/982070

**Carpenè Malvolti**
via Carpenè 1
31015 Conegliano TV
tel. 0438/364611

**Casa Vinicola Canella**
via Fiume 7
30027 S. Donà del Piave VE
tel. 0421/52446

**Col de' Salici**
Borgo degli Albizzi 14
50123 Firenze
tel. 055/243101

**Collalto**
via XXIV Maggio 1
31058 Susegnana TV
tel. 0438/738241

**Foss Marai**
strada Giulia 75
31040 Giulia in
Valdobbiadene TV
tel. 0423/900560

**Gregoletto**
via San Martino 1
31050 Premaor di Miane TV
tel. 0438/970463

**Il Colle**
via Colle 15
31020 S. Pietro di Feletto TV
tel. 0438/486926

**La Gioiosa**
via Erizzo 113/a
31035 Crocetta del Montello TV
tel. 0423/8607

**Toffoli**
via Liberazione 26
31020 Refrontolo TV
tel. 0438/894240

**Villa Sandi**
via Erizzo 112/b
31035 Crocetta
del Montello TV
tel. 0423/665033

**PROSECCO DI
CONEGLIANO
VALDOBBIADENE
FRIZZANTE** doc
*Vines: Prosecco (min. 85%)*

**Bortolomiol**
via Garibaldi 142
31049 Valdobbiadene TV
tel. 0423/955794

**Ca' Salina**
via S. Stefano 2
31049 Santo Stefano di
Valdobbiadene TV
tel. 0423/975296

**Canevel**
via Cal Piandre 25
31049 Valdobbiadene TV
tel. 0423/975940

**La Farra**
via San Francesco 44
31010 Farra di Soligo TV
tel. 0438/801242

**Mionetto**
via Colderove 2
31049 Valdobbiadene TV
tel. 0423/9707

**Montesel**
via San Daniele 42
31030 Colfosco TV
tel. 0438/781341

**Sorelle Bronca**
via Martiri 20
31020 Colbertaldo di Vidor TV
tel. 0423/987201

Vincenzo Toffoli
via Liberazione 26
31020 Refrontolo TV
tel. 0438/894240

### PROSECCO DI CONEGLIANO VALDOBBIADENE FERMO doc

*Vines: Prosecco (min. 85%)*

Adami Adriano
via Rovede 27
31020 Colbertaldo di Vidor TV
tel. 0423/982110

Bisol
via Fol 33
31049 Valdobbiadene TV
tel. 0423/900138

Col Vetoraz Spumanti
strada delle Tresiese 1
31040 Santo Stefano di
Valdobbiadene TV
tel. 0423/975291

Dal Din Spumanti
via Montegrappa 31
31020 Vidor TV
tel. 0423/987295

Dea-Rivalta
via Garibaldi 309/A
31049 Valdobbiadene TV
tel. 0423/971017

 Gregoletto
via San Martino 1
31050 Premaor di Miane TV
tel. 0438/970463

Il Colle
via Colle 15
31020 S. Pietro di Feletto TV
tel. 0438/486926

Le Groppe
strada Farra 4
31049 Valdobbiadene TV
tel. 0423/972305

Nino Franco Spumanti
via Garibaldi 147
31049 Valdobbiadene TV
tel. 0423/972051

### PROSECCO DI CONEGLIANO VALDOBBIADENE SUPERIORE CARTIZZE doc

*Vines: Prosecco (min. 85%)*

Adami Adriano
via Rovede 27
31020 Colbertaldo di Vidor TV
tel. 0423/982110

Bellenda
via Giardino 90
31029 Carpensica di Vittorio
Veneto TV
tel. 0438/920025

 Bisol
via Fol 33
31049 Valdobbiadene TV
tel. 0423/900138

Bortolomiol
via Garibaldi 142
31049 Valdobbiadene TV
tel. 0423/955794

Col Vetoraz Spumanti
strada delle Treziese 1
31040 Santo Stefano di
Valdobbiadene TV
tel. 0423/975291

Foss Marai
strada Giulia 75
31040 Giulia in
Valdobbiadene TV
tel. 0423/900560

Le Colture
via Fol 5 - fraz. Santo Stefano
31049 Valdobbiadene TV
tel. 0423/900192

Nino Franco Spumanti
via Garibaldi 147
31049 Valdobbiadene TV
tel. 0423/972051

 Ruggeri
via Prà Fontana
31049 Valdobbiadene TV
tel. 0423/9092

Villa Sandi
via Erizzo 112/b
31035 Crocetta
del Montello TV
tel. 0423/665033

### RECIOTO DELLA VALPOLICELLA doc

*Vines: Corvina veronese (dal 40 al 70%), Rondinella (dal 20 al 40%), Molinara (dal 5 al 25%), Negrara a/o Rossignola a/o Barbera a/o Sangiovese a/o Garganega (max 15%)*

Allegrini
via Giare 9/11
37022 Fumane
di Valpolicella VR
tel. 045/7701774

Brigaldara
via Brigaldara 1
frazione Floriano
37029 S. Pietro in Cariano VR
tel. 045/7701055

 Castellani Michele
via Granda 1 - fraz. Valgatara
37020 Marano
di Valpolicella VR
tel. 045/7701253

Corte Sant'Alda
località Fioi - via Capovilla 28
37030 Mezzane di Sotto VR
tel. 045/8880006

Le Salette
via Pio Brugnoli 11/c
37022 Fumane
di Valpolicella VR
tel. 045/7701027

Masi Agricola
via Monteleone
37020 Gargagnago di
Valpolicella VR
tel. 045/6832511

Montresor
via Ca' di Cozzi 16
37124 Verona VR
tel. 045/913399

Novaia
località Novaia 3
37020 Marano
di Valpolicella VR
tel. 045/7755129

Sartori
via Casette 2
37024 Negrar
di Valpolicella VR
tel. 045/6028011

### RECIOTO DELLA VALPOLICELLA SPUMANTE doc

*Vines: Corvina veronese (dal 40 al 70%), Rondinella (dal 20 al 40%), Molinara (dal 5 al 25%), Negrara a/o Rossignola a/o Barbera a/o Sangiovese a/o Garganega (max 15%)*

Cavaliere G.B. Bertani
loc. Novare - fraz. Arbizzano
37024 Negrar VR
tel. 045/6011211

### RECIOTO DI SOAVE docg

*Vines: Garganega (min 70%), Pinot Bianco a/o Chardonnay a/o Trebbiano di Soave (max 30%)*

Ca' Rugate
via Mezzavilla 12
37030 Brognoligo VR
tel. 045/6175082

Cecilia Beretta
via Sant'Eurosia - fraz. Mizzole
37030 Verona VR
tel. 045/8402021

Coffele
via Roma 5
37038 Soave VR
tel. 045/7680007

Gini
via Matteotti 42
37032 Monteforte D'Alpone VR
tel. 045/7611908

Roccolo Grassi
via San Giovanni di Dio 19
37030 Mezzane di Sotto VR
tel. 045/8880089

Santa Sofia
via Ca' Dede' 61
37020 Pedemonte di
Valpolicella VR
tel. 045/7701074

Sartori
via Casette 2
37024 Negrar VR
tel. 045/6028011

Tamellini
via Tamellini 4
37038 Costeggiola Soave VR
tel. 045/7575328

### SOAVE doc

*Vines: Garganega (min 70%), Pinot Bianco a/o Chardonnay a/o Trebbiano di Soave (max 30%)*

Bolla
piazza Cittadella 3
37122 Verona VR
tel. 045/8670911

Boscaini Paolo & Figli
via Ca' de Loi
37020 Marano
di Valpolicella VR
tel. 045/6832411

Ca' Rugate
via Mezzavilla 12
37030 Brognoligo VR
tel. 045/6175082

Campagnola
via Agnella 9
37020 Valgatara di
Valpolicella VR
tel. 045/7703900

Cantina di Soave
viale Vittoria 100
37038 Soave VR
tel. 045/6139811

Cecilia Beretta
via Sant'Eurosia - fraz. Mizzole
37030 Verona VR
tel. 045/8402021

Coffele
via Roma 5
37038 Soave VR
tel. 045/7680007

Fratelli Zeni
via Costabella 9
37011 Bardolino VR
tel. 045/7210022

Gini
via Matteotti 42
37032 Monteforte D'Alpone VR
tel. 045/7611908

Inama
via IV Novembre 1
37047 San Bonifacio VR
tel. 045/6101411

La Cappuccina
via San Brizio 125
37032 Monteforte d'Alpone VR
tel. 045/6175840

Masi Agricola
via Monteleone
37020 Gargagnago di
Valpolicella VR
tel. 045/6832511

Pasqua
via Belviglieri 30
37131 Verona VR
tel. 045/8402111

Pieropan
via Camuzzoni 3
37038 Soave VR
tel. 045/6190171

Portinari Umberto
frazione Brognoligo
via Santo Stefano 2
37032 Monteforte d'Alpone VR
tel. 045/6175087

Prà
via della Fontana 31
37032 Monteforte d'Alpone VR
tel. 045/7612125

Roccolo Grassi
via San Giovanni di Dio 19
37030 Mezzane di Sotto VR
tel. 045/8880089

Santi
via Ungheria 33
37031 Illasi VR
tel. 045/6520077

Sartori
via Casette 2
37024 Negrar
di Valpolicella VR
tel. 045/6028011 Soldi

Suavia
via Centro 14 - frazione Fittà
37038 Soave VR
tel. 045/7675089

Tamellini
via Tamellini 4
37038 Costeggiola Soave VR
tel. 045/7575328

Walter Balestri
via Monti 44
37038 Soave VR
tel. 045/7675393

Zenato
via San Benedetto 8
fraz. San Bendetto di Lugana
37010 Peschiera del Garda VR
tel. 045/7550300

## VALPOLICELLA CLASSICO E SUPERIORE doc

*Vines: Corvina veronese (dal 40 al 70%), Rondinella (dal 20 al 40%), Molinara (dal 5 al 25%), Negrara a/o Rossignola a/o Barbera a/o Sangiovese a/o Garganega (max 15%)*

Accordini
via Bolla 9
37020 Pedemonte di
Valpolicella VR
tel. 045/7701733

Allegrini
via Giare 9/11
37022 Fumane
di Valpolicella VR
tel. 045/7701774

Bolla
piazza Cittadella 3
37122 Verona VR
tel. 045/8670911

Boscaini Paolo & Figli
via Ca'de Loi 2
37020 Marano
di Valpolicella VR
tel. 045/6832411

Cantina Soc. della Valpantena
via Orfani di Guerra 5/b
37044 Quinto
di Valpantena VR
tel. 045/550032

Cantina Sociale della
Valpolicella
via Ca' Salgari 2
37024 Negrar VR
tel. 045/7500070

Casa Vinicola Santi
via Ungheria 33
37031 Illasi VR
tel. 045/6520077

Castellani Michele
via Granda 1 - fraz. Valgatara
37020 Marano
di Valpolicella VR
tel. 045/7701253

Cavaliere G.B. Bertani
loc. Novare - fraz. Arbizzano
37024 Negrar VR
tel. 045/6011211

Cecilia Beretta
via Sant'Eurosia - fraz. Mizzole
37030 Verona VR
tel. 045/8402021

Conti Guerrieri Rizzardi
via Verdi 4
37011 Bardolino VR
tel. 045/7210028

Corte Sant'Alda
località Fioi - via Capovilla 28
37030 Mezzane di Sotto VR
tel. 045/8880006

Dal Forno Romano
via Lodoletta 1
37030 Cellore d'Illasi VR
tel. 045/7834923

Fratelli Fabiano
via Verona 6 - 37060 Sona VR
tel. 045/6081111

Fratelli Tedeschi
via Verdi 4/a
37020 Pedemonte di
Valpolicella VR
tel. 045/7701487

Le Ragose
via Le Ragose 1
37020 Arbizzano di Negrar VR
tel. 045/7513171

Le Salette
via Pio Brugnoli 11/c
37022 Fumane
di Valpolicella VR
tel. 045/7701027

Masi Agricola
via Monteleone
37020 Gargagnago di
Valpolicella VR
tel. 045/6832511

Montresor
via Ca' di Cozzi 16
37124 Verona VR
tel. 045/913399

Novaia
località Novaia 3
37020 Marano
di Valpolicella VR
tel. 045/7755129

Pasqua
via Belviglieri 30
37131 Verona VR
tel. 045/8402111

Quintarelli
via Cerè 1
37024 Negrar
di Valpolicella VR
tel. 045/7500016

Roccolo Grassi
via San Giovanni di Dio 19
37030 Mezzane di Sotto VR
tel. 045/8880089

San Rustico
via Pozzo 2 - fraz. Valgatara
37020 Marano
di Valpolicella VR
tel. 045/7703348

Santa Sofia
via Ca' Dede' 61
37020 Pedemonte di
Valpolicella VR
tel. 0457/701074

Sartori
via Casette 2
37024 Negrar
di Valpolicella VR
tel. 045/6028011

Serego Alighieri
via Stazione 2
37020 Gargagnago di
Valpolicella VR
tel. 045/7703622

Tenuta Musella
località Monte del Drago
37036 San Martino Buon
Albergo VR
tel. 045/973385

Tenuta Sant'Antonio
via Ceriani 23
37037 San Zeno di Colognola
ai Colli VR
tel. 045/7650383

Trabuchi
località Monte Tenda 3
37031 Illasi VR
tel. 0458/755455 Cuore

Venturini
via Semonte 20
37029 S. Pietro in Cariano VR
tel. 0457/701331

Zenato
via San Benedetto 8
fraz. San Benedetto di Lugana
37010 Peschiera del Garda VR
tel. 045/7550300

### ROSSO IGT VERONESE

*Corvina + altre*

Accordini
via Bolla 9 - fraz. Pedemonte
37020 Pedemonte di
Valpolicella VR
tel. 045/7701733
*Passo* (Corvina+altre)

Castellani Michele
via Granda 1 - fraz. Valgatara
37020 Marano
di Valpolicella VR
tel. 045/7701253
*Sergio* (Corvina+altre)

Fratelli Tedeschi
via Verdi 4/a
37020 Pedemonte di
Valpolicella VR
tel. 045/7701487
*Rosso della Fabriseria*
(Corvina+altre)

Montresor
via Ca' di Cozzi 16
37124 Verona VR
tel. 045/913399
*Arcaio* (Corvina+altre)

Nicolis
via Villa Girardi 29
37029 S. Pietro in Cariano VR
tel. 045/7701261
*Testal* (Corvina+altre)

### ROSSO VERONESE IGT
### CORVINA

Allegrini
via Giare 9/11
37022 Fumane
di Valpolicella VR
tel. 045/7701774
*La Poja*

Campagnola
via Agnalla 9
37020 Valgatara di
Valpolicella VR
tel. 045/7703900
*Corte Agnella*

Corte Gardoni
via Gardoni 5
37067 Valeggio
sul Mincio VR
tel. 045/7950382
*Becco Rosso*

Pasqua
via Belviglieri 30
37131 Verona VR
tel. 045/8402111
*Kòrae*

Sartori
via Casette 2
37024 Negrar VR
tel. 045/6028011
*Regolo*

Anselmi
via San Carlo 46
37032 Monteforte D'Alpone VR
tel. 045/7611488
*I Capitelli* (Garganega)

La Cappuccina
via San Brizio 125
37032 Monteforte D'Alpone VR
tel. 045/6175840
*Armizio passito* (Garganega)

Montresor
via Ca' di Cozzi 16
37124 Verona VR
tel. 045/913399
*Terranatìa* (Garganega +
Sauvignon)

### VENETO IGT BIANCO

Anselmi
via San Carlo 46
37032 Monteforte D'Alpone VR
tel. 045/7611488
*Capitel Foscarino e Capitel
Croce* (Garganega)

### VENETO IGT
### PROSECCO PASSITO

Toffoli
via Liberazione 26
31020 Refrontolo TV
tel. 0438/894240

### VENETO IGT ROSSO

Masi Agricola
via Monteleone
37020 Gargagnago di
Valpolicella VR
tel. 045/6832511
*Toar* (Corvina+altre)

### VERONA IGT MOSCATO

Conti Guerrieri Rizzardi
via Verdi 4
37011 Bardolino VR
tel. 045/7210028
*Dogoli*

### FRIULI
### VENEZIA GIULIA

#### CARSO MALVASIA doc
*Vines: Malvasia*

Castelvecchio
via Castelnuovo 2
4078 Sagrado GO
tel. 0481/99742

Kante
località Prepotto 3
34011 San Pelagio TS
tel. 040/200761

#### CARSO REFOSCO DAL
#### PEDUNCOLO ROSSO doc
*Vines: Refosco dal Peduncolo
Rosso*

Castelvecchio
via Castelnuovo 2
34078 Sagrado GO
tel. 0481/99742

#### COLLI ORIENTALI DEL
#### FRIULI BIANCO doc

Ronchi di Cialla
frazione Cialla
33040 Prepotto UD
tel. 0432/731679
*Cialla Bianco* (Ribolla Gialla
+ Verduzzo + Picolit)

Walter Filiputti
piazza Abbazia 15
località Rosazzo
33044 Manzano UD
tel. 0432/759429
*Ronco del Monastero* (Tocai +
Sauvignon)

## COLLI ORIENTALI DEL FRIULI MALVASIA doc

*Vines: Malvasia*

Le Vigne di Zamò
via Abate Corrado 4
località Rosazzo
33040 Manzano UD
tel. 0432/759693

Ronco del Gnemiz
via Ronchi 5
33048 San Giovanni al
Natisone UD
tel. 0432/756238
tel. 0432/740414

## COLLI ORIENTALI DEL FRIULI PICOLIT doc

*Vines: Picolit*

Aquila del Torre
via Attimis 25
frazione Sarvognano del Torre
33040 Povoletto UD
tel. 0432/666428

Ca' Ronesca
località Lonzano 27
34070 Dolegna del Collio GO
tel. 0481/60034

*Picolit 1999*

Jucuss
viale Kennedy35/a
33040 Montino di Torreano UD
tel. 0432/715147

Livio Felluga
via Risorgimento 1
34070 Brazzano
di Cormons GO
tel. 0481/60203

Rocca Bernarda
via Rocca Bernarda 27
33040 Premariacca UD
tel. 0432/716914

Rodaro Paolo
via Cormons 8
33042 Spessa di Cividale UD
tel. 0432/716066

Ronchi di Cialla
frazione Cialla
33040 Prepotto UD
tel. 0432/731679

Ronchi di Manzano
via Orsaria 42
33044 Manzano UD
tel. 0432/740718

Tenuta di Angoris
località di Angoris
34071 Cormons GO
tel. 0481/60923

Torre Rosazza
località Poggiobello 12
33044 Manzano UD
tel. 0432/750180

Walter Filiputti
piazza Abbazia 15
località Rosazzo
33044 Manzano UD
tel. 0432/759429

Zof Daniele
via Papa Giovanni XXIII 32/a
33040 Corno
di Rosazzo UD
tel. 0432/759673

## COLLI ORIENTALI DEL FRIULI PIGNOLO doc

*Vines: Pignolo*

Davide Moschioni
loc. Gagliano 30
via Doria 30
33043 Cividale del Friuli UD
tel. 0432/730210

Le Vigne di Zamò
via Abate Corrado 4
località Rosazzo
33040 Manzano UD
tel. 0432/759693

Walter Filiputti
piazza Abbazia 15
località Rosazzo
33044 Manzano UD
tel. 0432/759429

## COLLI ORIENTALI DEL FRIULI RAMANDOLO docg

*Vines: Ramandolo*

Coos
via Ramandolo 15
33045 Nimis UD
tel. 0432/790320

Dri Giovanni
via Pescia 7
33045 Ramandolo di Nimis UD
tel. 0432/790260

Scubla
via Rocca Bernarda 22
33040 Ipplis
di Premariacco UD
tel. 0432/716258

## COLLI ORIENTALI DEL FRIULI REFOSCO DAL PEDUNCOLO ROSSO doc

*Vines: Refosco dal Peduncolo Rosso*

Ca' Ronesca
località Lonzano 27
34070 Dolegna del Collio GO
tel. 0481/60034

Cantarutti Alfieri
via Ronchi 9
33048 San Giovanni al
Natisone UD
tel. 0432/756317

Colutta Gianpaolo
via Orsaria 32
33044 Manzano UD
tel. 0432/510724

Conte d'Attimis - Maniago
via Sottomonte 21
33042 Buttrio UD
tel. 0432/674027

Ermacora
via Solzaredo 9
33040 Ipplis
di Premariacco UD
tel. 0432/716250

Gigante Adriano
via Rocca Bernarda 3
33040 Corno di Rosazzo UD
tel. 0432/755835

Girolamo Dorigo
via del Pozzo 5
33042 Buttrio UD
tel. 0432/674268

Le Vigne di Zamò
via Abate Corrado 4
località Rosazzo
33040 Manzano UD
tel. 0432/759693

Livio Felluga
via Risorgimento 1
34070 Brazzano
di Cormons GO
tel. 0481/60203

Livon
via Montarezza 33
33048 Dolegnano UD
tel. 0432/757173

Petrucco
via Morpurgo 12
33042 Buttrio UD
tel. 0432/674387

Ronchi di Cialla
frazione Cialla
33040 Prepotto UD
tel. 0481/61394

Torre Rosazza
località Poggiobello 12
33044 Manzano UD
tel. 0432/750180

Vigna Traverso
via Ronchi 73
33040 Prepotto UD
tel. 0432/713072

Volpe Pasini
via Cividale 16
33040 Togliano
di Torreano UD
tel. 0432/715151

**COLLI ORIENTALI
DEL FRIULI RIBOLLA
GIALLA** doc

*Vines: Ribolla Gialla*

Colutta Gianpaolo
via Orsaria 32
33044 Manzano UD
tel. 0432/510654

Eugenio Collavini
via della Ribolla Gialla
33040 Corno di Rosazzo UD
tel. 0432/753222

Perusini
via Torrione 13
33040 Corno di Rosazzo UD
tel. 0432/759151

Petrucco
via Morpurgo 12
33042 Buttrio UD
tel. 0432/674387

Ronco delle Betulle
via Abate Colonna 24
33034 Rosazzo di Manzano UD
tel. 0432/740547

Tenuta di Angoris
località di Angoris
34071 Cormons GO
tel. 0481/60923

Valle
via Nazionale 3
33042 Buttrio UD
tel. 0432/674289

Vigna Traverso
via Ronchi 73
33040 Prepotto UD
tel. 0432/713072

Volpe Pasini
via Cividale 16
33040 Togliano
di Torreano UD
tel. 0432/715151

**COLLI ORIENTALI
DEL FRIULI
SCHIOPPETTINO** doc

*Vines: Schioppettino*

Cantarutti Alfieri
via Ronchi 9
33048 San Giovanni al
Natisone UD
tel. 0432/756317

Colli Di Poianis
località Poianis 34/a
33040 Prepotto UD
tel. 0432/713185

Dal Fari
via Darnazzacco
33043 Cividale del Friuli UD
tel. 0432/7670770

Ermacora
via Solzaredo 9
33040 Ipplis
di Premariacco UD
tel. 0432/716250

Girolamo Dorigo
via del Pozzo 5
33042 Buttrio UD
tel. 0432/674268

Grillo
via Albana 60
33043 Cividale del Friuli UD
tel. 0432/713322

Jucuss
viale Kennedy 35/a
33040 Montino di Torreano UD
tel. 0432/715147

La Viarte
via Novacuzzo 50
33040 Prepotto UD
tel. 0432/759458

Rodaro Paolo
via Cormons 8
33042 Spessa di Cividale UD
tel. 0432/716066

Ronchi di Cialla
frazione Cialla
33040 Prepotto UD
tel. 0432/731679

Ronco del Gnemiz
via Ronchi 5
33048 San Giovanni al
Natisone UD
tel. 0432/756238

Vidussi
via Spessa 20
34070 Capriva del Friuli GO
tel. 0481/80072

Vigna Petrussa
via Albana 47
33040 Prepotto UD
tel. 0432/713021

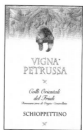

Vigna Traverso
via Ronchi 73
33040 Prepotto UD
tel. 0432/713072

**COLLI ORIENTALI
DEL FRIULI
TAZZELENGHE** doc

*Vines: Tazzelenghe*

La Viarte
via Novacuzzo 50
33040 Prepotto UD
tel. 0432/759458

**COLLI ORIENTALI
DEL FRIULI TOCAI** doc

*Vines: Tocai friulano*

Cantarutti Alfieri
via Ronchi 9
33048 San Giovanni al
Natisone UD
tel. 0432/756317

Colli Di Poianis
località Poianis 34/a
33040 Prepotto UD
tel. 0432/713185

Ermacora
via Solzaredo 9
33040 Ipplis
di Premariacco UD
tel. 0432/716250

Gigante Adriano
via Rocca Bernarda 3
33040 Corno di Rosazzo UD
tel. 0432/755855

Girolamo Dorigo
via del Pozzo 5
33042 Buttrio UD
tel. 0432/674268

Jucuss
viale Kennedy 35/a
33040 Montino di Torreano UD
tel. 0432/715147

La Tunella
via del Collio 14
33040 Ipplis
di Premariacco UD
tel. 0432/716030

La Viarte
via Novacuzzo 50
33040 Prepotto UD
tel. 0432/759458

Le Vigne di Zamò
via Abate Corrado 4
località Rosazzo
33040 Manzano UD
tel. 0432/759693

Livio Felluga
via Risorgimento 1
34070 Brazzano
di Cormons GO
tel. 0481/60203

Rodaro Paolo
via Cormons 8
33042 Spessa di Cividale UD
tel. 0432/716066

Ronco delle Betulle
via Abate Colonna 24
33034 Rosazzo di Manzano UD
tel. 0432/740547

Subida di Monte
località Monte 9
34071 Cormons GO
tel. 0481/61011

Valchiarò
Casali Laurini 3
33040 Torreano UD
tel. 0432/712393

Valentino Butussi
via Prà di Corte 1
33040 Corno di Rosazzo UD
tel. 0432/759194

Valle
via Nazionale 3
33042 Buttrio UD
tel. 0432/674289

**COLLI ORIENTALI DEL FRIULI VERDUZZO** doc

*Vines: Verduzzo*

Bandut di Colutta
via Orsaria 32
33044 Manzano UD
tel. 0432/740315

Butussi Valentino
via Pra di Corte 1
33040 Corno di Rosazzo UD
tel. 0432/759194

Colutta Gianpaolo
via Orsaria 32
33044 Manzano UD
tel. 0432/510654

Ermacora
via Solzaredo 9
33040 Ipplis
di Premariacco UD
tel. 0432/716250

Girolamo Dorigo
via del Pozzo 5
33042 Buttrio UD
tel. 0432/674268

Livon
via Montarezza 33
33048 Dolegnano UD
tel. 0432/757173

Rodaro Paolo
via Cormons 8
33042 Spessa di Cividale UD
tel. 0432/716066

Ronchi di Manzano
via Orsaria 42
33044 Manzano UD
tel. 0432/740718

Torre Rosazza
località Poggiobello 12
33044 Manzano UD
tel. 0432/750180

**COLLIO BIANCO** doc

Marco Felluga
via Gorizia 121
34072 Gradisca d'Isonzo GO
tel. 0481/99164
*Molamatta* (Ribolla Gialla +
Tocai + Pinot Bianco)

Maurizio Buzzinelli
Località Pradis 20
34071 Cormons GO
tel. 0481/60902
*Frututis Bianco* (Tocai +
Ribolla Gialla + Malvasia)

**COLLIO PICOLIT** doc

*Vines: Picolit*

Primosic
località Madonna di Oslavia
34070 Oslavia GO
tel. 0481/535153

**COLLIO RIBOLLA GIALLA** doc

*Vines: Ribolla Gialla*

Attems
via Giulio Cesare
34070 Lucinico GO
tel. 0481/393619

Castello di Spessa
via Spessa 1
34070 Capriva del Friuli GO
tel. 0481/639914

La Castellada
località Oslavia 1
34070 Oslavia GO
tel. 0481/33670

Livon
via Montarezza 33
33048 Dolegnano UD
tel. 0432/757173

Marco Felluga
via Gorizia 121
34072 Gradisca d'Isonzo GO
tel. 0481/99164

Roncada
località Roncada 5
34071 Cormons GO
tel. 0481/61394

Venica&Venica
via Mernico 42
34070 Dolegna del Collio GO
tel. 0481/60177

Villa Russiz
via Russiz 6
34070 Capriva del Friuli GO
tel. 0481/80047

## COLLIO TOCAI doc
*Vines: Tocai Friulano*

Alessandro Princic
località Pradis 5
34071 Cormons GO
tel. 0481/60723

Attems
via Giulio Cesare
34070 Lucinico GO
tel. 0481/393619

Borgo del Tiglio - Azienda
Agricola Manferrari
via San Giorgio 71
34070 Brazzano di Cormons GO
tel. 0481/62166

Ca' Ronesca
località Lonzano 27
34070 Dolegna del Collio GO
tel. 0481/60034

Cantina Produttori di Cormons
via Vino della Pace 31
34071 Cormons GO
tel. 0481/60579

Castello di Spessa
via Spessa 1
34070 Capriva del Friuli GO
tel. 0481/639914

Eugenio Collavini
via della Ribolla Gialla
33040 Corno di Rosazzo UD
tel. 0432/753222

La Boatina
via Corona 62
34071 Cormons GO
tel. 0481/60445

Livon
via Montarezza 33
33048 Dolegnano UD
tel. 0432/757173

Marco Felluga
via Gorizia 121
34072 Gradisca d'Isonzo GO
tel. 0481/99164

Polencic Isidoro
località Plessiva 12
34071 Cormons GO
tel. 0481/60655

Russiz Superiore
via Russiz 7
34070 Capriva del Friuli GO
tel. 0481/80328

Schioppetto
via Palazzo Arcivescovile 1
34070 Capriva del Friuli GO
tel. 0481/80332

Venica&Venica
via Mernico 42
34070 Dolegna del Collio GO
tel. 0481/60177

## FRIULIA ANNIA REFOSCO
## DAL PEDUNCOLO
## ROSSO doc
*Vines: Refosco dal Peduncolo
Rosso*

Bortolusso Cav. Emiro
via Oltregorgo
33050 Carlino UD
tel. 0431/924723

## FRIULIA ANNIA TOCAI
## FRIULANO doc
*Vines: Tocai friulano*

Bortolusso Cav. Emiro
via Oltregorgo
33050 Carlino UD
tel. 0431/67596

## FRIULI AQUILEIA
## REFOSCO DAL
## PEDUNCOLO ROSSO doc
*Vines: Refosco dal Peduncolo*

Mulino delle Tolle
via Mulino delle Tolle 15
33050 Bagnaria Arsa UD
tel. 0432/924723

Ca' Bolami
via Ca' Bolami 1
33052 Cervignano
del Friuli UD
tel. 0431/32670

Ca' Tullio
via Beligna 41
33051 Acquileia UD
tel. 0431/919700

Cantina Produttori di Cormons
via Vino della Pace 31
34071 Cormons GO
tel. 0481/60579

Villa Vitas
via San Marco 5
33050 Cervignano
del Friuli UD
tel. 0431/93083

Foffani
Piazza Giulia 13/14
33050 Clauiano Trivignano
Udinese UD
tel. 0432/999584

Tenuta Beltrame
località Antonini 6/8
33050 Bagnaria Arsa UD
tel. 0432/923670

## FRIULI AQUILEIA TOCAI
## FRIULANO doc
*Vines: Tocai friulano*

Mulino delle Tolle
via Mulino delle Tolle 15
33050 Bagnaria Arsa UD
tel. 0432/924723

Foffani
Piazza Giulia 13/14
33050 Clauiano Trivignano
Udinese UD
tel. 0432/999584

Tenuta Beltrame
località Antonini 6/8
33050 Bagnaria Arsa UD
tel. 0432/923670

## FRIULI GRAVE REFOSCO
## DAL PEDUNCOLO
## ROSSO doc
*Vines: Refosco dal Peduncolo
Rosso*

Borgo Magredo
via Basaldella 5
33097 Tauriano di
Spilimbergo PN
tel. 0427/51444

Cabert
via Madonna 27
33032 Bertiolo UD
tel. 0432/917434
tel. 0432/917768

Cantine San Simone
via Prata 30
33080 Porcia PN
tel. 0434/578633

Casa Vinicola Antonutti
via D'Antoni 21
33030 Colloredo di Prato UD
tel. 0432/662001

Di Leonardo
piazza Battisti 1
33050 Ontagnano di Gonars UD
tel. 0432/928633

Forchir - Viticoltori in Friuli
via Ciasutis 1/b
33095 Provesano
San Giorgio Richinvelda PN
tel. 0427/96037

Fratelli Pighin
viale Grado
frazione Risano
33050 Pavia di Udine UD
tel. 0432/675444

Principi di Porcia
e Brugnera
via Zuiano 29
33082 Azzano Decimo PN
tel. 0434/631001

Vigneti Le Monde
via Montarezza 33
33100 San Giovanni al
Natisone UD
tel. 0432/757173

Vines: Tocai friulano

Borgo Magredo
via Basaldella 5
33097 Tauriano di
Spilimbergo PN
tel. 0427/751444

Cabert
via Madonna 27
33032 Bertiolo UD
tel. 0432/917434

Casa Vinicola Antonutti
via D'Antoni 21
33030 Colloredo di Prato UD
tel. 0432/662001

Fratelli Pighin
viale Grado - frazione Risano
33050 Pavia di Udine UD
tel. 0432/675444

Le Due Torri
via Roma 68/b
33040 Prepotto UD
tel. 0432/759150

Vines: Malvasia

Lorenzon Enzo
I Feudi di Romans
via Ca' del Bosco 6
frazione Pieris
34075 S. Canzian d'Isonzo GO
tel. 0481/76445

Tenuta Villanova
via Contessa Beretta 29
34070 Farra d'Isonzo GO
tel. 0481/888013

Vines: Refosco dal Peduncolo
Rosso

Lorenzon Enzo
I Feudi di Romans
via Ca' del Bosco 6
frazione Pieris
34075 S. Canzian d'Isonzo GO
tel. 0481/76445

Luisa Eddi
via Cormons 19
frazione Corona
34070 Mariano in Friuli GO
tel. 0481/69680

Vines: Schioppettino

Bressan
via Conti Zoppini
34070 Farra d'Isonzo GO
tel. 0481/888131

Scolaris Vini
via Boschetto 4
34070 S. Lorenzo Isontino GO
tel. 0481/809920

Vines: Tocai friulano

Borgo San Daniele
via San Daniele 16
34071 Cormons GO
tel. 0481/60552

Lis Neris
via Gavinana 5
34070 S. Lorenzo Isontino GO
tel. 0481/80105

Lorenzon Enzo
via Ca' del Bosco 6
frazione Pieris
34075 S. Canzian d'Isonzo GO
tel. 0481/76445

Luisa Eddi
via Cormons 19 - fraz. Corona
34070 Mariano in Friuli GO
tel. 0481/69680

Masùt da Rive
via Manzoni 82
34070 Mariano in Friuli GO
tel. 0481/69200

Ronco del Gelso
via Isonzo 117
34071 Cormons GO
tel. 0481/61310

Vines: Verduzzo

Bressan
via Conti Zoppini
34070 Farra d'Isonzo GO
tel. 0481/888131

Cantina Produttori di Cormons
via Vino della Pace 31
34071 Cormons GO
tel. 0481/60579

Tenuta Beltrame
località Antonini 6/8
33050 Bagnaria Arsa UD
tel. 0432/923670

Bressan
via Conti Zoppini
34070 Farra d'Isonzo GO
tel. 0481/888131
Pignol (Pignolo)

La Viarte
via Novacuzzo 50
33040 Prepotto UD
tel. 0432/759458
Sìum (Picolit + Verduzzo)

Aquila del Torre
via Attimis 25
frazione Sarvognano del Torre
33040 Povoletto UD
tel. 432/666428

Girolamo Dorigo
via del Pozzo 5
33042 Buttrio UD
tel. 0432/674268

Ronchi di Manzano
via Orsaria 42
33044 Manzano UD
tel. 0432/740718

Russiz Superiore
via Russiz 7
34070 Capriva del Friuli GO
tel. 0481/80328

Torre Rosazza
località Poggiobello 12
33044 Manzano UD
tel. 0432/750180

### VDT BIANCHI

Ca' Ronesca
località Lonzano 27
34070 Dolegna del Collio GO
tel. 0481/60034
*Saramago* (Picolit + Verduzzo
+ Riesling Renano)

Ronco di Gramogliano
via Gramogliano 21
33040 Ronco Di Rosazzo UD
*Sghirat* (Tocai + Ribolla
Gialla + Pinot grigio)

### VDT ROSSI

Dri Giovanni
via Pescia 7
33045 Ramandolo di Nimis UD
tel. 0432/790260
*Rosso del Monte dei Carpini*
(Schioppettino + Refosco)

### EMILIA-ROMAGNA

#### ALBANA DI ROMAGNA AMABILE docg
*Vines: Albana*

Leone Conti
via Pozzo 1
48018 S. Lucia /Faenza RA
tel. 0546/6642149

#### ALBANA DI ROMAGNA DOLCE docg
*Vines: Albana*

Cantina Sociale Terre
Riminesi - Cevico
Via Fiumazzo 72
41100 Lugo RA
tel. 059/413411

Cantine Ronchi
V. Paurosa. 15 - 48022 Lugo RA
tel. 0545/23041

Casa Vinicola F.lli Bernardi
via Tenuta 91
47827 Villaverucchio RN
tel. 0541/678622

Coop. Agricola Brisighellese
via Strada 2
48013 Brisighella RA
tel. 0546/81103

Stefano Ferrucci
Via Casolana 3045/2
48014 Castelbolognese RA
tel. 0546/651068

#### ALBANA DI ROMAGNA PASSITO docg
*Vines: Albana*

C.S. Terre Riminesi - Cevico
Via Fiumazzo 72
41100 Lugo RA
tel. 0594/13411

Celli
viale Carducci 5
47032 Bertinoro FO
tel. 0543/445183

Colonna Spalletti
Via Matteotti. 62
47039 Savignano
sul Rubicone FC
tel. 0541/945111

Fattoria Zerbina
via Vicchio 11
48010 Marzeno/Faenza RA
tel. 0546/40022

Istituto Prof. per l'Agricoltura
via Firenze 194
48048 Faenza RA
tel. 0546/22932

Stefano Ferrucci
Via Casolana, 3045/2
48014 Castelbolognese RA
tel. 0546/651068

Tre Monti
Via Lola. 3 - 40026 Imola BO
tel. 0542/657116

U. Cesari
Via Stanzano, 1120
40050 Castel San Pietro BO
tel. 051/941896

#### ALBANA DI ROMAGNA SECCO docg
*Vines: Albana*

Gallegati
Via Isonzo. 4
48018 Faenza RA
tel. 0546/621149

Podere del Nespoli
Villa Rossini, 50
47012 Civitella di Romagna FC
tel. 0543/989637

Tre Monti
Via Lola. 3
40026 Imola BO
tel. 0542/657116

U. Cesari
Via Stanzano. 1120
40050 Castel San Pietro BO
tel. 0519/41896

Celli
viale Carducci 5
47032 Bertinoro FO
tel. 0543/445183

#### COLLI BOLOGNESI PIGNOLETTO docg
*Vines: Pignoletto (min. 85%)*

Gaggioli
via Raibolini 55
40069 Zola Pedrosa BO
tel. 051/753489

Bonfiglio
Via Cassola 21
40050 Monteveglio BO
tel. 051/830758

Vallona
frazione Fagnano
Via Sant'Andrea 203
40050 Castello di Serravalle BO
tel. 051/6703058

#### COLLI BOLOGNESI PIGNOLETTO FRIZZANTE doc
*Vines: Pignoletto (min. 85%)*

Isola
via Bernardi 3
40050 Monte San Pietro BO
tel. 0516/768428

Podere Riosto
Via di Riosto 12
40065 Pianoro BO
tel. 0517/77109

Tizzano
Via Marescalchi. 13
40033 Casalecchio di Reno BO
tel. 0515/71208

#### COLLI PIACENTINI BARBERA doc
*Vines: Barbera (min. 85%)*

Bonelli
via Roma 86
29029 Rivergano PC
tel. 0523/958621

La Stoppa
Loc. Ancarano
29029 Rivergaro PC
tel. 0523/958159

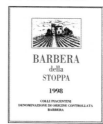

Terre dei Farnese
Via Newton. 13/A
42040 Gaida PC
tel. 0522/942135

Romagnoli
Via Genova. 20
29020 Villò di Vigolzone PC
tel. 0523/870129

## COLLI PIACENTINI BARBERA FRIZZANTE doc
*Vines: Barbera (min. 85%)*

Mossi
Fraz. Albareto, 80
29010 Ziano Piacentino PC
tel. 0523/860201

Podere Casale
località Vicobarone - via Creta
29010 Ziano Piacentino PC
tel. 0523/868302

## COLLI PIACENTINI BONARDA FERMO E FRIZZANTE doc
*Vines: Croatina (min. 85%)*

Cantina Valtidone
v. Moretta 58 - 29100 Borgonovo PC
tel. 0523/864086

Mossi
Fraz. Albareto, 80
29010 Ziano Piacentino PC
tel. 0523/860201

Romagnoli
via Genova, 20
29020 Villò di Vigolzone PC
tel. 0523/870129

Tenuta Pernice
località Pernice
29010 Castelnovo PC
tel. 0523/860050

Torre Fornello
località Fornello
29010 Ziano Piacentino PC
tel. 0523/861001

## COLLI PIACENTINI GUTTURNIO doc
*Vines: Barbera (min. 55, max 70%), Croatina, localmente detta Bonarda (min. 30%, max 45%)*

Cantina Valtidone
via Moretta 58
29100 Borgonovo Val Tidone PC
tel. 0523/864086

Cantina Vicobarone
via Creta 60
29010 Vicobarone di Ziano PC
tel. 0523/868522

Casa Bianca
Loc. Casa Bianca 1
29028 Pontedell'Olio
tel. 0523/877229

Conte Otto Barattieri
località Albarola
29020 Vigolzone PC
tel. 0523/875111

Gaetano Lusenti
frazione Vicobarone
casa Piccioni 67
29010 Ziano Piacentino PC
tel. 0523/868479

Il Poggiarello
Loc. Scrivellano-Statto
29020 Travo PC
tel. 0523/957241

La Stoppa
Loc. Ancarano
29029 Rivergaro PC
tel. 0523/958159

La Tosa
Località La Tosa
29020 Vigolzone PC
tel. 0523/870727

Montesissa
via Buffalora 48
29013 Rezzano
di Carpaneto PC
tel. 0523/850123

Mossi
Fraz. Albareto 80
29010 Ziano Piacentino (PC)
tel. 0523/860201

Romagnoli
via Genova 20 M
29020 Villò di Vigolzone PC
tel. 0523/870129

Tenuta Pernice
località Pernice
29010 Borgonovo Val Tidone PC
tel. 0523/860050

Torre Fornello
Loc. Fornello
29010 Ziano Piacentino PC
tel. 0523/861001

## COLLI PIACENTINI MALVASIA PASSITO doc
*Vitigno: Malvasia di Candia (min 85%)*

La Stoppa
Loc. Ancarano
29029 Rivergaro PC
tel. 0523/958159

## COLLI PIACENTINI MALVASIA doc
*Vitigno: Malvasia di Candia (min 85%)*

Gaetano Lusenti
fraz. Vicobarone - c. Piccioni 67
29010 Ziano Piacentino PC
tel. 0523/868479

La Tosa
Località La Tosa
29020 Vigolzone PC
tel. 0523/870727

Luretta
Cascina Costa
29010 Gazzola PC
tel. 0523/976500

Romagnoli
via Genova, 20
29020 Villò di Vigolzone PC
tel. 0523/870129

Torre Fornello
Loc. Fornello
29010 Ziano Piacentino PC
tel. 0523/861001

## COLLI PIACENTINI MALVASIA SPUMANTE doc
*Vitigno: Malvasia di Candia (min 85%)*

Cantina Valtidone
via Moretta 58
29100 Borgonovo VT PC
tel. 0523/864086

Il Poggiarello
Loc. Scrivellano di Statto
29020 Travo PC
tel. 0523/957241

Montesissa
via Buffalora 48
29013 Rezzano
di Carpaneto PC
tel. 0523/850123

Torre Fornello
Loc. Fornello
29010 Ziano Piacentino PC
tel. 0523/861001

## COLLI DI SCANDIANO E CANOSSA LAMBRUSCO GRASPAROSSA doc
*Vines: Lambrusco Grasparossa*

Moro di Rinaldini
via Patrioti 47
42049 Calerno di Sant'Ilario
d'Enza RE
tel. 0522/679190

## LAMBRUSCO GRASPAROSSA DI CASTELVETRO doc
*Vines: Lambrusco Grasparossa (min. 85%)*

Barbolini
via Fiori 40
41041 Casinalbo
di Formigine MO
tel. 059/550154

Cantina Soc. Coop. Formigine
via Pascoli 4
41043 Formigine MO
tel. 059/558122

Cavicchioli
via Gramsci 9
41030 San Prospero sul
Secchia MO
tel. 059/812411

Chiarli 1860
via Manin, 15
41100-Modena MO
tel. 059/310545

Coltiva Civ&Civ
via Polonia 85
41100 Modena MO
tel. 059/413411

Corte Manzini
via Modena 131
41014 Castelvetro MO
tel. 059/702658

Tenuta Pederzana
via Palona 12/a
41014 Castelvetro MO
tel. 059/799677

Villa di Corlo
Strada Cavezzo, 200
41040 Baggiovara MO
tel. 059/510736

## LAMBRUSCO SALAMINO DI SANTA CROCE doc
*Vines: Lambrusco Salamino (min 90%)*

Cavicchioli
via Gramsci 9
41030 San Prospero sul
Secchia MO
tel. 059/812411

Coltiva Civ&Civ
via Polonia 85
41100 Modena MO
tel. 059/413411

## LAMBRUSCO DI SORBARA doc
*Vines: Lambrusco di Sorbara (min 60%), Lambrusco Salamino (max 40)*

Barbolini
via Fiori 40
41041 Casinalbo MO
tel. 059/550154

Cantina Soc. Coop. Formigine
via Giovanni Pascoli 4
41043 Formigine MO
tel. 059/558122

Cavicchioli
via Gramsci 9
41030 San Prospero sul
Secchia MO
tel. 0598/12411

Chiarli 1860
via Manin, 15
41100 Modena MO
tel. 059/310545

Coltiva Civ&Civ
via Polonia 85
41100 Modena MO
tel. 0594/13411

Francesco Bellei
via per Modena 80
41030 Bomporto MO
tel. 059/818002

Villa di Corlo
Strada Cavezzo, 200
41040 Baggiovara MO
tel. 059/510736

## PAGADEBIT DI ROMAGNA doc
*Vines: Pagadebit è un sinonimo del Bombino Bianco*

Fattoria Paradiso
via Palmeggiana, 285
47032 Bertinoro FO
tel. 0543/445044

Colonna-Vini Spalletti
via Sogliano 100
47039 Savignano sul
Rubicone FC
tel. 0541/945111

## REGGIANO LAMBRUSCO DOLCE doc
*Vines: Lambrusco varie varietà (min. 85%) e Ancellotta*

Ca' De Medici
via della Stazione 34
42040 Località Cadè
Reggio Emilia
tel. 0522/942141

Medici Ermete
via Newton 13/A
42040 località Gaida
Reggio Emilia
tel. 0522/942135

## REGGIANO LAMBRUSCO doc
*Vines: Lambrusco varie varietà (min. 85%) e Ancellotta*

Ca' De Medici
via della Stazione 34
42040 Località Cadè
Reggio Emilia
tel. 0522/942141

Cavicchioli
piazza Gramsci 9
41030 San Prospero sul
Secchia MO
tel. 0598/12411

Medici Ermete
via Newton 13/A
42040 località Gaida
Reggio Emilia
tel. 0522/942135

Moro di Rinaldini
via Patrioti 47
42040 Calerno di Sant'Ilario
d'Enza RE
tel. 0522/679190M

Puianello Cantina Sociale
via Carlo Marx 19/A
42030 Località Puianello
Quattro Castella RE
tel. 0522/889120

Venturini Baldini
via Turati 42
42020 frazione Roncolo
Quattro Castella RE
tel. 0522/887080

## ROMAGNA ALBANA SPUMANTE doc
*Vines: Albana*

Fattoria Paradiso
via Palmeggiana, 285
47032 Bertinoro FC
tel. 0543/445044

Celli
viale Carducci 5
47032 Bertinoro FO
tel. 0543/445183

## SANGIOVESE DI ROMAGNA doc
*Vines: Sangiovese (min. 85%)*

C.S. Terre Riminesi Cevico
via Fiumazzo 72
41100 Lugo RA
tel. 059/413411

Casetto dei Mandorli
via Umberto I 21
47010 Predappio Alta FO
tel. 0543/922361

Castelluccio
via Tramonto 15
47015 Modigliana FC
tel. 0546/942486

Celli
viale Carducci 5
47032 Bertinoro FO
tel. 0543/445183

Coop. Agricola Brisighellese
via Strada 2
48013 Brisighella RA
tel. 0546/81103

Drei Donà
via del Tesoro 23
47100 località Massa di
Vecchiazzano - Forlì
tel. 0543/769371

Fattoria Paradiso
via Palmeggiana, 285
47032 Bertinoro FO
tel. 0543/445044

La Berta
via Pideura 48
48013 Brisighella RA
tel. 0546/84998

Le Rocche Malatestiane
via Emilia 104
47037 Rimini
tel. 0541/740163

Leone Conti
via Pozzo 1
48018 S. Lucia/Faenza RA
tel. 0546/6642149

Missiroli
via Andrea Costa 39/41
47010 Cusercoli FO
tel. 0543/989660

Podere del Nespoli
Villa Rossini 50
47012 Civitella
di Romagna FC
tel. 0543/989637

S. Patrignano
via San Patrignano 53
47052 Ospedaletto
di Coriano RN
tel. 0541/756436

Stefano Ferrucci
via Casolana 3045/2
48014 Castelbolognese RA
tel. 0546/651068

Tenuta Arpineto
Strada Arpineto-Pertinello 2
47010 Galeata FC
tel. 0543/983156

Tenuta Pandolfa
via Pandolfa 35
47010 Fiumana di Predappio FC
tel. 0543/940073

Tre Monti
via Lola 3 - 40026 Imola BO
tel. 0542/657116

U. Cesari
via Stanzano, 1120
40050 Castel San Pietro BO
tel. 0519/41896

## TREBBIANO DI ROMAGNA doc

*Vines: Trebbiano di Romagna (min 85%)*

Cantina Sociale Terre
Riminesi - Cevico
via Fiumazzo 72
41100 Lugo RA
tel. 0594/13411

Casetto dei Mandorli
via Umberto I 21
47010 Predappio Alta FE
tel. 0543/922361

Celli
viale Carducci 5
47032 Bertinoro FO
tel. 0543/445183

Coop. Agricola Brisighellese
via Strada 2
48013 Brisighella RA
tel. 0546/81103

Le Rocche Malatestiane
via Emilia 104
47037 Rimini
tel. 0541/740163

Spinetta
via Pozzo, 26
48018 Faenza RA
tel. 0546/642037

Tre Monti
via Lola 3 - 40026 Imola BO
tel. 0542/657116

## EMILIA IGT LAMBRUSCO

Villa di Corlo
Strada Cavezzo 200
4104 Baggiovara MO
tel. 059/510736
*Corleto* (Lambrusco)

Cantine dall'Asta
via Toscana 47
43100 Parma PR
tel. 0521/484086
*Le Viole* (Lambrusco)

## FORLÌ IGT BARBERA

Fattoria Cà Rossa
via Cellaimo 735
47032 Bertinoro FO
tel. 0543/445130

## FORLÌ IGT ROSSO

Podere del Nespoli
Villa Rossini 50
47012 Civitella di Romagna FC
tel. 0543/989637
*Borgo dei Guidi* (Sangiovese +
Cabernet + Raboso)

## FORLÌ IGT SANGIOVESE

Castelluccio
via Tramonto, 15
47015 Modigliana FC
tel. 0546/942486
*Ronco delle Ginestre*

Drei Donà
via del Tesoro, 23
47100 Massa
di Vecchiazzano FC
tel. 0543/769371
*Notturno*

Podere del Nespoli
Villa Rossini 50
47012 Civitella di Romagna FC
tel. 0543/989637
*Il Nespoli*

## MODENA IGT LAMBRUSCO

Barbolini
via Fiori 40
41041 Casinalbo
di Formigine MO
tel. 059/550154

Cavicchioli
via Gramsci 9
41030 San Prospero sul
Secchia MO
tel. 0598/12411

Coltiva Civ&Civ
via Polonia 85
41100 Modena MO
tel. 0594/13411

Chiarli 1860
v. Manin 15 - 41100 Modena
tel. 059/310545
*Vecchia Modena*

### RAVENNA IGT BIANCO

Ballardini e Ricci
via Borcellino 55
Bagnacavallo RA
(Trebbiano + altre)

### RAVENNA IGT ROSSO

Ballardini e Ricci
via Borcellino 55
Bagnacavallo RA
*Burson* (Longanesi)

Daniele Longanesi
via Borcellino 30
Bagnacavallo RA
tel. 0545/60289
*Burson* (Longanesi)

Ercolani
via Turati 6
48012 Bagnacavallo RA
tel. 0545/62381
*Burson* (Longanesi)

Istituto Prof. per l'Agricoltura
via Firenze 194
48048 Faenza RA
tel. 0546/22932
*Varrone* (Longanesi + Sangiovese)

Paolo Gordini
via Gabina 13/15
località Boncellino
48012 Bagnocavallo RA
tel. 0545/41154
*Burson* (Longanesi)

Tenuta Uccellina
via Palmeggiana 672
47032 Bertinoro FO
tel. 0544/580144
*Burson* (Longanesi)

### RUBICONE IGT SANGIOVESE

U. Cesari
via Stanzano, 1120
40050 Castel San Pietro BO
tel. 051/941896
*Tauleto*

### VDT ROSSO

Cà dè Medici
via della Stazione, 34
42040 Reggio Emilia RE
tel. 0522/942141
*Terra Calda* (Lambrusco)

### VDT SPUMANTE

Moro di Rinaldini
via Patrioti 47
42049 Calerno di Sant'Ilario
d'Enza RE
tel. 0522/679190
*Pjcol Rosso*

Venturini Baldini
via Turati 42 - fraz. Roncolo
42020 Quattro Castella RE
tel. 0522/887080
*Rubino del Cerro*

### MARCHE

### COLLI PESARESI
### SANGIOVESE doc
*Vines: Sangiovese (min. 85%)*

Claudio Morelli
viale Romagna 47/b
61032 Fano PU
tel. 0721/823352

La Collina - Cant. Bianchini
via Sant'Anna 15
61030 Cartoceto PU
tel. 0721/898440

### FALERIO DEI COLLI
### ASCOLANI doc
*Vines: Trebbiano toscano (dal
20 al 50%), Passerina (dal
10 al 30%) e Pecorino (dal
10 al 30%), altre
raccomandate a/o autorizzate
dalla provincia di Ascoli
Piceno (max 20%)*

Cantina dei Colli Ripani
via Tosciano 28
63038 Ripatransone AP
tel. 073/59505

Cantina Saladini Pilastri
via Saladini 5
63030 Spinetoli AP
tel. 0736/899580

Le Canniette
contrada Canali 23
63038 Ripatransone AP
tel. 0735/9200

San Giovanni
contrada Ciafone 41
63035 Offida AP
tel. 0736/889032

Velenosi Ercole
via Biancospini 11
63100 Ascoli Piceno AP
tel. 0736/341218

Villa Pigna
c.da Ciafone 63-63035 Offida AP
tel. 0736/87525

### LACRIMA DI MORRO
### D'ALBA doc
*Vines: Lacrima di Morro (min.
85%)*

La Vite - Monteschiavo
via Vivaio - Fraz. Monteschiavo
60030 Maiolati Spontini AN
tel. 0731/700297

Marotti Campi
località S. Amico 14
60030 Morro d'Alba AN
tel. 0731/618027

Stefano Mancinelli
via Roma 72
60030 Morro d'Alba AN
tel. 0731/63021

Umani Ronchi
S.S. 16 Km 310,400 74
60027 Osimo AN
tel. 071/7108019

### OFFIDA PASSERINA
### SPUMANTE doc

Tenuta Cocci Grifoni
contrada Messieri 12
63030 Ripatransone AP
tel. 0735/90143

### ROSSO CONERO doc
*Vines: Montepulciano (min.
85%), Sangiovese (max 15%)*

Alessandro Moroder
via Monteacuto 112
60029 Ancona AN
tel. 071/898232

Conte Leopardi Dittajutti
via Marina II 26
60026 Numana AN
tel. 071/7390116

Fattorie Le Terrazze
via Musone 4
60026 Numana AN
tel. 071/7390352

Fazi Battaglia
via Roma 117
60032 Castelpiano AN
tel. 0731/831444

La Vite - Monteschiavo
via Vivaio
Fraz. Monteschiavo
60030 Maiolati Spontini AN
tel. 0731/700385

Lanari
frazione Varano
60029 Ancona
tel.071/2861343

Serenelli
via del Conero 20/c
60129 Ancona AN
tel. 0171/31343

Umani Ronchi
S.S. 16 Km 310,400 74
60027 Osimo AN
tel. 071/7108019

## ROSSO
## PICENO doc

*Vines: Montepulciano
(dal 35 al 70%),
Sangiovese (dal 30 al 50%),
altre raccomandate a/o
autorizzate dalle provincie di
Asoli Piceno, Pesaro e Ancona
(max 15%)*

Cantina dei Colli Ripani
via Tosciano 28
63038 Ripatransone AP
tel. 0735/9505

Cantina Saladini Pilastri
via Saladini 5
63030 Spinetoli AP
tel. 0736/899534

Fratelli Bucci
via Cona 30
60010 Ostra Vetere AN
tel. 071/964179

Garofoli
via Arno 9 - 60025 Loreto AN
tel. 071/7820163

La Vite - Monteschiavo
fraz. Monteschiavo
60030 Maiolati Spontini AN
tel. 0731/700385

Le Canniette
contrada Canali 23
63038 Ripatransone AP
tel. 0735/9200

San Giovanni
contrada Ciafone 41
63035 Offida AP
tel. 0736/889032

Santa Barbara
borgo Mazzini 35
60010 Barbara AN
tel. 071/9674249

Tenuta De Angelis
via San Francesco 10
63030 Castel di Lama AP
tel. 0736/87429

Tenuta di Tavignano
località Tavignano
62011 Cingoli MC
tel. 0733/617303

Velenosi Ercole
via Biancospini 11
63100 Ascoli Piceno AP
tel. 0736/341218

## VERDICCHIO DEI
## CASTELLI DI JESI
## CLASSICO doc

*Vines: Verdicchio (min. 85%)*

Casalfarneto
via Farneto 16
60030 Serra de' Conti AN
tel. 0731/889001

Colonnara
via Mandriole 2
60034 Cupramontana AN
tel. 0731/780273

Fazi Battaglia
via Roma 117
60032 Castelpiano AN
tel. 0731/831444

Fratelli Bucci
via Cona 30
60010 Ostra Vetere AN
tel. 071/964179

Garofoli
via Arno 7 - 60025 Loreto AN
tel. 071/7820163

La Vite - Monteschiavo
via Vivaio
fraz. Monteschiavo
60030 Maiolati Spontini AN
tel. 0731/700385

Marotti Campi
località S. Amico 14
60030 Morro d'Alba AN
tel. 0731/618027

Santa Barbara
borgo Mazzini 35
60010 Barbara AN
tel. 071/9674249

Sartarelli
via Coste del Mulino 24
60030 Poggio S. Marcello AN
tel. 0731/89732

Tenuta di Tavignano
località Tavignano
62011 Cingoli MC
tel. 0733/617303

Umani Ronchi
S.S. 16 Km 310 400 74
60027 Osimo AN
tel. 071/7108019

Vallerosa Bonci
via Torre 13
60034 Cupramontana AN
tel. 0731/789129M

## VERDICCHIO DEI
## CASTELLI DI JESI
## PASSITO doc

*Vines: Verdicchio (min. 85%)*

Fazi Battaglia
via Roma 117
60032 Castelpiano AN
tel. 0731/831444

Garofoli
via Arno 9
60025 Loreto AN
tel. 071/7820163

Terre Cortesi Moncaro
via Piandole 7/a
60036 Montecarotto AN
tel. 0731/89245

## VERDICCHIO DI
## MATELICA doc

*Vitigno: Verdicchio (min. 85%)*

Belisario - C.S. di Matelica
Via Merloni, 12
62024 Matelica MC
tel. 0737/787247

Bisci
Via Fogliano, 120
62024 Matelica MC
tel. 0737/787490

Enzo Mecella
via Dante 112
60044 Fabriano AN
tel. 0732/21680

La Monacesca
C.da Monacesca, 1
62024 Matelica MC
tel. 0733/812602

San Biagio
via San Biagio, 32
62024 Matelica MC
tel. 0737/83997

## MARCHE IGT ROSSO

Claudio Morelli
viale Romagna 47/b
61032 Fano PU
tel. 0721/823352
*Suffragium* (Montepulciano + Vernaccia)

Colonnara
via Mandriole 6
60034 Cupramontana AN
tel. 0731/780273
*Tornamagno* (Montepulciano + Sangiovese)

San Biagio via San Biagio 32
62024 Matelica MC
tel. 0737/83997
*Bragnolo* (Ciliegiolo + Merlot)

Tenuta De Angelis
via San Francesco 10
63030 Castel di Lama AP
tel. 0736/87429
*Anghelos* (Montepulciano + Sangiovese + Cabernet)

## VDT
*Vernaccia Rossa*

Villa Ligi
località Zoccolanti 25/a
61045 Pergola PS
tel. 0721/734351
*Vernaculum*

## TUSCANY

### BIANCO DI PITIGLIANO doc
*Vines: Trebbiano Toscano (dal 50 all'80%), Greco a/o Malvasia Toscana a/o Verdello (max 20%), Grechetto, Chardonnay, Sauvignon, Pinot Bianco, Riesling Italico (congiuntamente max 30%, da soli max 15%), altri raccomandati a/o autorizzati dalla provincia di Grosseto (max 10%)*

Cantina Cooperativa del Morellino Scansano
località Saragiolo
58054 Scansano GR
tel. 0564/507288

Sassotondo
località Pian di Conati 52
58010 Sorano GR
tel. 0564/614218

Tenuta Roccaccia
località Poggio Cavalluccio
58017 Pitigliano GR
tel. 0564/617976

### BOLGHERI VERMENTINO doc
*Vitigno: Vermentino*

Guado al Tasso
località Belvedere 140
57020 Bolgheri LI
tel. 056/5749735

### BRUNELLO DI MONTALCINO docg
*Vines: Sangiovese*

Altesino
località Altesino
53024 Montalcino SI
tel. 0577/806208

Argiano
loc. Argiano - S. Angelo in Colle
53020 Montalcino SI
tel. 0577/844037

 Banfi
Castello di Poggio alla Mura
53024 Montalcino
tel. 0577/840111

Biondi Santi
via I Pieri 1
53024 Montalcino SI
tel. 0577/847121

Casanova di Neri
località Casanova - Torrenieri
53028 Montalcino SI
tel. 0577/834455

Castelgiocondo
località Castelgiocondo
53024 Montalcino SI
tel. 055/27141

Castello di Camigliano
località Camigliano
53024 Montalcino SI
tel. 0577/844068

Fattoria dei Barbi
località Pordenovi 170
53024 Montalcino SI
tel. 0577/740424

Fattoria Il Colle
casato Prime Donne
53024 Montalcino SI
tel. 0577/849421

Fattoria Lisini
Fattoria di S. Angelo in Colle
53024 Montalcino SI
tel. 0577/864040

La Gerla
località Canalicchio
podere Colombaio 5
53024 Montalcino SI
tel. 0577/848599

La Poderina Saiagricola
località Poderina
53020 Castelnuovo dell'Abate
Montalcino SI
tel. 0577/835737

Mastrojanni
fraz. Castelnuovo dell'Abate
53024 Montalcino SI
tel. 0577/835681

Pian delle Vigne
Località Pian delle Vigne
53024 Montalcino SI
tel. 0577/816066

Salvioni
piazza Cavour 19
53024 Montalcino SI
tel. 0577/848499

Siro Pacenti
località Pelagrilli
53024 Montalcino
tel. 0577/848662

Talenti
podere Pian di Conte
53020 Sant'Angelo al Colle SI
tel. 0577/864004

Tenimenti Angelini
località Val di Cava
53024 Montalcino SI
tel. 0577/80411

Tenuta La Fuga
Via dei Bardi 28
50125 Firenze
tel. 055/5200281

Tenuta Caparzo
SP del Brunello Km.1 700
53024 Montalcino SI
tel. 0577/849377

Tenuta Col d'Orcia
località Sant'Angelo in Colle
53020 Montalcino SI
tel. 0577/808001

Tenuta il Poggione
via Castello 14 - località
Sant'Angelo in Colle
53020 Montalcino SI
tel. 0577/844029

Tenuta Oliveto
fraz. Castelnuovo dell'Abate
Località Oliveto 53020
Montalcino SI
tel. 0577/835542

Tenute Silvio Nardi
località Casale del Bosco
53024 Montalcino SI
tel. 0577/808269

Uccelliera di Andrea Cortonesi
Fraz. Castelnuovo dell'Abate
podere Uccelliera 45
53024 Montalcino SI
tel. 0577/835729

**CARMIGNANO** docg
*Vines: Sangiovese (min 50%),
Cabernet Franc a/o Cabernet
Sauvignon (dal 10 al 20%),
Canaiolo Nero (max 20%),
Trebbiano toscano a/o
Canaiolo bianco a/o Malvasia
del Chianti (max 10%)*

Tenuta di Capezzana
via Capezzana 100
59042 Carmignano PR
tel. 055/8706005

Tenuta Farnete - Cantagallo
via Valicarda 35
50056 Capraia F.na FI
tel. 0571/910078

Piaggia
via Cegoli 47
59016 Poggio a Caiano PO
tel. 055/8705401

**CHIANTI** docg
*Vines: Sangiovese*

Cantine Leonardo Da Vinci
via del Torrino 19
50059 Vinci FI
tel. 0571/902444

Fattoria di Petrognano
via Bottinaccio 16
50056 Montelupo
Fiorentino FI
tel. 0571/542001

Poggio Capponi
via Poggio Capponi 9
50025 Montespertoli FI
tel. 0571/671914

**CHIANTI CLASSICO** docg
*Vines: Sangiovese (min 75%),
Canaiolo Nero (max 10%),
Trebbiano Toscano, Malvasia
Bianca, altri vines*

Agricola San Felice
località San Felice
53019 Castelnuovo
Berardenga SI
tel. 0577/39911

Agricoltori del Geografico
via del Mulinaccio 10
53013 Gaiole in Chianti
tel. 0577/719489

Antica Fattoria Nicolò
Macchiavelli
loc. Sant'Andrea in Percussina
50026 S. Casciano Val di Pesa
tel. 0577/989001

Concadoro
località Concadoro 67
53011 Castellina in Chianti SI
tel. 0577/741285

Lanciola
via Imprunetana 210
50023 Impruneta FI
tel. 055/208324

Badia a Coltibuono
località Badia a Coltibuono
53013 Gaiole in Chianti SI
tel. 0577/74481

Barone Ricasoli
Loc. Brolio
53013 Gaiole in Chianti SI
tel. 0577/7301

Brancaia
località Poppi 42/B
53017 Radda in Chianti SI
tel. 0577/742007

Cecchi
località Casina dei Ponti 56
53032 Castellina in Chianti
tel. 0577/743024

Castellare di Castellina
località Castellare
53011 Castellina in Chianti
tel. 0577/742903

Castelli del Gravepesa
via Grevignana 34 - località
Ponte del Gabbiano
50024 Mercatale di Val di
Pesa FI
tel. 055/821911

Castello d'Albola
località Pian d'Abola 31
53017 Radda in Chianti
tel. 0577/738019

Castello di Ama
Ama di Gaiole in Chianti
53013, Gaiole in Chianti SI
tel. 0577/746031

Castello di Fonterutoli
località Fonterutoli - via
Ottone III di Sassonia 5
53011 Castellina in Chianti SI
tel. 0577/73571

Castello di Monsanto
via Monsanto 8
50021 Barberino Val d'Elsa FI
tel. 055/8259000

Castello di Volpaia
piazza della Cisterna
53017 Radda in Chianti SI
tel. 0577/738066

Droandi
località Caposelvi 61
52025 Montevarchi AR
tel. 055/9707276

Fattoria Le Corti
località le Corti - via San Piero
di Sotto 1
50026 San Casciano
in Val di Pesa FI
tel. 055/820123

Fattoria Nittardi
località Nittardi 76
53011 Castellina in Chianti SI
tel. 0577/740269

Fattoria Viticcio
via San Cresci 12/A
50022 Greve in Chianti FI
tel. 055/854210

Felsina
SS 484 - Chiantigiana
53019 Castelnuovo
Berardenga SI
tel. 0577/355117

Il Palagio
frazione Castel San Giminiano
località Il Palagio
53030 Colle Val d'Elsa SI
tel. 0577/953004

 Isole e Olena
località Isole 1
50021 Barberino Val d'Elsa FI
tel. 055/8072763

La Sala
via Sorripa 34
50026 San Casciano
Val di Pesa FI
tel. 055/828111

Marchesi Antinori
piazza Antinori 3
50123 Firenze FI
tel. 055/23595

Melini
località Gaggiano
53036 Poggibonsi SI
tel. 0577/989001

Rocca delle Macie
località le Macie
53011 Castellina in Chianti SI
tel. 0577/7321

Rocca di Castagnoli
località Castagnoli
53013 Gaiole in Chianti SI
tel. 0577/731004

Rocca di Montegrossi
località San Marcellino 21
località Monti in Chianti
53013 Gaiole in Chianti SI
tel. 0577/747977

Tenimenti Ruffino
via Aretina 42/44
50065 Pontassieve FI
tel. 055/83605

Tenute Ambrogio e Giovanni
Folonari Tenuta di Nozzole
via De Bardi 28
50125 Firenze FI
tel. 055/200281

Villa Cafaggio
via San Martino in Cecione 5
50020 Panzano in Chianti FI
tel. 055/852949

## CHIANTI
## COLLI ARETINI
docg

*Vines: Sangiovese*

Villa Clinia
via Montoncello 27
52040 Bagnoro AR
tel. 0575/365017

## CHIANTI
## COLLI FIORENTINI
docg

*Vines: Sangiovese (min 75%),
Malvasia bianca, Trebbiano
Toscano, Canaiolo Nero ed
altri autorizzati sino ad un
max del 10%*

Castello di Poppiano Conte
Ferdinando Guicciardini
via Fezzana 45
50025 Montespertoli FI
tel. 055/82315

Castelvecchio
via Certaldese 30
50026 San Casciano
Val di Pesa FI
tel. 055/8248032

Fattoria di Fiano
via Firenze 11
50050 Fiano FI
tel. 0571/669048

Fattoria di Lilliano
via Lilliano e Meoli 82
50015 Grassima FI
tel. 055/644669

Fattoria Le Sorgenti
via Docciola 8
50012 Bagno a Ripoli FI
tel. 055/690604

Fattoria Sonnino
via Volterrana Nord 10
50025 Montespertoli FI
tel. 0571/609198

Fattoria Torre a Cona
località San Donato in Collina
50010 Rignano sull'Arno FI

Lanciola
via Imprunetana 210
50023 Impruneta FI
tel. 055/208324

Tenuta il Corno
via Malafrasca 64
50026 San Casciano
Val di Pesa FI
tel. 055/8248009

## CHIANTI
## COLLI SENESI docg

*Vines: Sangiovese (min 75%),
Malvasia bianca, Trebbiano
Toscano, Canaiolo Nero ed
altri autorizzati sino ad un
max del 10%*

Fattoria Belvedere
via Mantegazza 68
50022 Greve in Chianti FI
tel. 055/8544823

Il Palagio
frazione Castel San Giminiano
località Il Palagio
53030 Colle Val d'Elsa SI
tel. 057/7953004

La Vigna
Podere La Vigna 1
53049 Torrita di Siena SI
tel. 0577/669714

Salcheto
via di Villa Bianca 15
53045 Montepulciano SI
tel. 0578/799031

## CHIANTI COLLINE
## PISANE docg

*Vines: Sangiovese (min 75%),
Malvasia bianca, Trebbiano
Toscano, Canaiolo Nero ed
altri autorizzati sino ad un
max del 10%*

Sorelle Palazzi
via del Chianti 34
56030 Morrone PI
tel. 0587/654003

Tenuta Ghizzano
via della Chiesa 1
56030 Ghizzano di Peccioli PI
tel. 0587/630096

### CHIANTI MONTALBANO
docg
*Vines: Sangiovese*

Fattoria Bibbiani
Via Bibbiani 7
50150 Capraia e Limite FI
tel. 0571/57338 M

### CHIANTI MONTESPERTOLI docg
*Vines: Sangiovese (min 75%),
Malvasia bianca, Trebbiano
Toscano, Canaiolo Nero ed
altri autorizzati sino ad un
max del 10%*

Fattoria Sonnino
via Volterrana Nord 10
50025 Montespertoli FI
tel. 0571/609198

Poggio Capponi
via Poggio Capponi 9
50025 Montespertoli
tel. 0571/671914

### CHIANTI RUFINA docg
*Vines: Sangiovese (min 75%),
Malvasia bianca, Trebbiano
Toscano, Canaiolo Nero ed
altri autorizzati sino ad un
max del 10%*

Casa Vinicola Visco
S.S. Tosco-Romagnola km 106
50068 Rufina FI
tel. 055/8397886

Castello del Trebbio
via Santa Brigida 9
50060 Pontassieve FI
tel. 055/8304900

Colognole
via del Palagio 15
50068 Rufina FI
tel. 055/8319870

Fattoria di Basciano
viale Duca della Vittoria 159
50068 Rufina FI
tel. 055/8397034

Fattoria di Grignano
via di Grignano 22
50065 Pontassieve FI
tel. 055/8398490

Fattoria di Lavacchio
via di Montefiesole 55
50065 Pontassieve FI
tel. 055/8317472

Fattoria Selvapiana
località Selvapiana 43
50065 Pontassieve FI
tel. 055/8369848

Frascole
via di Frascole 27
50062 Dicomano FI
tel. 055/8386340

Nipozzano - Marchesi de'
Frescobaldi
via Santo Spirito 11
50125 Firenze FI
tel. 055/27141

Tenuta Bossi
via dello Stracchino 32
50065 Pontassieve FI
tel. 055/8317830

Travignoli
via Travignoli 78
50060 Pelago FI
tel. 055/8361098

### COLLINE LUCCHESI BIANCO doc
*Vines: Trebbiano toscano (dal
45 al 70%), Greco a/o
Grechetto a/o Malvasia del
Chianti a/o Vermentino (max
45%), Chardonnay a/o
Sauvignon (max 30%)*

Tenuta di Valgiano
via di Valgiano 7
55010 Capannori LU
tel. 0583/402271

### COLLINE LUCCHESI ROSSO doc
*Vines: Sangiovese (dal 45 al
70%), Canaiolo a/o Cigliegiolo
(max 30%), Merlot (max 15%)*

Tenuta di Forci
via Pieve di S. Stefano 7165
località Forci
55060 Lucca
tel. 0583/349007

Tenuta di Valgiano
via di Valgiano 7
55010 Capannori LU
tel. 0583/402271

### COLLINE LUCCHESI VERMENTINO doc
*Vines: Vermentino (min. 85%)*

Fattoria di Fubbiano
via per Fubbiano 6
frazione San Gennaro
55010 Capannori LU
tel. 0583/978011

Tenuta di Forci
via Pieve di Santo Stefano
7165 - località Forci
55060 Lucca LU
tel. 0583/349007

### ELBA ALEATICO doc
*Vines: Aleatico*

Acquabona
località Acquabona 1
57037 Portoferraio LI
tel. 0565/933013

Mola
località Gelsarello 2
57031 Porto Azzurro LI
tel. 0565/222089

Sapereta
località Mola
via Provinciale Ovest 73
57036 Porto Azzurro LI
tel. 0565/95033

### ELBA ROSSO doc
*Vines: Sangiovese minimo 60%
Altri Vines raccomandati a/o
autorizzatti dalla Prov. Di
Livorno max 40%*

Acquabona
località Acquabona 1
57037 Portoferraio LI
tel. 0565/933013

Mola
località Gelsarello 2
57031 Porto Azzurro LI
tel. 0565/222089
*Gelsarello*

Sapereta
località Mola
via Provinciale Ovest 73
57036 Porto Azzurro LI
tel. 0565/95033
*Thea*

### MONTECARLO BIANCO doc
*Vines: Trebbiano Toscano (dal
40 al 60%), Semillon, Pinot
Bianco, Pinot Grigio,
Sauvignon, Roussanne,
Vermentino (dal 40 al 60%)
purché almeno tre di essi
raggiungano singolarmente il
10%*

Fattoria del Buonamico
via Provinc. di Montecarlo 43
55015 Montecarlo LU
tel. 0583/22038

Fattoria del Teso
via Poltroniera
55015 Montecarlo LU
tel. 0583/286288

Fattoria La Torre
via Provinciale 7
55015 Montecarlo LU
tel. 0583/22981 M

Anna Maria Selmi
Via Della Pace 43
55015 Montecarlo LU
tel. 0583/22434

### MONTECARLO ROSSO doc

*Vines: Sangiovese (dal 50 al 75%), Canaiolo Nero (dal 5 al 15%), Cigliegiolo a/o Colorino a/o Malvasia nera a/o Merlot a/o Syrah a/o Cabernet Franc a/o Cabernet Sauvignon (dal 10 al 15%), altri raccomandati a/o autorizzati dalla provincia di Lucca (max 20%)*

Anna Maria Selmi
Via Della Pace 43
55015 Montecarlo LU
tel. 0583/22434

Fattoria del Buonamico
via Provinc. di Montecarlo 43
55015 Montecarlo LU
tel. 0583/22038

Fattoria del Teso
via Poltroniera
55015 Montecarlo LU
tel. 0583/286288

### MONTESCUDAIO BIANCO doc

*Vines: Trebbiano toscano (min. 50%), altri autorizzati a/o raccomandati dalla provincia di Pisa (max 50%)*

Fattoria di Sorbaiano
località Sorbaiano
56040 Montecatini
Val di Cecina PI
tel. 0588/30243

Fattoria Poggio Gagliardo
località Poggio Gagliardo
56040 Montescudaio PI
tel. 0586/6630775

### MONTESCUDAIO ROSSO doc

*Vines: Sangiovese (min. 50%), altri autorizzati a/o raccomandati dalla provincia di Pisa (max 50%)*

Fattoria di Sorbaiano
località Sorbaiano
56040 Montecatini
Val di Cecina PI
tel. 0588/30243

Fattoria Poggio Gagliardo
località Poggio Gagliardo
56040 Montescudaio PI
tel. 0586/6630775

### MORELLINO DI SCANSANO doc

*Vines: Sangiovese (min 85%)*

Aia della Macina
via Fosso Lombardo
58054 Scansano GR
tel. 0577/940600

Poliziano
via Fontago 1
53045 Montepulciano SI
tel. 0578/738171

Cantina Cooperativa del
Morellino Scansano
località Saragiolo
58054 Scansano GR
tel. 0564/507288

Cecchi - Tenuta Val Rose
località Casina dei Ponti 56
53032 Castellina in Chianti SI
tel. 0577/743024

Erik Banti
località Fosso dei Mulini
58054 Scansano GR
tel. 0564/602778

Fattoria Le Pupille
Piagge del Maiano 92/a
58040 Istia d'Ombrone GR
tel. 0564/409517

Fattoria Mantellassi
località Banditaccia 26
58051 Magliano in Toscana GR
tel. 0564/592037

Moris Farm
località Curanuova
58024 Massa Marittima GR
tel. 0566/919135

Poggio Argentiera
località Bandinella- Alberese
58010 Grosseto GR
tel. 0564/405099

### MOSCADELLO DI MONTALCINO doc

*Vines: Moscato bianco (min. 85%)*

Banfi
Castello di Poggio alla Mura
53024 Montalcino SI
tel. 0577/816001

La Poderina - Saiagricola
località Poderina
53020 Castelnuovo dell'Abate
Montalcino SI
tel. 0577/835737

Tenuta Caparzo
SP del Brunello Km.1 700
53024 Montalcino SI
tel. 0577/848390

Tenuta Col d'Orcia
località Sant'Angelo in Colle
53020 Montalcino SI
tel. 0577/808001

Tenuta il Poggione
piazza Castello 14
53020 Sant'Angelo in Colle SI
tel. 0577/844029

### ROSSO DI MONTALCINO doc

*Vines: Sangiovese*

Altesino
località Altesino
53024 Montalcino SI
tel. 0577/806208

Argiano
località Sant'Angelo in Colle
53028 Montalcino SI
tel. 0577/844210

Talenti
podere Pian di Conte
53020 Sant'Angelo al Colle
tel. 0577/864004

Banfi
Castello di Poggio alla Mura
53024 Montalcino SI
tel. 0577/808001

Casanova di Neri
località Casanova - Torrenieri
53028 Montalcino SI
tel. 0577/834455

Castelgiocondo
località Castelgiocondo
53024 Montalcino SI
tel. 055/27141

Castello di Camigliano
località Camigliano
53024 Montalcino SI
tel. 0577/844068

Castiglion del Bosco
località Castiglion del Bosco
53024 Montalcino SI
tel. 0577/807078

Collemattoni
podere Collemattoni 100
53020 Montalcino SI

Corte Pavone
località Casanova
53024 Montalcino SI
tel. 0577/848111

Fattoria Lisini
Fattoria di S. Angelo in Colle
53024 Montalcino SI
tel. 0577/864040

La Poderina Saiagricola
località Poderina
53020 Castelnuovo dell'Abate
Montalcino SI
tel. 0577/835737

Salvioni
piazza Cavour 19
53024 Montalcino SI
tel. 0577/848499

Tenimenti Angelini
località Val di Cava
53024 Montalcino SI
tel. 0577/80411

 Tenuta Caparzo
SP del Brunello Km.1,700
53024 Montalcino SI
tel. 0577/848390

 Tenuta Col d'Orcia
località Sant'Angelo in Colle
53020 Montalcino
tel. 0577/80891

Tenuta di Collosorbo
località Villa a Sesta 25 -
Castelnuovo Abate
53020 Montalcino SI
tel. 0577/835534

Tenuta il Poggione
piazza Castello 14
53020 Sant'Angelo in Colle SI
tel. 0577/844029

Tenuta Oliveto
fraz. Castelnuovo dell'Abate
Località Oliveto
53020 Montalcino SI
tel. 0577/835542

Tenute Silvio Nardi
viale Nardi 92
06017 Selci Lama
tel. 0577/808269

## ROSSO DI MONTEPULCIANO doc

*Vines: Sangiovese, localmente detto Prugnolo gentile (min. 70%), Canaiolo Nero (max 20%), altri vines autorizzatia/o raccomandati dalla provincia di Siena (max 10%)*

Avignonesi
via di Gracciano nel Corso 91
53045 Montepulciano SI
tel. 0578/757872

Bindella
via delle Tre Berte 10/A
53040 Acquaviva di
Montepulciano SI
tel. 0578/767777

 Boscarelli
via Montenero 28
località Cervognano
53040 Montepulciano SI
tel. 0578/767277

Carpineto
strada della Chiana 62
53042 Greve in Chianti FI
tel. 055/8549062

Contucci
via del Teatro 1
53045 Montepulciano SI
tel. 0578/757006

Fassati
frazione Gracciano
via di Graccianello 3/a
53040 Montepulciano SI
tel. 0578/708708

Fattoria del Cerro - Saiagricola
via Grazianella 5
frazione Acquaviva
53040 Montepulciano SI
tel. 0578/767722

La Braccesca
loc. Gracciano - S.S. 126 15
53040 Montepulciano SI
tel. 0578/724252

La Calonica
via della Stella 27
53040 Valiano di
Montepulciano SI
tel. 0578/724119

Le Casalte
via del Termine 2
53042 Sant'Albino di
Montepulciano SI
tel. 0578/799738

Poliziano
via Fontago 1
53045 Montepulciano SI
tel. 0578/738171

 Romeo
via di Totona 29
53045 Montepulciano SI
tel. 0578/708599

Salcheto
via di Villa Bianca 15
53045 Montepulciano SI
tel. 0578/799031

Tenuta Lodola Nuova
località Valiano - via Lodola 1
53045 Montepulciano SI
tel. 0578/724032

Tenuta Valdipiatta
via Ciarlana 25/A
53040 Gracciano di
Montepulciano SI
tel. 0578/757930

Vecchia Cantina di
Montepulciano - Redi
strada Provinciale 7
53045 Montepulciano SI
tel. 0578/716092

## VAL DI CORNIA ALEATICO PASSITO doc

*Vines: Aleatico*

Banti Jacopo
località Citerna24
57021 Campiglia LI
tel. 0565/838802

## VAL DI CORNIA BIANCO doc

*Vines: Trebbiano toscano
(min. 50%), Vermentino (max
20%), altri raccomandato a/o
autorizzati (max 20%)*

Banti Jacopo
località Citerna 24
57021 Campiglia LI
tel. 0565/838802

Gualdo del Re
località Notri 77
57028 Suvereto LI
tel. 0565/829888

## VAL DI CORNIA CIGLIEGIOLO doc

*Vines: Cigliegiolo (min. 85%)*

Banti Jacopo
località Citerna 24
57021 Campiglia LI
tel. 0565/838802

## VAL DI CORNIA ROSSO doc

*Vines: Sangiovese (min. 50%),
Cabernet Sauvignon a/o
Merlot (max 50%), altre
autorizzate a/o raccomandate
(max 20%)*

Bulichella
località. Bulichella 131
57028 Suvereto LI
tel. 0565/829892

 Petra
località San Lorenzo Alto 131
57028 Suvereto LI
tel. 0565/845180

Tenuta Il Vignale
località Vignale Rio Torto
57025 Piombino LI
tel. 0565/20812

## VAL DI CORNIA SANGIOVESE doc

*Vines: Sangiovese (min. 85%)*

Gualdo del Re
località Notri 77
57028 Suvereto LI
tel. 0565/829888

## VERNACCIA DI SAN GIMIGNANO docg

*Vines: Vernaccia di San
Gimignano (min 90%)*

 Agricoltori del Geografico
via del Mulinaccio 10
53013 Gaiole in Chianti SI
tel. 0577/719489

Casa alle Vacche
frazione Pancone
Località Lucignano 73/A
53037 San Gimignano SI
tel. 0577/955103

Fattoria Abbazie Monte Oliveto
località Monte Oliveto
53037 San Gimignano SI
tel. 0577/953004

Fattoria Cusona
località Cusona 5
53037 San Gimignano SI
tel. 0577/950028

Il Palagio
fraz. Castel S. Gimignano
53030 Colle Val d'Elsa SI
tel. 0577/953004

 La Lastra
via De Grada 9
53037 San Gimignano SI
tel. 0577/941781

La Rampa di Fugnano
località Fugnano 55
53037 San Gimignano SI
tel. 0577/941655

Melini
località Gaggiano
53036 Poggibonsi SI
tel. 0577/989001

Panizzi Giovanni
località Racciano 34
53037 San Gimignano SI
tel. 0577/941576

Pietrafitta
località Cortennarno
53037 San Gimignano SI
tel. 0577/943200

 Tenuta Mormoraia
località Sant'Andrea
53037 San Gimignano SI
tel. 0577/940096

Teruzzi & Puthod
Ponte a Rondolino
località Casale 19
53037 San Gimignano SI
tel. 0577/940143

## VIN SANTO COLLI DELL'ETRURIA CENTRALE doc

*Vines: Trebbiano toscano a/o
Malvasia del Chianti (min.
70%), altri vines autorizzati
a/o raccomandati per le
provincie di Firenze, Siena,
Pistoia, Arezzo, Pisa e Prato
(max 30%). Per la tipologia
Occhio di Pernice: come sopra
ma con Sangiovese (min 50%),
vines raccomandati a/o
autorizzati (max 50%)*

Fattoria Il Colle
casato Prime Donne
53024 Montalcino SI
tel. 0577/849421

## VIN SANTO DEL CHIANTI doc

*Vines: Trebbiano toscano a/o
Malvasia (min. 70%), altri
vines autorizzati a/o
raccomandati per le provincie
di Firenze, Siena, Pistoia,
Arezzo, Pisa e Prato (max
30%) Per la tipologia Occhio
di Pernice: come sopra ma con
Sangiovese (min 50%), vines
raccomandati a/o autorizzati
(max 50%)*

Castelvecchio
via Certaldese 30
50026 San Casciano
Val di Pesa FI
tel. 055/8248032

Fattoria Corzano e Paterno
via Paterno 8
50020 San Casciano
Val di Pesa FI
tel. 055/8248179

327

Fattoria Selvapiana
Giuntini Antinori Francesco
località Selvapiana 43
50068 Rufina FI
tel. 055/8369848

Fattoria Sonnino
via Volterrana Nord 10
50025 Montespertoli FI
tel. 0571/609198

Lanciola
via Imprunetana 210
50023 Impruneta FI
tel. 055/208324

Tenuta Ghizzano
via della Chiesa 1
56030 Ghizzano di Peccioli PI
tel. 0587/630096

### VIN SANTO DEL CHIANTI CLASSICO doc

*Vines: Trebbiano toscano a/o Malvasia (min. 70%), altri vines autorizzati a/o raccomandati per le province di Firenze, Siena, Pistoia, Arezzo, Pisa e Prato (max 30%). Per la tipologia Occhio di Pernice: come sopra ma con Sangiovese (min 50%), vines raccomandati a/o autorizzati (max 50%)*

Agricola San Felice
località San Felice
53019 Castelnuovo
Berardenga SI
tel. 0577/39911

Castello di Volpaia
località Volpaia
53017 Radda in Chianti SI
tel. 0577/738066 M

Isole e Olena
località Isole 1
50021 Barberino Val d'Elsa FI
tel. 055/8072763

Rocca di Montegrossi
località San Marcellino 21
Monti in Chianti
53010 Gaiole in Chianti SI
tel. 0577/747977

### VIN SANTO DI MONTEPULCIANO doc

*Vines: Grechetto bianco, localmnte detto Pulcinculo a/o Trebbiano toscano a/o Malvasia (min. 70%), altri vines autorizzati a/o raccomandati per la provincia di Siena (max 30%). Per la tipologia Occhio di Pernice: come sopra ma con Sangiovese, localmente detto Prugnolo gentile (min 50%), vines raccomandati a/o autorizzati (max 50%)*

Avignonesi
via di Gracciano nel Corso 91
53045 Montepulciano SI
tel. 0578/757872
*Occhio di Pernice*

Avignonesi
via di Gracciano nel Corso 91
53045 Montepulciano SI
tel. 0578/757872

Fattoria del Cerro - Saiagricola
via Grazianella 5
53040 Acquaviva di
Montepulciano SI
tel. 0578/767722

### VINO NOBILE DI MONTEPULCIANO docg

*Vines: Sangiovese (min 70%), Canaiolo Nero, Malvasia del Chianti*

Avignonesi
via di Gracciano nel Corso 91
53045 Montepulciano SI
tel. 0578/757872

Bindella
via delle Tre Berte 10/A
località Acquaviva
53040 Montepulciano SI
tel. 0578/767777

Boscarelli
via Montenero 28
località Cervognano
53045 Montepulciano SI
tel. 0578/767277

Carpineto
strada della Chiana 72
50020 Greve in Chianti FI
tel. 055/8549062

Fassati
frazione Gracciano
via di Graccianello 3/a
53040 Montepulciano SI
tel. 057/8708708

Fattoria del Cerro - Saiagricola
via Grazianella 5
località Acquaviva
53040 Montepulciano SI
tel. 0578/767722

La Braccesca
loc. Gracciano - S.S. 126 15
53040 Montepulciano SI
tel. 0578/724252

Le Casalte
via del Termine 2
53042 Sant'Albino di
Montepulciano
tel. 0578/799738

Poliziano
via Fontago 1
53040 Montepulciano SI
tel. 0578/738171

Romeo
via di Totona 29
53045 Montepulciano SI
tel. 0578/708599

Salcheto
via di Villa Bianca 15
53045 Montepulciano SI
tel. 0578/799031

Tenuta Valdipiatta
via Ciarlana 25/A
località Gracciano
53045 Montepulciano SI
tel. 0578/757930

Triacca
strada per Pienza 39
53045 Montepulciano SI
tel. 0578/757774

Vecchia Cantina di
Montepulciano - Redi
strada Provinciale 7
53045 Montepulciano SI
tel. 0578/716092

### MAREMMA TOSCANA IGT

Moris Farm - Fattoria Poggetti
località Curanuova
58020 Massa Marittima GR
tel. 0566/919135
*Avvoltore (Sangiovese + Cabernet)*

## TOSCANA CENTRALE IGT ROSSO

*Vines: Sangiovese + Altre*

San Luciano
località San Luciano 90
52048 Monte San Savino AR
tel. 0575/843518
*Colle Carpito*

San Luciano
località San Luciano 90
52048 Monte San Savino AR
tel. 0575/843518
*Boschi Salviati*

San Luciano
località San Luciano 90
52048 Monte San Savino AR
tel. 0575/843518
*D'Ovidio*

Castellare di Castellina
località Castellare
53011 Castellina in Chianti SI
tel. 0577/742903
*I Sodi di San Nicolò*

Tenuta di Fontodi
Via San Leonino 87
50020 Panzano FI
tel. 055/852005
*Flaccianello della Pieve*

## TOSCANA IGT BIANCO

*Vermentino + Altre*

Michele Satta
località Vigna al Cavaliere
57022 Castagneto Carducci LI
tel. 0565/773041 Costa di
*Giulia* cuore

## TOSCANA IGT

*Vitigno: Cesanese d'Affile*

Tenuta di Trinoro
53047 Sartenano SI
tel. 0578/267110

## TOSCANA IGT CILIEGIOLO

Sassotondo Azienda Agricola
località Pian di Conati 52
58010 Sorano GR
tel. 0564/614218

## TOSCANA IGT COLORINO

Tenuta Il Corno
via Malafrasca 64
50026 San Casciano
Val di Pesa FI
tel. 055/8248009

## TOSCANA IGT ROSSO

*(Sangiovese + Cabernet)*

Fattoria Corzano e Paterno
via Paterno 8 - San Pancrazio
50020 San Casciano
Val di Pesa FI
tel. 055/8248179

Il Corzano - Fattoria La Torre
via Provinciale 7
55015 Montecarlo LU
tel. 0583/22981
*Stringaio*

Marchesi Antinori
piazza Antinori 3
50123 Firenze
tel. 055/23595
*Tignanello*

Querciabella
via Carducci 16
20123 Milano MI
tel. 02/72002256
*Camartina*

Tenuta Ghizzano
via della Chiesa 1
56030 Ghizzano di Peccioli PI
tel. 0587/63009
*Veneroso*

Tenute Ambrogio
e Giovanni Folonari
via De Bardi 28
50125 Firenze FI
tel. 055/200281
*Cabreo Il Borgo*

## TOSCANA IGT ROSSO

*(Sangiovese + altre autoctone)*

Montevertine
località Montevertine
53017 Radda in Chianti SI
tel. 0577/738009
*Il Sodaccio*

Bibi Graetz
via di Vincigliata 19
Fiesole FI
tel. 055/599556
*Testamatta*

Capannelle
via Capannelle 13
53013 Gaiole in Chianti
tel. 0577/749691
*Capannelle*

Fattoria Gratena
località Pieve a Maiano
52100 Arezzo AR
tel. 0575/368664
*Rapozzo di Maiano*

## TOSCANA IGT ROSSO

*(Sangiovese + Merlot)*

I Giusti & Zanza Vigneti
via Puntoni 9
56043 Fauglia PI
tel. 0585/44354
*Belcore*

Brancaia
località Poppi 42/B
53017 Radda in Chianti SI
tel. 0577/742007
*Brancaia*

329

### TOSCANA IGT ROSSO
*(Sangiovese)*

Biondi Santi
via I Pieri 1
53024 Montalcino SI
tel. 0577/847121
*Sassolloro*

 Cantine Leonardo Da Vinci
via Provinciale Mercatale 291
50059 Vinci FI
tel. 0571/902444
*San Zio*

Castello di Querceto
via Dudda 61- Luculena
50020 Greve in Chianti FI
tel. 055/85921
*Cento*

Fattoria di Sorbaiano
località Sorbaiano
56040 Montecatini
Val di Cecina
tel. 0588/30243
*Pian del Conte*

 Felsina
SS 484 - Chiantigiana
53019 Castelnuovo
Berardenga SI
tel. 0577/355117
*Fontalloro*

 Isole e Olena
località Isole 1
50021 Barberino Val d'Elsa FI
tel. 055/8072763
*Cepparello*

Massanera
via Saltignano 76
località Chiesa di Nuova
50020 San Cassiano
Val di Pesa FI
tel. 055/8242222
*Prelato di Massanera*

 Michele Satta
località Vigna al Cavaliere
57022 Castagneto Carducci LI
tel. 0565/773041
*Cavaliere*

 Montevertine
località Montevertine
53017 Radda in Chianti SI
tel. 0577/738009
*Le Pergole Torte*

Rocca delle Macie
località le Macie 5
3011 Castellina in Chianti
tel. 0577/7321
*Ser Gioveto*

San Giusto a Rentennanno
fraz. Monte in Chianti
loc. S. Giusto a Rentennanno
53013 Gaiole in Chianti
tel. 077/747121
*Percarlo*

Tenuta Castello di
Vicchiomaggio
via Vicchiomaggio 4
50022 Greve in Chianti FI
tel. 055/854079
*Ripa delle More*

 Tenuta Sette Ponti
località Oreno
52020 S. Giustino Valdarno FI
tel. 055/977443
*Crognolo*

Tenuta Vecchie Terre
di Montefili
via San Cresci 45
50022 Greve in Chianti FI
tel. 055/853739

Villa Cafaggio
via San Martino in Cecione 5
50020 Panzano in Chianti FI
tel. 055/852949
*San Martino*

### TOSCANA IGT
### VERMENTINO NERO

Podere Scurtarola
via dell'Uva 3
54100 Massa MS
tel. 0585/833523

### TOSCANA IGT
### VERMENTINO

 Podere Scurtarola
via dell'Uva 3
54100 Massa MS
tel. 0585/833523

### VDT
*(Sangiovese)*

 Capannelle
via Capannelle 13
53013 Gaiole in Chianti SI
tel. 0577/749691

### UMBRIA

### ASSISI GRECHETTO doc
*Vines: Grechetto (min. 85%)*

Sportoletti
via Lombardia 1
06038 Spello PG
tel. 0742/651461

Tili
Frazione Campodacqua
via Cannella 2
06081 Assisi PG
tel. 075/8064370

### ASSISI ROSSO doc
*Vines: Sangiovese (dal 50 al
70%), Merlot (dal 10 al 40%),
altri autorizzati a/o
raccomandati dalla provincia
di Perugia (max 40%)*

Tili
Frazione Campodacqua
via Cannella 2
06081 Assisi PG
tel. 075/8064370

Sportoletti
via Lombardia 1
06038 Spello PG
tel. 0742/651461

### COLLI DEL TRASIMENO
### BIANCO doc
*Vines: Trebbiano (min. 40%),
Grechetto a/o Chardonnay a/o
Pinot Bianco a/o Pinot Grigio
(max 30%)*

Duca della Corgna
via Roma 236
06061 Castiglione del Lago PG
tel. 0759/653210

Pieve de Vescovo
via Giacomo Leopardi 82
06073 Corciano PG
tel. 0756/978874

Terre del Carpine
via Formanuova 87
06063 Magione PG
tel. 075/840298

Villa Po' del Vento
Via Po' del Vento 6
06062 Città della Pieve PG
tel. 0578/299950

## COLLI DEL TRASIMENO
### ROSSO doc

*Vines: Sangiovese (min. 40%),
Cigliegiolo a/o Gamey a/o
Merlot a/o Cabernet (max
30%), altri autorizzati a/o
raccomandati dalla provincia
di Perugia (max 30%)*

Duca della Corgna
via Roma 236
06061 Castiglione del Lago PG
tel. 0759/653210

Fanini
Vocabolo i Cucchi
06061 Petrignano del Lago PG
tel. 075/9528116

 Lamborghini
località Soderi 1
06064 Panicale PG
tel. 0758/350029

Pieve del Vescovo
via Giacomo Leopardi 82
06073 Corciano PG
tel. 0756/978874

Terre del Carpine
via Formanuova 87
06063 Magione PG
tel. 075/840298

Villa Po' del Vento
Via Po' del Vento 6
06062 Città della Pieve PG
tel. 0578/299950

## COLLI MARTIANI
### GRECHETTO doc

*Vines: Grechetto (min. 85%)*

Adanti
Vocabolo Arquata
06031 Bevagna PG
tel. 0742/360295

Arnaldo Caprai
località Torre di Montefalco
06036 Montefalco PG
tel. 0742/378802

Terre de Trinci
via Fiamenga 57
06034 Foligno PG
tel. 0742/320165

## COLLI MARTANI
### SANGIOVESE doc

*Vines: Sangiovese (min. 85%)*

Di Filippo
Via Conversino 153
06033 Cannara PG
tel. 0742/731242

Rocca di Fabbri
località Fabbri di Montefalco
06036 Montefalco PG
tel. 0742/399379

## MONTEFALCO ROSSO
### doc

*Vines: Sangiovese (dal 60 al
70%), Sagrantino (dal 10 al
15%), altri, per la restante
parte, autorizzati a/o
raccomandati dalla provincia
di Perugina*

Antonelli San Marco
località San Marco 59
06036 Montefalco PG
tel. 0742/379158

Arnaldo Caprai
località Torre di Montefalco
06036 Montefalco PG
tel. 0742/378802

Castello di Antignano
Loc.Bastia Umbra
06083 Bastia Umbra PG
tel. 075/8001501

Colpetrone
via della Collina 4
frazione Marcellano
06035 Guado Cattaneo PG
tel. 0578/767722

Rocca di Fabbri
località Fabbri di Montefalco
06036 Montefalco PG
tel. 0742/399379

Spoletoducale
località Petrognano 54
06049 Spoleto PG
tel. 0743/56224

Terre de Trinci
via Fiamenga 57
06034 Foligno PG
tel. 0742/320165

## MONTEFALCO
### SAGRANTINO docg

*Vines: Sagrantino*

Arnaldo Caprai
località Torre di Montefalco
06036 Montefalco PG
tel. 0742/378802

Azienda Agricola Antonelli
San Marco
località San Marco 59
06036 Montefalco PG
tel. 0742/379158

Castello di Antignano
Località Bastia Umbra
via degli Olmi 9
06083 Perugia
tel. 075/8001501

Colpetrone
via della Collina 4
frazione Marcellano
06035 Guado Cattaneo PG
tel. 0578/767722

Rocca di Fabbri
località Fabbri di Montefalco
06036 Montefalco PG
tel. 0742/399379

Spoletoducale
località Petrognano 54
06049 Spoleto PG
tel. 0743/56224

Tenuta San Lorenzo
località San Lorenzo Vecchio
06034 Foligno PG
tel. 0742/22553

Terre de Trinci
via Fiamenga 57
06034 Foligno PG
tel. 0742/320165

## MONTEFALCO
### SAGRANTINO
### PASSITO docg

*Vines: Sangiovese (dal 60 al
70%), Sagrantino (dal 10 al
15%), altri, per la restante
parte, autorizzati a/o
raccomandati dalla provincia
di Perugina*

Adanti
Vocabolo Arquata
06031 Bevagna PG
tel. 0742/360295

Arnaldo Caprai
località Torre di Montefalco
06036 Montefalco PG
tel. 0742/378802

Fattoria Milziade Antano
Località Colle Allodole
06031 Bevagna PG
tel. 0742/360371

Rocca di Fabbri
località Fabbri di Montefalco
06036 Montefalco PG
tel. 0742/399379

### ROSSO ORVIETANO doc

*Vines: Aleatico a/o Cabernet Sauvignon a/o Cabernet Franc a/o Canaiolo a/o Sangiovese a/o Pinot Nero a/o Cigliegiolo a/o Merlot a/o Montepulciano (min. 70%), Aleatico a/o Barbera a/o Cesanese comune a/o Colorino a/o Dolcetto (max 30%)*

Tenuta Le Velette
località Le Velette 23
05019 Orvieto TR
tel. 0763/29090

Tordimaro
località Tordimonte 37
05019 Orvieto TR
tel. 0763/304227
*Selvaia*

### ORVIETO doc

*Vines: Trebbiano toscano, localmente detto Procanico (dal 40 al 60%), Verdello (dal 15 al 25%), Grechetto a/o Canaiolo bianco, localmente detto Drupeggio a/o Malvasia toscana, globalmente per la restante parte, purché la Malvasia non superi il 20%. Altri autorizzati a/o raccomandati dalle province di Terni e Viterbo (max 15%)*

Antinori - Castello della Sala
frazione Sala
05016 Ficulle TR
tel. 0763/86051

Barberani - Azienda Agr.
Vallesanta
Via Michelamgeli 14
05018 Orvieto TR
tel. 0763/341820

 Bigi
località Ponte Giulio 3
05018 Orvieto TR
tel. 0763/316591

Cantina Monrubio
Loc. Le Prese 22
Monterubiaglio
05010 Castel Viscardo TR
tel. 0763/626064

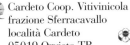 Cardeto Coop. Vitivinicola
frazione Sferracavallo
località Cardeto
05019 Orvieto TR
tel. 0763/341286

Decugnano dei Barbi
loc. Fossatello di Corbara 50
05019 Orvieto TR
tel. 0763/308255

La Carraia
località Tordimonte 56
05018 Orvieto TR
tel. 0763/304013

Palazzone
via Rocca Ripesana 66
05019 Orvieto TR
tel. 0763/344166

Sergio Mottura
loc. Poggio della Costa
01020 Civitella d'Agliano VT

Tenuta di Salviano
Località Civitella del Lago
Salviano 44
05020 Baschi TR
tel. 0744/950459

Tenuta Le Velette
località Le Velette 23
05019 Orvieto TR
tel. 0763/29090

Tenuta Poggio del Lupo
località Buzzaghetto 100
05010 Allerona TR
tel. 0763/628350

Tordimaro
località Tordimonte 37
05019 Orvieto TR
tel. 0763/304227

### TORGIANO BIANCO doc

*Vines: Trebbiano toscano (dal 50 al 70%), Grechetto (dal 15 al 40%), altre autorizzate a/o raccomandate della provincia di Perugia (max 15%)*

Lungarotti
via Mario Angeloni 16
06089 Torgiano PG
tel. 0759/880348

### TORGIANO ROSSO RISERVA docg

*Vines: Sangiovese (dal 50 al 70%), Canaiolo (dal 15 al 30%), Trebbiano toscano (max 10%), Cigliegiolo a/o Montepulciano (max 10%)*

Lungarotti
via Mario Angeloni 16
06089 Torgiano PG
tel. 0759/880348
*Rubesco*

### CILIEGIOLO IGT SPELLO

Tenuta San Lorenzo
località San Lorenzo Vecchio
06034 Foligno PG
tel. 0742/22553

### UMBRIA IGT ALEATICO

Cantina dei Colli Almerini
zona Industriale
05020 Fornole di Amelia TR
tel. 0744/989721
*Bartolomeo*

### UMBRIA IGT CANAIOLO

Fattoria Le Poggette
Fattoria Le Poggette 141
05026 Montecastrilli TR
tel. 0744/940338

### UMBRIA IGT GRECHETTO

Arnaldo Caprai
località Torre di Montefalco
06036 Montefalco PG
tel. 0742/378802

Falesco
Località artigiana Le Guardie
01027 Montefisacone VT
tel. 0761/825669

Fattoria Le Poggette
Fattoria Le Poggette 141
05026 Montecastrilli TR
tel. 0744/940338

Tordimaro
località Tordimonte 37
05019 Orvieto TR
tel. 0763/304227

### UMBRIA IGT ROSSO

Cardeto Coop. Vitivinicola
frazione Sferracavallo
località Cardeto
05019 Orvieto TR
tel. 0763/341286
*Sangiovese + Canaiolo + Montepulciano*

Castello delle Regine
Strada del Castelluccio
Amerino PG
tel. 0744/702005
*Princeps (Sangiovese + Merlot + Cabernet Sauvignon)*

Decugnano dei Barbi
loc. Fossatello di Corbara 50
05019 Orvieto TR
tel. 0763/308255
*IL* (Sangiovese + Canaiolo +
Montepulciano + altre)

Fattoria Le Poggette
Fattoria Le Poggette 141
05026 Montecastrilli TR
tel. 0744/940338
*Torre Maggiore*
(Montepulciano)

Giulio Freddano
Località Fossatello
05018 Orvieto TR
tel. 0763/308248
*Campo de' Massi* (Sangiovese
+ Cabernet)

I Girasoli di Sant'Andrea
Località Molino Vitelli
06019 Umbertide PG
tel. 0759/410837
*Cà Andrea* (Sangiovese +
Canaiolo)

I Girasoli di Sant'Andrea
Località Molino Vitelli
06019 Umbertide PG
tel. 0759/410837
*Il Doge* (Sangiovese + Merlot)

Tordimaro
località Tordimonte 37
05019 Orvieto TR
tel. 0763/304227
*Torriello* (Barbera +
Montepulciano + Canaiolo)

### UMBRIA IGT SANGIOVESE

Bigi
località Ponte Giulio 3
05018 Orvieto TR
tel. 0763/316591

Cantina dei Colli Almerini
zona Industriale
05020 Fornole di Amelia TR
tel. 0744/989721
*Torraccio*

Castello delle Regine
Strada del Castelluccio
Amerino PG
tel. 0744/702005

Fanini
Vocabolo i Cucchi
06061 Petrignano del Lago PG
tel. 075/5171141
*Vigna La Pieve*

La Carraia
località Tordimonte 56
05018 Orvieto TR
tel. 0763/304013

Poggio Bertaio
Frazione Casamaggiore
Frattavecchia 29
06061 Castiglione del Lago PG
tel. 0759/56921
*Cimbolo*

Tenuta San Lorenzo
località San Lorenzo Vecchio
06034 Foligno PG
tel. 0742/22553
*Chiostro*

### ABRUZZO

### MONTEPULCIANO D'ABRUZZO CERASUOLO doc

*Vitigno: Montepulciano (min. 85%)*

Camillo Montori
via Piane Tronto
64010 Controguerra PE
tel. 0861/809900

Cantina Tollo soc. Coop.
viale Garibaldi 68
66010 Tollo CH
tel. 0871/96251

Casal Bordino Soc. Coop
contrada Termine 38
66020 Casal Bordino CH
tel. 0873/918107

Casal Thaulero - Aprutina Vini
contrada Cuccullo 32
66026 Ortona CH
tel. 085/9032533

Consorzio Cooperative
Riunite d'Abruzzo
contrada Cuccullo
66026 Ortona CH
tel. 085/9031342

Fattoria Bruno Nicodemi
strada Provinciale 19 8
64024 Notaresco TE
tel. 085/895493

Fattoria Buccicatino
contrada Sterpara
66010 Vacri CH
tel. 0871/720273

Marramiero
contrada Sant'Andrea 1
65010 Rosciano PE
tel. 085/8505766

Masciarelli
66010 San Martino sulla
Marrucina CH
tel. 0871/85241

Tenuta Cataldi Madonna
località Piano 1
67025 Ofena AQ
tel. 0854/911680

Terre d'Aligi
contrada Piana La Fara 90
66041 Atessa CH
tel. 0872/897916

Valentini
via Del Baio 2
65014 Loreto Aprutini PE
tel. 085/8291138

### MONTEPULCIANO D'ABRUZZO doc

*Vitigno: Montepulciano (min. 85%)*

Agriverde
via Monte Maiella 118
66020 Caldari di Ortona CH
tel. 085/9032101

Barone Cornacchia
contrada Torri
64010 Torano Nuovo TE
tel. 0861/887412

Camillo Montori
via Piane Tronto
64010 Controguerra PE
tel. 0861/809900

Cantina Miglianico
via San Giacomo 40
66010 Miglianico
tel. 0871/950240

Cantina Tollo soc. Coop.
viale Garibaldi 68
66010 Tollo CH
tel. 0871/96251

Cantina Zaccagnini
contrada Da Pozzo
65020 Bolognano
tel. 085/8880195

Casal Bordino Soc. Coop
contrada Termine 38
66020 Casal Bordino
tel. 0873/918107

Casal Thaulero
Aprutina Vini
contrada Cuccullo 32
66026 Ortona CH
tel. 085/9032533

Consorzio Cooperative
Riunite d'Abruzzo
contrada Cuccullo
66026 Ortona CH
tel. 085/9031342

Dino Illuminati
contrada San Biagio 18
64010 Controguerra
tel. 086/1808008

Farnese Vini
piazza Porta Caldari 26
66026 Ortona CH
tel. 085/9067388

---

Fattoria Bruno Nicodemi
strada Provinciale 19 8
64024 Notaresco TE
tel. 085/895493

Fattoria Buccicatino
contrada Sterpaia
66010 Vacri CH
tel. 0871/720273

Marramiero
contrada Sant'Andrea 1
65010 Rosciano PE
tel. 085/8505766

Masciarelli
via Gamberale 1
66010 San Martino sulla
Marrucina CH
tel. 0871/85241

Orlandi Contucci Ponto
località Piana degli Ulivi 1
64026 Roseto degli Abruzzi
tel. 085/8944049

Tenuta Cataldi Madonna
località Piano 1
67025 Ofena AQ
tel. 0854/911680

Terre d'Aligi
contrada Piana La Fara 90
66041 Atessa
tel. 087/2897916

---

Valentini
via Del Baio 2
65014 Loreto Aprutino PE
tel. 085/8291138

TREBBIANO
D'ABRUZZO doc
Vitigno: Trebbiano (min. 85%)

Barone Cornacchia
contrada Torri
64010 Torano Nuovo TE
tel. 0861/887412

Camillo Montori
via Piane Tronto
64010 Controguerra PE
tel. 0861/809900

Cantina Miglianico
via San Giacomo 40
66010 Miglianico CH
tel. 0871/950240

Cantina Tollo soc. Coop.
viale Garibaldi 68
66010 Tollo CH
tel. 0871/96251

Cantina Zaccagnini
contrada Da Pozzo
65020 Bolognano
tel. 085/8880195

Casal Bordino Soc. Coop
contrada Termine 38
66020 Casal Bordino
tel. 0873/918107

Casal Thaulero - Aprutina Vini
contrada Cuccullo 32
66026 Ortona CH
tel. 085/9032533

Cons. Coop. Riunite d'Abruzzo
contrada Cuccullo
66026 Ortona CH
tel. 085/9031342

Dini Illuminati
contrada San Biagio 18
64010 Controguerra TE
tel. 0861/808008

---

Fattoria Bruno Nicodemi
strada Provinciale 19 8
64024 NotarescoTE
tel. 085/895493

Fattoria Buccicatino
contrada Sterpaia
66010 Vacri CH
tel. 0871/720273

Marramiero
contrada Sant'Andrea 1
65010 Rosciano PE
tel. 085/8505766

Masciarelli
via Gamberale 1
66010 San Martino sulla
Marrucina CH
tel. 0871/85241

Orlandi Contucci Ponto
località Piana degli Ulivi 1
64026 Roseto degli Abruzzi
tel. 085/8944049

Tenuta Cataldi Madonna
località Piano 1
67025 Ofena AQ
tel. 085/4911680

Terre d'Aligi
contrada Piana La Fara 90
66041 Atessa CH
tel. 0872/897916

Valentini
via Del Baio 2
65014 Loreto Aprutino PE
tel. 085/8291138

## LAZIO

### ALEATICO DI GRADOLI
doc

*Vines: Aleatico*

Cantina Sociale di Gradoli
Via Roma 81
01010 Gradoli
tel. 076/1456087

### CASTELLI ROMANI BIANCO doc

*Vines: Malvasia Bianca di Candia a/o puntinata a/o Trebbiano toscano, romagnolo, di Soave, verde e giallo, altri autorizzati a/o raccomandati dalla provincia di Roma e Latina (max 30%)*

Cantina Cerquetta
via Fontana Candida 20
00040 Monteporzio Catone RM
tel. 06/9424147
(Malvasia+Trebbiano)

Casalgentile
Via Casale Paoloni 13
00133 Roma
tel. 06/72602022

CO.PRO.VI. Velletri
via Pontina km 55
04011 Campoverde
di Aprilia LT
tel. 06/92903212

Gotto d'Oro
via Divino Amore 115
00040 Frattocchie
di Marino RM
tel. 06/9302221

La Selva
via La Selva
03018 Paliano FR
tel. 0775/533125

### CASTELLI ROMANI ROSSO doc

*Vines: Cesanese a/o Merlot a/o Montepulciano a/o Nero buono a/o Sangiovese, altri autorizzati a/o raccomandati dalla provincia di Roma e Latina (max 15%)*

Cantina Cerquetta
via Fontana Candida 20
00040 Monteporzio
Catone RM
tel. 06/9424147

Casalgentile
via Casale Paoloni 13
00133 Roma
tel. 06/72602022

CO.PRO.VI. Velletri
via Pontina km 55
04011 Campoverde
di Aprilia LT
tel. 06/92903212

Gotto d'Oro
via Divino Amore 115
00040 Frattocchie
di Marino RM
tel. 06/9302221

La Selva
via La Selva
03018 Paliano FR
tel. 0775/533125

### CERVETERI BIANCO doc

*Vines: Trebbiano toscano, localmente detto Procanico a/o Trebbiano giallo (min. 50%), Malvasia di Candia a/o Malvasia del Lazio (max 35%), altri autorizzati a/o raccomandati dalla provincia di Roma e Viterbo (max 30%)*

Cantina Cerveteri
via Aurelia Km 42.700
00052 Cerveteri RM
tel. 06/9905677

### CERVETERI ROSSO doc

*Vines: Sangiovese (min. 25%) e Montepulciano (min. 25%), però congiuntamente (min. 60%) e Cesanese comune (max. 25%), altri raccomandati a/o autorizzati dalle provincie di Roma e Viterbo (max 30%)*

Cantina Cerveteri
via Aurelia Km 42.700
00052 Cerveteri RM
tel. 06/9905677

### CESANESE DEL PIGLIO doc

*Vines: Cesanese di Affile a/o Cesanese comune (min. 90%), Sangiovese a/o Montepulciano, a/o Barbera a/o Trebbiano toscano a/o Bombino bianco (max 10%)*

Cantina Sociale Cesanese del Piglio
via Prenestina km 42
03010 Piglio FR
tel. 0775/502356

Casale della Ioria
Azienda Agricola Perinelli
piazza Regina Margherita 1
03010 Acuto FR
tel. 0775/56031

Giovanni Terenzi
via Forese 13
03010 La Forma-Serrone FR
tel. 0775/595466

La Selva
via La Selva
03018 Paliano FR
tel. 0775/533125

Marcella Giuliani
via Anticolana Km. 5
03012 Anagni FR
tel. 0775/744331

Terre del Cesanese
Via Maggiore 105
03010 Piglio FR
tel. 0775/502356

### COLLI ALBANI doc

*Vines: Malvasia di Candia, localmente detta Malvasia rossa (max 60%), Trebbiano toscano, a/o romagnolo, a/o giallo a/o di Soave (dal 25 al 50%), Malvasia del Lazio, localmente detta Malvasia puntinata (dal 5 al 45%), altri autorizzati a/o raccomandati dalla provincia di Roma (max 10%)*

Cantine S. Tommaso
via Appia Vecchia km 3.5
00045 Genzano di Roma RM
tel. 06/9375863

Cantine Volpetti
via Nettunese Km 7800, 21
00040 Ariccia RM
tel. 06/9342000

Donnardea
via Fosso di Valle Caia 7
00040 Ardea RM
tel. 06/9115435

Fontana di Papa
via Nettunense Km 10,800
00040 Ariccia RM
tel. 06/9340071-2-3

**COLLI LANUVINI** doc

*Vines: Malvasia bianca di
Candia a/o puntinata (max
70%), Trebbiano Toscano a/o
verde a/o giallo (min. 30%),
altri autorizzati a/o
raccomandati dalla provincia
di Roma (max 10%)*

Cooperativa Agricola Andreassi
via Montecagnolo 25
00045 Genzano RM
tel. 06/9370271

La Selva
via La Selva
03018 Paliano FR
tel. 0775/533125

Cantine S. Tommaso
via Appia Vecchia km 3,5
00045 Genzano di Roma RM
tel. 06 /9375863

Covarelli
via Vigne Nuove 53
00045 Genzano di Roma RM
tel. 06/93709135

**EST! EST!! EST!!! DI
MONTEFIASCONE** doc

*Vines: Trebbiano toscano, qui
chiamato Procanico (65%
circa), Trebbiano giallo, qui
chiamato Rossetto (15%
circa), Malvasia bianca
toscana (20% circa)*

 Bigi-Grupo Italiano Vini
località Ponte Giulio 3
05018 Orvieto TR
tel. 07/63316224

Cantina Stefanoni
via Stefanoni 48
01027 Montefiascone VT
tel. 0761/827031

 Mazziotti
località Mecona-Bonvino
via Cassi Km 110
01023 Bolsena VT
tel. 0761/799049

Trappolini
via del Rivellino 65
01024 Castiglione
in Teverina VT
tel. 0761/948381

**FRASCATI** doc

*Vines: Malvasia bianca di
Candia a/o Trebbiano
toscano (min. 70%), Greco a/o
Malvasia del Lazio (max
30%), altri autorizzati a/o
raccomandati dalla provincia
di Roma (max 10%)*

Cantine San Marco
via di Mola Cavona 26/28
00044 Frascati RM
tel. 06/9422689

 Falesco
località Artigiana-Le Guardie
01027 Montefiascone VT
tel. 0761/825669

Casale Marchese
via di Vermicino 68
00044 Frascati RM
tel. 06/9408932

Casale Mattia
via Buttarelli 16
00044 Frascati RM
tel. 06/9426249

 Castel de Paolis
via Val De Paolis
00046 Grottaferrata RM
tel. 06/9413648

Conte Zandotti
00132 Roma RM
tel. 06/20609000

Fontana Candida
via Fontana Candida 11
00040 Monteporzio Catone RM
tel. 06/9420066

Gotto d'Oro
via Divino Amore 115
00040 Frattocchie
di Marino RM
tel. 06/93022200

L'Olivella
via Colle Pisano 5
00044 Frascati RM
tel. 06/9424527

Pallavicini
via Casilina Km 25 500
00030 Colonna RM
tel. 06/9438816

Villa Simone Piero Costantini
via Frascati Colonna 29
00040 Monte Porzio
Catone RM
tel. 06/3603575

Tenuta di Pietra Porzia
via Pietra Porzia 60
00044 Frascati RM
tel. 06.9464392

**FRASCATI CANELLINO** doc

*Vines: Malvasia bianca di
Candia a/o Trebbiano toscano
(min. 70%), Greco a/o
Malvasia del Lazio (max
30%), altri autorizzati a/o
raccomandati dalla provincia
di Roma (max 10%)*

Cantine San Marco
via di Mola Cavona 26/28
00044 Frascati RM
tel. 06.9422689

Casale Mattia
via Buttarelli 16
00044 Frascati RM
tel. 06/9426249

Castel de Paolis
via Val De Paolis
00046 Grottaferrata RM
tel. 06/9413648

Villa Simone Piero Costantini
via Frascati Colonna 29
00040 Monte Porzio
Catone RM
tel. 06/3603575

**MARINO** doc

*Vines: Malvasia bianca di
Candia, localmente detta
Malvasia rossa (max
60%),Trebbiano toscano a/o
romagnolo a/o giallo a/o di
Soave (dal 25 al 55%),
Malvasia del Lazio, localmente
detta Malvasia puntinata (dal
5 al 45%), altri autorizzati a/o
raccomandati dalla provincia
di Roma (max 10%)*

Dino Limiti
corso Vittoria Colonna 170
00047 Marino RM
tel. 06/9385051

Galassini
via G.Prati
00040 Santa Maria delle
Mole-Marino RM
tel. 06/9309383

Gotto d'Oro
via Divino Amore 115
00040 Frattocchie
di Marino RM
tel. 06/9302221

Paola di Mauro-Colle Picchioni
via Colle Picchioni 46
00040 Frattocchie
di Marino RM
tel. 06/93546329

## MONTECOMPATRI COLONNA doc
*Vines: Malvasia bianca a/o puntinata (max 70%), Trebbiano toscano a/o verde a/o giallo (min. 30%), Bellone, Bonvino, che è un sinonimo del Bombino bianco, (max 10%)*

Cantina Cerquetta
via Fontana Candida 20
00040 Monteporzio Catone RM
tel. 06/9424147

Tenuta Le Quinte
via delle Marmorelle 71
00040 Montecompatri RM
tel. 06/9438756

## TARQUINIA BIANCO doc
*Vines: Trebbiano toscano, detto localmente Procanico, a/o giallo (min. 50%), Malvasia bianca di Candia a/o Malvasia del Lazio (max 35%), altri autorizzati a/o raccomandati dalla province di Roma e Viterbo, ad esclusione del Pinot Grigio (max 30%)*

Castello di Torre in Pietra
via di Torre in Pietra 247
00050 Torrimpietra RM
tel. 06/61697070

## TARQUINIA ROSSO doc
*Vines: Sangiovese (min. 25%) e Montepulciano (min. 25%), però congiuntamente (min. 60%) e Cesanese comune (max. 25%), altri autorizzati a/o raccomandati dalle provincie di Roma e Viterbo (max 30%)*

Castello di Torre in Pietra
via di Torre in Pietra 247
00050 Torrimpietra RM
tel. 06/61697070

## VELLETRI BIANCO doc
*Vines: Malvasia bianca del Lazio a/o puntinata (max 70%), Trebbiano toscano a/o verde a/o giallo (min. 30%), Bellone e Bonvino e altri autorizzati a/o raccomandati dalle provincie di Roma e Latina (max 20%)*

CO.PRO.VI.
via Pontina Km 55 +
04011 Campoverde
di Aprilia LT
tel. 06/92900017

## VELLETRI ROSSO doc
*Vines: Montepulciano (dal 30 al 50%), Cesanese comune e/o di Affile (min. 10%), Sangiovese (dal 10 al 45%), Bombino nero a/o Merlot a/o Ciliegiolo a/o altri raccomandati a/o autorizzati dalle provincie di Roma e Latina (max 30%)*

CO.PRO.VI.
via Pontina Km 55 +
04011 Campoverde
di Aprilia LT
tel. 06/92900017

## FRUSINATE IGT BIANCO PASSERINA

Cantina Sociale Cesanese
del Piglio
via Prenestina km 42
03010 Piglio FR
tel. 0775.502356

## LAZIO IGT CESANESE

Pallavicini
via Casilina Km 25 500
00030 Colonna RM
tel. 06/9438816

## LAZIO IGT ALEATICO

Falesco
via San Domenico Savio 28
01027 Monterubiaglio VT
tel. 0761/834011

Trappolini
via del Rivellino 65
01024 Castiglione
in Teverina VT
tel. 0761/948381
*Idea*

## LAZIO IGT BIANCO

L'Olivella
via Colle Pisano 5
00044 Frascati RM
tel. 6/9424527
*Tre Grome (Malvasia+altri)*

## LAZIO IGT BOMBINO BIANCO

Donnardea
via Fosso di Valle Caia 7
00040 Ardea RM
tel. 06/9115435

## LAZIO IGT GRECHETTO

Sergio Mottura
Loc. Poggio della Costa 1
01020 Civitella d'Agliano VT
tel. 07/61914533
*Latour a Civitella*
*Il Poggio della Costa*

## LAZIO IGT MALVASIA

Belardi Maria Dolores
via della Fontanella 19
Genzano di Roma RM
tel. 06/9370389

Cantina Cerveteri
via Aurelia Km 42.7
00052 Cerveteri RM
tel. 06/9905677

Casale Mattia
via Buttareli 16
00044 Frascati RM
tel. 06/9426249

Conte Zandotti
casella Postale 46
000044 Frascati RM
tel. 06/20609000
*Rumon*

Fontana Candida
via Fontana Candida 11
00040 Monteporzio Catone RM
tel. 06/9420066
*Terre dei Grifi*

Gotto d'Oro
via Divino Amore 115
00040 Frattocchie
di Marino RM
tel. 06/9302221

Pallavicini
via Casilina Km 25 500
00030 Colonna RM
tel. 06/9438816

## LAZIO IGT MOSCATO DI TERRACINA

Cantina Sant'Andrea
via Renibbio 1720
Borgo Vodice
04019 Terracina LT
tel. 0773/755028

## LAZIO IGT ROSSO

Donnardea
via Fosso di Valle Caia 7
00040 Ardea RM
tel. 06/9115435
*Re Turno (Cesanese + Montepulciano)*

Cantine Volpetti
via Nettunese Km 7800 21
00040 Ariccia RM
tel. 06/9342000
*Elegie Romane (Sangiovese + Montepulciano + altre)*

Paola di Mauro
Colle Picchioni
via Colle Picchioni 46
00040 Frattocchie
di Marino RM
tel. 06/93546329
*Picchioni Rosso (Sangiovese + Montepulciano + altre)*

## LAZIO IGT SANGIOVESE

Cantine Volpetti
via Nettunese Km 7800 21
00040 Ariccia RM
tel. 06/9342000
*Le Pianate*

Trappolini
01024 Castiglione
in Teverina VT
via del Rivellino 65
tel. 0761/948381
*Paterno*

## CAMPANIA

### AGLIANICO DEL TABURNO doc
*Vines: Aglianico (min. 85%)*

Cantina del Taburno
via Sala
82030 Foglianise BN
tel. 0824/871338

Fattoria La Rivolta
Contrada Rivolta
82030 Torrecuso BN
tel. 0824/872921

Fontanavecchia - Orazio Rilllo
contrada Fontanavecchia
82030 Torrecuso BN
tel. 0824/876275

Ocone
via del Monte 56
Località La Madonnella
83030 Ponte BN
tel. 0824/874040

### CAMPI FLEGREI BIANCO doc
*Vines: Falanghina (min. 50, max 70%), Biancolella e Coda di Volpe (insieme o da soli min. 10, max 30%), altri vines autorizzati max 30%*

Caputo
via Garibaldi 64
81030 Teverola CE
tel. 081/5033955

Grotta del Sole
via Spinelli 2
80010 Quarto NA
tel. 081/8762566

Vinicola Pietraspaccata
via G. Di Vittorio C/1
80016 Marano di Napoli NA
tel. 081/5865834

### CAMPI FLEGREI PIEDIROSSO doc
*Vines: Piedirosso localmente detto Pér 'e palummo (min. 90%)*

Caputo
via Garibaldi 64 M
81030 Teverola CE
tel. 081/5033955

Grotta del Sole
via Spinelli 2
80010 Quarto NA
tel. 081/8762566

### CILENTO AGLIANICO doc
*Vines: Aglianico (min. 85%)*

Rotolo Francesco
via San Cesario 18
84070 Rutino SA
tel. 0974/830050

### FALERNO DEL MASSICO BIANCO doc
*Vines: Falangina*

Moio
Viale Margherita 6
81034 Mondragone CE
tel. 0823/978017

Villa Matilde
SS Domitiana 18
81030 Cellole CE
tel. 0823/932088

FALERNO DEL MASSICO

VILLA MATILDE

### FALERNO DEL MASSICO PRIMITIVO doc
*Vines: Falangina*

Moio
viale Margherita 6
81034 Mondragone CE
tel. 0823/978017

### FALERNO DEL MASSICO ROSSO doc
*Vines: Aglianico (min. 60, max 80%), Piedirosso (min. 20, max 40%), possono concorrere Primitivo e Barbera (max 20%) complessivamente*

Villa Matilde
SS Domitiana 18
81030 Cellole CE
tel. 0823/932088

### FIANO DI AVELLINO doc
*Vines: Fiano (min. 85%)*

Antonio Caggiano
Contrada da Sala
83030 Taurasi AV
tel. 0827/74043

Colli Irpini
Loc. Serra
83038 Serra di Montefusco AV
tel. 0825/627252

D'Antiche Terre Vega
Contrada da Lo Piano
83030 Manocalzati AV
tel. 0825/675358

Feudi di San Gregorio
Località Cerza Grossa
83050 Sorbo Serpico AV
tel. 0825/986266

Marianna
v. Filande 6 - 83100 Avellino AV
tel. 0825/627252

Mastroberardino
via Manfredi, 75/81
83042 Atripalda AV
tel. 0825/614111

Pietracupa
via Vadiaperti 17
83030 Montefredane AV
tel. 0825/607418

Terredora
via Serra
83030 Montefusco AV
tel. 0825/968215

Vadiaperti
Fraz. Arcella Cont. da Vadiaperti
83030 Montefredane AV
tel. 0825/607270

### GRECO DI TUFO doc
*Vines: Greco (min 85%), Coda di Volpe (max 15%)*

Colli Irpini
Loc. Serra
83038 Serra di Montefusco AV
tel. 0825/963972

D'Antiche Terre Vega
Contrada Lo Piano-SS7bis
83030 Manocalzati AV
tel. 0825/675359

Feudi di San Gregorio
Località Cerza Grossa
83050 Sorbo Serpico AV
tel. 0825/986611

Mastroberardino
via Manfredi 75/81
83042 Atripalda AV
tel. 0825/614111

Pietracupa
via Vadiaperti 17
83030 Montefredane AV
tel. 0825/607418

Struzziero Giovanni
via Cadorna 214
83030 Venticano AV
tel. 0825/965065

Terredora
via Serra
83030 Montefusco AV
tel. 0825/968215

### SANNIO AGLIANICO doc
*Vines: Aglianico (min. 85%)*

Cantine Terre di Lavoro
via Ettore Concioni 75
81031 Aversa CE
tel. 081/5033955

Caputo
via Garibaldi 64
81030 Teverola CE
tel. 081/5033955

Colli Irpini
Loc. Serra
83038 Serra di Montefusco AV
tel. 0825/963972

Corte Normanna
Contrada da Sapienze
20emergente
82034 Guardia
Sanframondi BN
tel. 0824/817004

De Lucia
Contrada da Starze
82034 Guardia
Sanframondi BN
tel. 0824/864259

Vinicola del Sannio
via Sannitica 171
82030 Castelvenere BN
tel. 0824/940207

### SANNIO BARBERA doc
*Vines: Barbera (min. 85%)*

Antica Masseria Venditti
via Sannitica, 122
82030 Castelvenere BN
tel. 0824/940306

### SANNIO BIANCO doc
*Vines: Trebbiano toscano (min. 50%), altri vines autorizzati o raccomandati per la provincia di Benevento*

Antica Masseria Venditti
via Sannitica 122
82030 Castelvenere BN
tel. 0824/940306

### SANNIO FALANGHINA doc
*Vines: Falanghina (min. 85%)*

Antica Masseria Venditti
via Sannitica, 122
82030 Castelvenere BN
tel. 0824/940306

Caputo
via Garibaldi 64
81030 Teverola CE
tel. 081/5033955

Corte Normanna
Contrada da Sapienze 20
82034 Guardia
Sanframondi BN
tel. 0824/817004

De Lucia
Contrada da Starze
82034 Guardia
Sanframondi BN
tel. 0824/864259

Di Meo
Contrada da Coccovoni 1
83050 Salza Irpina AV
tel. 0825/981419

### SANNIO FALANGHINA PASSITO doc
*Vines: Falanghina (min. 85%)*

Corte Normanna
Contrada da Sapienze 20
82034 Guardia
Sanframondi BN
tel. 0824/817004

### SANT'AGATA DE' GOTI AGLIANICO doc
*Vines: Aglianico (min. 90%)*

Mustilli
via dei Fiori, 20
82019 S. Agata dei Goti BN
tel. 0823/717433

### SANT'AGATA DE' GOTI FALANGHINA doc
*Vines: Falanghina (min. 90%)*

Mustilli
via dei Fiori, 20
82019 S. Agata dei Goti BN
tel. 0823/717433

### SANT'AGATA DE' GOTI GRECO doc
*Vines: Greco (min. 90%)*

Mustilli
via dei Fiori 20
82019 S. Agata dei Goti BN
tel. 0823/717433

### SANT'AGATA DE' GOTI PIEDIROSSO doc
*Vines: Piedirosso (min. 90%)*

Mustilli
via dei Fiori 20
82019 S. Agata dei Goti BN
tel. 0823/717433

### SOLOPACA AGLIANICO doc
*Vines: Aglianico (min. 85%)*

Cantina Sociale di Solopaca
via Bebiana 44
82036 Solopaca BN
tel. 0824/977921

## SOLOPACA ROSSO doc

*Vines: Sangiovese (min. 50, max 60%), Aglianico (min. 20%, max 40%), altri vines raccomandati a/o autorizzati dalla provincia di Benevento (max 30%)*

Antica Masseria Venditti
via Sannitica 122 M
82030 Castelvenere BN
tel. 0824/940306

Cantina Sociale di Solopaca
via Bebiana 44
82036 Solopaca BN
tel. 0824/977921

Corte Normanna
Contrada da Sapienze 20
82034 Guardia
Sanframondi BN
tel. 0824/817004

## TABURNO CODA DI VOLPE doc

*Vines: Coda di Volpe (min. 85%)*

Cantina del Taburno
via Sala
82038 Foglianise BN
tel. 0824/871338

Fattoria La Rivolta
Contrada Rivolta
82030 Torrecuso BN
tel. 0824/872921

Ocone
via Monte-Loc. La Madonnella
83030 Ponte BN
tel. 0824/874040

## TABURNO FALANGHINA doc

*Vines: Falanghina (min. 85%)*

Cantina del Taburno
via Sala
82038 Foglianise BN
tel. 0824/871338

Fattoria La Rivolta
Contrada Rivolta
82030 Torrecuso BN
tel. 0824/872921

Ocone
via Monte-Loc. La Madonnella
83030 Ponte BN
tel. 0824/874040

## TABURNO GRECO doc

*Vines: Greco bianco (min. 85%)*

Cantina del Taburno
via Sala
82038 Foglianise BN
tel. 0824/871338

Ocone
via Monte-Loc. La Madonnella
83030 Ponte BN
tel. 0824/874040

## TABURNO PIEDIROSSO doc

*Vines: Piedirosso (min. 85%)*

Ocone
via Monte-Loc. La Madonnella
83030 Ponte BN
tel. 0824/874040

## TAURASI docg

*Vines: Aglianico (min. 85%)*

Antonio Caggiano
Contrada da Sala
83030 Taurasi AV
tel. 0827/74043

D'Antiche Terre Vega
Contrada Lo Piano- SS 7 bis
83030 Manocalzati AV
tel. 0825/675358

Marianna
via Filande 6
83100 Avellino AV
tel. 0825/627252

Di Meo
Contrada Coccovoni 1
83050 Salza Irpina AV
tel. 0825/981419

Feudi di San Gregorio
Località Cerza Grossa
83050 Sorbo Serpico AV
tel. 0825/986611

Mastroberardino
via Manfredi 75/81
83042 Atripalda AV
tel. 0825/614111

Pietracupa
via Vadiaperti 17
83030 Montefredane AV
tel. 0825/607418

Salvatore Molettieri
via Musanni 19
83040 Montemarano AV
tel. 0827/63424

Terredora
via Serra
83030 Montefusco AV
tel. 0825/968215

## VESUVIO BIANCO, LACRYMA CHRISTI doc

*Vines: Coda di Volpe, nota localmente come Caprettone, (min. 35%), Verdeca (congiuntamente min. 80%), Falanghina a/o Greco (max 20%)*

Caputo
via Garibaldi 64 CE
81030 Teverola
tel. 081/5033955

De Falco Vini
via Figliola
80040 San Sebastiano Al
Vesuvio NA
tel. 081/7713755

Grotta del Sole
v. Spinelli 2 - 80010 Quarto NA
tel. 081/8762566

Mastroberardino
via Manfredi 75/81
83042 Atripalda AV
tel. 0825/614111

Sorrentino
via Casciello 5
80042 Boscotrecase NA
tel. 081/8584194

## VESUVIO ROSSO, LACRYMA CHRISTI doc

*Vines: Piedirosso, noto localmente come Palombina, (min. 50%), Sciascinoso, noto localmente come Olivella (congiuntamente min. 80%), Aglianico (max 20%)*

Cantine Terre di Lavoro
via Ettore Concioni 75
81031 Aversa CE
tel. 081/5048645

Caputo
via Garibaldi 64
81030 Teverola CE
tel. 081/5033955

De Angelis
via Marziale 14
80067 Sorrento NA
tel. 081/8781648

De Falco Vini
via Figliola
80040 San Sebastiano Al
Vesuvio NA
tel. 081/7713755

Grotta del Sole
via Spinelli 2
80010 Quarto NA
tel. 081/8762566

Mastroberardino
via Manfredi, 75/81
83042 Atripalda AV
tel. 0825/614111

## BENEVENTANO IGT FALANGHINA

Colli Irpini
Loc. Serra
83038 Serra di Montefusco AV
tel. 0825/963982

## BENEVENTO IGT AGLIANICO

Cantina del Taburno
via Sala
82030 Foglianise BN
tel. 0824/871338
*Bue Apis e Delius*

De Falco Vini
via Figliola
80040 San Sebastiano Al
Vesuvio NA
tel. 081/7713755

## IRPINIA IGT AGLIANICO

Di Meo
Contrada Coccovoni 1
83050 Salza Irpina AV
tel. 0825/981419
*Vigna Olmo*

Feudi di San Gregorio
Località Cerza Grossa
83050 Sorbo Serpico AV
tel. 0825/986611
*Serpico*

Terredora
via Serra
83030 Montefusco AV
tel. 0825/968215
*Il Principio*

Mastroberardino
via Manfredi 75/81
83042 Atripalda AV
tel. 0825/614111
*Naturalis Historia*

---

Salvatore Molettieri
via Musanni 19
83040 Montemarano AV
tel. 0827/63424

### IRPINIA IGT CODA DI VOLPE

Marianna
via Filande 6
83100 Avellino AV
tel. 0825/627252

Di Meo
Contrada Coccovoni 1
83050 Salza Irpina AV
tel. 0825/981419

### PAESTUM IGT AGLIANICO

De Conciliis
località Querce 1
84060 Prignano Cilento SA
tel. 0974/831090
*Naima e Donnaluna*

### PAESTUM IGT FIANO

Rotolo Francesco
via San Cesario 18
84070 Rutino SA
tel. 0974/830050
*Valentina*

De Conciliis
località Querce 1
84060 Prignano Cilento SA
tel. 0974/831090
*Vigna Perella*

---

### POMPEIANO IGT BIANCO

Mastroberardino
via Manfredi 75/81
83042 Atripalda AV
tel. 0825/614111
*Avalon* (Coda di Volpe)

### POMPEIANO IGT PIEDIROSSO

Terradora
via Serra
83030 Montefusco AV
tel. 0825/968215

### POMPEIANO IGT ROSSO

Mastroberardino
via Manfredi 75/81
83042 Atripalda AV
tel. 0825/614111
*Avalon* (Piedirosso + Aglianico)

## MOLISE

### BIFERNO BIANCO doc
*Vines: Trebbiano toscano (dal 65% al 75%); Bombino bianco (dal 25% al 30%); Malvasia bianca (dal 5% al 10%)*

Cantine Borgo di Colloredo
Contrada Da Zezza 8/b
86042 Campomarino CB
tel. 0875/57453

Di Majo Norante
Contrada Ramitelli 4
86032 Campomarino CB
tel. 0875/57208

---

### BIFERNO ROSATO doc
*Vines: Montepulciano (dal 60% al 70%); Trebbiano toscano (dal 15% al 20%); Malvasia bianca (dal 15% al 20%)*

Cantine Borgo di Colloredo
Contrada Da Zezza 8/b
86042 Campomarino CB
tel. 0875/57453

Di Majo Norante
Contrada Ramitelli 4
86032 Campomarino CB
tel. 0875/57208

### BIFERNO ROSSO doc
*Vines: Montepulciano (dal 60% al 70%); Trebbiano toscano (dal 15% al 20%); Malvasia bianca (dal 15% al 20%)*

Cantine Borgo di Colloredo
Contrada Da Zezza 8/b
86042 Campomarino CB
tel. 0875/57453

Di Majo Norante
Contrada Ramitelli 4
86032 Campomarino CB
tel. 0875/57208

### MOLISE AGLIANICO doc
*Vitigno: Aglianico (min. 85%)*

Di Majo Norante
Contrada Ramitelli 4
86032 Campomarino CB
tel. 0875/57208

### MOLISE FALANGINA doc
*Vines: Falanghina (min. 85%)*

Cantine Borgo di Colloredo
Contrada Da Zezza 8/b
86042 Campomarino CB
tel. 0875/57453

Di Majo Norante
Contrada Ramitelli 4
86032 Campomarino CB
tel. 0875/57208

### MOLISE
### MONTEPULCIANO doc
(diventerà ROSSO
MOLISE)

*Vines: Montepulciano (min.
85%). Il nome della doc
cambierà in Rosso del Molise*

Cantine Borgo di Colloredo
Contrada Da Zezza 8/b
86042 Campomarino CB
tel. 0875/57453

Di Majo Norante
Contrada Ramitelli 4
86032 Campomarino CB
tel. 0875/57208

### MOLISE
### MOSCATO doc

*Vines: Moscato bianco (min.
85%)*

Di Majo Norante
Contrada Ramitelli 4
86032 Campomarino CB
tel. 0875/57208

### TERRE DEGLI
### OSCI IGT

 Cantine Borgo di Colloredo
Contrada Da Zezza 8/b
86042 Campomarino CB
tel. 0875/57453
(Sangiovese)

Di Majo Norante
Contrada Ramitelli 4
86032 Campomarino CB
tel. 0875/57208
*Prugnolo (Sangiovese)*

### BASILICATA

### AGLIANICO DEL
### VULTURE doc

*Vines: Aglianico*

 Basilisco
via Umberto I 129
85028 Rionero in Vulture PZ
tel. 0972/720032

Cantina della Riforma
Fondiaria di Venosa
contrada Vignali
85029 Venosa PZ
tel. 0972/36702

 Cantine del Notaio
via Roma 159
85028 Rionero in Vulture PZ
tel. 0972/717111

Cantine Di Palma
via Potenza 13
85028 Rionero in Vulture PZ
tel. 0972/722515

Cantine Sasso
via Appia 123
85100 Potenza PZ
tel. 0971/470709

Consorzio Viticoltori Associati
del Vulture
S.S. 93
85022 Barile PZ
tel. 0972/770386

D'Angelo
via Provinciale 8
85028 Rionero in Vulture PZ
tel. 0972/721517

Paternoster
via Nazionale 23
85022 Barile PZ
tel. 0972/770224

Tenuta del Portale
Strada Provinciale 8
Località le Querce
85022 Barile PZ
tel. 0972/724691

 Tenuta Le Querce
Via Appia 123
85100 Potenza PZ
tel. 0971/470709

### PUGLIA

### BRINDISI ROSATO doc

*Vines: Negroamaro (min.
70%), Malvasia nera di
Brindisi a/o Sussumaniello a/o
Montepulciano a/o Sangiovese
(max 30%)*

 Agricole Vallone
via XXV Luglio 5
73100 Lecce LE
tel. 0832/308041

### BRINDISI ROSSO doc

*Vines: Negroamaro (min.
70%), Malvasia nera di
Brindisi a/o Sussumaniello a/o
Montepulciano a/o Sangiovese
(max 30%)*

Agricole Vallone
via XXV Luglio 5
73100 Lecce LE
tel. 0832/308041

Cantina Due Palme
via San Marco 130
72020 Cellino San Marco BR
tel. 0831/617865

Coop. Agricola Santa Barbara
via Maternità e Infanzia 23
72027 S. Pietro Vernotico BR
tel. 0831/652749

Lomazzi & Sarli
contrada Partemio S.S. 7
72022 Latiano BR
tel. 0831/725898

Tenuta Rubino
via Medaglie d'Oro 15/A
72100 Brindisi
tel. 0831/502912

### CACC'E MMITTE DI
### LUCERA doc

*Vines: Uva di Troia,
localmente chiamata
Sumarello (dal 35 al 60%),
Montepulciano a/o Sangiovese
a/o Malvasia nera di Brindisi
(dal 25 al 35%), Trebbiano
toscano a/o Bombino bianco
a/o Malvasia del Chianti (dal
15 al 30%)*

Cooperativa Svevo
viale Orazio 1
71036 Lucera
tel. 0881/542301

 Azienda Paolo e Paola Petrilli
Località Motta Caropresa
71036 Lucera FG
tel. 0881/523980

## CASTEL DEL MONTE AGLIANICO doc

*Vines: Aglianico (min. 90%)*

Rivera
S.S. 98 Km 19,8
70031 Andria BA
tel. 0883/569501
*Cappellaccio*

## CASTEL DEL MONTE ROSATO doc

*Vines: Uva di Troia (anche 100%), Aglianico (anche 100%), Bombino nero (anche 100%), altri autorizzati a/o raccomandati dalla provincia di Bari (max 35%)*

Rivera
S.S. 98 Km 19,8
70031 Andria BA
tel. 0883/569501

Torrevento
località Castel del Monte -
S.S. 170 Km 28
70033 Corato BA
tel. 080/8980929

## CASTEL DEL MONTE ROSSO doc

*Vines: Uva di Troia (anche 100%), Aglianico (anche 100%), Montepulciano (anche 100%), altri autorizzati a/o raccomandati dalla provincia di Bari (max 35%)*

Rivera
S.S. 98 Km 19,8
70031 Andria BA
tel. 0883/569501
*Il Falcone* (Uva di Troia + Montepulciano)

Rivera
S.S. 98 Km 19 8
70031 Andria BA
tel. 0883/569501
*Puer Apuliae* (Uva di Troia)

Rivera
S.S. 98 Km 19 8
70031 Andria BA
tel. 0883/569501
*Rupicolo* (Uva di Troia + Montepulciano)

Santa Lucia
Strada Comunale S. Vittore 1
70033 Corato BA
tel. 0808/721168
(Uva di Troia + Malbec)

Tormaresca
via Maternità e Infanzia 21
72027 S. Pietro Vernotico BR
tel. 0804/771392
*Bocca di Lupo* (Aglianico + Cabernet)

Torrevento
località Castel del Monte -
S.S. 170 Km 28
70033 Corato BA
tel. 080/8980929
*Vigna del Pedale* (Uva di Troia)

Torrevento
località Castel del Monte -
S.S. 170 Km 28
70033 Corato BA
tel. 0808/980929
(Bombino Nero + Aglianico)

## CASTEL DEL MONTE BIANCO doc

*Vines: Pampanuto, anche chiamato Pampanino (anche 100%), Chardonnay (anche 100%), Bombino bianco (anche 100%), altri autorizzati a/o raccomandati dalla provincia di Bari (max 35%)*

Rivera
S.S. 98 Km 19 8
70031 Andria BA
tel. 0883/569501
(Bombino Bianco + altri)

Torrevento
località Castel del Monte -
S.S. 170 Km 28
70033 Corato BA
tel. 080/8980929
(Bombino Bianco + altri)

## COPERTINO ROSSO doc

*Vines: Negroamaro (min. 70%), Malvasia nera di Brindisi a/o Malvasia nera di Lecce a/o Sangiovese a/o Montepulciano (max 30%)*

Cantina Sociale di Copertino
via Martiri del Risorgimento 6
73043 Copertino LE
tel. 0832/947031

Conti Leone De Castris
via Senatore De Castris
73015 Salice Salentino LE
tel. 0832/731112

Marco Maci
via San Marco 61
72020 Cellino San Marco BR
tel. 0831/617689

Masseria Monaci
località Tenuta Monaci
73043 Copertino LE
tel. 0832/947512

## GIOIA DEL COLLE BIANCO doc

*Vines: Trebbiano toscano (dal 50 al 70%), altri raccomandati a/o autorizzati dalla provincia di Bari (dal 30 al 50%)*

Cantine Coppi
via Martinelli 10
70010 Turi BA
tel. 080/8911990

### GIOIA DEL COLLE PRIMITIVO doc

*Vines: Primitivo*

Cantine Coppi
via Martinelli 10
70010 Turi BA
tel. 080/8911990

Vini Classici Cardone
via Martiri della Libertà 28
70010 Locorotondo BA
tel. 080/4311624

### GIOIA DEL COLLE ROSATO doc

*Vines: Primitivo (dal 50 al 60%), Montepulciano a/o Sangiovese a/o Malvasia nera (max 10%) a/o Negroamaro (complessivamente dal 40 al 50%)*

Cantine Coppi
via Martinelli 10
70010 Turi BA
tel. 080/8911990

### GIOIA DEL COLLE ROSSO doc

*Vines: Primitivo (dal 50 al 60%), Montepulciano a/o Sangiovese a/o Malvasia nera (max 10%) a/o Negroamaro (complessivamente dal 40 al 50%)*

Cantine Coppi
via Martinelli 10
70010 Turi BA
tel. 0808/8911990

### GRAVINA doc

*Malvasia del Chianti (dal 40 al 65%); Greco di Tufo a/o Bianco d'Alessano (dal 35 al 60%); Bombino Bianco a/o Trebbiano Toscano a/o Verdeca (max 10%)*

Botromagno
via Fratelli Cervi 12
70024 Gravina in Puglia BA
tel. 080/3265865

### LEVERANO BIANCO doc

*Vines: Malvasia bianca (min. 50%), Bombino bianco (max 40%), altri autorizzati a/o raccomandati dalla provincia di Lecce (max 30%)*

Conti Zecca
via Cesarea
73045 Leverano LE
tel. 0832/925613

### LEVERANO ROSATO doc

*Vines: Negroamaro (min. 50%), Malvasia nera di Lecce a/o Montepulciano a/o Sangiovese (max 40%), altri autorizzati a/o raccomandati dalla provincia di Lecce (max 30%)*

Conti Zecca
via Cesarea
73045 Leverano LE
tel. 0832/925613

### LEVERANO ROSSO doc

*Vines: Negroamaro (min. 50%), Malvasia nera di Lecce a/o Montepulciano a/o Sangiovese (max 40%), altri autorizzati a/o raccomandati dalla provincia di Lecce (max 30%)*

Cantina Sociale Cooperativa Vecchia Torre
via Marche 1
73045 Leverano LE
tel. 0832/925053

Conti Zecca
via Cesarea
73045 Leverano LE
tel. 0832/925613

### LIZZANO BIANCO doc

*Vines: Trebbiano toscano (dal 40 all'60%), Chardonnay a/o Pinot Bianco (min. 30%), Malvasia bianca (max 10%), Sauvignon a/o Bianco di Alessandro (max 25%)*

Cantina Sociale di Lizzano
corso Europa 37/39
74020 Lizzano TA
tel. 0999/552013

### LIZZANO ROSSO doc

*Vines: Negroamaro (dal 60 all'80%), Bombino nero a/o Montepulciano a/o Sangiovese a/o Pinot Nero (max 40), Malvasia nera di Lecce a/o di Brindisi (max 10%)*

Cantina Sociale di Lizzano
corso Europa 37/39
74020 Lizzano TA
tel. 0999/552013

### LOCOROTONDO doc

*Vines: Verdeca (da 50 a 65%), Bianco d'Alessano (da 35 a 50%)*

Borgo Canale
via Canale di Pirro 23
72015 Fasano BR
tel. 080/4331351

Cantina Sociale di Locorotondo
via Madonna della Catena 99
70015 Locorotondo BA
tel. 080/4311644

Conti Leone De Castris
via Senatore De Castris
73015 Salice Salentino LE
tel. 0832/731112

I Pastini
via Alberobello 232
70010 Locorotondo BA
tel. 080/8980923

### MARTINA doc

*Vines: Verdeca (da 50 a 65%), Bianco d'Alessano (da 35 a 50%)*

Vinicola Miali
via Madonna Piccola 1
74015 Martina Franca TA
tel. 080/4303222

### MOSCATO DI TRANI doc

*Vines: Moscato bianco, localmente detto Moscato reale (min. 85%)*

Fratelli Nugnes
via Barletta S.S. 16231
70059 Trani BA
tel. 0883/586837

Rivera
S.S. 98 Km 19 8
70031 Andria BA
tel. 0883/569501

Torrevento
località Castel del Monte
S.S. 170 Km 28
70033 Corato BA
tel. 080/8980929

### PRIMITIVO DI MANDURIA doc

*Vines: Primitivo*

Cantina Soc. di Locorotondo
via Madonna della Catena 99
70015 Locorotondo BA
tel. 080/9311644

Consorzio Produttori Vini
via Massimo 19
74024 Manduria TA
tel. 099/935332

Conti Leone De Castris
via Senatore De Castris
73015 Salice Salentino LE
tel. 0832/731112

Felline
Accademia dei Racemi
via Santo Stasi Primo
74024 Manduria TA
tel. 099/9711660

Masseria Pepe
Accademia dei Racemi
via Santo Stasi Primo
74024 Manduria TA
tel. 099/9711660

Miali
via Madonna Piccola 1
74015 Martina Franca TA
tel. 080/4303222

Pervini
via Santo Stasi Primo
74024 Manduria TA
tel. 099/9738929

Sinfarosa - Accademia dei Racemi
via Santo Stasi Primo
74024 Manduria TA
tel. 099/9711660

Vinicola Mediterranea
via Maternità Infanzia 22
72027 S. Pietro Vernotico BR
tel. 0831/676323

**PRIMITIVO DI MANDURIA DOLCE** doc
*Vines: Primitivo*

Cantina Sociale di Lizzano
corso Europa 37/39
74020 Lizzano TA
tel. 099/9552013

Cantina Sociale di Sava
S.S 7 Km 17 8 - 74028 Sava TA
tel. 099/9726199

Consorzio Produttori Vini
via Massimo 19
74024 Manduria TA
tel. 099/9791021

Pervini
via Santo Stasi Primo
74024 Manduria TA
tel. 099/9738929

**SALICE SALENTINO ROSSO** doc
*Vines: Negroamaro (min. 80%), Malvasia nera di Lecce a/o di Brindisi (max 20%)*

Cantele
via Vincenzo Balsamo 13
73100 Lecce LE
tel. 0832/240962

Cantina Due Palme
via San Marco 130
72020 Cellino San Marco BR
tel. 0831/617865

Cantina Soc. Coop. di Leverano
via Marche 1
73045 Leverano LE
tel. 0832/925053

Conti Leone De Castris
via Senatore De Castris
73015 Salice Salentino LE
tel. 0832/731112
*Donna Lisa*

Conti Zecca
via Cesarea
73045 Leverano LE
tel. 0832/925613

Cosimo Taurino
strada Statale 605
73010 Guagnano LE
tel. 0832/706242

Francesco Candido
via Diaz 54
72025 Sandonaci BR
tel. 0831/635674

Pervini
via Santo Stasi Primo - Z.I.
74024 Manduria TA
tel. 099/9738929

Torrevento
località Castel del Monte -
S.S. 170 Km 28
70033 Corato BA
tel. 080/8980929

Vallone
via XXV Luglio 5
73100 Lecce LE
tel. 0832/308041

**SAN SEVERO ROSATO** doc
*Vines: Montepulciano (min. 70%), Sangiovese (max 30%)*

Cantine D'Alfonso del Sordo
contr. S. Antonio S.S.89 Km 5
71016 San Severo FG
tel. 0882/221444

Torretta Zamarra
via Croce Santa 48
71016 San Severo FG
tel. 0882/374295

**SAN SEVERO ROSSO** doc
*Vines: Montepulciano (min. 70%), Sangiovese (max 30%)*

Cantine D'Alfonso del Sordo
contr. S. Antonio S.S.89 Km 5
71016 San Severo FG
tel. 0882/221444

Torretta Zamarra
via Croce Santa 48
71016 San Severo FG
tel. 0882/374295

**SAN SEVERO BIANCO** doc
*Vines: Bombino bianco (dal 40 al 60%), Trebbiano toscano (dal 40 al 60%), Malvasia bianca a/o Verdeca (max 20%)*

Cantine D'Alfonso del Sordo
contr. S. Antonio S.S.89 Km 5
71016 San Severo FG
tel. 0882/221444

Torretta Zamarra
via Croce Santa 48
71016 San Severo FG
tel. 0882/374295

### SQUINZANO ROSSO doc

*Vines: Vines: Negroamaro (min. 70%), Malvasia nera di Lecce a/o di Brindisi a/o Sangiovese (max 30%)*

 Cantina Due Palme
via San Marco 130
72020 Cellino San Marco BR
tel. 0831/617875

Coop. Agricola Santa Barbara
via Maternità e Infanzia 23
72027 S. Pietro Vernotico BR
tel. 0831/652749

### DAUNIA IGT ROSSO

Cantine D'Alfonso del Sordo
contr. S. Antonio S.S.89 Km 5
71016 San Severo FG
tel. 0882/221444
*Contrada del Salto* (Uva di Troia+Montepulciano)
*Casteldrione* (Sangiovese + Uva di Troia + Montepulciano)

### FIANO IGT MURGIA

Santa Lucia
strada Comunale S. Vittore 1
70033 Corato BA
tel. 080/8721168

### PUGLIA IGT ALEATICO

Cantine Coppi
via Martinelli 10
70010 Turi BA
tel. 080/8911990

Santa Lucia
str. Comunale San Vittore 1
70033 Corato BA
tel. 080/8721168

### PUGLIA IGT BIANCO

Torre di Quarto
Strada Torre Quarto 5
71042 Cerignola FG
tel. 0885/418453
(Bombino Bianco + Greco + Trebbiano)

### PUGLIA IGT MOSCATO

Cantina Sociale di Locorotondo
via Madonna della Catena 99
70015 Locorotondo BA
tel. 080/9311644
*Olimpia*

Conti Leone De Castris
via Senatore De Castris
73015 Salice Salentino LE
tel. 0832/731112
*Pierale*

### PUGLIA IGT NEGROAMARO

 Calatrasi - Allora
via Cellino San Marco Km 1,5
73012 Campi Salentina LE
tel. 091/8576767

Feudo Monaci
Contrada Monaci
73015 Salice Salentino LE
tel. 0831/666071

### PUGLIA IGT ROSATO

Torre di Quarto
Contrada Quarto 5
71042 Cerignola FG
tel. 0885/418453
(Bombino Nero + Montepulciano)

### PUGLIA IGT ROSSO

 Castel di Salve
piazza Castello 8
73030 Depressa LE
tel. 0833/771012
*Il Volo di Alessandro* (Sangiovese)

Felline - Accademia dei Racemi
via Santo Stasi Primo
74024 Manduria TA
tel. 099/9711660
*Vigna del Feudo* (Primi + Ottavianello + Malvasia Nera)

Le Fabbriche
contrada Le Fabbriche
74020 Maruggio TA
tel. 030/984136
(Negroamaro + Malvasia + Cabernet)

Tormaresca
via Maternità e Infanzia 21
72027 S. Pietro Vernotico BR
tel. 080/4771392
(Negroamaro + Merlot)

Torre di Quarto
Contrada Quarto 5
71042 Cerignola FG
tel. 0885/418453
(Aglianico + Nero di Troia + Montepulciano + Cabernet)

Torre di Quarto
Contrada Quarto 5
71042 Cerignola FG
tel. 0885/418453
*Nero di Troia* (Nero di Troia)

### ROSSO IGT MURGIA

Botromagno
via Fratelli Cervi 12
70024 Gravina in Puglia BA
tel. 080/3265865
*Pier delle Vigne* (Montepulciano + Aglianico)

### SALENTO IGT ALEATICO

Conti Leone De Castris
via Senatore De Castris
73015 Salice Salentino LE
tel. 0832/731112
*Negrino*

Lomazzi & Sarli
contrada Partemio S.S. 7
72022 Latiano BR
tel. 0831/725898
*Dimastro Donato*

### SALENTO IGT BIANCO

Castel di Salve
piazza Castello 8
73030 Depressa LE
tel. 0833/771012
*Santi Medici* (Malvasia Bianca+Bombino Bianco)

Conti Zecca
via Cesarea
73045 Leverano LE
tel. 0832/925613
*Donna Marzia* (Malvasia Bianca+Bombino Bianco)

Lomazzi & Sarli
contrada Partemio S.S. 7
72022 Latiano BR
tel. 0831/725898
*Partemio* (Malvasia Bianca)

### SALENTO IGT PRIMITIVO

Cantina Sociale Cooperativa Vecchia Torre
via Marche 1
73045 Leverano LE
tel. 0832/925053

Conti Leone De Castris
via Senatore De Castris
73015 Salice Salentino LE
tel. 0832/731112

Cooperativa Agricola
Santa Barbara
via Maternità e Infanzia 23
72027 S. Pietro Vernotico BR
tel. 0831/652749

Le Fabbriche
contrada Le Fabbriche
74020 Maruggio TA
tel. 030/984136

Lomazzi & Sarli
contrada Partemio S.S. 7
72022 Latiano BR
tel. 0831/725898
*Latias*

Marco Maci
via San Marco 61
72020 Cellino San Marco BR
tel. 0831/617689

Masseria Monaci
località Tenuta Monaci
73043 Copertino LE
tel. 0832/947512

Tenuta Rubino
via Medaglie d'Oro 15/A
72100 Brindisi
tel. 0831/502912

## SALENTO IGT ROSATO

Cantina Sociale di Sava
S.S 7 Km 17.8
74028 Sava TA
tel. 099/9726199
(Negroamaro)

Conti Leone De Castris
via Senatore De Castris
73015 Salice Salentino LE
tel. 0832/731112
*Five Roses*
(Negroamaro+Malvasia)

Conti Zecca
via Cesarea
73045 Leverano LE
tel. 0832/925613
*Donna Marzia*
(Negroamaro+Malvasia)

Duca Guarini
largo Frisari 1
73020 Scorrano LE
tel. 0836/460288
(Negroamaro)

Michele Calò & Figli
via Masseria Vecchia 1
73058 Tuglie LE
tel. 0833/596242
(Negroamaro+Malvasia)

Rosa del Golfo
via Garibaldi 56
73011 Alezio LE
tel. 0331/993198
*Rosa del Golfo*
(Negroamaro+Malvasia)

## SALENTO IGT ROSSO

Cantina Sociale di Lizzano
corso Europa 37/39
74020 Lizzano TA
tel. 099/9552013
(Negroamaro)

Cantine di Al Bano Carrisi
contrada Bosco
72020 Cellino San Marco TA
tel. 0831/619211
*Nostalgia* (Negroamaro)

Cantine di Al Bano Carrisi
contrada Bosco
72020 Cellino San Marco TA
tel. 0831/619211
*Platone*
(Primitivo+Negroamaro)

Castel di Salve
piazza Castello 8
73030 Depressa LE
tel. 0833/771012
*Santi Medici* (Negroamaro)

Castel di Salve
piazza Castello 8
73030 Depressa LE
tel. 0833/771012
*Armecolo* (Negroamaro +
Malvasia)

Castel di Salve
piazza Castello 8
73030 Depressa LE
tel. 0833/771012
*Rosso Priante* (Negroamaro +
Montepulciano)

Conti Leone De Castris
via Senatore De Castris
73015 Salice Salentino LE
tel. 0832/731112
*Illemos* (Primitivo +
Negroamaro + Montepulciano
+ Merlot)

Conti Zecca
via Cesarea
73045 Leverano LE
tel. 0832/925613
*Donna Marzia*
(Negroamaro + Malvasia)

Felline-Accademia dei Racemi
via Santo Stasi Primo
74024 Manduria TA
tel. 099/9711660
*Alberello*
(Primitivo+Negroamaro)

Francesco Candido
via Diaz 54
72025 Sandonaci BR
tel. 0831/635674
*Duca d'Aragona*
(Negroamaro+Montepulciano)

Francesco Candido
via Diaz 54
72025 Sandonaci BR
tel. 0831/635674
*Immensum*
(Negroamaro+Cabernet
Sauvignon)

Lomazzi & Sarli
contrada Partemio S.S. 7
72022 Latiano BR
tel. 0831/725898
*Terre di Tacco*
(Negroamaro+Malvasia)

Rosa del Golfo
via Garibaldi 56
73011 Alezio LE
tel. 0331/993198
*Portulano* (Negroamaro +
Primitivo + Aglianico)

Torreguaceto-Accademia dei
Racemi
via Santo Stasi Primo
74024 Manduria TA
tel. 099/9711660
*Dèdalo* (Ottavianello)

### SANGIOVESE IGT MURGIA

Cantina Cooperativa della
Riforma Fondiaria
via Sosta San Riccardo 1
70031 Andria BA
tel. 0883/542912

### PUGLIA IGT PRIMITIVO
*Vines: Primitivo*

Cantine Coppi
via Martinelli 10
70010 Turi BA
tel. 080/8911990

Feudo Monaci
Contrada Monaci
73015 Salice Salentino LE
tel. 0831/666071

Calatrasi Puglia
via Cellino San Marco Km 1,5
73012 Campi Salentina LE
tel. 091/8576767

Rivera
S.S. 98 Km 19,8
70031 Andria BA
tel. 0883/569501
*Triusco*

### PRIMITIVO IGT TARANTINO
*Vines: Primitivo*

Azienda Vinicola I Pastini
via Alberobella 232
70010 Locorotondo BA
tel. 080/8980973

Cantina Sociale di Lizzano
corso Europa 37/39
74020 Lizzano TA
tel. 099/9552013

Cantina Sociale di Sava
SS Taranto Lecce
S.S 7 Km 17 8
74028 Sava TA
tel. 099/9726199

Masseria La Corte
via Piave 28
73051 Novoli LE
tel. 055/9707594
*Zinfandel La Corte*

Sinfarosa - Accademia dei
Racemi
via Santo Stasi Primo
74024 Manduria TA
tel. 099/9711660

### SPUMANTE

Cantine d'Arapri
via Petrarca 17
71016 San Severo FG
tel. 0882/227643
Spumante Pas Dosé (Bombino
Nero + Montepulciano)

Cantine d'Arapri
via Petrarca 17
71016 San Severo FG
tel. 0882/227643
Spumante Riserva Nobile
(Bombino Bianco)

Cantine d'Arapri
via Petrarca 17
71016 San Severo FG
tel. 0882/227643
Spumante Rosè
(Montepulciano + Pinot Nero)

### CALABRIA

### CIRÒ BIANCO doc
*Vines: Greco bianco (min. 90%)*

Cantine Ippolito
Via Tirone 118
88811 Cirò Marina KR
tel. 0962/31106

Caparra & Siciliani
Bivio S.S.106
88811 Cirò Marina KR
tel. 0962/371435

Enotria
S.S.106
Località S. Gennaro 88811
Cirò Marina KR
tel. 0962/371181

Fattoria San Francesco
Strada Provinciale
ex S.S.106 - loc. Quattromani
888013 Cirò Marina KR
tel. 0962/32228

Librandi
S.S. 106
Località San Gennaro
88811 Cirò Marina KR
tel. 0962/31518

Linardi
Via Nazionale SS106
88812 Crucoli Torretta KR
tel. 0962/34094

### CIRÒ ROSATO doc
*Vines: Gaglioppo (min 95%)*

Cantina Enotria
S.S.106
Località S. Gennaro
88811 Cirò Marina KR
tel. 0962/371181

Caparra & Siciliani
Bivio S.S.106
88811 Cirò Marina KR
tel. 0962/371435

Cantine Ippolito
Via Tirone 118
88811 Cirò Marina KR
tel. 0962/31106

Fattoria San Francesco
Strada Provinciale ex S.S.106
località Quattromani
888013 Cirò Marina KR
tel. 0962/32228

Librandi
S.S. 106 - Località San
Gennaro
88811 Cirò Marina KR
tel. 0962/31518

Linardi
via Nazionale SS106
88812 Crucoli Torretta KR
tel. 0962/34094

### CIRÒ ROSSO doc
*Vines: Gaglioppo (min 95%)*

Cantine Ippolito
Via Tirone 118
88811 Cirò Marina KR
tel. 0962/31106

Caparra & Siciliani
Bivio S.S.106
88811 Cirò Marina KR
tel. 0962/371435

Enotria
S.S.106
Località S. Gennaro
88811 Cirò Marina KR
tel. 0962/371181

Fattoria San Francesco
Strada Provinciale ex S.S.106
località Quattromani
888013 Cirò Marina KR
tel. 0962/32228

Librandi
S.S. 106 - Loc. San Gennaro
88811 Cirò Marina KR
tel. 0962/31518

Linardi
Via Nazionale SS106
88812 Crucoli Torretta KR
tel. 0962/34094

**LAMEZIA BIANCO** doc
*Vines: Greco (max 50%),
Trebbiano toscano (max
40%), Malvasia bianca (min.
20%), altri raccomandati a/o
autorizzati dalla provincia di
Catanzaro (max 20%)*

Cantine Lento
via del Progresso 1
88046 Lamezia Terme CZ
tel. 0968/28028

**LAMEZIA GRECO** doc
*Vines: Greco (min. 85%)*

Cantine Lento
via del Progresso 1
88046 Lamezia Terme CZ
tel. 0968/28028

---

Statti
Tenuta Lenti
88046 Lamezia Terme CZ
tel. 0968/456138

**LAMEZIA
ROSSO** doc
*Vines: Nerello Mascalese a/o
Nerello Cappuccio (dal 30 al
50%), Gaglioppo a/o
Magliocco (dal 25 al 35%),
Greco Nero e Marsigliana (dal
25 al 35%), altri autorizzati
a/o raccomandati dalla
provincia di Catanzaro (max
20%)*

Cantine Lento
via del Progresso 1
88046 Lamezia Terme CZ
tel. 0968/28028

**SAVUTO** doc
*Vines: Gaglioppo, localmente
chiamato Magliocco o Arvino
(dal 35 al 45%), Greco Nero
a/o Nerello a/o Cappuccio a/o
Magliocco canino a/o
Sangiorese (dal 30 al 40%),
di cui Sangiorese (max 10%),
Malvasia bianca a/o Pecorino
(max 25%)*

 Odoardi
viale della Repubblica 143
87100 Cosenza CZ
tel. 0984/29961

**SCAVIGNA
BIANCO** doc
*Vines: trebbiano toscano (max
50%), Chardonnay (max
30%), Greco (max. 20%),
Malvasia bianca (max 10%),
altri raccomandati a/o
autorizzati dalla provincia di
Catanzaro (max 35%)*

Odoardi
viale della Republica 143.
87100 Cosenza CZ
tel. 0984/29961

---

**SCAVIGNA ROSATO** doc
*Vines: Gaglioppo (max
60%), Nerello Cappuccio
(max 40%), altri
raccomandati a/o
autorizzati dalla provincia
di Catanzaro (max 40%)*

Odoardi
viale della Repubblica 143
87100 Cosenza CZ
tel. 0984/29961

**SCAVIGNA ROSSO** doc
*Vines: Gaglioppo (max
60%), Nerello Cappuccio
(max 40%), altri
raccomandati a/o
autorizzati dalla provincia
di Catanzaro (max 40%)*

Odoardi
viale della Repubblica 143
87100 Cosenza CZ
tel. 0984/29961

**CALABRIA IGT BIANCO**

Vintripodi
via Vecchia Comunale 28
89051 Archi RC
tel. 0965/48438
*Magna Grecia (Inzolia +
Greganico + Trebbiano)*

**CALABRIA IGT ROSSO**

Vivacqua
Contrada San Vito
87040 Luzzi CZ
tel. 0984/543404
*Marinò Rosso (Gaglioppo +
Merlot)*

**PELLARO IGT**

Vintripodi
via Vecchia Comunale 28
89051 Archi RC
tel. 0965/48438
(Nerello + Alicante + altre)

---

**VAL DI NETO IGT BIANCO**

Dattilo
Loc. Marina di Strongoli
Contrada Da Dattilo
88815 Crotone KR
tel. 0962/865613
*Petelia Bianco (Greco +
Chardonnay)*

Vintripodi
via Vecchia Comunale 28
89051 Archi RC
tel. 0965/48438
(Inzolia+Greganico+Trebbiano)

**VAL DI NETO IGT ROSSO**

Dattilo
Loc. Marina di Strongoli
Contrada Da Dattilo
88815 Crotone KR
tel. 0962/865613
*Petraro Rosso (Gaglioppo +
Montepulciano + Cabernet)*

Librandi
S.S. 106 - Loc. San Gennaro
88072 Cirò Marina CZ
tel. 0962/31518
*Magno Megonio (Magliocco)*

Librandi
S.S. 106 - Loc. San Gennaro
88072 Cirò Marina CZ
tel. 0962/31518
*Gravello (Gaglioppo+Cabernet)*

Statti
Tenuta Lenti
88046 Lamezia Terme CZ
tel. 0968/456138
*Arvino (Gaglioppo +
Cabernet)*

## SICILY

### ALCAMO doc

*Vines: Catarrato (min. 60%), Inzolia, localmente chiamata Ansonica a/o Grillo a/o Grecanico a/o Chardonnay a/o Muller Thurgau a/o Sauvignon (max 40%), altre raccomandate a/o autorizzate dalla provincie di Trapani e Palermo (max 20%)*

Cantine Rallo
via Vincenzo Florio 2
91025 Marsala TP
tel. 0923/721633

Cossentino
via Principe Umberto 241
90047 Partinico PA
tel. 0918/782569

Cusumano
Contrada S.Carlo S.S. 113
90047 Partinico PA
tel. 091/8903456

Miceli
via Denti di Pirano 7
90142 Palermo PA
tel. 091/6396111

Pollara Aziende Agricole
C.da Malvello Sp. 4bis km. 2
90046 Monreale PA
tel. 091/8462922

Rapitalà Tenute - Gruppo Italiano Vini
via Segesta 9
90141 Palermo PA
tel. 091/332088

Spadafora
via Ausonia 90
90146 Palermo PA
tel. 091/514952

Vinci Vini
c.da S. Venera - via Trapani 7
91025 Marsala TP
tel. 0923/989300

### CERASUOLO DI VITTORIA doc

*Vines: Frappato (min. 40%), Calabrese (max 60%), Grosso Nero a/o Nerello Mascalese (max 10%)*

Avide
Corso Italia 131
97100 Ragusa RG
tel. 0932/967456

Cos
piazza del Popolo 34
97019 Vittoria RG
tel. 0932/864042

Hauner Carlo
via Umberto 1 - Loc. Lingua
98050 S. Marina Salina ME
tel. 0909/843141

Maggio Vini
str. Comunale Marangio 31
97019 Vittoria RG
tel. 0932/984771

Mediterranea
piazza Duomo 52
97012 Chiaramonte Gulfi RG
tel. 0932/922342

Torrevecchia
contrada Torrevecchia
97011 Acate RG
tel. 0932/990951

Valle dell'Acate
Contrada Bidini
97011 Acate RG
tel. 0932/875114

### CONTEA DI SCLAFANI BIANCO doc

*Vines: Cataratto a/o Inzolia, localmente detta Ansonica a/o Grecanico (min. 50%), altri autorizzati a/o raccomandati per le provincie di Palermo, Agrigento e Caltanissetta*

Tasca D'Almerita
contrada Regaleali
93010 Vallelunga di Pratameno CL
tel. 0921/544011
*Nozze d'Oro*

### CONTEA DI SCLAFANI ROSSO doc

*Vines: Nero d'Avola a/o Perricone (min. 50%), altri autorizzati a/o raccomandati per le provincie di Palermo, Agrigento e Caltanissetta*

Tasca D'Almerita
contrada Regaleali
93010 Vallelunga di Pratameno CL
tel. 0921/544011

### ELORO NERO D'AVOLA doc

*Vines: Nero d'Avola (min. 90%)*

Cantina Sociale Elorina
via Minghetti 80
96019 Rosolini SR
tel. 0931/857068

### ELORO PACHINO doc

*Vines: Nero d'Avola (min. 80%), Pignatello a/o Frappato (max 20%)*

Cantina Sociale Elorina
via Minghetti 80
96019 Rosolini SR
tel. 0931/857068

### ELORO ROSSO doc

*Vines: Nero d'Avola a/o Frappato a/o Pignatello (min. 90%)*

Cantina Sociale Elorina
via Minghetti 80
96019 Rosolini SR
tel. 0931/857068

Duca di Salaparuta
via Nazionale S.S. 113
90014 Casteldaccia PA
tel. 091/945201

### ETNA BIANCO doc

*Vines: Carricante (min. 60%), Catarratto (max 40%), Trebbiano a/o Minella a/o altre non aromatiche (max 15%)*

Barone Scaccamacca del Murgo
tenuta San Michele
95121 Santa Venerina CT
tel. 0959/50520

Benanti
via Garibaldi 475
95029 Viagrande CT
tel. 0957/893533

### ETNA ROSSO doc

*Vines: Nerello Mascalese (min. 80%), Nerello Cappuccio (max 20%), altre a bacca bianca, non aromatiche (max 10%)*

Barone Scaccamacca del Murgo
tenuta San Michele
95121 Santa Venerina CT
tel. 0959/50520

Benanti
via Garibaldi 475
95029 Viagrande CT
tel. 0957/893533

Pellegrino
via del Fante 39
91025 Marsala TP
tel. 0923/719911

Tenuta Scillio di Valle Galfina
viale delle Provincie 52
95014 Giarre CT
tel. 0959/33694

**FARO** doc
*Vines: Nerello Mascalese (dal
45 al 60%), Nocera (dal 5 al
10%), Nerello Capuccio (dal
15 al 30%), Nero d'Avola,
localmente detto Calabrese
a/o Gaglioppo a/o Sangiovese
(max 15%)*

Casa Vinicola Grasso
via Albero 5
98057 Milazzo ME
tel. 090/981082997

Di Stefano
C.da Corso Faro Superiore
98100 Messina ME
tel. 090/9227997

Palari
Loc. Santo Stefano Briga
98137 Villa Geraci MS
tel. 090/694281

**MALVASIA
DELLE LIPARI** doc
*Vines: Malvasia delle Lipari
(max 95%), Corinto Nero (da
5 all'8%)*

Azienda Agricola Fenech
via Fratelli Mirabito
98050 Malfa ME
tel. 0771/512422

Cantine Colosi
via Militare Ritiro 23
98152 Messina ME
tel. 090/53852

Feudo Solaria
contrada Sulleria
98059 Rodi Milici ME
tel. 090/9227997

Hauner Carlo
via Umberto 1 - Loc. Lingua
98050 S. Marina Salina ME
tel. 090/9843141

**MARSALA TIPOLOGIE
AMBRA E ORO** doc
*Vines: Grillo a/o Catarratto
a/o Inzolia, localmente detta
Ansonica a/o Damaschino*

Alagna Giuseppe
via Salemi 752
91025 Marsala TP
tel. 0923/981022

Baglio Hopps
via Salemi C.da Biesina
91025 Marsala TP
tel. 0923/967020

Cantine Florio
via Vincenzo Florio 1
91025 Marsala TP
tel. 0923/781111

Cantine Mothia
via Sappusi 12
91025 Marsala TP
tel. 0923/7327295

Cantine Rallo
via Vincenzo Florio 2
91025 Marsala TP
tel. 0923/721633

Lombardo F.lli
via Vincenzo Florio17
91025 Marsala TP
tel. 0923/721666

Marco De Bartoli c.da
Fornara Samperi 292
91025 Marsala TP
tel. 0923/962093

Pellegrino
via del Fante 39
91025 Marsala TP
tel. 0923/951177

Vinci Vini
contrada Santa Venera
via Trapani 7
91025 Marsala TP
tel. 0923/989300

**MARSALA RUBINO** doc
*Vines: Perricone, localmente
chiamato Pignatello a/o Nero
d'Avola, localmente chiamato
Calabrese a/o Nerello
Mascalese. Grillo a/o
Catarratto a/o Inzolia,
localmente detta Ansonica a/o
Damaschino (max 30%)*

Pellegrino
via del Fante 39
91025 Marsala TP
tel. 0923/719911

**MOSCATO DI NOTO** doc
*Vines: Moscato bianco*

Cantina Sociale Elorina
via Minghetti 80
96019 Rosolini SR
tel. 0931/857068

**MOSCATO DI NOTO
LIQUOROSO** doc
*Vines: Moscato bianco*

Cantina Sociale Elorina
via Minghetti 80
96019 Rosolini SR
tel. 0931/857068

**MOSCATO DI
PANTELLERIA** doc
*Vines: Zibibbo, localmente
detto Moscatellone (min. 95%)*

Bonsulton
Contrada Bonsulton 10
91017 Pantelleria TP
tel. 095/7893438

Cantine Rallo
via Vincenzo Florio 2
91025 Marsala TP
tel. 0923/721633

Donnafugata
via Lipari 18
91025 Marsala TP
tel. 0923/724200

Garche del Barone
C.da Rukia
91017 Pantelleria TP
tel. 06/30311298

Marco De Bartoli
c.da Fornara Samperi 292
91025 Marsala TP
tel. 0923/962093

Miceli
via Denti di Pirano 7
90142 Palermo PA
tel. 091/6396111

Murana Salvatore
contrada Khamma 276
91017 Pantelleria TP
tel. 0923/915231

 Nuova Agricoltura
via Napoli 22
91017 Pantelleria TP
tel. 0923/691009

*Vines: Zibibbo, localmente
detto Moscatellone (min. 95%)*

 Abraxas
via Enrico Albanese 29
90100 Palermo PA
tel. 091/6110051

Benanti
via Garibaldi 475
95029 Viagrande CT
tel. 0957/893533

Bonsulton
Contrada Bonsulton 10
91017 Pantelleria TP
tel. 095/7893438

Cantine Rallo
via Vincenzo Florio 2
91025 Marsala TP
tel. 0923/721633

 Donnafugata
via Lipari 18
91025 Marsala TP
tel. 0923/724200

Garche del Barone
C.da Rukia
91017 Pantelleria TP
tel. 06/30311298

 Marco De Bartoli
c.da Fornara Samperi 292
91025 Marsala TP
tel. 0923/962093

Miceli
via Denti di Pirano 7
90142 Palermo PA
tel. 091/6396111

Murana Salvatore
contrada Khamma 276
91017 Pantelleria TP
tel. 0923/915231

 Nuova Agricoltura
via Napoli 22
91017 Pantelleria TP
tel. 0923/691009

 Pellegrino
via del Fante 39
91025 Marsala TP
tel. 0923/719911

Promed
via Toscanini 6
91026 Mazzara del Vallo TP
tel. 0923/670214

*Vines: Moscato bianco*

Pupillo
contrada Targia
96100 Siracusa SR
tel. 0931/494029

Calatrasi - Terre di Ginestra
contrada Piano Piraino
90040 Loc. San Ciperello -
Palermo
tel. 091/8576767

Avide
Corso Italia 131
97100 Ragusa RG
tel. 0932/967456
*Herea*

 Valle dell'Acate
Contrada Bidini
97011 Acate RG
tel. 0932/874166

Abbazia Santa Anastasia
contrada Santa Anastasia
90013 Castelbuono PA
tel. 0921/671959
*Passomaggio* (Nero d'Avola
+Merlot)

Agareno
via Crispi 4
Menfi AG
tel. 0925/570409
*Moscafratta* (Nero d'Avola
+Cabernet Sauvignon)

Avide
corso Italia 131
97100 Ragusa RG
tel. 0932/967456
*Sigillo* (Nero d'Avola +
Cabernet Sauvignon)

Cantina Sociale di Trapani
c.da Ospedaletto Fontanelle
91100 Trapani TP
tel. 0923/539349
*Forti Terre di Sicilia* (Nero
d'Avola +Cabernet Sauvignon)

Casa Vinicola Grasso
via Albero 5
98057 Milazzo ME
tel. 090/9281082
*Caporosso* (Nero d'Avola +
Sangiovese)

 Ceuso
via Enea 18
91011 Alcamo TP
tel.0924/507860
*Ceuso Austera* (Nero d'Avola
+ Cabernet + Merlot)

Cusumano
Contrada S. Carlo S.S. 113
90047 Partinico PA
tel. 091/8903456
*Noà* (Nero d'Avola+Cabernet
+Merlot)

Donnafugata
via Lipari 18
91025 Marsala TP
tel. 0923/724200
*Angheli* (Nero d'Avola
+Merlot)

Duca di Salaparuta
via Nazionale S.S. 113
90014 Casteldaccia PA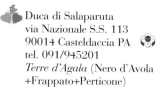
tel. 091/945201
*Terre d'Agala* (Nero d'Avola
+Frappato+Perticone)

Feudo Solaria
contrada Sullaria
98059 Rodi Milici ME
tel. 0909/227997
*Sullaria*

Firriato Casa Vinicola
via Trapani 4
91027 Paceco TP
tel. 0923/882755
*Sant'Agostino Rosso* (Nero
d'Avola +Syrah)

Marco De Bartoli
c.da Fornara Samperi 292
91025 Marsala TP
tel. 0923/962093
*Rosso di Marco* (Nero d'Avola
+Merlot)

Planeta
c.da Dispensa - largo Arancio
92013 Sambuca AG
tel. 0925/80009
*Segreta Rosso* (Nero d'Avola
+Merlot)

Settesoli Cantine
Strada Statale 115
92013 Menfi AG
tel. 0925/77111
(Nero d'Avola + Cabernet)

Tenute Rapitalà
Gruppo Italiano Vini
via Segesta 9
90141 Palermo
tel. 091/332088
*Nuhar* (Nero d'Avola + Pinot
Nero)

## SICILIA IGT SPUMANTE DOLCE

Fazio Wines
via Capo Rizzo 39
91010 Fulgatore Erice TP
tel. 0923/811700
*Petali* (Moscato)

## SICILIA IGT INZOLIA

Avide
Corso Italia 131
97100 Ragusa RG
tel. 0932/967456
*Herea;*
*Vigne d'Oro*

Valle dell'Acate
Contrada Bidini
97011 Acate RG
tel. 0932/874166

Cottanera
C.da Innazzo-Strada Prov. 89
95030 Castiglione di Sicilia CT
tel. 0942/963601

Cusumano
Contrada S. Carlo S.S. 113
90047 Partinico PA
tel. 091/8903456
*Cubia*

Duca di Salaparuta
via Nazionale S.S. 113
90014 Casteldaccia PA
tel. 091/953988
*Bianca di Valguarnera*

Fazio Wines
via Capo Rizzo 39
91010 Fulgatore Erice TP
tel. 0923/811700
*Torre dei Venti*

Maggio Vini
str. Comunale Marangio 31
97019 Vittoria RG
tel. 0932/984771
*Pitoi*

Miceli
via Denti di Pirano 7
90142 Palermo PA
tel. 091/6396111

Terre di Shemir
contrada Guarrato
91100 Trapani TP
tel. 0923/865323
*Ispirazione*

## SICILIA IGT MOSCATO PASSITO

Alagna Giuseppe
via Salemi 752
91025 Marsala TP
tel. 0923/981022

Fazio Wines
via Capo Rizzo 39
91010 Fulgatore Erice TP
tel. 0923/811700
*Ky*

## SICILIA IGT GRILLO

Duca di Salaparuta
via Nazionale S.S. 113
90014 Casteldaccia PA
tel. 091/945201
*Kados*

## SICILIA IGT BIANCO
*(Inzolia + Altre)*

Cantina Sociale di Trapani
c.da Ospedaletto Fontanelle
91100 Trapani TP
tel. 0923/539349
*Forti Terre di Sicilia*
(Inzolia+Chardonnay)

Duca di Salaparuta
via Nazionale S.S. 113
90014 Casteldaccia PA
tel. 091/945201
*Corvo Platino; Corvo Bianco*
(Inzolia +Cataratto + Grillo +
Altre)

Fazio Wines
via Capo Rizzo 39
91010 Fulgatore Erice TP
tel. 0923/811700
*Torre dei Venti*
(Inzolia+Chardonnay)

Feudo Solaria
contrada Sullaria
98059 Rodi Milici ME
tel. 090/9227997
*Sullaria* (Inzolia +Cataratto +
Grillo + Altre)

## SICILIA IGT NERO D'AVOLA

Adragna
C.da Ospedaletto Fontanelle
91100 Trapani TP
tel. 0923/26401

Barone La Lumia
contrada Castel Pozzillo
92027 Licata AG
tel. 0922/891709
*Don Totò*

Benanti
via Garibaldi 475
95029 Viagrande CT
tel. 095/7893438
*Il Monovitigno*

Calatrasi - Terre di Ginestra
contrada Piano Piraino
90040 Loc. San Ciperello -
Palermo
tel. 091/8576767

Cantina Sociale di Trapani
c.da Ospedaletto Fontanelle
91100 Trapani TP
tel. 0923/539349

Valle dell'Acate
Contrada Bidini
97011 Acate RG
tel. 0932/874166
*Il Moro*

Cusumano
Contrada S. Carlo S.S. 113
90047 Partinico PA
tel. 091/8903456
*Saganà*

Duca di Salaparuta
via Nazionale S.S. 113
90014 Casteldaccia PA
tel. 091/945201
*Duca Enrico*

Duca di Salaparuta
via Nazionale S.S. 113
90014 Casteldaccia PA
tel. 091/945201
*Triskelè*

Fazio Wines
via Capo Rizzo 39
91010 Fulgatore Erice TP
tel. 0923/811700
*Torre dei Venti*

Feudo Principi di Butera
contrada Deliella
93011 Butera CL
tel. 0934/347726

Miceli
via Denti di Pirano 7
90142 Palermo PA
tel. 091/6396111
*Fiammato*

Morgante
contrada Racalmare
92020 Agrigento AG
tel. 0922/945579
*Don Antonio*

Pellegrino
via del Fante 39
91025 Marsala TP
tel. 0923/719911
*Cent'Are*

Planeta
c.da Dispensa - largo Arancio
92013 Sambuca AG
tel. 0925/80009
*Santa Cecilia*

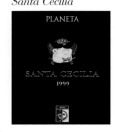

Settesoli Cantine
Strada Statale 115
92013 Menfi AG
tel. 0925/77111
*Mandrarossa*

## SARDINIA

### ALGHERO ROSSO doc
*Vines: Tutti quelli
raccomandati a/o autorizzati
dalla provincia di Sassari,
con esclusione dei vines
aromatici*

Sella & Mosca
07041 Alghero SS
località I Piani
tel. 079/997700
*Tanca Farrà (Cannonau +
Cabernet)*

### CANNONAU DI SARDEGNA doc
*Vines: Cannonau (min. 90%)*

Alberto Loi
09100 Cagliari CA
viale Trieste 61
tel. 070/240866

Antichi Poderi Jerzu
via Umberto I 1
08044 Jerzu NU
tel. 0782/70028

Argiolas
via Roma 56/58
09040 Serdiana CA
tel. 070/740606

Cantina Coop. di Oliena
via Nuoro 112
08025 Oliena NU
tel. 0784/287509

Cantina Delle Vigne di Piero
Mancini
zona Industriale st.1
07026 Olbia SS
tel. 078/950717

Cantina Soc. Dolianova
S.S. 387 Km 17 150
09041 Dolianova CA
tel. 070/744101

Cantina Soc. di Dorgali
via Piemonte 11
08022 Dorgali NU
tel. 0784/96143

Cantina Soc. S. Maria La
Palma
loc. Santa Maria La Palma
07040 Alghero SS
tel. 079/999008

Cherchi
via Ossi 22
07049 Usini SS
tel. 079/380273

Contini
via Genova 48/50
09072 Cabras OR
tel. 0783/290806

Gabbas
via Trieste 65
08100 Nuoro NU
tel. 0784/31351

Gostolai
via Nino Bixio 87
Località Sant'Esu
08025 Oliena NU
tel. 078/4288417

Meloni
via A. Gallus 79
09047 Selargius CA
tel. 070/852822

Sella & Mosca
località I Piani
07041 Alghero SS
tel. 079/997700

## CANNONAU DI SARDEGNA ROSATO doc
*Vines: Cannonau (min. 90%)*

Alberto Loi
viale Trieste 61 M
09100 Cagliari CA
tel. 070/240866

Cherchi
località Sa Pala e Sa Chessa
07049 Usini SS
tel. 079/380273

Gostolai
via Nino Bixio 87
08025 Oliena NU
tel. 0784/288417

## CARIGNANO DEL SULCIS doc
*Vines: Carignano (min. 85%)*

Cantina Soc. di Santadi
via Su Pranu 12
09010 Santadi CA
tel. 0781/950127

Cantine Soc. Sardus Pater
via Rinascita 46
09017 Sant'Antioco CA
tel. 0781/800274

Sella & Mosca
località I Piani
07041 Alghero CC
tel. 079/997700

## MALVASIA DI CAGLIARI doc
*Vines: Malvasia di Cagliari*

Cantina Soc. di Quarto
Sant'Elena
via Marconi 489
09045 Quartu Sant'Elena CA
tel. 070/826033

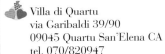
Villa di Quartu
via Garibaldi 39/90
09045 Quartu San'Elena CA
tel. 070/820947

## MONICA DI SARDEGNA doc
*Vitigno: Monica min. 90%*

Argiolas
via Roma 56/58
09040 Serdiana CA
tel. 070/740606

Cantina Soc. Dolianova
S.S. 387
09041 Dolianova CA
tel. 070/744101

Pala
via Verdi 7
09040 Serdiana CA
tel. 070/740284

Cantina Soc. della Trexenda
viale Piemonte 28
09040 Senorbì CA
tel. 070/9808863

## MOSCATO DI CAGLIARI doc
*Vines: Moscato bianco*

Cantina Soc. Dolianova
S.S. 387 Km 17 150
Località Sant'Esu
09041 Dolianova CA
tel. 070/744101

Cantina Soc. di Quarto
Sant'Elena
via Marconi 489
09045 Quartu San'Elena CA
tel. 070/826033

Meloni
via A. Gallus 79
09047 Selargius CA
tel. 070/852822

Villa di Quartu
via Garibaldi 39/90
09045 Quartu San'Elena CA
tel. 070/820947

## MOSCATO DI SARDEGNA SPUMANTE doc
*Vines: Moscato bianco (min. 90%)*

Cantina Soc. di Gallura
via Val di Cossu 9
07029 Tempio Pausania SS
tel. 079/631241

Meloni
via A. Gallus 79
09047 Selargius CA
tel. 070/852822

## VERMENTINO DI GALLURA docg
*Vines: Vermentino (min. 95%)*

Piero Mancini
zona Industriale st.1
07026 Olbia SS
tel. 078/950717

Cantina Soc. del Vermentino
via San Paolo 1
07020 Monti
tel. 0789/944012

Cantina Soc. di Gallura
via Val di Cossu 9
07029 Tempio Pausania SS
tel. 079/631241

Cantina Soc. Giogantinu
via Milano 30
07022 Berchidda SS
tel. 079/704163

Capichera
località Capichera
07021 Arzachena SS
tel. 0789/80612

Depperu
via Udine 2
07025 Luras SS
tel. 079/648121

Pedra Majore
via Roma 106
07020 Monti SS
tel. 0789/43185

### VERMENTINO DI SARDEGNA doc

*Vines: Vermentino (min. 85%)*

Argiolas
via Roma 56/58
09040 Serdiana CA
tel. 070/740606

Cantina Soc. Dolianova
S.S. Km 17,5
09041 Dolianova CA
tel. 070/744101

Cantina Soc. della
Trexenta
viale Piemonte 28
09040 Senorbì CA
tel. 070/9808863

Cantina Soc. di Santadi
via Su Pranu 12
09010 Santadi CA
tel. 0781/950127

Cherchi
località Sa Pala e Sa Chessa
07049 Usini SS
tel. 079/380273

Contini
via Genova 48/50
09072 Cabras OR
tel. 0783/290806

Meloni
via A. Gallus 79
09047 Selargius CA
tel. 070/852822

Sella & Mosca
località I Piani
07041 Alghero SS
tel. 079/997700

Tenute Soletta
via Sassari 77
Regione Signar'Anna Florinas
07030 Loc. Condrongianos SS
tel. 079/438160

### VERNACCIA DI ORISTANO doc

*Vines: Vernaccia di Oristano*

Cantina Josto Puddu
via San Lussorio 1
09070 San Severo Milis OR
tel. 0783/53329

Contini
via Genova 48/50
09072 Cabras OR
tel. 0783/290806

Meloni
via A. Gallus 79
09047 Selargius CA
tel. 070/852822

### ROMANGIA IGT

Tenute Dettori
Località Badde Nigolosu S.P.
29 Km 10
07036 Sennori SS
tel. 079/514711
*Tuderi*

Tenute Dettori
Località Badde Nigolosu S.P.
29 Km 10
07036 Sennori SS
tel. 079/514711
*Tenores*

Tenute Dettori
Località Badde Nigolosu S.P.
29 Km 10
07036 Sennori SS
tel. 079/514711
*Dettori Rosso* (Cannonau)

### ISOLA DEI NURAGHI IGT ROSSO

Argiolas
via Roma 56/58
09040 Serdiana CA
tel. 070/740606
*Turriga* (Cannonau+altre)

Cherchi
via Ossi 22
07049 Usini SS
tel. 079/380273
*Luzzana*
(Cannonau+altre)

Pala
via Verdi 7
09040 Serdiana CA
tel. 070/740284
*S'Arai* (Cannonau+altre)

### VDT BIANCO

Tenute Dettori
Località Badde Nigolosu S.P.
29 Km 10
07036 Sennori SS
tel. 079/514711
*Muscadeddu* (Moscato)

### VINO DA TAVOLA LIQUOROSO

Sella & Mosca
località I Piani
07041 Alghero SS
tel. 079/997700
*Anghelu Rujo*
(Cannonau)

# Index

# Index to Wine Producers by Category